Harnessing AI for Point-of-Sale Optimization

Nozha Erragcha
https://orcid.org/0000-0002-0534-0309
University of Jendouba, Tunisia

Maher Toukabri
https://orcid.org/0000-0003-3190-2472
Northern Border University, Saudi Arabia & University of Jendouba, Tunisia & Laboratory ARBRE, University of Tunis, Tunisia

IGI Global
Scientific Publishing
Publishing Tomorrow's Research Today

Vice President of Editorial Melissa Wagner
Director of Acquisitions Mikaela Felty
Director of Book Development Jocelynn Hessler
Production Manager Mike Brehm
Cover Design Jose Rosado

Published in the United States of America by
IGI Global Scientific Publishing
701 East Chocolate Avenue
Hershey, PA, 17033, USA
Tel: 717-533-8845 | Fax: 717-533-7115
Website: https://www.igi-global.com E-mail: cust@igi-global.com

Library of Congress Cataloging-in-Publication Data

LCCN: 2025029103 (CIP Data Pending)
ISBN13: 979-8-3373-4392-1
Isbn13Softcover: 979-8-3373-4393-8
EISBN13: 979-8-3373-4394-5

British Cataloguing in Publication Data
A Cataloguing in Publication record for this book is available from the British Library.

Table of Contents

Detailed Table of Contents

Central to its success is the integration of Artificial Intelligence, which enables real-time demand forecasting, dynamic route optimization, micro-inventory management, and personalized customer interactions. AI technologies such as machine learning, predictive analytics, and computer vision empower Q-commerce platforms to operate with precision, speed, and scalability.

This chapter explains how artificial intelligence can upgrade point-of-sale (POS) systems by joining three goals—smarter promotions, stronger fraud detection, and tighter security—into one decision layer at checkout. It first describes the AI-enabled POS landscape and the data foundations needed for reliable learning, including clean event streams, privacy-safe identity, feature stores, and delayed labels. It then shows how uplift-based personalisation, basket-aware recommendations, and guardrailed dynamic incentives raise incremental margin without adding friction. For fraud, the chapter combines supervised models with anomaly, sequence, and graph methods to spot refund abuse, coupon misuse, and organised schemes in real time while keeping false positives low. For security, it presents adaptive authentication, endpoint and network analytics, cryptography and tokenisation health checks, and device integrity monitoring, all designed to react quickly and safely.

A key component of retail marketing is the study of consumer behavior, which helps with decision-making about the layout of the product mix that is presented. In the past, retailers found it challenging to forecast customer behavior because the process was expensive and time-consuming due to the large amount of data that needed to be analyzed. However, access to consumer data has become less expensive and time-consuming due to the substantial developments in information and communications technology. Processing this data and turning it into marketing decisions that support customer requirements and aspirations has been made easier by artificial intelligence. Technologies such as machine learning, deep learning, robotics, facial recognition, and augmented reality have been used at retail points of sale by well-known brands like Adidas, Sephora, IKEA, and Amazon Go to understand and meet customer needs.

This study examines the influence of touchpoint frequency, message consistency, and response time on consumer decision-making, offering valuable insights for businesses aiming to enhance customer engagement. A total of 268 respondents were surveyed using a stratified random sampling technique, ensuring demographic diversity. Employing a cross-sectional research design, the data was analyzed using multiple regression analysis to quantify the relationships between the independent variables and customer decisions. The study found that frequent touchpoints, consistent messaging, and prompt responses significantly enhance the likelihood of favorable consumer decisions. These findings have profound implications for businesses seeking to enhance customer experience, underscoring the importance of integrating these factors for more effective marketing strategies and improved customer satisfaction

The luxury industry is undergoing a profound transformation driven by Artificial Intelligence (AI), which is redefining consumer expectations, brand interactions, and value creation. This chapter examines the impact of AI on luxury consumer behaviour and experience by integrating theoretical insights with illustrative case studies from global luxury brands. The study begins by introducing the growing role of AI in the luxury sector and outlining its significance for personalization, exclusivity, and consumer engagement. The conceptual background explores key frameworks that link AI-driven innovations such recommendation systems, chatbots, virtual try-ons, and predictive analytics with shifts in consumer attitudes, purchase intentions, and loyalty.Selected case studies highlight how leading luxury brands leverage AI to strengthen brand equity while navigating challenges of authenticity and data ethics. The analysis discusses the dual dimensions of AI adoption: the

This chapter explores the application of machine learning (ML) techniques for detecting and preventing fraud in digital marketing and promotional campaigns. It examines common fraud types, including click fraud, coupon abuse, identity manipulation, and network-based schemes, and reviews supervised, unsupervised, and deep learning approaches for anomaly detection. Key challenges, such as data quality, model interpretability, real-time processing, and ethical considerations, are discussed. Emerging trends, including predictive AI, hybrid models, and graph-based analytics, highlight future directions for robust, adaptive, and trustworthy promotional fraud detection systems.

This study explores the factors influencing consumers' intention to click on e-commerce advertisements using Partial Least Squares Structural Equation Modeling Artificial Neural Networks (PLS-SEM ANN). The main objectives of the research are to identify the key factors affecting click-through rates (CTR), assess the moderating role of privacy concerns, and predict the most significant factors influencing click behavior. A survey was conducted with 528 valid responses from consumers using e-commerce platforms such as Shopee, Lazada, and TikTok Shop, as well as companies operating on those platforms in Vietnam. The results show that Trust (T) and Information Quality (IQ) are the most significant predictors of click-through intention, with path coefficients of 0.352 ($p < 0.01$) and 0.770 ($p < 0.01$), respectively. Privacy Concern (PC) negatively affects click intention, with a path coefficient of -0.411 ($p < 0.01$), indicating that as privacy concerns increase, consumers are less likely to engage with advertisements. Additionally, Artificial Intelligence (AI) was found to have a positive impact on Trust, with a path coefficient of 0.656 ($p < 0.01$), enhancing the relevance and personalization of advertisements. Integrating PLS-SEM and ANN provides a comprehensive approach to modeling both linear and nonlinear relationships. The ANN model achieves an R^2 value of over 0.85 for predicting click intention, demonstrating its ability to capture complex relationships that PLS-SEM

Preface

INTRODUCTION

Artificial intelligence (AI) is transforming point-of-sale management by automating and optimizing various functions. Through real-time data analysis, AI enables better inventory management by predicting demand and avoiding stockouts or overstocks. It also improves the customer experience through personalized recommendation systems and chatbots for after-sales service. AI algorithms optimize shelf layouts and dynamic pricing, increasing sales. Facial recognition and behavioral analytics help understand customer journeys to adapt store layouts. Finally, checkout automation with computer vision reduces queues. In short, AI makes retail outlets more efficient, profitable, and responsive to consumer expectations, while reducing operational costs.

OBJECTIVES OF THE BOOK

This book aims to critically explore how artificial intelligence (AI) can improve efficiency, profitability, and the customer experience in retail outlets. This theme also aims to demonstrate how AI is transforming retail outlets into smarter, more responsive, and consumer-centric systems. The main objectives include: Improving the customer experience through the use of chatbots, facial recognition, or optimized shopping journeys. Examining the personalization of recommendations. Analyzing purchasing behaviors and proposing targeted offers.

CONTENTS OF THE BOOK

This book is a collection of 11 chapters that address key issues for understanding the transformative power of artificial intelligence and digital transformation in the domain of retail and distribution, because AI is radically transforming point-of-sale systems into strategic tools and no longer just transactional ones.

Chapter 1, titled " A study on the impact of predictive analysis on the marketing activities of companies", (by Jeet Singh, Preeti Yadav, Padam Bhushan, Manjit Kour and Anupam Jain) explores that "The predictive analytics is used by companies, especially in manufacturing, credit facilities, and underwriting, marketing, fraud detection, supply chain, human resources, etc. Nowadays, marketing managers use predictive analysis to find out the future trends, especially in the buying behaviour of customers. The process of predictive analysis involves in guessing the move of the customer, whether the customer will buy the product or not, and how they will engage in a particular channel. The present study is based on secondary data, highlighting the way the companies use predictive analysis. The study concludes with the fact that predictive analysis converts information into knowledge. The paper concludes that predictive analysis in marketing leads to lead generation. The analysis identifies potential leads, creation of personalized campaigns, reducing waste, product offerings, increasing efficiency, and determining marketing channels".

Chapter 2, titled " AI in Quick Commerce Technologies, Models, and Market Drivers ", (by J R Ashlin Nimo and S Pradeep Kumar), explores "how AI underpins the operational backbone of Quick commerce (Q-commerce), driving innovation and redefining convenience in modern digital retail. Q-commerce represents a transformative shift in the retail and e-commerce landscape, emphasizing ultra-fast delivery within minutes. Driven by rising consumer expectations for instant gratification and seamless service, Q-commerce has gained momentum in urban areas, especially for groceries, personal care, and medicines. Central to its success is the integration of Artificial Intelligence, which enables real-time demand forecasting, dynamic route optimization, micro-inventory management, and personalized customer interactions. AI technologies such as machine learning, predictive analytics, and computer vision empower Q-commerce platforms to operate with precision, speed, and scalability".

Chapter 3, titled "AI-powered promotional campaigns, fraud detection and security enhancement", (by S. Ida Evangeline), "explains how artificial intelligence can upgrade point-of-sale (POS) systems by joining three goals—smarter promotions, stronger fraud detection, and tighter security—into one decision layer at checkout. It first describes the AI-enabled POS landscape and the data foundations needed for reliable learning, including clean event streams, privacy-safe identity, feature stores, and delayed labels. It then shows how uplift-based personalisation, basket-aware recommendations, and guardrailed dynamic incentives raise incremental margin without adding friction. For fraud, the chapter combines supervised models with anomaly, sequence, and graph methods to spot refund abuse, coupon misuse, and organised schemes in real time while keeping false positives low. For security, it presents adaptive authentication, endpoint and network analytics, cryptography and tokenisation health checks, and device integrity monitoring, all designed to react quickly and safely “.

Chapter 4, titled “AI's contribution to predicting consumer behavior in retail stores”, (by Brahim boutaleb and Maher Toukabri), affirms that “A key component of retail marketing is the study of consumer behavior, which helps with decision-making about the layout of the product mix that is presented. In the past, retailers found it challenging to forecast customer behavior because the process was expensive and time-consuming due to the large amount of data that needed to be analyzed. However, access to consumer data has become less expensive and time-consuming due to the substantial developments in information and communications technology. Processing this data and turning it into marketing decisions that support customer requirements and aspirations has been made easier by artificial intelligence. Technologies such as machine learning, deep learning, robotics, facial recognition, and augmented reality have been used at retail points of sale by well-known brands like Adidas, Sephora, IKEA, and Amazon Go to understand and meet customer needs”.

Chapter 5, titled ” Customer Journey Analysis: Insights from a Quantitative Approach on Consumer Behavior across Touch points” (by Mahima Dogra, Pawan Kumar and Chahat Sahni), examines “The influence of touchpoint frequency, message consistency, and response time on consumer decision-making, offering valuable insights for businesses aiming to enhance customer engagement. A total of 268 respondents were surveyed using a stratified random sampling technique, ensuring demographic diversity. Employing a cross-sectional research design, the data was analyzed using multiple regression analysis to quantify the relationships between the independent variables and customer decisions. The study found that frequent touchpoints, consistent messaging, and prompt responses significantly enhance the likelihood of favorable consumer decisions. These findings have profound implications for businesses seeking to enhance customer experience, underscoring the importance of integrating these factors for more effective marketing strategies and improved customer satisfaction”.

Chapter 6, titled ” Impact of Artificial Intelligence on Luxury Consumer Behavior and Experience” (by Guruprasanna G Hegde and Ganesha K S), observes that “The luxury industry is undergoing a profound transformation driven by Artificial Intelligence (AI), which is redefining consumer expectations, brand interactions, and value creation. This chapter examines the impact of AI on luxury consumer behaviour and experience by integrating theoretical insights with illustrative case studies from global luxury brands. The study begins by introducing the growing role of AI in the luxury sector and outlining its significance for personalization, exclusivity, and consumer engagement. The conceptual background explores key frameworks that link AI-driven innovations such recommendation systems, chatbots, virtual try-ons, and predictive analytics with shifts in consumer attitudes, purchase intentions, and loyalty.Selected case studies highlight how leading luxury brands leverage AI to strengthen brand equity while navigating challenges of authenticity and data ethics. The analysis discusses the dual dimensions of AI adoption: the benefits of enhanced personalization, efficiency, and predictive value, as well as the challenges of over-automation".

Chapter 7, titled "Leveraging AI for promotional campaigns" (by J R Ashlin Nimo and S Pradeep Kumar), discusses "how AI has revolutionized up-to-date marketing strategies, how it is gradually taking over different activities in promotional campaigns. Starting with the overview of the emergence of AI in marketing, this chapter defines major AI technologies and machine learning applications that allow making smarter and data-driven decisions. This chapter also talks about the techniques of AI that are used to personalize campaigns based on the behavior of consumers and to make campaigns efficient and to delight customers. As a result, it acknowledges the effectiveness of promoting campaigns driven by AI and includes measurable outcomes through case studies of real-life situations. Through this thorough analysis, it is important to note that AI can transform the promotional efforts, with companies getting a competitive advantage in this digital age. "

Chapter 8, titled" Leveraging AI on Sales Management – A Data- driven Strategy" (by Roshan Kumar Shiva and Geetha Manoharan), affirms that "Using data-driven tactics that improve decision-making, forecasting, and overall sales performance, this chapter examines how artificial intelligence (AI) confers authority onto sales management. In order to improve pipeline management, identify high-potential prospects, and design tailored outreach, sales managers may take use of the capabilities of artificial intelligence in the areas of predictive analytics, lead scoring, customer behavior analysis, and real-time insights respectively. With the use of artificial intelligence, workloads may be simplified by automating common processes and generating suggestions that can be implemented. This enables sales teams to concentrate on high-value activities and maximize win rates. In addition, coaching tools that are powered by artificial intelligence will assist managers in cultivating talent and enhancing the efficiency of their teams. By continually improving tactics based on emerging data patterns, integrating AI into sales management supports agility, precision, and sustained revenue development".

Chapter 9, titled " Machine Learning Models for Fraud Detection in Promotional Activities " (by Munir Ahmad, Kanchon Kumar Bishnu, Rasibul Islam and Khalilor Rahman), explore that " The application of machine learning (ML) techniques for detecting and preventing fraud in digital marketing and promotional campaigns.

It examine common fraud types, including click fraud, coupon abuse, identity manipulation, and network-based schemes, and reviews supervised, unsupervised, and deep learning approaches for anomaly detection. Key challenges, such as data quality, model interpretability, real-time processing, and ethical considerations, are discussed. Emerging trends, including predictive AI, hybrid models, and graph-based analytics, highlight future directions for robust, adaptive, and trustworthy promotional fraud detection systems".

Chapter 10 titled " Modeling Click Intention in E-Commerce Advertising A Hybrid PLS-SEM and ANN Approach: Modeling Click Intention in E-Commerce Advertising" (by Minh Ly, Van and Trung Quang Ngo), explore "The factors influencing consumers' intention to click on e-commerce advertisements using Partial Least Squares Structural Equation Modeling Artificial Neural Networks (PLS-SEM ANN). The main objectives of the research are to identify the key factors affecting click-through rates (CTR), assess the moderating role of privacy concerns, and predict the most significant factors influencing click behavior. A survey was conducted with 528 valid responses from consumers using e-commerce platforms such as Shopee, Lazada, and TikTok Shop, as well as companies operating on those platforms in Vietnam. The results show that Trust (T) and Information Quality (IQ) are the most significant predictors of click-through intention, with path coefficients of 0.352 (p < 0.01) and 0.770 (p < 0.01), respectively. Privacy Concern (PC) negatively affects click intention, with a path coefficient of -0.411 (p < 0.01), indicating that as privacy concerns increase, consumers are less likely to engage with advertisements".

Chapter 11 titled " Optimizing Sales and Inventory Performance Using AI and Business Intelligence in POS Environments" (by Lal Tlan Sang, Ravikumar R N, Aarthi S and Thian Lian Ben), explore "How integrating Artificial Intelligence (AI) with Power BI enhances B2B Point-of-Sale (POS) operations through intelligent visualization and analytics. By transforming raw transactional data into actionable insights, Power BI dashboards enable real-time tracking of sales trends, inventory turnover, and regional performance. The analysis demonstrates improvements in sales forecasting accuracy by 27%, inventory efficiency by 21%, and decision-making speed by 35%. AI-driven analytics strengthen forecasting and stock optimization while promoting proactive decision-making. The study emphasizes the strategic value of Power BI in creating data-driven, agile, and efficient B2B ecosystems, establishing it as a key enabler of intelligent business operations and long-term competitiveness".

Chapter 1
A Study on the Impact of Predictive Analysis on the Marketing Activities of Companies

Jeet Singh
https://orcid.org/0000-0003-1444-5134
Guru Jambeshwar University, Moradabad, India

Preeti Yadav
Amity University, India

Padam Bhushan
Chandigarh University, India

Manjit Kour
https://orcid.org/0000-0003-1043-3187
Chandigarh University, Mohali, India

Anupam Jain
https://orcid.org/0009-0003-3192-7837
Amity University, India

ABSTRACT

Predictive analytics is used by companies, especially in manufacturing, credit facilities, and underwriting, marketing, fraud detection, supply chain, human resources, etc. Nowadays, marketing managers use predictive analysis to find out the future trends, especially in the buying behaviour of customers. The process of predictive analysis involves in guessing the move of the customer, whether the customer will

DOI: 10.4018/979-8-3373-4392-1.ch001

buy the product or not, and how they will engage in a particular channel. The present study is based on secondary data, highlighting the way the companies use predictive analysis. The study concludes with the fact that predictive analysis converts information into knowledge. The paper concludes that predictive analysis in marketing leads to lead generation. The analysis identifies potential leads, creation of personalized campaigns, reducing waste, product offerings, increasing efficiency, and determining marketing channels.

INTRODUCTION

Predictive analysis is a part of advanced analytics that forecasts future trends. Various companies use this analysis to make decisions by identifying trends, events, and behaviours. The predictive analysis uses various techniques, to name a few are machine learning, statistical algorithms, along historical data. Based on the above, we can present a few key elements of predictive analysis, such as:

- *Machine Learning*: Here, neural networks, decision tree analysis, support vector machines, and other algorithms are used for predictive analysis. These all help in managing large and complex data.
- *Statistical Algorithms*: Various statistical tools and techniques, such as time series analysis, regression analysis, are used to identify the relationships between variables and find out the future trends.
- *Historical Data*: To find out the trends and patterns, past data is essential. There are various sources from which we can collect the historical data, for example, social media, consumer behaviour, sensor outputs, etc.
- *Predictive Models*: A model is framed, tested and validated on the data, which is obviously historical data. Once finalised, the model is used for forecasting future trends.

Predictive analysis is applied in various sectors such as Business, healthcare, finance, retail, and manufacturing etc. Marketing is essential for every kind of business; therefore, marketing managers use predictive analysis to find out the future trends, especially in the buying behaviour of customers. Previously, simple methods of statistics were used, but now with the advent of artificial intelligence, predictive analysis uses machine learning and complex algorithms in predicting the future. The process of predictive analysis involves in guessing the move of the customer, whether the customer will buy the product or not, and how they will engage in a particular channel. Marketing is greatly impacted by predictive analysis by using historical and current data to forecast the behaviour of the customers and the upcoming trends of the market and through which the companies frame their strategies. The outcomes of all these efforts are efficient allocation and use of resources, enhancement of return on investment, customer segmentation is improved, various marketing campaigns are personalized, etc.

Steps of Predictive Analysis

Followed in a structured workflow, the various steps of predictive analysis are highlighted below:

Table 1. Steps of Predictive Analysis

S. No.	Steps	Particulars
1.	Define the objective	The first step to indentify the business problem which needs to be solved, for instance, sales forecast, customer demand, etc.
2.	Collection of Data	Historical data along with latest data should be collected from different sources.
3.	Pre-processing of Data (Cleaning)	Find out the missing values. Remove the duplicates if any. Find out inconsistent data and correct the errors if any. Data should be normalized and scaled.
4.	Data Exploration and Graphical Presentation	The trends and patterns should be explored. The relationships in the data should also be explored. It is better to use graphical presentation for instance, scatter plots, histograms, charts, boxplots, etc. It is also essential to find out correlation between variables and outliers also.
5.	Feature Engineering	Raw data should be transformed in to a meaningful variable or what we called as features. So, generate new features which were not available in the original dataset. The features that are present should be modified if necessary. The relevant features should be selected to include in the model, the irrelevant features should be discarded.
6.	Splitting of Data	It is an important step in ML model development. This step ensures efficient training, tuning and evaluation of model. The subsets of the data splitting are: Training set: It is used to train the ML model comprising of 70% - 80% of the total data. Test Set: This is used to find out the performance of the model on different and new data. This shows how the model works on unseen and real world examples. This comprises of 20% to 30% of the data. Validation: This helps in the selection of best model configuration.
7.	Selection of Model	Based on the business problem, select the most suitable predictive techniques for instance, decision tree, logistic regression, linear regression, time series, deep learning, neural networks.
8.	Training of Model	With the help of training dataset, there is a need for training of model.
9.	Evaluation of Model	To evaluate the performance of the model, we have to use the test dataset or validation.
10.	Deployment of Model	Make Model available to production department or other systems so that it is accessible to the business users.
11.	Maintenance and Monitoring	Regular maintenance of model is essential. Also regular monitor the performance of model. Model drift should be detected.

REVIEW OF LITERATURE

Predictive analytics has a long history and has been used extensively in various fields for decades, but because of technological advancements and data dependence, we are living in the age of predictive analytics. Predictive analytics is becoming popular among businesses looking to boost profits and bottom lines. (Sue Korn, 2011)

According to Bouveret (2019), the 1980s and 1990s saw the widespread use and formalization of predictive analytics. During this period, businesses began to recognize the value of using past data to predict future trends and behaviors. Database management systems (DBMS) and data warehousing made it easy for organizations to collect, store, and manage massive amounts of data. The term "predictive analytics" started to gain traction as statistical techniques improved.

According to Bromiley, et.al. (2015), the early 2000s saw the start of the big data revolution. The widespread use of the internet and social media, led to a significant increase in the quantity, variety, and velocity of data generated. In this era, the need for large data-handling systems and more advanced analytical techniques was emphasized. Businesses were able to manage and analyze massive amounts of data more efficiently with the creation of Hadoop, an open-source framework for distributed storage and processing of large datasets. During this period, significant advancements were also made in ML algorithms, which are crucial to predictive analytics.

A systematic review by Chen et al. (2022) highlights the integration of big data with predictive analytics, emphasising its role in enhancing business intelligence. The study categorises applications into e-commerce, smart healthcare, and predictive maintenance, noting advancements in tools like Hadoop and XL Miner to improve prediction accuracy and scalability.

According to Bzdok, et.al. (2018), a paradigm change was marked in the 2010s by the use of machine learning and artificial intelligence (AI) for predictive analytics. In particular, deep learning has enabled the development of increasingly complex and precise predictive models. Techniques like image recognition and natural language processing (NLP) expanded the applications of predictive analytics.

Aluri et al., 2019 have concentrated on applying machine learning to engage dynamic clients with the loyalty program brand in order to ascertain the worth of customers in the hospitality sectors, such as restaurants and hotels. Additionally, their findings demonstrate how well machine learning algorithms recognize clients who are more valuable in particular campaigns. In a framework that employs a dynamic model for customer interaction, they have expanded both the theoretical and practical knowledge of automated learning in the value chain of client loyalty.

According to Moedjionom et al., a multimedia services company that offers a wide range of services in an effort to gain market share is likely to have loyal customers.

In order to apply the classification and proportion of accuracy in customer loyalty rating research, this study uses data pertaining to the segmentation and splitting of potential customers based on the RFM model. Even if the C4.5 approach with k-mean segmentation produces superior results, there are a few crucial steps that can be added to the search: choosing features using an optimization algorithm or modifying the label value to produce a more accurate model.

According to Chollet (2018), Internet of Things devices, such as smart meters and sensors, continuously generate large amounts of data. These devices are crucial for collecting data in real time from a range of sources, including automobiles, industrial machines, and consumer electronics.

Statistical software packages like SAS and R offer a comprehensive set of tools for statistical analysis and predictive modeling. These tools enable analysts to use a range of techniques, including regression analysis, hypothesis testing, and time series analysis, to extract knowledge from data.

Predictive analytics is a valuable tool for e-commerce platforms because it analyzes browsing and purchase behavior. Predictive analytics can analyze user behavior on e-commerce websites, including search terms, page views, and past purchases, to find trends and preferences that guide tailored suggestions. E-commerce platforms are able to provide relevant and targeted product recommendations by basing these recommendations on the likelihood that a user will buy particular things (Ahmad, et. al., 2024, Bello, et. al., 2022, Olaboye, et. al., 2024). By showing customers products, they are more likely to purchase, personalization improves the shopping experience, boosts user engagement, and increases revenue. E-commerce companies can better target marketing campaigns and discounts to particular groups by using predictive analytics to better understand client segmentation and behavior. This increases conversion rates and fosters customer loyalty.

An investigation of predictive analysis in the e-commerce industry with a focus on men's apparel. Predictive analysis is perhaps primarily examined in this study in relation to the men's clothing e-commerce market. To predict trends, demand patterns, and consumer preferences, it can include examining past data. Inventory control, product recommendations, and marketing tactics specific to this specialized market could all benefit from the findings (Merceline Anitha, 2023).

In order to reduce client attrition in e-commerce platforms, this study focuses on using machine learning approaches within the field of business intelligence. In order to keep customers, it might investigate customer segmentation, predictive modeling, and tailored interventions. The study may help improve client retention tactics and maximize company performance in the e-commerce industry (Bamini Rajasekaran, 2023)

Client turnover forecasts are crucial in e-commerce. Predictive modeling can help consumers (Xiahou, Harada, 2022; Bauer & Jannach, 2018). Customer turnover can be shown by analyzing data and finding forecasting models. Businesses may utilize the data to develop retention measures like commitment, targeted discounts, and improved customer service. Customer connections are not strengthened by this. It increases long-term earnings while reducing buying costs.

Predictive analytics is used to estimate the chance of a condition happening or the likely future outcome of an occurrence. It is the area of data mining that deals with forecasting future trends and probabilities.

To identify different risks and possibilities, predictive models examine historical data to find patterns. In order to estimate the risks associated with a specific set of variables and guide decision-making for possible transactions, forecasting models incorporate correlations between numerous aspects. Time series tracking, sequential pattern analysis, and data profiling are the three fundamental methods of predictive analytics.

By forecasting customer behavior, predictive modeling informs marketing professionals about future trends. Based on data analysis, marketers can modify their engagement and conversion tactics. E-commerce requires modeling when a lot of information is available (Ba-taineh et al., 2023). When evaluating cause-related initiatives, prediction models are essential. Rego and Hamilton (2022) state that strategic configuration changes pertaining to management strategy modification and resource restructuring are facilitated by insightful data. This understanding could lead to successful cause-related marketing in Jordan's digital commerce sector. As a result, Kennedy et al. (2021) show how analytics could predict social network sign efficiency. Their study demonstrates how predictive designs look at how social networks affect customer engagement.

OBJECTIVES OF THE STUDY

The research on “A study on the impact of predictive analysis on the marketing activities of companies” aims to achieve the following objectives:

1) To find out the impact of predictive analysis on the marketing activities of companies.
2) To highlight the ways organisation uses predictive analysis in their marketing events.
3) To study the Cases of selected companies using predictive analysis

The present study is based on secondary data, highlighting the way the companies use predictive analysis. The study took into consideration the research articles written on predictive models and predictive analysis

ANALYSIS AND INTERPRETATION

Predictive Analysis in Marketing

Predictive analysis is a revolutionary attempt by which business organisations plan and execute their marketing strategies. Industries from finance to marketing and insurance to manufacturing use predictive analysis to make major decisions. The analysis is done on the basis of examining current as well as historical data. The companies use various models of predictive analysis, such as regression analysis, decision tree analysis, neural networks, etc. Now we have access to abundant data, companies are recognising the potential use of predictive analysis.

Common Applications in Marketing

The various applications of predictive analysis in Marketing are mentioned below:

Table 2. Applications of Predictive Analysis

S. No.	Application	Details	Examples
1.	Customer Segmentation	On the basis of demographic profile or previous interaction, predictive analysis helps in predicting future buying behaviours.	Amazon segments its users by using predictive models.
2.	Churn Prediction	By using predictive models, companies identify the customers who are likely to stop purchasing the product or availing the service.	Netflix identifies at-risk subscribers and tries to adopt retention strategies.
3.	Lead Scoring	Companies try to identify which leads are likely to be converted into sales.	To prioritise the sales efforts, Salesforce uses AI-based lead scoring.
4.	Product Recommendation	Predictive analysis helps companies to develop products based on users' tastes and preferences, and behaviour.	Based on listening history, Spotify recommends playlists and songs by using predictive analysis.
5.	Strategies related to the pricing and promotion of products and services	Predictive analysis helps in knowing how customers will react to the price changes.	Based on demand forecasts, Walmart optimises the pricing in real time.
6.	Marketing Campaign	Predictive analysis helps in forecasting the best time and place for marketing campaigns.	Coca-Cola determines the effectiveness of marketing campaigns in various market segments.

Steps of Predictive Analysis for Marketing Techniques

To have effective marketing strategies, predictive analysis is an important tool. There are various steps involved in predictive analysis for developing effective marketing techniques. The steps of predictive analysis for marketing techniques are mentioned below:

1) *Step 1 - Define the marketing objective*: The first step is to determine the specific marketing objective or goal, for instance,
   - Will the customer purchase the product?
   - Which customers are likely to buy the product?
   - Whether the marketing campaign effective?
2) *Step 2 - Collection of Data pertaining to Marketing*: The next step is to collect marketing data that is relevant at present times. There are various sources from which data can be gathered, such as customer relationship management, website analytics, social media (an important source nowadays), sales history of the company, various platforms such as email campaign platforms, etc.
3) *Step 3 - Pre-processing of Data*: Once data is collected, it is to be processed, or we call it cleaning of data, whereby duplicate data should be removed, missing demographic details should be handled, and timestamps (time of occurrence of a particular event) should be converted into usable features.
4) *Step 4 - Feature Engineering*: Marketing raw data should be transformed into a meaningful variable or which we call features. So, generate new features that were not available in the original dataset. The features that are present should be modified if necessary. The relevant features should be selected to include in the model, and the irrelevant features should be discarded.
5) *Step 5 - Splitting of Data*: It is an important step in ML model development. This step ensures efficient training, tuning, and evaluation of the model. The subsets of the data splitting are: (a) Training set: It is used to train the ML model, comprising of 70% - 80% of the total data. (b) Test Set: This is used to find out the performance of the model on different and new data. This shows how the model works on unseen and real-world examples. This comprises 20% to 30% of the data. (c) Validation: This helps in the selection of the best model configuration.
6) *Step 6 - Selection of Model*: Based on the business problem, select the most suitable predictive techniques, for instance, decision tree, logistic regression, linear regression, time series, deep learning, and neural networks.
7) *Step 7 - Training of Model*: With the help of the training dataset, there is a need for training of model. It is better to use the marketing data.

8) *Step 8 - Evaluation of Model*: To evaluate the performance of the model, we have to use the test dataset or a validation. There are various performance metrics which are related to marketing, such as Root Mean Squared Error, Mean Absolute Error, and Coefficient of Determination. These are common regression models for evaluation. There are other marketing-specific key performance indicators that tell us how effectively business and marketing objectives are achieved by the company. These include conversion rate (uplift), customer lifetime value, and the profitability of a marketing campaign measured by the return on investment method.
9) *Step 9 - Deployment of Model*: Make the Model available to the marketing department or other systems so that it is accessible to the marketing executives. Here, the marketing personnel will launch the tailored campaigns targeting the high-likelihood customers. Also, product recommendations should be done through an automated personalised system.
10) *Step 10 - Maintenance and Monitoring*: Marketing officials should track how the predictions are aligned to actual results. Regular maintenance of the model is essential. Also, regularly monitor the performance of the model. Model drift should be detected. Also, the models should be updated with the passage of time as the customer behaviour changes, and the marketing strategies should also be modified.

Case Studies of Selected Companies Using Predictive Analysis

In marketing, predictive analytics is a major tool that companies use to forecast customer behaviour, manage campaigns, and more. Various companies use predictive models in their marketing strategies. The details are mentioned below:

1) **Amazon:** The company uses predictive analysis to recommend products and personalise promotions by analysing the past purchases, browsing history, and other similar customer behaviour. Generally, we come across a statement "Customers who bought this also bought......", which is because of a predictive model. This helps the company with cross-selling (selling additional products that complement the original purchase) and upselling (convincing the customer to purchase a more premium version of the product they are already considering). Amazon is successful in improving customer experience and conversion rates. The company uses behavioural analytics and collaborative filtering algorithms to identify what customers are likely to buy next time. The company recommends its products on the emails, checkout pages, and homepage.
2) **Google:** The search engine and multinational technology company predicts the advertisement performance through Google Ads Smart Bidding. Machine

Learning helps in predicting the likelihood of a conversion or a click. This all helps to maximise the return on investment.

3) **Walmart:** The company forecasts its demand and plans its promotional campaign by predicting which products will sell region-wise on the basis of trends, season, and taste, etc. This helps the company reduce understocking or overstocking and also enhances the return on investment from marketing campaigns.
4) **Netflix:** The OTT Platform personalises the content recommendations and forecasts what content the user is likely to see and enjoy next with the help of viewing history and preferences. This helps the OTT platform to increase the watch time of the programme, and also subscription cancellations are minimised. The OTT platform has increased user engagement and reduced the churn of the audience. The platform had collected data related to the viewing behaviour of the audience to find out what users would like to watch. It developed a predictive model to suggest content to the audience, to personalise thumbnails, etc. The platform has come out with push notifications and personalized newsletters recommending new releases and shows.
5) **Spotify:** A global audio streaming service provider uses predictive models to predict playlists and organise campaigns to engage users. The predictive analytics through machine learning helps in predicting music taste as it evolves. This helps the service provider in gaining a premium subscription and increasing loyalty.
6) **American Express:** A multinational financial services corporation uses predictive analysis to find out customer churn and to provide offers for the retention of customers. The company developed a predictive model that analysed customer transaction data, customer service interactions, usage patterns, complaint history, etc. The company now offers personalised credit card offers and upgrades, and launched a retention campaign. With the help of predictive analysis, the organisation benefited in the form of reduced churn as the company offers loyalty benefits and personalised services.
7) **Hindustan Unilever Limited:** The company optimises digital advertisement spending along with campaign targets. The company uses predictive models to find out which type of audience will respond to a particular advertisement. The company benefited in the form of brand engagement and an increase in advertisement efficiency.
8) **Coca-Cola:** The soft drink manufacturer forecasts the impact of its marketing campaign, and for this, it uses social listening and the data related to the previous campaign. This leads to predicting the success of new advertisements and other promotions. The company uses predictive models and artificial intelligence to analyse the trends, social media data, and responses to the advertisement. It tries to predict which visuals would perform best in further campaigns. With the

help of predictive analysis, the company can easily allocate marketing budgets more efficiently and effectively. Now the company can understand the consumer sentiments and launch campaigns that become successful.

9) **Meta:** Meta or Facebook uses predictive analysis in targeting of audience. The company observes the activity of the users or audience on the platform, through which the company predicts user or audience behaviour and interests. This benefits the company by enabling advertisers to target the audience and other most likely converters through personalised messaging.
10) **Marriott Hotels:** The hospitality company uses models to predict pricing and promotional campaigns. In order to forecast demand, the company combines booking patterns with customer behaviour. This helps the company in sending various offers to customers or users to book the rooms and other services. This benefited the company in the form of an increased occupancy rate.

It is clear from the above cases that predictive analysis helps all types of companies, whether it is the consumer goods sector, or hospitality sector, or media and entertainment sector, or banking and financial services or, the e-commerce and retail sector, or the tech and digital services sector, etc.

Based on the above cases, we can highlight the various application areas in marketing where predictive analysis plays an important role. The important ones are:

- *Customer Segmentation*: Predictive models in this application domain aid in predicting the kind of users who are most likely to react to particular offers.
- *Churn Prediction*: Predictive models in this application domain help in identifying the customers who are likely to leave and thus target them with incentives or other retention offers.
- *Optimisation of Timing*: Predictive models in this application domain help in predicting when the audience or user will look at the message. This helps in finding out the engagement timings of the user.
- *Optimisation of Campaign*: Predictive models in this application domain help in finding out which creative advertisement will perform better or which platform is best suited for the campaign.
- *Next Best Offer*: Predictive models in this application domain help in recommending what to sell next.

Impact of Predictive Analysis on the Marketing Activities of Companies

By using data, statistical algorithms, and machine learning to foresee future events, predictive analysis dramatically improves and changes businesses' marketing efforts. The impact of predictive analysis on the market activities of companies is highlighted below:

1) **Targeting customers:** Based on prior behavior and preferences, predictive analytics assists in determining which clients are most likely to react to particular marketing initiatives. For instance, personalized product recommendations can be sent to customers by an e-commerce platform based on their browsing and past purchases.
2) **Increased return on investment on marketing campaigns:** Businesses can cut waste and increase the return on investment for marketing expenditures by concentrating resources on the most promising leads or high-value clients. Thus, increased conversion rates and lower acquisition costs are the outcomes of the predictive analysis.
3) **Dynamic Customer Segmentation:** Businesses can develop more precise and dynamic client segments by using predictive models to find hidden trends in customer data. For instance, campaigns can be customized for particular demographics, customer behaviours, or lifecycle stages.
4) **Optimising Time**: By identifying the most effective moments to contact clients, predictive analytics raises engagement and conversion rates. For instance, sending marketing emails at a time when the user is free and has sufficient time to open and respond.
5) **Hyper-personalised marketing**: Hyper-personalised marketing on digital platforms is made possible by combining automation and predictive analytics. For instance, Amazon uses this to advise products, and Netflix and Spotify use it to recommend content.
6) **Customer Retention:** Businesses may identify which clients are most likely to go and take proactive measures to keep them around with tailored support or offers. Thus, companies achieve higher lifetime value and lower customer attrition.
7) **Optimising product and content:** Based on anticipated consumer preferences and performance projections, marketing teams can test and improve product offerings, creatives, and content. For instance, using predictive models in conjunction with A/B testing (split testing) can result in quicker and more precise decision-making.
8) **Detecting Fraud:** Additionally, predictive analytics can assist in spotting irregularities and possible fraud, which is particularly helpful in digital advertising.
9) **Effective supply chain management**: By predicting demand based on campaigns, predictive analytics links marketing and the supply chain. Thus, prevents overstock or stockouts.

10) **New Marketing Opportunities:** Predictive analytics can find new localized areas where advertising can be done. It also finds new market opportunities by examining trends and behaviors in different regions. Predictive analysis helps in informed decisions for geographic expansion or region-wise promotional campaigns.

So, with the help of predictive analytics, the companies benefited a lot in the form of more precise and tailor-made campaigns, higher engagement rates, higher retention rates, effective return on investment on marketing campaigns, actionable customer groups, improved customer experience, effective campaigns, real-time marketing adaptation, focus on high-value prospects, bejavour based marketing actions or events, smart selection of influencers or collaborators, align supply with marketing driven demand, and reduced financial and reputational risks.

RISKS AND NEGATIVE EFFECTS OF PREDICTIVE ANALYSIS ON MARKETING ACTIVITIES

On the one hand, predictive analysis facilitates personalization and informed decision-making; on the other hand, it has some negative effects if not managed carefully. The few risks associated with predictive analysis are mentioned below:

1) **Overuse of Algorithms and Data**: It has been noticed that companies are heavily using predictive models, and as a result, the companies are ignoring human creativity. Due to this, the strategies of marketing become mechanical without any emotions and are unable to connect with the customers.
2) **Biasness of Data**: The effectiveness of predictive analysis depends on the quality of data. If data is biased and incomplete, predictive analysis becomes misleading. Due to this, the decisions relating to marketing become useless, and the wrong audience can be targeted.
3) **Customer Distrust**: Predictive analysis leads to personalized marketing, which may be manipulative. It looks like the privacy and trust of the customers are broken.
4) **Focus is short-term**: The measurable gains, which are generally short-term, are often emphasized by predictive analysis, for instance, click-through rates. Due to that, long-term brand building is neglected by marketing professionals.
5) **Security concerns**: Marketers collect and analyse the customers' data. There are chances that this data may be misused, and so the question of privacy arises. There are chances of data breaches. All this leads to a degradation of the company's reputation.

6) **Heavy cost**: A Lot of infrastructure, various software, and learned scientists are involved in the system of predictive analytics, and all these involve huge costs. Big companies can easily afford this cost, but small companies can't afford such a huge cost, and if they somehow incur such a cost, it leads to low ROI.
7) **Adaptability is limited in many cases**: The past or historical data is used in the predictive models, which may be outdated, and due to that, new trends may not be reflected. That's why many marketing strategies are not meeting expectations.
8) **Misinterpretations**: Tough statistical methods and complex algorithms are used in predictive analysis. Those executives who are not aware of these methods may misinterpret the results, which leads to faulty decisions.
9) **Violation of Laws**: Sometimes predictive models may violate advertising norms and standards, due to which legal penalties may be imposed on the companies, thereby damaging the reputation of the company.
10) **Trust concerns**: Personalised messages along with predictive advertisements are termed as invasive to the customers because customers feel that everything about them is known to the companies. This leads to loss of trust.

INSTANCES WHERE COMPANIES FACED LOSSES, BACKLASH, OR NEGATIVE CONSEQUENCES DUE TO PREDICTIVE ANALYSIS IN MARKETING ACTIVITIES

There are some noteworthy real-world instances where predictive analytics caused businesses to suffer financial losses, public backlash, or reputational harm. The few ones are mentioned herein below:

1. **Netflix:** When Netflix attempted to utilize similar predictive models for marketing and new show investments, the algorithms overestimated anticipated audience interest in specific episodes. Netflix first introduced its "Cinematch" predictive algorithm with the goal of recommending content customers would adore. A number of expensive ventures did not draw the anticipated number of viewers. As a result, Netflix incurred heavy losses on the production of content, and its budget was wasted. After that, Netflix changed its strategy to incorporate both human creativity and statistical analysis.
2. **Target Corporation**: The USA-based company analyzes the purchase patterns of its customers and predicts pregnancy among women shoppers. Due to predictive analysis, the company identified a pregnant girl, but her family was not aware of the pregnancy. The company dispatched maternity-related coupons, and as a result father of the girl complained. The story went viral, and the company

had to face public criticism on a large scale. The company lost the trust of its customers, which compelled it to alter its data policies.

3. **Amazon**: The company used personalized pricing whereby it shows different prices to different customers depending on their purchase history and the chances of buying the product. Later on, it came to the knowledge of the customers that they are paying a higher price as compared to other customers, and it was a public outcry. Customers' trust was trashed, forcing the company to drop the idea of charging different prices to different customers. The company faced long-term damage to its reputation.
4. **Coca-Cola**: The company uses predictive analysis to find out the demand for its products to optimise the marketing and distribution activities. But in few areas, the analysis turned out to be disaster because it overestimated the consumer demand which leads to overproduction and huge expenses on marketing and publicity. The company incurs huge losses due to excess stock and ineffective marketing campaigns. So, due to defective data analytics and overconfidence in its predictive analysis, the company suffers huge losses.
5. **Microsoft**: To engage younger users, Microsoft introduced "Tay", a predictive learning-powered Twitter chatbot. Users trained Tay to create racist and offensive videos in a matter of hours, startling viewers. It was a predictive learning effort with a focus on brand interaction, but it wasn't a conventional marketing campaign. The initiative was immediately shelved due to severe brand embarrassment; Microsoft's reputation was momentarily damaged by unfavorable media attention.
6. **Amazon**: To determine which job candidates would be hired, Amazon created an internal artificial intelligence system. The algorithm learned to devalue resumes with terms like "women's" because it was educated on historical data that showed a male-dominated workforce. Before it was fully implemented, the tool was discarded. Amazon was criticized for its lack of accountability and algorithmic prejudice.
7. **COMPAS**: Black defendants were shown to be disproportionately affected by COMPAS, a tool used by U.S. courts to assess the likelihood of reoffending. Black people had significantly higher false-positive rates in the model, according to a ProPublica analysis. Public criticism of "algorithmic justice" is widespread. Public demands that predictive algorithms be regulated and made transparent. Public confidence in automated decision-making systems was eroded.
8. **Facebook / Cambridge Analytica**: Predictive models anticipated voter behavior and had an impact on political campaigns. Millions of Facebook users' personal information was collected without their permission and used to target false information and political advertisements. Public indignation and worldwide controversy arose. The FTC penalized Facebook $5 billion.

9. **United Airlines**: The airline used the Predictive Booking Model. The airlines use Predictive analytics to minimize empty seats and maximize flight reservations. One person was forcibly removed from an overbooked flight as a result of the predictive model's overbooking of planes. All of this results in international censure and viral backlash. For a brief period, the stock price fell by almost $1 billion.
10. **British Airways**: The airline used a dynamic pricing model. To adjust ticket pricing in response to demand and search activity, the airline uses predictive algorithms. Customers experienced that as more and more searches are made by them about the flights, the prices increased every time. This results in significant media coverage and public criticism. Regulatory authorities looked at the transparency of algorithmic pricing. This all leads to reduced consumer confidence in the fairness of internet pricing.

So, it is clear that companies have violated the privacy of the customers, used inadequate predictive models, over-relied on algorithms, and failed on ethical grounds. Due to all these, there was a loss of reputation and trust, financial losses, poor marketing decisions, and public criticism.

SUGGESTIONS FOR ORGANISATIONS USING PREDICTIVE MODELS

To enhance decision-making and boost return on investment, companies are using predictive models and predictive analysis. However, it should be used carefully and strategically. Based on the above analysis, the researchers recommend certain suggestions for companies using predictive models in their marketing activities:

1) There are various marketing goals of the companies, such as reducing churn, enhancing customer conversion rates, providing personalized content or messages, etc. It is to ensure that predictive models align with the marketing goals and objectives.
2) There should be a measurable purpose of using predictive models; therefore, avoid using predictive analytics unnecessarily.
3) It is to ensure that whatever data companies are using is relevant and of good quality. Also, ensure that different types of data are included, such as transactional data, behavioural data, demographic data, etc. Also, sources of data should be updated and revised, and a proper audit of sources should be done.

4) Care should be taken to choose the correct predictive models. The models must suit the goals and objectives of the organisation. There are various models, such as decision trees, logistic regression, time series, etc.
5) It is suggested that customers or audience should be grouped according to lifecycle stages, behaviours, or potential value. Once the segmentation is done, tailor-made messages or content should be sent to the audience or potential customers to increase the effectiveness of the messages. Tailored campaigns can also be organized according to the group of customers.
6) The taste and preferences of the customers change with the passage of time. Also, the behaviour of the customers and the conditions of the market change regularly. Therefore, predictive models should be updated regularly so that the accuracy of the model is maintained.
7) The companies must take corrective actions wherever necessary. Therefore, whatever analysis is received from the predictive models should be followed. For instance, if a predictive model shows a high risk of churn, then the company should start the corrective measures, such as a retention campaign or other events to retain the customers.
8) Provide training and development programmes to the marketing professionals so that they can understand what predictions mean and how to act or react on them. It is suggested that dashboards or tools should be developed to simplify the output for non-technical marketing team members.
9) It is suggested that those companies that are using predictive models for the first time should start at a smaller level and slowly and gradually go on to a larger scale. Suppose at the starting level, the companies are predicting churning of customers, so go for that, but afterwards, more areas should be included, such as content recommendations, lifetime value forecasting, pricing, etc.

CONCLUSION

Predictive analytics has become an indispensable tool in marketing functions. It offers insights into the strategic decision and enhances customer engagement. Organisations can harness the full potential of predictive analysis to stay competitive in this dynamic environment by adopting advanced methodologies. Predictive analytics offers companies a competitive edge in marketing by enhancing the decision-making process, personalised customer experiences, and enhancing ROI, along with efficient resource allocation. So, instead of just implementing the models, companies should use them ethically, strategically, and carefully. Predictive analysis, when done in the right direction, boosts marketing performance, strengthens customer relationships and enhances the growth of the organisation on a long-term basis.

To conclude, we can say that a robust toolkit for comprehending and predicting customer behaviour across several domains is provided by predictive analytics. It improves consumer happiness and streamlines inventory management in the retail sector. It increases sales and makes personalised recommendations possible for e-commerce platforms. It makes targeted campaigns easier and boosts return on investment in marketing and advertising. Businesses may make data-driven decisions, stay competitive in a market that is changing quickly, and obtain important insights into customer behavior by utilizing AI and sophisticated analytical methodologies. Applications for predictive analytics are expected to grow as the technology develops further, giving companies even more chances to improve operations and establish strong customer relationships.

REFERENCES

Ahmad, I. A. I., Akagha, O. V., Dawodu, S. O., Obi, O. C., Anyanwu, A. C., & Onwusinkwue, S. (2024). Innovation management in tech start-ups: A review of strategies for growth and sustainability. *International Journal of Science and Research Archive*, *11*(1), 807–816. DOI: 10.30574/ijsra.2024.11.1.0150

Aluri, A., Price, B. S., & McIntyre, N. H. (2019). Using machine learning to co-create value through dynamic customer engagement in a brand loyalty program. *Journal of Hospitality & Tourism Research (Washington, D.C.)*, *43*(1), 78–100. DOI: 10.1177/1096348017753521

Bauer, J., & Jannach, D. (2018). Optimal pricing in e-commerce based on sparse and noisy data. *Decision Support Systems*, *106*, 53–63. DOI: 10.1016/j.dss.2017.12.002

Bello, O. A., Folorunso, A., Ogundipe, A., Kazeem, O., Budale, A., Zainab, F., & Ejiofor, O. E. (2022). Enhancing cyber financial fraud detection using deep learning techniques: A study on neural networks and anomaly detection. *International Journal of Network and Communication Research*, *7*(1), 90–113.

Bouveret, A. (2019). Estimation of losses due to cyber risk for financial institutions. *Journal of Operational Risk*, *14*(2), 1–20. DOI: 10.21314/JOP.2019.224

Bromiley, P., McShane, M., Nair, A., & Rustambekov, E. (2015). Enterprise risk management: Review, critique, and research directions. *Long Range Planning*, *48*(4), 265–276. DOI: 10.1016/j.lrp.2014.07.005

Bzdok, D., Altman, N., & Krzywinski, M. (2018). Statistics versus machine learning. *Nature Methods*, *15*(4), 233–234. DOI: 10.1038/nmeth.4642 PMID: 30100822

Chen, Y., Li, C., & Wang, H. (2022). Big data and predictive analytics for business intelligence: A bibliographic study (2000–2021). *Forecasting*, *4*(4), 767–786. DOI: 10.3390/forecast4040042

Chollet, F. (2018). *Deep learning with Python*. Manning Publications.

Kennedy, H., Kunkel, T., & Funk, D. C. (2021). Using predictive analytics to measure effectiveness of social media engagement: A digital measurement perspective. *Sport Marketing Quarterly*, *30*(4), 265–277. DOI: 10.32731/SMQ.304.1221.02

Moedjiono, S., Isak, Y. R., & Kusdaryono, A. (2016). Customer loyalty prediction in multimedia service provider company with K-means segmentation and C4.5 algorithm. In *2016 International Conference on Informatics and Computing (ICIC)* (pp. 210–215). IEEE. DOI: 10.1109/IAC.2016.7905717

Olaboye, J. A., Maha, C. C., Kolawole, T. O., & Abdul, S. (2024). Promoting health and educational equity: Cross-disciplinary strategies for enhancing public health and educational outcomes. *International Journal of Applied Research in Social Sciences*, *6*(6), 1178–1193. DOI: 10.51594/ijarss.v6i6.1179

Rego, M. M., & Hamilton, M. A. (2022). The importance of fit: A predictive model of cause marketing effects. *Journal of Marketing Theory and Practice*, *30*(2), 172–190. DOI: 10.1080/10696679.2021.1901594

Shobana, J., Gangadhar, C., Arora, R. K., Renjith, P., Bamini, J., & Chincholkar, Y. D. (2023). E-commerce customer churn prevention using machine learning-based business intelligence strategy. (Publication details missing—journal or conference needed for full APA citation). Korn, S. (2011). The opportunity of predictive analytics in finance. HPC Wire. (URL optional in APA; provide if required.)

Society of Petroleum Engineers. (2019). Natural language understanding for safety and risk management in oil and gas plants [Paper presentation]. Abu Dhabi International Petroleum Exhibition and Conference (ADIPEC 2019). DOI: 10.2118/197668-MS

Xiahou, X., & Harada, Y. (2022). B2C e-commerce customer churn prediction based on K-means and SVM. *Journal of Theoretical and Applied Electronic Commerce Research*, *17*(2), 458–475. DOI: 10.3390/jtaer17020024

Chapter 2
AI in Quick Commerce:
Technologies, Models, and Market Drivers

Zokir Mamadiyarov
Termez University of Economics and Service, Uzbekistan

Sindor Sapaev
Urgench State University, Uzbekistan

Gularam Masharipova
Alfraganus University, Uzbekistan

Munir Ahmad
https://orcid.org/0000-0003-4836-6151
Survey of Pakistan, Islamabad, Pakistan

ABSTRACT

This chapter explores how AI underpins the operational backbone of Quick commerce (Q-commerce), driving innovation and redefining convenience in modern digital retail. Q-commerce represents a transformative shift in the retail and e-commerce landscape, emphasizing ultra-fast delivery within minutes. Driven by rising consumer expectations for instant gratification and seamless service, Q-commerce has gained momentum in urban areas, especially for groceries, personal care, and medicines. Central to its success is the integration of Artificial Intelligence, which enables real-time demand forecasting, dynamic route optimization, micro-inventory management, and personalized customer interactions. AI technologies such as machine learning, predictive analytics, and computer vision empower Q-commerce platforms to operate with precision, speed, and scalability.

DOI: 10.4018/979-8-3373-4392-1.ch002

INTRODUCTION

Q-commerce, also known as quick commerce, is the newest trend in the retail and e-commerce business world, which has been centered on getting items to the customer in minutes as opposed to hours or even days (A. Gupta & Jha, 2025a; Kavitha & Santhanalaxmi, 2025). As opposed to the common e-commerce operation, which is based on a wide selection of products and the efficiency of logistics at the expense of speed, Q-commerce is focused on providing an ultralow delivery speed. Q-commerce emerged through the combination of on-demand services and the trend towards digitalization of retailers and quickly acquired popularity in cities with a high population density, which also allows consumers to opt out of immediate satisfaction. This model is particularly notable in the industry of groceries, personal care products, and over-the-counter medicine, where the speed of delivery is directly related to the decision to buy (Astini et al., 2024; Chavhan & Dutta, 2024; Schorung, 2024).

The Q-commerce is all about addressing the growing consumer demand in terms of convenience and immediacy (Harter et al., 2024; Naik & Gupta, 2025; Rathee et al., 2025). In today's society, where people are used to the immediacy of online services, delays are becoming a hindrance to satisfaction. It is no longer a luxury to be fast, but it is the minimum requirement needed in competitive markets. One of the key distinguishing factors is convenient accessibility; convenience is not only obtained through speedy delivery, but also user-friendly, flexible payment, and on-demand delivery. These upheaved expectations are directly answered by adopting the transition of hyper-local fulfillment centers or even by what is known as dark stores, combined with dedicated delivery fleets. In that regard, the effectiveness of Q-commerce is dependent on the possibility of demand prediction, optimization of delivery routes, and micro-inventory management, as close to perfect as possible.

Artificial intelligence (AI) has a disruptive effect on scaling Q-commerce in line with such operational obstacles (S. Gupta et al., 2025; Presskila et al., 2025a). Inventory management can be managed through AI systems in terms of predicting the inventory, so that products will be stocked according to the current time trends about consumption, as well as local preferences. Machine learning algorithms study huge amounts of data the weather schedule, the traffic flow, etc., to predict the delay and recommend the best way to deliver a good. Chatbots and recommendation engines fueled by artificial intelligence make the process even more individual, which leads to engagement and repeat purchases. Also, with computer vision technologies, one can have an automated warehousing or quality control system, eliminating the need to rely on manual workers and avoiding errors. In sum, AI is the foundation that enables Q-commerce platforms to work productively, dynamically react, and provide exceptional service levels in a high-pressure, low-latency setting

CORE TECHNOLOGIES POWERING AI IN QUICK COMMERCE

Real-Time Data Analytics and Demand Forecasting

Real-time data analytics becomes essential to the quick commerce ecosystem (Q-commerce), or the ability to react continuously to the shifting economic landscape and customer patterns. In sharp contrast to the tasks of traditional analytics based on historical data, which should also be processed over long periods of time, real-time analytics is based on stream processing of information, which can be analyzed and decided instantly. This is a must in the fast-paced world of Q-commerce, where tastes, consumer demand, and logistic factors may vary by the minute.

It starts with the gathering of large and wide-ranging data. They comprise transactional databases like past buying history and frequency, behavioural data through mobile applications and websites like browsing patterns, clicks, and duration of time on products, geo-location data which depicts movement of consumers and closeness to delivery centres, and lastly contextual data like weather changes, local events, and local holidays. More and more, the analytics platforms are incorporating data that is not structured like social media onto them, where the value of sentiment and trend analysis can surface new product requirements or customer preference changes before they jump out in purchasing patterns.

These algorithms use machine learning to carry out predictions based on this complex data to predict demand at a hyper-local scale, sometimes to the level of individual neighborhoods or zip codes (Spiliotis et al., 2022; Zohdi et al., 2022). These predictions are not fixed; rather, they are continuously updated as new information is fed. To illustrate a more real-life situation, in case a sudden rainstorm starts somewhere in one of the parts of the city, the AI tools will be able to match this with a probable increase in the number of orders of umbrellas or hot drinks, initiating the replenishment of relevant micro-fulfillment facilities automatically. Likewise, seasonal insights allow platforms to be ready in advance to expect seasonal changes, e.g., high snack/drinks orders could be anticipated during a sporting event or a festival.

Demand forecasting is also crucial in streamlining the work and the logistics in the warehouse. Having the right information about the appropriate quantity that should be carried at any given time results in reduced expenses that are accrued in case of either large quantities (tied up capital and space) or stockouts (loss of sales and disappointing the customer). The visibility into the rates of consumption and the amount of in-stock, as provided on a real-time basis, will aid in streamlining the coordination efforts in procurement and supply chains, hence having the right products readily available near the point of need.

Along with the inventory and supply chain, dynamic pricing models rely on real-time analytics. An AI will be able to set prices by demand spikes, stock levels, and the pricing of the competitors, as well as user-driven aspects like past orders or buying capabilities. This covers the aspect of pricing competitively, keeping the profit margins as high as possible. In addition, AI-based insights feed personalized promotions and targeted marketing, i.e., providing the customer with suggestions on products that apply to them, at the same time being in line with the current state of supply.

AI-Powered Route Optimization

The logistical efficiency is not only a favorable aspect in high-pressure systems such as Q-commerce, where delivery windows can span between 10 to 30 minutes, but it is also an essential aspect within the system. The current approaches to delivery planning used in the industry are not sufficient in this case, because they cannot react to developments in real-time, road-based variations in demand, or the availability of vehicles. Here, the AI-based route optimization and delivery technologies come in handy, as one uses intelligent algorithms and the learning process to coordinate accurate, timely, and cost-efficient delivery of orders (Bhargava et al., 2022; Raha et al., 2023; Reis & Nordqvist, 2021; Zhang et al., 2024).

Machine learning and predictive analytics are the main features of the route optimization engines that lie in the core of these systems. These engines combine several sources of real-time data, which may include up-to-date information about traffic congestion, road closures, weather disturbances, public transport delays, and areas of deliveries to determine the most efficient and fastest ways to deliver particular orders. Instead of using fixed maps and delivery areas, AI is continuously adjusted to the changing situation. An example is that in case there arises a traffic jam arises on one of the routes that was planned delivery routes, the system may automatically route the rider through an alternate route in order to prevent time wastage and to meet the estimated time of arrival (ETA).

In addition, AI improves the prediction of ETA by learning from past delivery events. With improvements over time, AI models can and should get better at predicting by analyzing patterns, e.g., which routes are expected to experience bottlenecks during peak hours, how long passengers wait at the building entrances, or where routes are likely to get stuck during the rush hour. This not only benefits customers since they have realistic expectations on when their orders would be delivered, but it is also beneficial to the operational managers who use the information to base schedules and fleet usage.

Automated dispatching is one of the strongest AI applications of Q-commerce logistics. The AI-based systems will instead match the orders with available delivery people based on factors like rider location, their current workload, how fast they recently delivered, the distance to the delivery, and even the type of vehicle they deliver (e.g., an electric bike and a motorbike). This intelligent allocation also saves the idle time of the rider, including assuring that the available human resources will be used to the best of their capacity, and this is particularly relevant to the peak hour of demand.

Moreover, the predictive workload feature is also appearing in the delivery systems, where the AI can estimate incoming volumes of orders according to the previous trends, weather, time of the day, or special occasions (e.g., holidays, sporting events). That enables platforms to pre-populate the delivery workforce in highly active areas or to dynamically increase the capacity of the fleet before the surge occurs. Moreover, in certain situations, AI even gets incorporated into workforce management platforms to propose changes to shifts or redistribute automatic requests for more riders to a gig pool.

It is not only that the implementation of these AI-enabled technologies accelerates delivery, but the overall cost-efficiency and burden on the environment are also enhanced by these technologies. What the platforms can do is decrease their carbon footprint by cutting fuel usage by utilizing better routing, as well as by reducing pointless trips, which will also increase profitability. In cities where the use of vehicles is already limited by traffic density or green belts, the AI can even allow prioritizing the economy-friendly vehicles for some deliveries.

Smart Inventory Management

Inventory management is a problem and a rather important success factor in the hyper-fast and precision-oriented environment and domain of quick commerce (Q-commerce). The pace of picking, packing, and delivering products also requires real-time access to the stock levels, place of stock, and product freshness, particularly in high turnover categories such as grocery and personal care. Manual checks or regular audits take too much time and are prone to error to sustain the operating capacity of Q-commerce. Here is where computer vision, the Internet of Things (IoT), or inventory management systems powered by AI enter the picture and turn warehouses into smart, self-controlled spaces (Fang & Chen, 2022; Javaid et al., 2022; Mashayekhy et al., 2022; Villegas-Ch et al., 2024).

Computer vision technology is an advanced technology in image recognition and video analytics, and can read the physical information transmitted by cameras and sensors deployed in warehouses or micro-fulfillment centers (Javaid et al., 2022; Villegas-Ch et al., 2024). Such systems can identify the displaced items, full or misaligned shelves, and even the damaged or expired products by the visual image. An example is that, AI-powered cameras placed above and monitoring shelves can log real-time changes on particular goods without the input of human beings whenever it is taken off the shelf or restocked. In the event of placing a wrong product in its wrong section, the system could help identify the error and alert the warehouse employees before delivery accuracy is affected. This will eliminate a lot of human error in order picking, and is highly accurate, as well as helping in continuous inventory tracking (even in high velocity environments where you need possibly hundreds of transactions per hour).

The Internet of Things (IoT) machines go one step further, connecting directly to the physical space and placing intelligence as hardware in the environment. With smart shelves that are connected to IoT, weight sensors help to monitor the inventory by indicating the difference during product removal or addition, giving a minute-by-minute notification on the inventory (Bose et al., 2022; Fang & Chen, 2022; Mashayekhy et al., 2022; Soori et al., 2023). These shelves are programmed to give alerts, when necessary, when levels are reached, e.g., when items are below required threshold limits or when there are harmonic usage patterns. Simultaneously with this, RFID (Radio Frequency Identification) tags or QR codes give the ability to track individual products at each and every supply chain step, including receiving and shelving, picking and packing, etc.

Another great advantage of integrating IoT is environmental monitoring. The variables being monitored, such as temperature and humidity, can be monitored using sensors placed inside storage facilities. The variables are important, especially on perishables such as dairy products, meat, and ice cream products. When temperatures increase beyond safe limits, the system can automatically send alerts or start backup cooling, thus reducing spoilage and making food safe. Such environmental data is also injected into inventory algorithms to predict shelf-life and relevant dynamic rotations (e.g., with FIFO - First In, First Out- logics).

The inventory management systems administer all data gathered by computer vision and IoT systems with the assistance of AI. They are machine learning systems that predict demand, estimate rates of depletion of stock, and optimum replenishment timings. To illustrate, when the computer AI recognizes a pattern where the demand for cold beverages may go up in a heatwave, it will stock appropriate micro-fulfillment centers more in advance and automatically generate purchase orders to their manufacturers. In the same way, AI systems can suggest decreasing stock rankings of some SKUs (stock-keeping units) in case they are not operating properly to decrease deadstock. Such AI systems also enable dynamic slotting, which involves moving high-volume orders closer to picking stations so that the entire process takes less time to fulfill orders. In addition, the predictive intelligence and visual analytics will enable a business to proactively manage inventory aging, slow products, and wastages by timely markdown or promotion in bundles.

Computer vision, IoT, and AI together will make the warehouses smart, i.e., that constantly check and adjust themselves according to internal and external environment. It is particularly essential when small-scale fulfillment centers are built in cities with such characteristics as poor availability of space and high turnover of premises. These intelligent systems enable these centers to run lean, and their models allow just-in-time stocks, where they do not need much space to store their products, yet they have a good supply. They are also reducing the number of man-hours that are wasted in the warehouse, which requires the warehouse personnel to spend time on exception handling as well as quality control in trying to eliminate manual stock checks.

NLP for Customer Service and Chatbots

Quick commerce (Q-commerce) functions best on speed, especially not only in delivery but also in communication. With the high speed of transactions, customers feel that customer service should be expected as soon as possible. Customers would like to receive instant and precise answers on tracking an order, cancellation of a payment, or making sure that certain products are available. There is a subfield of artificial intelligence, called Natural Language Processing (NLP), which is concerned with computer-human language interaction, and as such, fulfills this expectation by providing customers with automated, intelligent, and intuitive customer service experiences (Doshi, 2021; Olujimi & Ade-Ibijola, 2023; Sood et al., 2024).

The chatbots and virtual assistants embodying NLP are the solutions that make customer support in Q-commerce apps, websites, and messaging systems possible. The training challenges of the conversation systems use large sets of data of actual customer queries, product descriptions, delivery challenges, and frequently asked questions. Consequently, they can read and act on user inputs using natural human language. Considering the example, when a customer poses the question: Where is my order? the chatbot can interpret, look at the backend system, and give an up-to-date report of the item tracking.

In addition to the simple query resolution, context-sensitive dialogue management can be achieved using advanced NLP, where bots will be able to keep conversation threads between several turns. It implies that a user will be able to continue the conversation by asking such questions as What time will it be delivered? Or can I alter the address and get reasonably understandable and useful answers? This ability goes a long way in increasing customer satisfaction in that a lot of human input will not be necessary, and the customer will not have to keep on explaining the same problem to a human in order to be heard.

Current NLP tools are now trained with deep learning models, including transformer-based models (e.g., BERT, GPT), which are well suited to modeling the many subtleties of language and slang, misspellings, and conversational language etc., as human actors in the real world do. As an example, the user who says, "My pack has not arrived" or "The milk was not in good shape," is a colloquial language. A customer care system based on NLP will be able to identify the actual intent (i.e., delivery delay or product quality complaint) and take relevant response measures such as refunds, transfer to human contact, or re-delivery.

NLP models further conduct emotion analysis to determine the position of the emotional tone of the customers. This enables the system to respond by priority, in emergency and emotional situations. As an example, an exasperated message which is identified as a negative sentiment message (I am really upset, this is the third time that it was late!), can be rerouted instantaneously to a live agent, whereas the routine enquiries can be attended to automatically. This smart triaging makes sure that the important matters are dealt with on time, and the issues are processed by a machine.

Q-commerce platforms have a tendency to cover linguistically diverse people, particularly within urban areas. NLP also supports cross-language communication so that the user communicates in the language of choice. Using AI models of translation, it is a smooth operation where user inquiries into the system are translated into the system's base language, the request is processed, and a response can be in the same language that the customer typed in, i.e., English, Spanish, Urdu, Arabic, etc. Such inclusivity leads to an extension of the market and an overall improved experience of non-English-speaking consumers. The other frontier is voice-based NLP, and this is especially applicable to mobile-first users and poorly digitally literate users. The system can be integrated with voice interfaces (e.g., Google Assistant), where customers can take or alter their orders, follow their deliveries, or resolve their problems with the help of spoken instructions. Such interfaces utilize the automatic recognition of speech (ASR) with the NLP to detect the intent, which makes the interaction hands-free and accessible.

Analyzing customer feedback is one of the most strategic applications of NLP in Q-commerce. NLP tools can help to detect patterns and find out what matters to several customers, frequent complaints, or rising discontent patterns by examining reviews, chat history, online surveys, and social media comments. This not only assists in the fine-tuned operations (i.e., packaging complaints addressed or partnering delivery attitudes) but is also helpful to the customer retailing strategies. Platforms may be able to actively communicate with unhappy customers that can provide them with compensation, an apology, or loyalty rewards, according to the information obtained during sentiment and keyword analysis.

Besides, the use of NLP strengthened by customer relationship management (CRM) systems enables automated but customized communication. As an example, when there is a common order of baby products, the system may provide a special offer on this type of purchase, and chances are high that such an offer may attract a repeat order and strengthen brand loyalty.

Machine Learning Models for Personalization and Recommendation

Personalization emerged as an essential element of quick commerce (Q-commerce) following the development of a highly competitive environment and the necessity to build user satisfaction and repeat engagement levels. Machine learning (ML) is a key factor that allows such customization, as it reads large amounts of user data with the aim of predicting their preferences and adjusting the shopping experience based on it. The inputs to reference these models include browsing history, purchase frequency, cart behavior, demographic information, and pattern of interaction with a customer in order to develop a unique profile of a customer. This means that the sites will be able to provide very relevant product recommendations, offers, and even an interface change, aligning with a person and her needs and behaviors (Chiu et al., 2021; L. Liu, 2022).

Collaborative filtering and content-based filtering are the two most popular ML methods to implement in Q-commerce recommendation systems (Eliyas & Ranjana, 2022; Widayanti et al., 2023). Collaborative filtering helps in establishing the pattern of a group of customers that exhibit similar actions concerning the purchase of products and then making a recommendation to an individual customer by suggesting a product that has been bought by other customers who have similar interests. On the other hand, content-based filtering concentrates on the features of the products themselves: category, brand, price, and features, and compares them with the preferences of the user. Several platforms also have hybrid models whereby a mixture of the two methods is used to be more accurate. These systems get even more efficient as they retrieve information in the long run due to the consistent learning process, which takes into account choices of other users, or their purchases, clicks, or skips, to optimize and make changes to their future advice.

In addition to simple recommendations, Q-commerce machine learning models can engage in contextual and time-aware personalization. This way, they can consider such criteria as time of day, location, weather conditions, and even current events so that what is presented to the user can be made specific. As an example, on rainy evenings, a platform can focus on wellness packaging proposals, hot beverages, ready meals, etc. Likewise, people who visit the stores early in the morning may be presented with breakfast foods or hygienic products. With this kind of responsiveness, the user experience is changed to one where it feels natural and up-to-date.

One of the most important elements about such systems is a feedback loop that drives continuous improvement. Each interaction, be it a click on a product, neglecting an item, buying, or reviewing it, is new training information for the algorithm. This will enable the recommendation engine to change with the evolving habits of the customer over time. When a user changes preferences and goes to ordering health-conscious snacks rather than the usual ones, the system will pick it up and, as time goes on, start feeding the user recommendations based on the new preference.

Reinforcement Learning for Logistics Decision-Making

Reinforcement learning (RL) has now been shown to be a practical machine learning programming framework that can be used in addressing dynamic and surprising difficulties of logistics in quick commerce (Q-commerce). In contrast to more classical supervised learning, which relies on pre-collected static labeled data, RL is adapted to the situation when choices have to be made sequentially and the outcome of the choice is experienced in time. RL models offer a smart structure in the context of Q-commerce, where speed, efficiency, and flexibility are the key. The basic mechanism of these models is an interaction between an agent (e.g., the delivery management system) and the environment (urban logistics networks): the agent performs actions in the environment and is rewarded or given a penalty under the consequences of the actions. This feed-forward mechanism enables the system to learn from its experience in making better decisions, as opposed to hard-coded rules (H. Liu et al., 2024; Yan et al., 2022; Zong et al., 2021).

Among the most salient examples of RL in use in Q-commerce would be in information gathering with regard to optimal routing and sequencing of delivery. An example is the ability of a reinforcement learning agent to compute the most optimal sequence of pickup and drop off by the delivery men, and at the same time accounting for other factors such as the state of the traffic, time, capacity of the vehicle, and the fatigue of the riders. In contrast to static routing algorithms, which can only perhaps have as a goal achieving the shortest paths, the use of RL-based systems can find more global solutions that consider concurrently the delivery time, efficiency of a given route, and customer satisfaction. In the event that a specific routing strategy delivers goods in shorter periods of time and elicits good customer responses, then the strategy will be rewarded and encouraged in the model. This allows constant adjustment and innovation in an elaborate delivery ecosystem.

In addition to the routing technique, reinforcement learning is also being used in dynamic resource allocation, another very important process in Q-commerce logistics. RL models can learn how to decide how many riders to put on the road and in different locations at various times, by looking at the historical demand trends, weather, or at what is happening in real time in the app. As an example, the RL system can also suggest redistributing riders between low- and high-demand areas during peak-hour time or on the sudden increase of orders because of a local event. In a similar way, RL algorithms can make decisions as to when to introduce surge pricing or encourage more riders to go online, or to address excessive demand that cannot be handled without affecting the quality of services. Although these decisions are minor compared to one another by themselves, the consequences of all these decisions play an important role in terms of efficiency on platforms and customer experiences.

The reinforcement learning is an effective fit for the Q-commerce logistics because it operates under uncertainty. In practice, things are always moving in the delivery business in cities- roads are blocked, others cancel consignments, and the capacity to deliver varies. RL agents learn to deal with this kind of variability by changing their policies on the fly as a response to the feedback provided by the running of operations. Due to this, Q-commerce platforms will be able to move beyond the reactive approach of managing logistics to being able to make proactive and predictive decisions, making the overall kit more resilient and scalable.

Predictive Analytics for Stock and Trend Anticipation

Predictive analytics is a critical part of enabling Q-commerce platforms to proactively sense and forecast customer needs and streamline operations to experience and always stay ahead of the game in an industry where speed and accuracy are the driving force. Predictive analytics also allows businesses to know the product required, the quantity, and at what time, which artificial intelligence reactive systems do not possess, as they only react when there are already surges in demand, when it is already too late. This forward-looking is possible with the help of AI models that process huge amounts of data covering past sales experience and trends in consumer behavior revealed by attention to location area conducted, and various external parameters, including weather conditions, national holidays, or community events (Kumar & Manikandan, 2025; Manasa et al., 2023).

Stock out forecasting and replenishment can be claimed as one of the most viable uses of predictive analytics in Q-commerce. As another example, given that sales of ice cream go through the roof when it gets extremely hot in the past, and a heatwave is predicted in a particular city, the system could actively initiate reordering of the cold storage-based products to central micro-fulfillment facilities within its environs. This is a preventive strategy that makes in-demand products available where, when, and how they are required, thus avoiding stockouts and lost sales opportunities. On the other hand, the system can also help to avoid overstocking because it will be able to detect when the demand for some seasonal products will decrease in order to reduce its storage cost as well as the wastage of products.

Besides the predictions done at a product level, predictive analytics is also useful in detecting trends. Artificial intelligence models programmed to look at search behavior patterns, social media posts, and even the activity on real-time mobile applications can detect the initial indicators of the emergence of a new trend, be it a new snack brand suddenly catching on, or a new obsession with plant-based products. It enables Q-commerce platforms to add popular products quicker, market them to the correct customer cohorts, and act at a shorter notice than conventional retailers. Not only does such responsiveness enhance satisfaction levels of customers, but it also enhances brand credibility as a platform that is on top of the game.

In order to carry out these tasks, different forecasting methods are applied on the platforms. Older methods of statistical analysis, such as ARIMA (AutoRegressive Integrated Moving Average) and exponential smoothing, can be applied to structured and time-related sales data. More advanced models based on AI, like Prophet, developed at Meta, and Long Short-Term Memory (LSTM) neural networks, however, have increasingly entered use due to their capability to handle innately complex seasonal trends, non-linear connections, and contingent interdependencies. The models are capable of operating with large amounts of multivariate data and can respond to emerging patterns, i.e., a surge behavior in consumers as a result of a sudden occurrence or an economic change.

Neural Networks Applications in Dynamic Pricing

In a quick and competitive environment of Q-commerce, price agility plays the pivoting role of attracting customers, maintaining inventory, and maximizing revenue. One crucial strategic lever has emerged: the possibility of adjusting prices in real time as a response to an unlimited combination of factors, namely, dynamic pricing. Neural networks are playing a central role in making this possible. The latter deep learning models work so well in that they can be trained to know complex, non-linear systems of many variables that can affect customer purchase behavior. Compared to rule-based systems, which act based on rigid application of predetermined logic, neural networks can adjust and correct themselves as time goes by, and thus they are very adept at the dynamism and situational sensitivity of pricing in Q-commerce (Chenavaz & Dimitrov, 2025; Famil Alamdar & Seifi, 2023; Iyer et al., 2021).

Neural networks involved in dynamic pricing take in a wide variety of data, both structured and unstructured. Structured data could contain product characteristics, past sales data, time of day, location, inventory, and competitor prices. Improperly structured data sets, e.g., product reviews, social media sentiment, or even product imagery, are also amenable to neural networks, e.g., convolutional neural networks (CNNs) or recurrent neural networks (RNNs). CNNs are normally employed when the input to be analyzed is visual or there is a spatial relationship involved; hence, they will be applicable to determine any visual effects that could influence the attractiveness of products. Instead, RNNs are extremely useful when dealing with time-based or sequential data, as the historical prices change, and customer response will enable the model to identify temporal patterns that can drive the sensitivity to prices.

Neural networks are powerful because they can learn the historical results and apply the knowledge gained to new cases. As an example, a Q-commerce platform can find out that customers in one region are very price-sensitive in the afternoons of the weekdays, whereas customers in another region are more likely to respond to the higher pricing on weekends. Neural networks learn through the backpropagation and gradient descent algorithms that change internal parameters in response to feedback, either conversion rates, abandonment rates, or increases/decreases in basket size, as a consequence of prior pricing decisions. This would facilitate a constant learning process and refinement of the pricing mechanism that would match with a given customer profile and market dynamics.

Additionally, the models are created to react to changes in real-time. If a competitor suddenly changes the prices of a popular product, or the event of an unpredicted surge in product demand because of a local occasion, weather condition, a neural network can instantly suggest or execute a price correction. This degree of responsiveness makes it possible not only to retain customer interest but to prevent the occurrence of inventory dislocations either by speeding up the flow of popular products or locking in increased value in hot products.

The dynamic prices through the neural networks approach are well balanced to help the customer as well as the business. To customers, it guarantees the competitive and contextually correct pricing that can be based on their preferences and purchasing habits. In the case of businesses, it helps in optimizing revenues, achieving effective turnover of boots, and depends less on manual pricing interventions in ensuring better demand management. With the further growth and differentiation of Q-commerce, neural networks in dynamic pricing will be more and more central to the profitability, customer satisfaction, and market competitiveness of the firms. Table 1 shows the summary of the core technologies powering AI in quick commerce, organized by technology, description, key functions, and benefits.

Table 1. Core Technologies and AI Models Powering Quick Commerce

Category	Technology/Model	Description	Key Functions	Benefits
Data Analytics & Forecasting	Real-Time Data Analytics & Demand Forecasting	Uses live and historical data to anticipate demand and optimize inventory & fulfillment	- Track user behavior, location, and trends - Forecast hyper-local demand	- Lower stockouts/ overstock - Agile supply planning - Better responsiveness
Logistics Optimization	AI-Powered Route Optimization & Delivery Systems	Calculates efficient routes and allocates deliveries based on real-time and historical logistics data	- Route planning - Rider-task matching - ETA prediction	- Faster deliveries - Reduced cost - Higher fleet productivity
Smart Warehousing	Computer Vision, IoT & Smart Inventory Management	Automates inventory monitoring and environment tracking using AI and sensors	- Track stock levels - Detect spoilage/ misplacement - Auto reorder	- Improved accuracy - Lower spoilage/ loss - Faster picking and fulfillment
Conversational AI	NLP for Customer Service and Chatbots	Automates customer interaction through AI-powered language understanding	- Handle FAQs and support - Multilingual and voice-enabled support - Sentiment detection	- 24/7 support - Higher customer satisfaction - Efficient issue handling
Personalization & UX	ML for Personalization and Recommendations	Suggests products based on individual preferences and behavior patterns	- User profiling - Personalized product suggestions - Cross-sell/upsell tactics	- Increased engagement - Higher conversion rates - Better user retention
Adaptive Decision-Making	Reinforcement Learning for Logistics	Continuously optimizes logistics decisions based on real-world feedback	- Dynamic dispatching - Fleet management - Delivery timing strategies	- Smart adaptation to uncertainty - Higher efficiency and resource utilization
Trend Prediction & Stock Planning	Predictive Analytics	Anticipates future demand patterns using time-series and behavioral analysis	- Product lifecycle planning - Seasonal inventory adjustments - Event-driven stocking	- Better availability - Reduced waste - Increased agility
Pricing Optimization	Neural Networks for Dynamic Pricing	Adjusts prices in real time using deep learning on market, user, and demand data	- Real-time price updates - Competitive pricing - Promotional strategies	- Maximized revenue - Balanced inventory turnover - Personalized price incentives

MARKET DRIVERS AND STRATEGIC ENABLERS

Shifting Consumer Behavior and Digital Adoption

One of the strongest market forces stimulating Q-commerce is the swift need to keep up with the ever-changing consumer demands. As modern consumers, and those in the city, particularly, become more concerned about convenience, speed, and smooth processes in the digital world. Immediacy is no longer a luxury, but a given in the on-demand culture, which has been formulated by the food delivery apps, cab services, and streaming-media-on-demand services. Consumers have changed and now demand products like groceries, over-the-counter drugs, and other personal care products within a few minutes of when they place the order.

Another cause of this behavior change has been further fueled by the high levels of digitalization, especially after the COVID-19 pandemic. Digital-first transactions became a normal part of life with lockdowns, remote employment, and social distancing, which increased the user base of e-commerce platforms and caused the penetration of these services in the rest of the population that lacked digitalization. With the increasing popularity of smartphone usage and online accessibility to internet services overall, customers are going to spend more time browsing Q-commerce websites and even skipping conventional purchasing altogether. Such tendencies contribute to a more comprehensive digital economy and create favorable conditions under which the rapid growth of quick commerce can take place.

Competitive Differentiation and Speed-to-Customer

Speed of delivery has become another differentiator in a crowded e-commerce market that is considered price sensitive. The traditional online retailers might be able to ship the next day or the same day, but the Q-commerce firms are likely to promise within 10-30 minutes, either to deliver or fulfill the customer. Not only does this ultra-fast model meet the pressing needs, but it also creates brand loyalty by exceeding expectations.

Speed-to-customer as a competitive weapon is considered strategic. Q-commerce platforms, which are always faster than competitors, will achieve a greater share of wallet, stickiness, and warrant a premium price or service fee. In addition, the densely populated region offers a first-mover advantage to the players, where early players are likely to acquire hyperlocal bases of riders, warehouses, and loyal customers, of which the new entrants can hardly compete unless they invest greatly. The need to stay fast is an innovation force behind developing routing algorithms, micro-fulfillment infrastructure, and real-time inventory, all supported by AI and data analytics.

Urbanization and Hyperlocal Fulfillment Centers

One of the drivers of Q-commerce is urbanization. Population density in cities rises with more citizens moving into the cities, meaning a perfect environment to implement the hyperlocal delivery models. The ability to have a high order volume at a small, local geographic concentration enables Q-commerce operators to operate micro-fulfillment centers (referred to as "dark stores") at a smaller and more decentralized location, which can quickly fulfill neighborhoods existing within a radius of 13 km. These facilities are specialized in speed, not in-store shopping, and so their layout and inventory management systems are engineered according to fast picking and dispatching of products (Tariq, 2025; Umair, 2026).

The fast growth of Q-commerce in cities can also be attributed to high technology infrastructure, such as superior road connectivity, increased broadband penetration, and access to gig-economy delivery labor. These city logistics systems allow the platforms to deliver products at the shortest time possible at the lowest cost. Moreover, geospatial data analytics, as well as location intelligence, along with AI, assist in determining the best location to build a fulfillment center, foreseeing the demand based on a certain region or neighbourhood, and optimizing the supply chain in real time. This urban-centric way of having Q-commerce will be more economically and ecologically viable as more cities become urbanized.

Partnerships, Data Ecosystems, and Investor Interest

The expansion of Q-commerce is not occurring in a vacuum, although the rapid growth in these areas is sprouting up with a thick network of strategic partnerships, strong data ecosystems, and eager investor support. FMCG brands, logistics companies, and payment gateways are strategic partners with platforms that allow them to provide quicker and more reliable service. As an example, the collaboration with the large grocery suppliers enables Q-commerce players to get direct-to-warehouse replenishments of the inventory, minimizing delays and enhancing the freshness of the goods. Fleet scaling using collaboration with third-party logistics or the last-mile delivery startups within a short time with less capital investment, is also possible. In addition, Q-commerce also works in closed data environments more and more. They use not only the data of internal transactions but also third parties such as weather APIs, social media trends, and traffic feeds. This abundance of data nourishes AI applications that optimize all stages of the operation, including customer profiling through delivery routing and demand forecasting.

The interest of investors in Q-commerce has really played a major role, as venture capitalists and other privately owned equity firms have invested billions of dollars into the sector all over the world. The funds invested are used in expansion, technology innovation, and tapping the population in new geographies. The availability of deep-pocketed investors in most cases enables these companies to achieve a growth that can be described as aggressive, including customer subsidies, as well as beating their competition in brand building and customer acquisitions. A healthy unit economics driven by the efficiencies of AI and the sheer size of potential consumers, as the digital retail trend continues to expand, are common drivers in investor confidence.

CHALLENGES AND ETHICAL CONSIDERATIONS

Data Privacy and Algorithmic Transparency

Since the Q-commerce platforms gather and process a huge volume of data about the users (their location, purchasing patterns, history, and interaction with the behavior), a threat to data privacy is a critical ethical issue. Sensitive information can be used as input into AI models driving personalized recommendations, dynamic pricing, and just-in-time logistics (Wu, 2024). Lack of defined reference protocols and an effective way of data governance might lead such systems to possible infringement of user rights or data breaches.

Moreover, the transparency of algorithms is vital, but in most AI-related processes are usually absent. The process of making decisions themselves is not known to most of the consumers, i.e., why a particular product is priced differently to them or why they are given a particular recommendation. Such a lack of transparency may create distrust, particularly as algorithmic biases create discriminatory prices, low quality of service in poorer neighborhoods, or customer targeting. Regulators and users themselves want the development of explainable AI (XAI) models, data use disclosures, which will make transparent what data are gathered, processed, and how they affect user experience. Transparency not only makes it possible to keep the law on data protection (such as GDPR or the Personal Data Protection Bill currently in the process of being enacted in Pakistan) but also brings about long-term consumer trust.

Labor Displacement and Gig Economy Ethics

The utilization of automation and gig workers poses ethical and socioeconomic issues to Q-commerce. On the one hand, AI-related efficiencies (questions of automated warehouse, smart dispatch systems, and autonomous delivery solutions) minimize human activity in numerous computational operations. In the long run, it causes job loss, particularly among those with low skills in the warehousing/

logistics department and who will find it hard to adjust to the new functions of a digital economy (Tan et al., 2021; Tariq, 2025).

Meanwhile, the boom in Q-commerce is strongly associated with using workers in the gig economy, dispatch riders, and part-time warehouse workers who are employed in unpleasant conditions. Such workers can be exposed to excessive working hours, health insurance or the lack of it, scant protection under the law, and algorithmic guidance of workers, on the basis of which they can be assigned or supervised and, in some cases, replaced or dismissed without human involvement. The ethical issues are associated with fair wages, safety, job security, and algorithms responsibility. We desperately require some rules and platform-initiated regulations that promote decent jobs, clear performance indicators, and ensure that the gig workers are also included in the benefits plans. Otherwise, Q-commerce would help to ramp up labor exploitation but enjoy the productivity gains that AI can bring.

Scalability Issues in Emerging Markets

Although the Q-commerce business has developed quickly in the developed and urbanized areas, the expansion of such a business in developing markets is a different difficulty altogether. Most developing nations have to deal with a lack of infrastructure, including an unstable electrical supply, non-existent or inadequate surface transport systems, low capacity in the last-mile logistics, and gaps in internet connectivity, all of which limit the efficiency of real-time service models and AI-driven systems.

In addition, such scenarios can be characterized by a shortage of data availability and quality, which are crucial to the development of machine learning models. This may prevent the use of route optimization algorithms, such as the lack of details address systems or location data, for example. Moreover, local dialects and languages might not be highly represented by the natural language processing (NLP) datasets, which only affects the accuracy of chats and customer interactions (Zampieri et al., 2020). Digital literacy is another problem; the consumers might not be conversant or comfortable with the ordering system by use of apps.

The solution to such challenges is implementing local models in Q-commerce platforms, such as hybrid models between digital and physical technologies, voice technologies in native languages, and less technologically advanced delivery (such as couriers by bicycle or community hubs). Scalability of these markets should not only be determined through technological changes, but through collaborations with domestic companies and government aid to enhance the overall enabling environment.

Green AI-Based Q-Commerce

The guarantee of hyper-speed delivery has its price on the environment. More deliveries, more single-use packaging, energy required in micro-fulfillment sites, and the use of AI processing all require more data center energy, which leads to a greater carbon footprint. Fragmented deliveries (several small orders within a short period) that are proposed by Q-commerce benefit its customers and the on-demand system as a goloshi (A. Gupta & Jha, 2025b; Presskila et al., 2025b). The fragmented type is less environmentally friendly than focused delivery or stores, having exploited vehicles, because it follows non-stop last-minute shopping and protects cars and trucks that deliver goods. Also, much energy is needed, including non-renewable energy, to maintain the infrastructure needed to service AI, including server farms where data is stored as well as training models. This creates fear of the practicality of large-scale AI implementation, especially when Q-commerce starts gaining more ground in different places.

To reduce these consequences, Q-commerce platforms need to consider environmentally-friendly solutions, e.g., go green packaging, use electric vehicles to deliver, and have energy-efficient data centres. The AI, in its turn, can be applied to hone in on sustainability as well, e.g., optimize delivery batches and the number of trips that have to be made, or predictive analytics to reduce food wastage rates by adjusting the position of different stocks. However, to come to actual sustainability, it is necessary to integrate environmental impact analysis with business models and use the principles of the circular economy in the supply chain.

CONCLUSION

The potential of AI-enabled Quick Commerce (Q-commerce) is being established at the level of an increasingly intelligent, self-governing, and self-optimizing ecosystem, which breaks the frame of conventional e-commerce. A significant frontier area that can have the greatest amount of change is autonomous delivery technologies, including drones and ground-based robots. Such advancements will revolutionize the last-mile logistics by minimizing human intervention, cutting costs of operation, and serving places that are inaccessible or crowded with traffic. Firms are already testing drone deliveries of small-weight goods to the suburbs and cities, with delivery robots being used to deliver goods, contact-free and at curbside. These technologies will conversely become part of scalable, 24/7 delivery models, as they develop, and regulatory frameworks possibly do as well.

The other important trend is the use of Generative AI to interact with customers. Generative AI has the potential to compose interactive and situational dialogues similar to human empathy and creativity, in contrast to traditional chatbots. This means that Q-commerce platforms can and will not only provide real-time help but also an interactive product discovery experience and dedicated shopping advisors, as well as relationship management after the sale with no significant level of human supervision. The systems can write individual messages, come up with product recommendations depending on the changing trends, and even design custom content that can be used as a marketing tool to make the customer involvement more active and emotionally appealing.

At the same time, real-time supply chain automation will be dramatically enhanced by developments in automation. The complete chain of supply, including the sourcing of suppliers, movement of inventory to be picked, and 3PL orders, as well as the delivery, would be coordinated through an AI-driven system in the near future without the involvement of a human. Predictive analytics will be used to predict interruptions in the supplies, and robotic process automation (RPA) will be utilized to run complex logistics and procurement operations in no more than milliseconds. The hyper-automation will allow the platforms to deal with demand surges, shorter lead times, and continue delivering services under such volatile circumstances.

Finally, hyper-personalization, which means that all elements of the user experience (visibility of products, their price, time, and communication) will be customized to personal needs in real-time, will characterize the next stage of Q-commerce. Integrating all these efforts, AI will create super-relevant consumer experiences that will be second nature and feel natural to consumers. Such a move to hyper-personalization will not only enhance engagement with the user but also boost lifetime value because platforms will be highly sensitive to individual habits and needs.

REFERENCES

Astini, R., Royanti, I., & Ramli, Y. Tafiprios, Imaningsih, E. S., & Imaroh, T. S. (2024). The Impact of Quick Commerce that Influence the Purchase Decision of E-Grocery. *Przestrzeń Społeczna (Social Space), 24*(1), 110–128. https://socialspacejournal.eu/menu-script/index.php/ssj/article/view/336

Bhargava, A., Bhargava, D., Kumar, P. N., Sajja, G. S., & Ray, S. (2022). Industrial IoT and AI implementation in vehicular logistics and supply chain management for vehicle mediated transportation systems. *International Journal of System Assurance Engineering and Management, 13*(1), 673–680. DOI: 10.1007/s13198-021-01581-2

Bose, R., Mondal, H., Sarkar, I., & Roy, S. (2022). Design of smart inventory management system for construction sector based on IoT and cloud computing. *E-Prime - Advances in Electrical Engineering. Electronics and Energy*, *2*, 100051. DOI: 10.1016/j.prime.2022.100051

Chavhan, R., & Dutta, P. (2024). Redesigning quick commerce fresh and short food supply chains: Circular economy strategies for sustainable last-mile operations. *British Food Journal*, *127*(5), 1676–1701. DOI: 10.1108/BFJ-05-2024-0560

Chenavaz, R. Y., & Dimitrov, S. (2025). Artificial intelligence and dynamic pricing: A systematic literature review. *Journal of Applied Econometrics*, *28*(1), 2466140. Advance online publication. DOI: 10.1080/15140326.2025.2466140

Chiu, M. C., Huang, J. H., Gupta, S., & Akman, G. (2021). Developing a personalized recommendation system in a smart product service system based on unsupervised learning model. *Computers in Industry*, *128*, 103421. DOI: 10.1016/j.compind.2021.103421

Doshi, J. (2021). Chatbot User Interface for Customer Relationship Management using NLP models. *Proceedings - 2021 1st IEEE International Conference on Artificial Intelligence and Machine Vision, AIMV 2021*. DOI: 10.1109/AIMV53313.2021.9670914

Eliyas, S., & Ranjana, P. (2022). Recommendation Systems: Content-Based Filtering vs Collaborative Filtering. *2022 2nd International Conference on Advance Computing and Innovative Technologies in Engineering, ICACITE 2022*, 1360–1365. DOI: 10.1109/ICACITE53722.2022.9823730

Famil Alamdar, P., & Seifi, A. (2023). Dynamic pricing of differentiated products under competition with reference price effects using a neural network-based approach. *Journal of Revenue and Pricing Management*, *23*(6), 575–587. DOI: 10.1057/s41272-023-00444-8

Fang, X., & Chen, H. C. (2022). Using vendor management inventory system for goods inventory management in IoT manufacturing. *Enterprise Information Systems, 16*(7), 1885743. Advance online publication. DOI: 10.1080/17517575.2021.1885743

Gupta, A., & Jha, D. (2025a). The Rise of Quick Commerce. *Sustainable Digitalization Strategies in Business and Healthcare*, 93–116. : Gupta, A., & Jha, D. (2025b). The Rise of Quick Commerce: Redefining Retail Through Digital Innovation and Sustainable Practices. In *Sustainable Digitalization Strategies in Business and Healthcare* (pp. 93–116). IGI Global Scientific Publishing.DOI: 10.4018/979-8-3373-5087-5.ch004

Gupta, S., Sharma, V., & Tomar, R. (2025). Impact of AI-Driven Personalized Experience in Shaping Consumer Loyalty Towards Quick Commerce. *ESIC 2025 - 5th International Conference on Emerging Systems and Intelligent Computing, Proceedings*, 955–960. DOI: 10.1109/ESIC64052.2025.10962778

Harter, A., Stich, L., & Spann, M. (2024). The Effect of Delivery Time on Repurchase Behavior in Quick Commerce. *Journal of Service Research*. Advance online publication. DOI: 10.1177/10946705241236961

Iyer, P., Sharma, V., Gupta, R., & Chopra, R. (2021). Leveraging Reinforcement Learning and Neural Networks for Optimized Dynamic Pricing Strategies in B2C Markets. *Australian Advanced AI Research Journal, 10*(7). https://aaairj.com/index .php/v1/article/view/6

Javaid, M., Haleem, A., Singh, R. P., Rab, S., & Suman, R. (2022). Exploring impact and features of machine vision for progressive industry 4.0 culture. *Sensors International, 3*, 100132. DOI: 10.1016/j.sintl.2021.100132

Kavitha, S., & Santhanalaxmi, K. (2025). Methods and Applications of Quick Commerce (Q-Commerce). *Methods and Applications of Quick Commerce (Q-Commerce)*, 261–298. : Kumar, C. R., & Manikandan, S. (2025). A Literature Review on Predictive Data Analytics and Learning Models in Stock Market Trend Analysis. *Lecture Notes in Electrical Engineering, 1274 LNEE*, 1175–1180. https:// doi.org/DOI: 10.4018/979-8-3373-1712-0.ch010

Liu, H., Zhang, J., Zhou, Z., Dai, Y., & Qin, L. (2024). A Deep Reinforcement Learning-Based Algorithm for Multi-Objective Agricultural Site Selection and Logistics Optimization Problem. *Applied Sciences 2024, Vol. 14, Page 8479, 14*(18), 8479. DOI: 10.3390/app14188479

Liu, L. (2022). e-Commerce Personalized Recommendation Based on Machine Learning Technology. *Mobile Information Systems, 2022*(1), 1761579. DOI: 10.1155/2022/1761579

Manasa, N., Praveenraj, D. W., & Lakshmi, S. R. (2023). Predictive Analytics for Stock Market Trends using Machine Learning. *2023 4th International Conference on Computation, Automation and Knowledge Management, ICCAKM 2023*. DOI: 10.1109/ICCAKM58659.2023.10449528

Mashayekhy, Y., Babaei, A., Yuan, X. M., & Xue, A. (2022). Impact of Internet of Things (IoT) on Inventory Management: A Literature Survey. *Logistics 2022, Vol. 6, Page 33, 6*(2), 33. DOI: 10.3390/logistics6020033

Naik, A., & Gupta, D. (2025). *Beyond Instant Delivery: Industry Challenges, Market Gaps, and the Future of Quick Commerce*. 402–437. DOI: 10.2991/978-94-6463-766-3_20

Olujimi, P. A., & Ade-Ibijola, A. (2023). NLP techniques for automating responses to customer queries: A systematic review. *Discover Artificial Intelligence, 3*(1), 1–19. DOI: 10.1007/s44163-023-00065-5 PMID: 40478082

Presskila, X. A., Raj, J. R. F., Kumar, P. S., Sankar, G. R., Rajkumar, G. V., & Sundaravadivel, P. (2025a). A Hybrid Learning-Based Q-Commerce Framework Evolving from E-Commerce. *2nd International Conference on Machine Learning and Autonomous Systems, ICMLAS 2025 - Proceedings*, 295–302. DOI: 10.1109/ICMLAS64557.2025.10968475

Presskila, X. A., Raj, J. R. F., Kumar, P. S., Sankar, G. R., Rajkumar, G. V., & Sundaravadivel, P. (2025b). A Hybrid Learning-Based Q-Commerce Framework Evolving from E-Commerce. *2025 International Conference on Machine Learning and Autonomous Systems (ICMLAS)*, 295–302. DOI: 10.1109/ICMLAS64557.2025.10968475

Raha, A. D., Munir, M. S., Adhikary, A., Qiao, Y., Park, S. B., & Hong, C. S. (2023). An Artificial Intelligent-Driven Semantic Communication Framework for Connected Autonomous Vehicular Network. *International Conference on Information Networking, 2023-January*, 352–357. DOI: 10.1109/ICOIN56518.2023.10049005

Rathee, R., Singh, M., & Maurya, I. (2025). Decoding Consumer Emotions in Quick Commerce. *Methods and Applications of Quick Commerce (Q-Commerce)*, 51–74. :
Reis, A., & Nordqvist, S. (2021). *AI utilization in route planning for delivery trucks within the supply chain*. https://lup.lub.lu.se/student-papers/record/9050694DOI: 10.4018/979-8-3373-1712-0.ch003

Schorung, M. (2024). Quick commerce and the evolving business models of the food retail industry - Investigating the quick commerce supply chain and the urban impacts of dark stores. *Transportation Research Procedia, 79*, 305–312. DOI: 10.1016/j.trpro.2024.03.041

Sood, P., Tanwar, H., Singh, J., Ruhela, A. K., Gupta, N., & Kumar, R. (2024). Revolutionizing Customer Service: An AI-powered Chatbot Approach using Advanced NLP Techniques. *Proceedings of the 2024 3rd Edition of IEEE Delhi Section Flagship Conference, DELCON 2024*. DOI: 10.1109/DELCON64804.2024.10866078

Soori, M., Arezoo, B., & Dastres, R. (2023). Internet of things for smart factories in industry 4.0, a review. *Internet of Things and Cyber-Physical Systems, 3*, 192–204. DOI: 10.1016/j.iotcps.2023.04.006

Spiliotis, E., Makridakis, S., Semenoglou, A. A., & Assimakopoulos, V. (2022). Comparison of statistical and machine learning methods for daily SKU demand forecasting. *Operations Research, 22*(3), 3037–3061. DOI: 10.1007/s12351-020-00605-2

Tan, Z. M., Aggarwal, N., Cowls, J., Morley, J., Taddeo, M., & Floridi, L. (2021). The ethical debate about the gig economy: A review and critical analysis. *Technology in Society, 65*, 101594. Advance online publication. DOI: 10.1016/j.techsoc.2021.101594

Tariq, M. U. (2025). Balancing Flexibility and Precarity: Ethical Implications and Sustainable Practices in Global Gig Economies. In *Sustainability and Adaptability of Gig Economies in Global Business* (pp. 323–346). IGI Global Scientific Publishing.

Umair, M. (2026). Hyperlocal Supply Chains for Quick Commerce: An Indian Perspective. In *Methods and Applications of Quick Commerce (Q-Commerce)* (pp. 367–398). IGI Global Scientific Publishing.

Villegas-Ch, W., Navarro, A. M., & Sanchez-Viteri, S. (2024). Optimization of inventory management through computer vision and machine learning technologies. *Intelligent Systems with Applications, 24*, 200438. DOI: 10.1016/j.iswa.2024.200438

Widayanti, R., Chakim, M. H. R., Lukita, C., Rahardja, U., & Lutfiani, N. (2023). Improving Recommender Systems using Hybrid Techniques of Collaborative Filtering and Content-Based Filtering. *Journal of Applied Data Sciences, 4*(3), 289–302. DOI: 10.47738/jads.v4i3.115

Wu, C. (2024). Data privacy: From transparency to fairness. *Technology in Society, 76*, 102457. Advance online publication. DOI: 10.1016/j.techsoc.2024.102457

Yan, Y., Chow, A. H. F., Ho, C. P., Kuo, Y. H., Wu, Q., & Ying, C. (2022). Reinforcement learning for logistics and supply chain management: Methodologies, state of the art, and future opportunities. *Transportation Research Part E, Logistics and Transportation Review, 162*, 102712. DOI: 10.1016/j.tre.2022.102712

Zampieri, M., Nakov, P., & Scherrer, Y. (2020). Natural language processing for similar languages, varieties, and dialects: A survey. In *Natural Language Engineering* (Vol. 26, Issue 6). DOI: 10.1017/S1351324920000492

Zhang, R., Mao, J., Wang, H., Li, B., Cheng, X., & Yang, L. (2024). A Survey on Federated Learning in Intelligent Transportation Systems. *IEEE Transactions on Intelligent Vehicles*, •••, 1–17. DOI: 10.1109/TIV.2024.3446319

Zohdi, M., Rafiee, M., Kayvanfar, V., & Salamiraad, A. (2022). Demand forecasting based machine learning algorithms on customer information: An applied approach. *International Journal of Information Technology : an Official Journal of Bharati Vidyapeeth's Institute of Computer Applications and Management*, *14*(4), 1937–1947. DOI: 10.1007/s41870-022-00875-3

Zong, Z., Feng, T., Xia, T., Jin, D., & Li, Y. (2021). Deep Reinforcement Learning for Demand Driven Services in Logistics and Transportation Systems: A Survey. *ACM Transactions on Knowledge Discovery from Data*. Advance online publication. DOI: 10.1145/3708325/ASSET/62683674-8B9D-4E3C-A6C2-15CCB80B1F9C

Chapter 3
Ai-Powered Promotional Campaigns, Fraud Detection and Security Enhancement

S. Ida Evangeline
https://orcid.org/0000-0003-2997-7897
Government College of Engineering, Tirunelveli, India

ABSTRACT

This chapter explains how artificial intelligence can upgrade point-of-sale (POS) systems by joining three goals—smarter promotions, stronger fraud detection, and tighter security—into one decision layer at checkout. It first describes the AI-enabled POS landscape and the data foundations needed for reliable learning, including clean event streams, privacy-safe identity, feature stores, and delayed labels. It then shows how uplift-based personalisation, basket-aware recommendations, and guardrailed dynamic incentives raise incremental margin without adding friction. For fraud, the chapter combines supervised models with anomaly, sequence, and graph methods to spot refund abuse, coupon misuse, and organised schemes in real time while keeping false positives low. For security, it presents adaptive authentication, endpoint and network analytics, cryptography and tokenisation health checks, and device integrity monitoring, all designed to react quickly and safely.

1 INTRODUCTION

Point-of-sale systems have moved from simple billing terminals to intelligent, connected touchpoints that influence what customers buy, how payments are pro-

DOI: 10.4018/979-8-3373-4392-1.ch003

tected, and how stores defend themselves against threats. As retail becomes more digital and omni-channel, the POS is no longer the end of the journey; it is a live decision surface where pricing, promotion, fraud screening, and security controls must operate together in real time. This chapter examines how artificial intelligence strengthens that surface by improving promotional effectiveness, detecting fraud with speed and precision, and enhancing the security posture of the entire POS ecosystem.

AI adds value at the POS because it can learn from high-velocity data without slowing down checkout. Transaction logs, item attributes, loyalty profiles, device signals, and store context form patterns that are too complex for static rules. Machine learning models can recognise who is likely to respond to an offer, which items tend to be purchased together, and when a sudden change in behaviour hints at misuse or collusion. At the same time, threat-detection models watch the health of terminals and networks, noticing anomalies in firmware, keys, or connections that may indicate tampering or intrusion (Dey et al. 2019). These capabilities turn a traditionally reactive function into a proactive one, where the system adapts to each basket, each customer, and each risk condition.

Promotional optimisation, fraud detection, and security enhancement are interdependent in practice. A personalised discount that increases basket size is valuable only if it does not trigger false fraud declines or expose sensitive data. Fraud controls that aggressively block transactions may reduce chargebacks but will also reduce revenue and harm customer trust if they are not calibrated with marketing goals in mind. Security controls that add friction can frustrate shoppers and staff unless AI tailors the level of authentication to the risk of the moment. Thinking about these three areas together helps retailers design a single intelligence fabric at the POS, rather than three separate systems that work at cross-purposes.

The promise of AI at checkout comes with constraints. Inference must be fast enough to keep queues short. Models must be resilient to seasonality, assortment changes, and data drift across stores and regions. Privacy and consent requirements limit how personal data can be used, and explainability matters when a transaction is declined or when an offer appears at the till. Small retailers often rely on vendor platforms and need simple, trustworthy options; large enterprises must integrate AI into complex estates with legacy POS software, multiple payment processors, and strict governance (Santos & Bacalhau, 2023). These differences affect how solutions are selected, deployed, and measured.

This chapter sets out a practical path. It begins by mapping the AI-enabled POS landscape and the data foundations needed for safe and effective learning. It then details how AI powers promotional campaigns at the point of decision, covering segmentation, propensity and uplift modelling, and basket-aware offers. Next, it explains real-time fraud detection methods, from supervised models to anomaly and graph approaches, and how to balance precision with customer experience. The security section shows how AI supports biometric and risk-based authentication, device integrity monitoring, tokenisation health checks, and network threat detection. Subsequent sections discuss deployment patterns across edge and cloud, metrics for marketing lift and fraud outcomes, compliance and ethics, operating models for teams, and differences between small and large retailers. The chapter closes with near-term trends such as federated learning and edge inference, and with a set of actionable takeaways for phased adoption.

2 THE AI-ENABLED POS LANDSCAPE

Point-of-sale systems have grown from stand-alone cash registers into connected platforms that sit at the centre of store operations. A modern POS often includes a touch screen terminal, a payment pin pad, barcode and RFID scanners, receipt printers, and sometimes cameras or weight sensors. The same store can also run mobile POS on tablets, self-checkout lanes, vending kiosks, and order-ahead counters. All these touchpoints speak to back-office systems for pricing, inventory, loyalty, and payments. The POS is therefore both a checkout tool and a real-time data source that reflects what is happening in the aisle, at the counter, and online.

Connectivity has changed how intelligence is delivered. Many retailers now use a small "edge" computer in the store to handle low-latency tasks, while heavier analytics run in the cloud. Edge inference helps when every millisecond counts, for example when scanning an item and showing a basket-aware offer, or when a fraud score must be ready before authorising a card. Cloud services are used to train models, aggregate data across stores, and push updated models back to the edge. This split keeps queues short while still learning from large datasets (Cui et al. 2022).

Omnichannel patterns also shape the landscape. A shopper may browse online, add items to a wishlist, and then buy in store. Loyalty programmes and digital receipts tie these actions together. When consent is present, the POS can use this context to personalise offers and reduce friction at payment. The same link across channels is useful for fraud detection, because abnormal behaviour often appears when comparing actions across web, app, and store visits. In this setting, identity resolution and tokenisation are important so that data can be matched without exposing sensitive details.

Operational constraints define what AI can do at checkout. Latency budgets are tight, so models must be compact and fast. Terminals go offline at times, so systems need fallbacks that keep selling without losing audit trails or security controls. Stores vary by size, network quality, and staff skills, so deployments must tolerate different hardware and still deliver consistent outcomes (Esch et al. 2021). Legacy POS software and payment rails are common, which means AI services integrate through well-defined APIs, event streams, and message queues rather than deep rewrites.

Security and governance are built into the landscape from the start. Devices are locked down, updates are staged, and keys are rotated on schedule. Data flows are logged for audit. Access is granted on least-privilege rules to reduce insider risk. In this environment, AI does not replace these controls; it sits beside them, monitoring signals from transactions, devices, and networks to guide promotions, flag suspicious activity, and protect the system. This mix of hardware, software, connectivity, and controls is the foundation on which the rest of the chapter builds specific methods for marketing lift, fraud reduction, and stronger security at the POS (Oosthuizen et al. 2021).

3 DATA FOUNDATIONS FOR POS INTELLIGENCE

Strong AI at the point of sale depends on strong data. The POS produces a fast stream of events: items scanned, quantities, prices, discounts applied, payment attempts, approvals, declines, returns, voids, cashier sign-ins, terminal health checks, and network status. Around this stream sit slower but important sources such as item master data, store information, shift rosters, loyalty profiles, promotion calendars, and fraud or incident logs. Bringing these sources together in a clean, timely, and secure way is the first requirement before any model can help with promotions, fraud, or security.

The most common failure is poor event quality. If timestamps are missing or recorded in different time zones, it becomes hard to match a scan with an authorisation or a refund with the original sale. If terminals lose connectivity and buffer events, the order may arrive late and out of sequence. A simple rule helps: always capture event time at source, keep a monotonic sequence per terminal, and include stable keys such as terminal ID, store ID, cashier ID, basket ID, and a privacy-safe customer token when consent exists. When data comes late, systems should still accept it but mark its arrival time, so training pipelines can reconstruct the true order of actions.

Identity resolution at the POS must be privacy-aware. Many use cases work with hashed or tokenised identifiers rather than raw personal data. For example, a loyalty ID can be converted to a rotating token that still lets the system recognise repeat visits without exposing identity. Payment cards should be handled by the payment processor, with only tokens and truncated numbers used downstream. When a customer does not identify themselves, models can still work with basket context, time of day, and store patterns, but should avoid inferring sensitive attributes.

Features are the signals that models learn from. Useful promotional features include basket composition, price elasticity from past purchases, response to previous offers, and seasonality around festivals or paydays. Fraud features include velocity of refunds, frequency of manual overrides, mismatch between scanned items and expected weights, and unusual patterns in cashier shifts or terminal usage. Security features come from device telemetry, such as firmware version changes, failed update attempts, and odd network connections (Jagannathan et al. 2023). A feature store helps manage these signals by defining how each feature is computed, where it is used, and how versions change over time. It also supports online features for real-time decisions and offline features for training, so that the values seen at checkout match the values used in model development.

Labels are equally important and often delayed. For promotions, the right label is not just "did the customer buy," but "did this offer change the purchase compared to what would have happened without it." That requires careful experiment design and holdouts. For fraud, the final truth may arrive weeks later as a chargeback outcome, which means models must learn from delayed feedback and avoid training on their own biased decisions. For security, confirmed incidents are rare, so teams use simulated attacks, red-team exercises, and enriched telemetry to create enough examples for training and testing. All labels should carry a clear provenance record so audits can trace how conclusions were made.

Pipelines need to support both streaming and batch. Real-time inference at checkout uses a streaming path that cleans, enriches, scores, and responds within tight latency budgets. Training and analytics use a batch path that builds daily or weekly datasets, runs quality checks, and retrains models. Data contracts between POS software, payment processors, and AI services set expectations for fields, formats, null handling, and change control (Al Kautsaf et al. 2023). When schemas evolve, backward-compatible fields and deprecation windows reduce breakage in stores.

Monitoring closes the loop. Data drift alerts show when feature distributions move due to assortment changes, new promotions, or a change in store traffic. Freshness dashboards show whether events are arriving on time. Integrity checks compare online features with offline recomputations to detect leakage or skew. Where possible, the store edge keeps a small cache of recent features so that decisions remain stable during short network outages. Every data flow should be logged with correlation IDs to make incident investigation and reconciliation simple.

Governance anchors all of this. Access to raw events is limited on a need-to-know basis. Sensitive attributes are minimised or removed. Retention periods match business and legal needs, with automatic deletion of expired records. Model inputs and outputs are catalogued, and any field that could introduce unfairness is reviewed. Customers are informed about data use in plain language, and their choices are respected at the counter and online (Ji et al. 2025).

4 AI-DRIVEN PROMOTIONAL CAMPAIGNS

AI changes promotions at the point of sale from broad, static discounts to timely, relevant offers that respect customer preferences and business constraints. The aim is not to show the most aggressive price cut, but to present the right incentive to the right person at the right moment, while protecting margin, brand positioning, and customer trust (Ediriweera et al. 2024). This section explains how segmentation, propensity and uplift models, next-best-offer logic, basket-aware recommendations, dynamic price and discount controls, and continuous experimentation come together at checkout.

4.1 Segmentation and micro-cohorts at the POS

Traditional segments such as "value seekers" or "premium shoppers" are too coarse for real-time decisions. AI improves on them by forming micro-cohorts based on recent behaviour, basket composition, visit frequency, and responses to past promotions. A customer who buys staples every week but rarely tries new items benefits from a gentle nudge to sample a related product; another who explores categories widely may be more responsive to bundle suggestions. These cohorts are not fixed labels. They are refreshed as new transactions arrive, so the system remains sensitive to pay-cycle effects, festival seasons, weather changes, and local events that move demand (Di Caro, 2022). When consent is limited or identity is absent, the system falls back to context signals such as time of day, store location, and current basket, which still support useful cohorting without personal data.

4.2 Foundations of Causal Inference

Effective promotional strategies, fraud controls, and security interventions at the point of sale require more than predictive accuracy—they demand clarity on cause and effect. Causal inference provides this foundation, allowing AI systems not just to predict what is likely, but to estimate what would change under an intervention, such as showing a discount, flagging a transaction, or prompting an authentication step.

Pearl (2000) introduced structural causal models (SCMs), which formalize cause-effect relationships using directed graphs and counterfactual reasoning. This framework, along with the potential outcomes approach developed in Rubin's causal model, underpins modern thinking on interventions and their effects.

Wager (2024) advanced this area with causal forests, an adaptation of random forests designed for heterogeneous treatment effect estimation. These models are particularly useful in retail, where treatment effects vary by customer, product, and context. Sheth et al. (2021) and Rossi (2018) emphasize the necessity of experimental design, control groups, and robust estimation methods in marketing analytics, especially when observational data is used.

Recent reviews such as He and Rao (2024) provide a consolidated view of causal inference methods in marketing—spanning difference-in-differences, instrumental variables, regression discontinuity, and synthetic control. These tools help marketers and risk managers answer "what-if" questions with statistical discipline, enabling counterfactual comparisons that go beyond correlations.

In the context of POS AI systems, causal inference is essential for:

- Estimating the incremental lift of personalised promotions
- Measuring the true deterrent effect of fraud prevention steps
- Understanding the impact of security interventions on customer throughput and trust

By grounding decision systems in causal logic, retailers can optimise for long-term outcomes—revenue, trust, and resilience—rather than chasing surface-level metrics.

4.3 Propensity and uplift modelling for offer selection

A propensity model estimates the likelihood that a shopper will take an action, such as accepting a coupon. On its own, high propensity can waste incentives by rewarding purchases that would have happened anyway. Uplift modelling addresses this by estimating the incremental impact of an offer compared to the no-offer case. At the POS, uplift is crucial because every incentive touches margin (Zhang et al. 2021). The system should prefer offers with positive and material uplift, rather than the easiest wins. This requires clean experimentation data with proper control groups, because the true counterfactual is not observed in live traffic (Wang et al. 2024). Over time, the model learns that some shoppers respond better to small, well-timed prompts than to deep discounts, and that certain items drive attachment of profitable complements.

4.4 Real-time experimentation without slowing checkout

Continuous testing keeps promotions honest. The system runs small, persistent holdouts to measure true incremental lift and avoids the trap of believing every declining price is a success. To protect the customer experience, experimentation logic is lightweight and lives close to the decision engine, with randomisation keys derived from basket IDs or privacy-safe tokens.

4.5 Reinforcement Learning in Marketing

While causal inference estimates the effect of isolated actions, reinforcement learning tackles the sequential nature of decisions—where each action influences future states and rewards. This is especially relevant at the point of sale, where a sequence of offers, interventions, or prompts must optimize not only immediate conversion but long-term customer value, trust, and operational stability.

At its core, RL is a framework where an agent learns to make decisions by interacting with an environment to maximize cumulative reward. Sutton and Barto (1998) provides the foundational taxonomy—value functions, policies, and exploration-exploitation trade-offs. In marketing, this translates to systems that learn over time which offers, recommendations, or fraud interventions yield the best long-term outcomes (Abe et. 2004).

Initial applications focused on multi-armed bandits, where algorithms select among competing offers or channels without full feedback. Extensions to contextual bandits—which incorporate customer and basket features—enable more personalised and efficient learning. Sawant et al. (2018) and Zhou et al. (2023) showed how contextual bandits can estimate both uplift and value while balancing exploration and exploitation, bridging causal inference and decision-making.

In POS settings, reinforcement learning enhances:

- Next-best-offer engines that evolve based on real-time acceptance and redemption data
- Fraud and security step-up strategies that adapt based on prior false positive rates and staff intervention success
- Experimentation platforms that explore alternative offer formats or authentication flows with bounded risk

By using RL methods tuned for real-time constraints, guardrails, and sequential outcomes, AI systems at checkout can shift from static rule-based logic to adaptive learning systems that optimise not just for revenue but for sustainable, trusted retail operations.

4.6 Operating the promotion engine in production

Reliable promotions depend on good engineering. A feature store keeps online signals consistent with training data, preventing drift between development and production. Versioned models allow safe rollback if performance degrades. Circuit breakers turn off offer families that exceed error budgets or conflict with stock conditions. Store staff need clear guidance on how offers appear on screens and receipts, and how to handle customer questions. Marketing, pricing, and store operations share dashboards so they see the same truth about uplift, margin, and customer experience. These routines make AI-driven promotions a stable part of daily retail rather than a one-time experiment.

5 REAL-TIME FRAUD DETECTION AT POS

Fraud at the point of sale is a moving target. Tactics range from counterfeit or stolen cards to refund and returns abuse, coupon and discount misuse, and collusion between staff and external actors. Effective defence at checkout requires models that can see patterns within a transaction, across a shift, and across the wider network of stores and devices. The goal is not only to catch bad activity but to do so with minimal disruption to genuine customers (Manoharan et al. 2024).

5.1 Features that reveal fraud without sensitive data

The richest signals are often non-personal. Transaction structure yields item counts, mix of high-risk categories, average item value, basket entropy, scan-to-pay latency, and the sequence of voids, re-scans, and overrides. Device and network telemetry add terminal ID, firmware version, failed update attempts, and unusual IP paths. Payment context contributes entry mode, contactless versus chip, fallback to magstripe, number of retries, and issuer responses. Store context covers time of day, shift start and end, rostered cashier, lane traffic, and whether the store is in a known hotspot for a given pattern (Deng et al. 2024). Loyalty and identity are used only in tokenised form when consent exists, with rotation to reduce tracking risk. A feature store computes these attributes consistently for both streaming inference and batch training so that online values match offline expectations.

5.2 Balancing precision, recall, and customer experience

Fraud is rare, which makes accuracy metrics deceptive. Teams monitor precision and recall at the operating threshold, but they also track false positives per 1,000 transactions, customer-initiated disputes, approval rate for loyal customers, and abandonment after a declined attempt. The business sets acceptable bounds for these outcomes and revisits them before tightening thresholds during a surge. To avoid sudden shocks, new models run in shadow mode to compare live scores with the incumbent (Seera et al. 2024). A small, continuously rotating control group bypasses the model to measure true loss and catch self-reinforcing bias, for example when blocked transactions never receive labels and the model appears better than it is.

5.3 Governance and privacy for durable trust

Fraud prevention relies on careful handling of sensitive data and clear accountability. Access to transaction details is limited by role, model inputs that could introduce bias are reviewed, and retention respects legal timelines. Explanations for adverse actions are captured at the time of decision so that the business can respond to complaints and improve the model (Lalotra et al. 2022). Third-party providers are assessed for their own controls, and changes to model logic follow documented approval and testing steps. These practices reduce legal and reputational risk while making the system easier to audit.

6 SECURITY ENHANCEMENT WITH AI

Security at the point of sale is strongest when it adapts to risk without slowing the lane. AI helps by turning raw device signals, network traces, transaction context, and operator behaviour into timely decisions about authentication, access, and threat response. Instead of relying only on fixed rules, the system learns what "normal" looks like for each store, terminal, and shift, and reacts when something deviates in a meaningful way (Vignesh Saravanan et al. 2023). The aim is a layered defence that protects cardholder data and store systems while keeping checkout smooth.

6.1 Threat detection for POS networks and endpoints

POS terminals and their attached peripherals are attractive targets because they handle sensitive data and often run for long periods without attention. AI-driven endpoint and network analytics build a baseline of process behaviour, file changes, registry activity where applicable, and connection patterns for each terminal type. The model notices when a payment application spawns an unexpected helper process, when a new binary appears outside the approved update window, or when a terminal begins contacting domains that do not fit its usual profile. On the network, the system watches DNS queries, TLS handshakes, and east–west traffic for command-and-control markers or data exfiltration attempts (Fadi et al. 2022). Alerts are prioritised with context such as store criticality, exposure of payment flows, and correlation with recent vendor advisories, so that scarce security staff focus on what matters first.

6.2 Privacy-preserving analytics for security insight

Security analytics need data, but they do not need to expose identity. Tokenised identifiers, purpose-limited feature sets, and short retention windows allow models to learn from behaviour without tracking people. Where cross-store learning is important, federated techniques train models at the store edge and aggregate only the updates, not the raw events. Differential privacy can add calibrated noise to aggregated metrics used for tuning thresholds, so that no single transaction can be reconstructed (Stutz et al. 2024). Sensitive fields are masked before logging, and access to raw traces is restricted to a small set of responders under audit. These practices keep defences strong while honouring consent, law, and customer expectations.

6.3 Human factors and store readiness

Most incidents involve people, not just code. AI can support staff by nudging better behaviour rather than policing after the fact. If a cashier repeatedly overrides price checks or leaves a session unlocked, the system suggests short training and adjusts session timeouts for that terminal. When a phishing simulation runs for store email accounts, the model adapts content by role and records which topics cause confusion (Singhal et al. 2024). Insights are shared with managers in plain language, with actions that fit store realities, such as changing the placement of terminals to reduce shoulder surfing or scheduling updates outside peak hours. Success is measured by fewer risky patterns over time, not only by the number of blocked events.

7 SYSTEM DESIGN AND DEPLOYMENT PATTERNS

Designing AI for the point of sale is a practical engineering problem before it is a research exercise. The system must meet strict latency targets, run reliably in busy stores, and evolve without breaking checkout. A good design separates training from inference, places the right work at the edge and in the cloud, and uses disciplined MLOps so models can change quickly and safely (Kreuzberger et al. 2023). This section describes the main patterns that make such deployments dependable.

The first choice is where to run inference. Edge inference keeps scoring close to the terminal, usually on a small in-store server or on the POS device itself if resources allow. This reduces round-trip time and shields the lane from network hiccups. It suits offer selection, fraud screening, and risk-based authentication where a decision must come back in a few tens of milliseconds. Cloud inference helps when the model is heavy, when features depend on cross-store context, or when centralising simplifies governance. Many retailers use a hybrid: the edge holds compact models and a cache of recent features for speed, while the cloud trains models, aggregates learning across stores, and periodically pushes signed model bundles down to each site. If connectivity drops, the store continues on the last approved bundle and synchronises events when the link returns.

MLOps practices make model changes routine rather than risky. Every model, feature view, and configuration is versioned. New models run in shadow beside the incumbent, scoring the same traffic without affecting decisions, so their drift and stability are visible before promotion. Promotions use canary rollout by store, time window, or traffic slice, with automatic rollback if error budgets are breached (Warnett & Zdun, 2025). Monitoring covers more than accuracy. It watches input freshness, feature distributions, latency percentiles, approval and decline rates, override frequencies, and the gap between online features and an offline recomputation. Each decision carries a correlation ID so incidents can be traced across logs, cases, and receipts.

Operations depend on clear observability and human-readable playbooks. Store dashboards show terminal health, queue time, approval rate, and offer take-up, with simple red-amber-green states rather than raw model metrics. Central teams see fleet-wide patterns, drift alerts, and can trigger controlled actions such as pausing a campaign, raising a fraud threshold, or rolling back a model in a region (Eken et al. 2024). When an alert fires, the playbook names the likely cause and the safe action, for example isolating a terminal, switching to safe-mode offers, or re-seeding a feature cache. Each action is reversible and logged.

Cost and performance are managed by right-sizing. Edge hardware is selected to meet peak lane throughput with headroom for short bursts. Models are compressed or distilled if they cannot meet the latency budget. Batch windows for training align with business rhythms, such as daily price updates or weekly promotion changes, so compute is not wasted. Cloud resources scale with traffic, and cold paths for audit data are moved to cheaper storage tiers after the active learning window closes.

Rollout follows a steady, low-risk rhythm. A pilot runs in a small group of stores with full instrumentation. Feedback from cashiers and managers is folded into product changes, not treated as noise. The next wave expands to diverse store formats to surface edge cases. Only after stable results does the programme scale network-wide (Bayram & Ahmed, 2025). Throughout, marketing, risk, security, and store operations review the same evidence and share ownership of outcomes so that the system reinforces business goals rather than a single function.

8 MEASUREMENT, KPIS, AND ROI

AI at the point of sale must prove its value in numbers that business leaders trust. Measurement begins with a clean baseline and a disciplined counterfactual. For promotions, the right question is not how many offers were redeemed, but how many incremental purchases were created compared to what would have happened without the offer. That requires persistent control groups or rotating holdouts at store, lane, or customer-token level, with enough duration to cover seasonality and pay cycles.

Commercial KPIs should connect directly to contribution margin. Incremental revenue is useful only when paired with the change in discount cost, cannibalisation of higher-margin items, and operational impacts such as longer scan-to-pay times. Attachment rate, average basket value, and repeat-purchase cadence indicate whether offers created lasting behaviour or a one-time spike. In fraud, approval rate for genuine customers, false positives per thousand transactions, and the value-weighted precision and recall at the operating threshold matter more than raw model accuracy (Mahapatra et al. 2024). For security, mean time to detect and mean time to recover quantify resilience, while terminal integrity scores, patch compliance, and key rotation timeliness show cryptographic hygiene in practice. These indicators should be reported with their denominators and confidence ranges so that trends are not mistaken for improvements.

Operational health metrics keep AI from winning on paper while losing in the lane. Latency at the ninety-fifth and ninety-ninth percentiles, cache hit rates for online features, and the share of decisions falling back to safe mode reveal whether the experience is stable at peak. Staff-facing signals—price overrides, manager interventions, and refund handling time—show whether the system adds friction. Customer trust can be tracked through dispute rates, complaint themes, and opt-out behaviour for personalised offers. When fairness and compliance are in scope, periodic bias audits and explanation quality reviews ensure that uplift or risk scoring does not systematically disadvantage protected groups.

Finally, measurement is continuous and reversible. New models run in shadow until their impact is visible on the same KPIs as the incumbent. Canary rollouts protect the network while learning from live traffic. When any metric crosses its error budget—whether latency, approval rate, or incident volume—automatic rollback returns the system to a known-good state, and a brief post-mortem updates playbooks and thresholds (Kurniawan et al. 2023). With this discipline, AI at the POS earns trust: leaders see clear financial value, store teams see stable operations, and customers experience a checkout that is faster, fairer, and more secure.

9 COMPLIANCE, ETHICS, AND CUSTOMER TRUST

Compliance is not a final box to tick after models go live; it is a design constraint that shapes how POS intelligence is built and operated. Laws on payments and privacy, card-scheme rules, and sector codes all meet at the checkout, and customers judge the retailer not only by speed and price but by how respectfully their data and choices are handled. Trust grows when legal duties, ethical standards, and clear communication reinforce one another.

A lawful basis for data use must be established before any learning begins. Much of POS processing is necessary to perform a transaction, but personalisation, loyalty enrichment, biometrics, and cross-channel profiling often rely on explicit consent (Damanik et al. 2025). Consent should be informed, unbundled, and easy to withdraw, with simple cues on the customer display, concise notices near the till, and clear language on digital receipts and account pages. When identity is unknown or consent is absent, the system should switch to context-only decisions that avoid tying behaviour to a person.

Explainability is essential when the system affects a customer's outcome. If an offer appears at the till, a short, human-readable reason helps it feel helpful rather than manipulative. If a transaction requires a step-up or is declined, the receipt or follow-up channel should provide a concise reason code and a route to human review. Internally, every automated decision is linked to a traceable record of inputs, feature versions, and model configuration so that auditors and complaint handlers can reconstruct what happened (Adeolu et al. 2024).. These explanations are specific without revealing internal defences that would aid attackers

Fairness demands active testing, not good intentions. Promotional models should be checked for disparate outcomes, for example whether certain protected groups consistently receive lower-value offers after controlling for relevant context, or whether uplift estimates are biased by historical under-promotion. Fraud scorers should be calibrated so that false-positive burdens do not fall disproportionately on particular cohorts, cards, or geographies. When bias is detected, the response combines feature review, constraint-aware optimisation, reweighting or re-sampling during training, and process changes such as targeted outreach or adjusted frequency caps. Results of these audits are reviewed by a cross-functional governance group, not only by the model owners.

Security obligations sit alongside privacy. Cardholder data environments must remain within scope and under strict controls, with encryption, tokenisation, key rotation, and tamper-evident hardware enforced by policy and verified by telemetry. Third-party providers that touch POS data are vetted for their own controls, contractual data-processing terms are clear on purpose and deletion, and changes to integrations follow change management with rollback plans. Incident handling is rehearsed: alerts carry correlation IDs, evidence is preserved automatically, and notifications follow legal timelines without speculation or blame.

Ethics reaches beyond formal rules. The system avoids dark patterns at checkout, such as hiding the full price behind a promotion, forcing consent through nudges, or exploiting impulsive buying with aggressive prompts. It respects vulnerable customers and minors by suppressing certain categories of offers and by limiting profiling where appropriate. It balances commercial goals with shopper wellbeing, for example by preferring loyalty rewards or bundles over deep discounts that could trigger regret or complaints (Vazquez Melendez et al. 2024).

Trust is earned in the lane through clear signals and responsive service. Staff can explain, in plain words, why an offer appeared or why a step-up was requested. Customers can change preferences without friction and can access a simple privacy centre that lists the kinds of data used at the POS. Complaints are analysed systematically to improve models and messages, and opt-out rates, dispute trends, and explanation quality are tracked as first-class indicators alongside financial KPIs. When mistakes happen, the retailer owns them quickly, fixes the cause, and closes the loop with the customer.

The design of POS intelligence systems must do more than comply on paper—it must embed the principles of GDPR into everyday operations. Voigt and Von dem Bussche (2017) argue for privacy by design as a structural foundation, requiring that data minimisation, purpose limitation, and transparency be built into systems from the outset rather than retrofitted. Tikkinen-Piri et al. (2018) extend this view by highlighting the operational burdens GDPR imposes on personal data–collecting companies, including the need to track consent granularity, limit cross-border transfers, and respond to data subject rights through automated systems. Your chapter's use of rotating tokens, fallback logic when consent is absent, and edge-first learning architectures directly addresses these constraints. Hoofnagle et al. (2019) further situate GDPR as a shift in data governance philosophy—one that elevates individual rights over organisational convenience, particularly in the context of profiling and automated decision-making. By enabling explainability, auditability, and real-time fairness testing, POS systems can honour not only the letter but also the spirit of GDPR, supporting customer trust through transparent, reversible, and respectful interactions at checkout.

10 ORGANISATION, SKILLS, AND GOVERNANCE

AI at the point of sale succeeds when people, process, and technology move together. The operating model should make clear who owns outcomes, who builds and runs the systems, and how decisions are made when marketing goals, fraud risk, and security posture pull in different directions. A simple structure works well: a small central team owns platforms and standards, while embedded specialists sit with marketing, risk, and store operations to shape use cases and measure value. Central ownership keeps feature stores, model registries, data contracts, and observability consistent across brands and regions; embedded practitioners ensure that models answer real store problems and adapt to local context.

Skills cluster into a few roles that must collaborate daily. Data engineers design reliable streams from POS software and payment processors and maintain the online and offline feature views. Machine learning engineers and data scientists build and tune models, compress them for edge inference, and monitor drift, calibration, and latency. Security engineers and fraud analysts define signals that matter, test defences, and respond to incidents with clear playbooks. Product managers balance business goals with operational constraints, sequence the roadmap, and own the KPI ledger that reconciles promotional lift, avoided loss, and stability. Store enablement leads train cashiers and managers, collect feedback from the lane, and translate it into product changes rather than ad-hoc workarounds (Wang et al. 2023). Legal and privacy partners set boundaries and review releases so that designs remain inside policy without slowing the pace of improvements.

Governance turns intent into safe practice. Model risk management starts at design time with purpose statements, input and output reviews, and impact assessments for privacy and fairness. Before deployment, each release passes a checklist that covers training data provenance, evaluation on holdouts, latency budgets, failover behaviour, and explanation quality for adverse decisions. After deployment, dashboards show the same truth to all functions: lift and margin for promotions, approval and false-positive rates for fraud, mean time to detect and recover for security, and the error budgets that trigger automatic rollback. Decisions that materially affect customers or store operations are logged with correlation IDs, model versions, and feature hashes so that audits and complaint handling can reconstruct events precisely.

Clear decision rights prevent stalemates. Thresholds and guardrails for offers, declines, and step-ups are owned jointly by marketing and risk, with security holding a veto when a change would weaken protection. Store operations can pause a campaign or loosen a threshold within defined bounds if queues form or terminals misbehave, and the system records these actions for later review. When trade-offs arise, the team uses an agreed playbook: state the customer impact, estimate financial effect, review compliance constraints, and choose the least disruptive reversible step, then follow up with experimentation or model changes rather than permanent exceptions.

Change management keeps the network steady while it learns. New models run in shadow, then progress through canary phases by store type and region, with rollback always available. Release notes explain what changed in plain language for store staff, and short videos or on-device tips show how offers or prompts will look at the till (Dubey & Das, 2022). Training is brief, repeated, and tied to observed issues, for example handling step-ups gracefully or answering a customer's question about an offer reason. Metrics from the first week after a change receive extra scrutiny so that small drifts do not become habits.

Vendor and partner management needs the same discipline. Contracts specify data boundaries, tokenisation requirements, model ownership, service-level targets for latency and uptime, and obligations for incident reporting and deletion at end of term. Integrations land on documented interfaces rather than custom forks of POS software, and third-party models go through the same risk review as internal ones. Joint runbooks define who acts first when fraud spikes or terminals show tamper signs, and shared drills test that responsibilities are clear.

A mature organisation treats stores as part of the design loop, not just endpoints. Cashiers and managers report friction and odd behaviour through simple channels, and these notes are triaged alongside automated alerts. Small suggestions—clarifying an on-screen message, adjusting an offer explanation, shortening a timeout—often prevent bigger problems. Recognition for stores that improve approval rates or reduce overrides turns adoption into pride rather than compliance.

With this operating model, the retailer can change models frequently without chaos, prove outcomes on a shared KPI ledger, and handle incidents calmly. The skills are well placed, governance is lightweight but firm, and store teams feel supported. AI then becomes a normal part of running the POS—quietly improving conversion, reducing loss, and strengthening security—rather than a fragile project that depends on a few experts (Velte, 2024).

11 SMB vs. Enterprise Implementation Notes

Small and mid-sized retailers usually need outcomes quickly, with minimal technical overhead. The best path is to start with managed services that bundle offer selection, fraud scoring, and basic device telemetry, exposed through simple APIs and lightweight POS plugs. Cloud inference is acceptable if latency remains within the checkout budget; an inexpensive in-store gateway can cache features and model responses to ride out short network issues. Data handling should be narrow and purpose-bound: tokenised payment outcomes, basic basket context, and opt-in loyalty signals are enough to deliver visible lift without building a large data platform. Configuration, not code, drives most behaviour so store managers can adjust frequency caps, discount ceilings, and review thresholds without specialist help. Training focuses on cashiers and supervisors, with clear messages on-screen and short playbooks for step-up checks or refund reviews. Reporting stays simple, showing incremental margin, approval rate, and incident counts in a single dashboard that compares this week to last week.

Large enterprises face scale, heterogeneity, and governance demands. They benefit from a hybrid edge–cloud design, with compact models running in stores and central training across chains and regions. A shared feature store prevents inconsistencies between brands, while a model registry, canary rollout, and shadow evaluation make continuous change safe. Integration lands at defined seams—event streams from POS software, decision topics back to the lane, and tokenised payment signals from processors—so upgrades do not break certifications or partner contracts. Security and compliance are first-class: device attestation, key lifecycle monitoring, federated learning where policy requires local training, and audit-ready explanations for adverse decisions (Akpan & Ibidunni, 2023). Cross-functional governance reconciles promotional lift, avoided fraud, and resilience on a single KPI ledger, preventing double-counting and clarifying trade-offs when thresholds tighten.

A practical migration path avoids big-bang rewrites. Start with one or two high-value use cases, such as basket-aware offers and refund risk scoring, in a small set of diverse stores. Keep a clean control group to measure true incremental value, and leave an easy rollback to a safe, rules-only mode. As confidence grows, add device integrity signals, expand to more stores and formats, and introduce graph or sequence models for organised patterns. For SMBs, success means stable lanes and clear gains with vendor-led tooling (Wynn & Olayinka, 2021). For enterprises, success means a repeatable operating model where models update often, stores stay resilient, and marketing, risk, and security share the same source of truth.

12 SHORT CASE SNAPSHOTS

A national grocer launched basket-aware offers at self-checkout. The model listened to the live basket and store stock rules, then suggested small, relevant add-ons such as fruit with breakfast staples or blades with razors. Guardrails enforced minimum margin and frequency caps. A permanent control group measured true incremental effect. Over six weeks the chain recorded higher attachment without longer queues, with incremental margin rising even when average discount depth fell. Customer complaints about "pushy" promos dropped because the reasoning on the screen was short and clear.

A fashion retailer faced refund abuse clustered around a few stores. Traditional rules caught some cases but raised many false positives. The team added a light-weight risk graph linking cards, receipts, cashiers, terminals, and coupon codes. Risk propagated across the graph and highlighted small communities with abnormal patterns, such as repeated refunds to the same instrument after closing time.

Reviewers saw the transaction timeline and related nodes in one view, approved genuine refunds quickly, and routed suspect cases to manager sign-off. Chargebacks decreased while approval rates for ordinary returns stayed high, and staff reported fewer tense conversations at the counter.

A convenience chain experienced sporadic terminal tampering. Device telemetry from boot state, secure element checks, and peripheral changes streamed to an edge model trained on each store's baseline. When one terminal began showing an unusual sequence of reboots and a new USB profile, the system isolated it at the switch, forced key rotation, and shifted the lane to safe-mode offers (Saad et al. 2021). A technician confirmed a rogue skimmer. Because actions and evidence were logged with correlation IDs, the chain completed forensics and vendor notifications quickly, avoided data exposure, and restored normal operation without disrupting the evening rush.

13 FUTURE DIRECTIONS

The next wave of POS intelligence will be shaped by models that learn closer to the lane, stricter privacy expectations, and tighter integration between marketing, risk, and security decisions. Edge-native learning will move beyond simple inference. Compact models will adapt in store using privacy-safe updates, while a central service aggregates gradients or parameters rather than raw events. This federated pattern will shorten feedback loops for promotions and fraud, reduce exposure of personal data, and make performance less dependent on perfect connectivity (Hussein et al. 2024). Distillation techniques will help by compressing rich central models into lightweight edge versions that retain most of the accuracy within the tight latency budget of checkout.

Privacy-preserving computation will mature from optional to default. Differential privacy will protect aggregate metrics used to tune thresholds and measure uplift. Confidential computing will run sensitive scoring inside hardware-backed enclaves on store gateways, reducing the blast radius of compromise. Tokenisation will remain the norm for payment and loyalty identifiers, but identity will also gain finer controls: rotating tokens that limit linkage over time, purpose tags attached to features, and auditable consent states that travel with each decision. These changes will not only meet legal requirements but also enable more granular data minimisation without sacrificing model quality.

Models will become more context-rich. Multimodal signals—vision from smart scales or cameras, audio cues in staffed lanes, and richer device telemetry—will give models a fuller view of what is happening at the counter while operating under strict privacy and signage rules. Basket-aware recommenders will include real-time inventory and shelf-life predictions so that offers move stock responsibly rather than chasing short-term redemption. Fraud scoring will lean more on graph-based foundations that learn patterns across cards, coupons, terminals, and stores, improving early detection of organised schemes without flooding reviewers with noise.

Decisioning will become more causal and more constrained. Instead of optimising on proxy metrics such as acceptance, promotion engines will use uplift models calibrated with robust holdouts and causal bandits that explore safely within guardrails (Mutashar & Flayyih, 2024). Reinforcement learning will appear in narrow, well-controlled pockets—such as selecting one of a few pre-approved offers—while business constraints on margin, fairness, and frequency act as hard boundaries the learner cannot cross. This approach will keep experimentation alive in production without sacrificing brand trust or profitability.

Security intelligence will keep pace with attackers that target both software and hardware. Device attestation will be continuous, not periodic, with terminals proving their firmware and configuration before accepting model updates. Supply-chain assurance will combine serial-range analytics with shipping telemetry to spot substitution risks. Network analytics will rely more on learned baselines per store, using unsupervised models that adapt as layouts, peripherals, and local conditions change. In parallel, cryptography will prepare for post-quantum threats by introducing quantum-resistant key exchange and signing algorithms in pilot, coordinated with payment partners to avoid fragmented rollouts.

Finally, evaluation will expand beyond accuracy to include trust and resilience. Uplift will be reported with confidence intervals and cannibalisation estimates. Fraud performance will account for delayed labels and positive-unlabelled bias. Security posture will be scored on mean time to detect, mean time to recover, and the fraction of terminals operating in attested, up-to-date states (Rasool & Bhat, 2025). Customer trust will be measured through dispute rates, opt-outs, and explanation comprehension checks, and those indicators will carry as much weight in release decisions as revenue and avoided loss.

14 CONCLUSION

AI at the point of sale works best when it is treated as an operating system for decisions rather than a set of add-on tools. Promotions, fraud control, and security are not separate tracks. They share the same data, the same latency constraints, and the same duty to protect customers while keeping checkout smooth. When these functions are designed together, the POS becomes a single intelligence layer that can nudge purchases responsibly, stop abuse without noise, and defend devices and networks quietly in the background.

The journey starts with foundations. Clean events, privacy-safe identity, well-governed features and labels, and a reliable edge–cloud pipeline allow models to act with confidence. Deployment patterns that include shadow evaluation, canary rollout, and fast rollback make change safe in busy stores. Clear metrics close the loop. Incremental margin, approval and false-positive rates, and resilience indicators show real value rather than vanity numbers. Compliance and ethics shape the design from the start so that explanations are simple, consent is respected, and fairness is tested rather than assumed.

People and process make the system durable. A small central platform team, embedded specialists with marketing, risk, security, and store operations, and shared KPI ledgers keep incentives aligned. SMBs can win with managed services and tight configuration. Enterprises can scale with a common feature store, model registry, and audit-ready decision trails across regions and brands.

With these habits in place, future advances such as federated learning, richer multimodal signals, and post-quantum security can be adopted without disruption. The result is a checkout that is faster, safer, and more trustworthy. Customers feel respected, stores run smoothly, and leaders see measurable impact on margin and risk.

REFERENCES

Abe, N., Verma, N., Apte, C., & Schroko, R. (2004, August). Cross channel optimized marketing by reinforcement learning. In *Proceedings of the tenth ACM SIGKDD international conference on Knowledge discovery and data mining* (pp. 767-772). DOI: 10.1145/1014052.1016912

Adeolu, A. A., Salamntu, L. T. P., & Paschal, I. M. (2024, March). Point of Sales (POS) Terminals for Bank Service Delivery, the needs for Management of Information Security: A case of Nigeria's Banking Sectors. In *2024 Conference on Information Communications Technology and Society (ICTAS)* (pp. 150-160). IEEE. DOI: 10.1109/ICTAS59620.2024.10507146

Akpan, I. J., & Ibidunni, A. S. (2023). Digitization and technological transformation of small business for sustainable development in the less developed and emerging economies: A research note and call for papers. *Journal of Small Business and Entrepreneurship*, *35*(5), 671–676. DOI: 10.1080/08276331.2021.1924505

Al Kautsaf, F. M. bin Mohd Nizam, M. N., & Harun, K. S. (2023, January). A system implementation: Point-of-sales (POS) system integrated with business intelligence (BI) capability focused on SME in Indonesia. In *2023 15th International Conference on Developments in eSystems Engineering (DeSE)* (pp. 287-292). IEEE.

Bayram, F., & Ahmed, B. S. (2025). Towards trustworthy machine learning in production: An overview of the robustness in mlops approach. *ACM Computing Surveys*, *57*(5), 1–35. DOI: 10.1145/3708497

Cui, Y., van Esch, P., & Jain, S. P. (2022). Just walk out: The effect of AI-enabled checkouts. *European Journal of Marketing*, *56*(6), 1650–1683.

Damanik, E. O., Tarigan, W. J., Tampubolon, J., Simanjuntak, D. C. Y., Sihombing, S. D., Saragih, D. Y., Simarmata, P. P., & Simarmata, H. M. P. (2025). Digital Transformation of PT Pos: Customer Loyalty In The Era of Security and Data Technology. *Jurnal Ekuilnomi*, *7*(2), 547–560. DOI: 10.36985/88gt8930

Deng, T., Bi, S., & Xiao, J. (2024, December). Transformer-based financial fraud detection with cloud-optimized real-time streaming. In *Proceedings of the 2024 5th International Conference on Big Data Economy and Information Management* (pp. 702-707). DOI: 10.1145/3724154.3724271

Dey, A., Jain, S., & Nandi, S. (2019, March). New method of POS based on artificial intelligence and cloud computing. In *2019 International Conference on Recent Advances in Energy-efficient Computing and Communication (ICRAECC)* (pp. 1-6). IEEE. DOI: 10.1109/ICRAECC43874.2019.8995078

Di Caro, V. N. (2022). Preterite indicative Pseudo-Coordination and morphomic patterns: The case of the W-Pattern in the dialect of Delia. In *Pseudo-Coordination and Multiple Agreement Constructions* (pp. 99–128). John Benjamins Publishing Company. DOI: 10.1075/la.274.04dic

Dubey, V. K., & Das, A. (2022). Role of governance on SME exports and performance. *Journal of Research in Marketing and Entrepreneurship*, *24*(1), 39–74. DOI: 10.1108/JRME-08-2020-0109

Ediriweera, C., Fernando, M. T., & Pramudika, H. (2024). AI-driven sustainable video marketing strategies: Harnessing deep learning algorithms to sustainable advertising campaigns with special reference to the education industry. *Asian Journal of Marketing Management*, *3*(01). Advance online publication. DOI: 10.31357/ajmm.v3i01.7304

Eken, B., Pallewatta, S., Tran, N., Tosun, A., & Babar, M. A. (2024). A multivocal review of mlops practices, challenges and open issues. *ACM Computing Surveys*.

Esch, P. V., Cui, Y., & Jain, S. P. (2021). Stimulating or intimidating: The effect of AI-enabled in-store communication on consumer patronage likelihood. *Journal of Advertising*, *50*(1), 63–80. DOI: 10.1080/00913367.2020.1832939

Fadi, O., Karim, Z., & Mohammed, B. (2022). A survey on blockchain and artificial intelligence technologies for enhancing security and privacy in smart environments. *IEEE Access : Practical Innovations, Open Solutions*, *10*, 93168–93186. DOI: 10.1109/ACCESS.2022.3203568

He, Z. D., & Rao, V. R. (2024). Methods for Causal Inference in Marketing. *Foundations and Trends® in Marketing, 18*(3-4), 176-309.

Hoofnagle, C. J., Van Der Sloot, B., & Borgesius, F. Z. (2019). The European Union general data protection regulation: What it is and what it means. *Information & Communications Technology Law*, *28*(1), 65–98. DOI: 10.1080/13600834.2019.1573501

Hussein, M. K., Krmln, N. Q., Flayyih, H. H., & Noori, R. B. (2024, June). Harnessing technological innovation and artificial intelligence in Iraqi commercial banks to achieve sustainability. In *International Conference on Explainable Artificial Intelligence in the Digital Sustainability* (pp. 280-296). Cham: Springer Nature Switzerland. DOI: 10.1007/978-3-031-63717-9_18

Jagannathan, S. K., & Bizel, G., JV, T. A., Kannan, G., Sankaradass, V., & Navulla, D. (2023, May). A Smart Innovation of Business Intelligence Based Analytical Model by Using POS Based Deep Learning Model. In *2023 International Conference on Disruptive Technologies (ICDT)* (pp. 63-67). IEEE. DOI: 10.1109/ICDT57929.2023.10151080

Ji, F., Zheng, X., Xue, H., & Wang, J. (2025, April). A study on the application of artificial intelligence in personalized Go-to-market strategy in retail industry. In *Proceedings of the 2025 International Conference on Machine Learning and Neural Networks* (pp. 217-222). DOI: 10.1145/3747227.3747262

Kreuzberger, D., Kühl, N., & Hirschl, S. (2023). Machine learning operations (mlops): Overview, definition, and architecture. *IEEE Access : Practical Innovations, Open Solutions, 11*, 31866–31879. DOI: 10.1109/ACCESS.2023.3262138

Kurniawan, A. C., Harsono, I. N. O., & Ruswandi, N. (2023). Determination of Warehouse Performance Measurement Indicators at PT Pos Logistik Indonesia with The Balanced Scorecard Method. *Majalah Ilmiah Bijak, 20*(1), 132–146. DOI: 10.31334/bijak.v20i1.3120

Lalotra, G. S., Kumar, V., Bhatt, A., Chen, T., & Mahmud, M. (2022). iReTADS: An Intelligent Real-Time Anomaly Detection System for Cloud Communications Using Temporal Data Summarization and Neural Network. *Security and Communication Networks, 2022*(1), 9149164. DOI: 10.1155/2022/9149164

Mahapatra, M., Raut, P., & Dharaskar, A. (2024, June). Effect of CRM on retail POS (point of sale) system. In *1st International Conference, 'Resonance': on Cognitive Approach, Social Ethics and Sustainability* (pp. 77-98). Routledge. DOI: 10.4324/9781003397175-6

Manoharan, G., Dharmaraj, A., Sheela, S. C., Naidu, K., Chavva, M., & Chaudhary, J. K. (2024, May). Machine learning-based real-time fraud detection in financial transactions. In *2024 International Conference on Advances in Computing, Communication and Applied Informatics (ACCAI)* (pp. 1-6). IEEE. DOI: 10.1109/ACCAI61061.2024.10602350

Mutashar, S. S., & Flayyih, H. H. (2024). The Impact of Artificial Intelligence on Accounting Performance: Sustainable Development as a Mediating Variable. *International Journal of Economics and Finance Studies, 16*(2), 36–54.

Oosthuizen, K., Botha, E., Robertson, J., & Montecchi, M. (2021). Artificial intelligence in retail: The AI-enabled value chain. *Australasian Marketing Journal, 29*(3), 264–273. DOI: 10.1016/j.ausmj.2020.07.007

Pearl, J. (2000). Models, reasoning and inference. *Cambridge, UK: Cambridge University Press, 19*(2), 3.

Rasool, N., & Bhat, J. I. (2025). Artificial intelligence in restaurant. In *Artificial intelligence in the food industry* (pp. 171–205). CRC Press.

Rossi, P. E. (2018). 6. Causal inference in marketing applications. *Handbook of Marketing Analytics: Methods and Applications in Marketing Management, Public Policy, and Litigation Support*, 135.

Saad, M., Qin, Z., Ren, K., Nyang, D., & Mohaisen, D. (2021). e-PoS: Making proof-of-stake decentralized and fair. *IEEE Transactions on Parallel and Distributed Systems, 32*(8), 1961–1973. DOI: 10.1109/TPDS.2020.3048853

Santos, V., & Bacalhau, L. M. (2023). Digital transformation of the retail point of sale in the artificial intelligence era. In *Management and Marketing for Improved Retail Competitiveness and Performance* (pp. 200–216). IGI Global. DOI: 10.4018/978-1-6684-8574-3.ch010

Sawant, N., Namballa, C. B., Sadagopan, N., & Nassif, H. (2018). Contextual multi-armed bandits for causal marketing. *arXiv preprint arXiv:1810.01859.*

Seera, M., Lim, C. P., Kumar, A., Dhamotharan, L., & Tan, K. H. (2024). An intelligent payment card fraud detection system. *Annals of Operations Research, 334*(1), 445–467. DOI: 10.1007/s10479-021-04149-2 PMID: 34121790

Sheth, P., Jeong, U., Guo, R., Liu, H., & Candan, K. S. (2021, October). Cause-Box: A Causal Inference Toolbox for BenchmarkingTreatment Effect Estimators with Machine Learning Methods. In *Proceedings of the 30th ACM International Conference on Information & Knowledge Management* (pp. 4789-4793). DOI: 10.1145/3459637.3481974

Singhal, D., Ahuja, L., & Seth, A. (2024). POSMETER: Proof-of-stake blockchain for enhanced smart meter data security. *International Journal of Information Technology : an Official Journal of Bharati Vidyapeeth's Institute of Computer Applications and Management, 16*(2), 1171–1184. DOI: 10.1007/s41870-023-01653-5

Stutz, D., de Assis, J. T., Laghari, A. A., Khan, A. A., Andreopoulos, N., Terziev, A., ... & Grata, E. G. (2024). Enhancing security in cloud computing using artificial intelligence (AI). *Applying Artificial Intelligence in Cybersecurity Analytics and Cyber Threat Detection*, 179-220.

Sutton, R. S., & Barto, A. G. (1998). *No. 1* (Vol. 1). Reinforcement learning: An introduction. MIT press.

Tikkinen-Piri, C., Rohunen, A., & Markkula, J. (2018). EU General Data Protection Regulation: Changes and implications for personal data collecting companies. *Computer Law & Security Review*, *34*(1), 134–153. DOI: 10.1016/j.clsr.2017.05.015

Vazquez Melendez, E. I., Bergey, P., & Smith, B. (2024). Blockchain technology for supply chain provenance: Increasing supply chain efficiency and consumer trust. *Supply Chain Management*, *29*(4), 706–730. DOI: 10.1108/SCM-08-2023-0383

Velte, P. (2024). Sustainable board governance and environmental performance: European evidence. *Business Strategy and the Environment*, *33*(4), 3397–3421. DOI: 10.1002/bse.3654

Vignesh Saravanan, K., Jothi Thilaga, P., Kavipriya, S., & Vijayalakshmi, K. (2023). Data protection and security enhancement in cyber-physical systems using AI and blockchain. In *AI models for blockchain-based intelligent networks in IoT systems: Concepts, Methodologies, tools, and applications* (pp. 285–325). Springer International Publishing. DOI: 10.1007/978-3-031-31952-5_13

Voigt, P., & Von dem Bussche, A. (2017). The eu general data protection regulation (gdpr). *A practical guide, 1st ed., Cham: Springer International Publishing*, *10*(3152676), 10-5555.

Wager, S. (2024, September). *Causal inference: A statistical learning approach.*

Wang, A., Ho, D. C. W., Lai, L. W. C., & Chau, K. W. (2023). Public preferences for government supply of public open space: A neo-institutional economic and lifecycle governance perspective. *Cities (London, England)*, *141*, 104463. DOI: 10.1016/j.cities.2023.104463

Wang, D., Xu, Q., Feng, Y., Ignatius, J., Yin, Y., & Xiao, D. (2024). Uplift modeling and its implications for appointment date prediction in attended home delivery. *Decision Support Systems*, *185*, 114303. DOI: 10.1016/j.dss.2024.114303

Warnett, S. J., & Zdun, U. (2025, March). Bridging the Gap Between MLOps and RLOps: An Industry 4.0 Case Study on Architectural Design Decisions in Practice. In *2025 IEEE 22nd International Conference on Software Architecture (ICSA)* (pp. 232-242). IEEE.

Wynn, M., & Olayinka, O. (2021). E-business strategy in developing countries: A framework and checklist for the small business sector. *Sustainability (Basel)*, *13*(13), 7356. DOI: 10.3390/su13137356

Zhang, W., Li, J., & Liu, L. (2021). A unified survey of treatment effect heterogeneity modelling and uplift modelling. *ACM Computing Surveys*, *54*(8), 1–36.

Zhou, H., Li, S., Jiang, G., Zheng, J., & Wang, D. (2023, June). Direct heterogeneous causal learning for resource allocation problems in marketing. *Proceedings of the AAAI Conference on Artificial Intelligence, 37*(4), 5446–5454. DOI: 10.1609/aaai.v37i4.25677

KEY TERMS AND DEFINITIONS

A/B/n Testing: Running controlled experiments with two or more variants at the POS to measure true impact, not just redemptions.

AI Decisioning: The use of machine learning models to make or support real-time decisions at checkout, such as offers, approvals, or step-ups.

Basket-Aware Recommendation: Suggestions that consider items already in the cart, stock status, and margin guardrails.

Cannibalisation: Sales gained by a promotion that merely replace higher-margin or full-price sales, reducing overall profit.

Chargeback: A cardholder dispute that reverses a transaction after settlement; a key fraud outcome label.

Cloud Inference: Running heavier models in the cloud and sending back decisions; useful for cross-store context and central governance.

Cost-Sensitive Thresholding: Setting decision cut-offs using expected financial value (avoided loss vs. friction cost), not only raw scores.

Dynamic Discount Guardrails: Business limits that cap discount depth, protect margins, respect brand rules, and prevent over-incentivising.

Edge Inference: Running AI models on devices in the store (or a small on-site gateway) so decisions return quickly even if the network is slow.

False Positive / False Negative: A genuine transaction incorrectly flagged as risky (false positive) or a fraudulent one missed by the model (false negative).

Feature Store: A managed catalog of input signals (features) used by models, with consistent online/offline definitions and versions.

Holdout Group: A small, always-on control population that does not receive a treatment, used to estimate incremental lift.

Incremental Lift: The extra revenue or conversion caused by a campaign versus what would have happened without it.

Next-Best-Offer (NBO): The most relevant incentive or recommendation to show now, given the current basket, context, and business rules.

Point of Sale (POS): The place and system where a customer pays for goods or services—includes terminals, scanners, payment pads, self-checkout, and mobile POS.

Precision / Recall: Precision is the share of flagged transactions that were truly risky; recall is the share of all risky transactions the model caught.

Propensity Model: A model that predicts the likelihood a shopper will take an action (for example, redeem an offer).

Refund/Returns Abuse: Illegitimate returns or inflated refunds, often detected by timing, velocity, or pattern anomalies.

Streaming Pipeline: A data flow that processes events (scans, refunds, authorisations) as they happen for low-latency scoring.

Sweethearting: Collusion where a cashier gives unauthorised discounts or free items to an accomplice.

Uplift Modelling: Predicting the incremental effect of an offer compared to showing nothing, so discounts are used only when they change behaviour.

Chapter 4
Ai's Contribution to Predicting Consumer Behavior in Retail Stores

Brahim Boutaleb
https://orcid.org/0009-0006-0228-4328
University of Boumerdes, Algeria

Maher Toukabri
https://orcid.org/0000-0003-3190-2472
Northern Border University, Saudi Arabia & University of Jendouba, Tunisia & Laboratory ARBRE, University of Tunis, Tunisia

ABSTRACT

A key component of retail marketing is the study of consumer behavior, which helps with decision-making about the layout of the product mix that is presented. In the past, retailers found it challenging to forecast customer behavior because the process was expensive and time-consuming due to the large amount of data that needed to be analyzed. However, access to consumer data has become less expensive and time-consuming due to the substantial developments in information and communications technology. Processing this data and turning it into marketing decisions that support customer requirements and aspirations has been made easier by artificial intelligence. Technologies such as machine learning, deep learning, robotics, facial recognition, and augmented reality have been used at retail points of sale by well-known brands like Adidas, Sephora, IKEA, and Amazon Go to understand and meet customer needs.

DOI: 10.4018/979-8-3373-4392-1.ch004

INTRODUCTION

The field of information technology (IT) has seen considerable development since the year 2000, with the rise of cloud computing. Organizations may now archive and manage vast amounts of data for a low cost and with greater security (Singh & Gill, 2023). Cloud computing has helped firms improve the efficiency and efficacy of processing market information, resulting in a considerable increase in dependence on it in marketing. However, this has created a new challenge for businesses: ensuring information security (Alam, 2021). The IT industry kept evolving, leading to the emergence of artificial intelligence as one of the most effective tools in the field of information management. This new technology has been used in numerous scientific, academic, economic, and even medical fields. Marketing, in turn, has benefited greatly from it in market research, Predicting consumer behaviour, and marketing mix design.

The proliferation of smartphones has also made it possible to employ artificial intelligence for data collection. Smartphones are a necessary part of modern life, and people's reliance on them has grown since COVID-19 was introduced (Boutaleb, 2024). In order to handle the enormous volume of data sent by internet-connected smartphones, this situation has made it possible for computer programs and algorithms to proliferate. As a result, businesses are using this knowledge to create smartphones that satisfy the expanding internet demands and preferences of their customers (Boutaleb & Toukabri, 2024). The growing use of smartphones in a variety of scientific, medical, educational, marketing, and social domains has benefited artificial intelligence. Software has been created to recognize symptoms in order to solve problems (Çelik et al, 2024; Mantena et al 2021; Jin et al 2024)and find commercial exploitation opportunities (Kietzmann et al, 2018; Oosthuizen et al, 2021), as well as to recognize trends and influence them (Nugroho, 2025; Okeleke, 2024; Lee et al, 2022; Bharti and Dongre, 2024).

For the business, customers are essential because they are the primary source of its revenue and ensure its viability in a volatile and fiercely competitive market. This implies that a business that has a deeper understanding of its customers can create a product that fulfills their requirements and expectations, making it a competitive option (Boutaleb, 2024). Predicting consumer behaviour is critical for firms to succeed in today's competitive market. With the rapid progress of Artificial Intelligence (AI) technology, businesses are increasingly turning to AI-powered solutions to get important insights into consumer preferences and purchasing patterns (Babu et al, 2023). AI approaches have transformed consumer behavior prediction by allowing both the creation of realistic data and the extraction of useful insights from massive, unstructured datasets.

The use of artificial intelligence (AI) to manage marketing operations has grown in significance due to the current state of business and information and communications technologies. Since the marketing process begins with predicting consumer behavior, we will look at how AI technology can be used to research and forecast consumer behavior in the retail industry. After providing an overview, we shall define artificial intelligence (AI), list its various forms, and discuss related procedures. Next, we'll talk about how it has influenced contemporary marketing in general and the retail industry in particular. We'll also look at how AI can be employed to predict customer behavior.

WHAT IS ARTIFICIAL INTELLIGENCE (AI)?

One of the most significant areas of modern science and technology is artificial intelligence. It seeks to create systems that can think, reason, solve problems, interpret language, and learn from past experiences—tasks that normally call for human intelligence (Russell & Norvig, 2021). Depending on their area of study, researchers have defined artificial intelligence (AI) differently. Some define it in terms of the behavior a system appears to display when interacting with its surroundings, while others concentrate on mental processes that resemble human thought processes (Poole & Mackworth, 2017). AI is able to connect data, identify trends, and produce results across geographical and domain barriers. AI can replace humans in monotonous or boring work, be more consistent than humans, and swiftly adjust to changing inputs. All of these are instances of technological prowess that are readily interpreted as promoting human wellbeing since they improve comprehension and provide new insights into a range of phenomena (Stahl, 2021).

Today, AI is regarded as a discipline of engineering that applies new ideas and approaches to complicated problems. With constant advances in technological speed, capacity, and software programming, computers may someday be as intelligent as humans. Contemporary cybernetics and biosynthetic machines has made a significant contribution to the development of AI (Hamet & Tremblay, 2017). The notion of artificial intelligence (AI) dates back to the mid-twentieth century, when Alan Turing raised the fundamental question, "Can a machine think?" (Turing. 1950). Since then, the discipline has expanded to include a variety of schools, ranging from symbolic AI based on logical rules to statistical AI based on machine learning and deep neural networks (Nilsson 2009). An important part of the global cultural system is artificial intelligence. It suggests things for us to read, watch, listen to, and purchase. It establishes the number of viewers for our shared material. It also assists us in choosing aesthetics when creating media. AI has been used in professional cultural creation to create architecture, music albums, fashion items, product and website designs, movie trailers, and more. To assist us consider the cultural applications of AI both now and in the future, Lev Manovich (2018) has offered a methodological framework. In order to comprehend media, design, and aesthetics in the era of artificial intelligence, he presents new ideas and talks about existing ones

Mc Cartney (2007) answered the question: What is artificial intelligence? as follows: It is the science and technology of creating intelligent machines, specifically computer programs. It is related to the problem of utilizing computers to study human intellect, but AI does not have to constrain itself to physiologically observable ways. According to Nilsson (2009), is "a set of activities aimed at enabling machines to perform functions that would be considered intelligent if performed by humans." For Russell and Norvig (2021), it provides a theoretical and applied framework for researching "intelligent entities," such as machines or humans.

According to Poole and Mackworth (2017), it is an interdisciplinary science that draws from computer science, logic, mathematics, and cognitive science with the goal of creating agents with the capacity for perception, learning, and rational behavior. Which is consistent with the definition provided by Schank (1991) who considered AI as the process by which a computer tries to explain how the (human) system it is modeling behaves. Holmes et al (2004) in turn, defined it as a science and engineering field focused on understanding intelligent behaviour and creating models that demonstrate it.

A thorough definition of artificial intelligence that includes the majority of the components included in all of the above definitions can be created by going over the earlier definitions again: AI is a multidisciplinary area of computing and psychology that focuses on developing computer programs and systems able to modeling human cognitive skills such as comprehension, learning, reasoning, problem-solving, and decision-making, as well as the ability to adapt to new environments and learn from past interactions. Artificial intelligence is built on a foundation of mathematical equations, algorithms, and logic.

TYPES OF AI

According to previous literature, artificial intelligence has been classified according to two criteria: functionality and capabilities.

1. The four types of AI based on functionalities

There are four fundamental categories of artificial intelligence, each with its own variations in complexity and abilities: reactive systems, limited-memory systems, systems with a theory of mind, and self-aware systems.

1.1 Reactive machines are the most basic types of AI. They follow pre-programmed algorithms without remembering or learning from previous experiences. For example, the well-known chess software Deep Blue defeated world champion Garry Kasparov in 1997. It was based on instantaneous location processing with no flexibility for adaptation (Nilsson 2009).

1.2. Limited-memory systems are more common today. They can gain knowledge from previous data under specific constraints and then apply that information to improve future performance. Self-driving automobiles are a popular example, as they make immediate judgments based on previous sensor data (such as the speed of neighboring vehicles or traffic lights) (Russell & Norvig, 2021).

1.3. Theory of Mind. AI systems are theoretical algorithms under investigation that aim to imitate human social and emotional capacities, such as comprehending other people's intentions, beliefs, and feelings. If achieved, this category could transform human-machine interactions, particularly in healthcare and education (Kaplan & Haenlein, 2019).

1.4. Self-aware Artificial intelligence systems represent the most ambitious future step. AI systems are fundamentally different from humans in terms of self-awareness and consciousness. Self-awareness is a key aspect of consciousness, allowing individuals to distinguish themselves from their surroundings. Achieving this feature in AI is challenging because to its intricacy and the nature of consciousness (Watchus, 2024).

2. The three kinds of AI based on capabilities

Artificial intelligence is divided into three types according to capabilities (IBM Data and AI Team, 2023):

2.1. Artificial Narrow AI

Artificial Narrow Intelligence, often known as Weak AI (or Narrow AI), is the only type of AI that currently exists. Any other type of AI is theoretical. It can be trained to accomplish a particular or specific task much faster and better than a human mind.

However, it is unable to perform outside of its assigned mission. Instead, it focuses on a certain subset of cognitive talents and progresses along that range.

Siri, Amazon Alexa, and IBM Watson are instances of narrow AI. Even OpenAI's ChatGPT is classified as Narrow AI because it is limited to a single task: text-based communication.

2.2. General AI

Today, Strong AI, another name for Artificial General Intelligence (AGI), is simply a theoretical idea. Without requiring humans to train the underlying models, AGI may apply prior knowledge and abilities to complete new tasks in a different context. AGI can learn and carry out any intellectual work that a human can thanks to its capability.

2.3. Super AI

Like AGI, super AI is purely theoretical and is often referred to as artificial superintelligence. Super AI would be able to understand, reason, learn, make decisions, and have cognitive capacities that are superior to those of humans if it were ever developed. Applications with Super AI capabilities will have advanced past the point where they can comprehend human emotions and experiences to be able to feel emotions, have wants, and have their own opinions and desires.

Processes relating to AI

As stated below, the AI programs will possess cognitive abilities (reasoning), problem-solving, learning, perception, and self-correction (Sharma & Garg, 2021).

1. Reasoning process

It is the scientific process of using algorithms to predict a specific behaviour, make a decision, extrapolate a phenomenon, or provide specific conclusions.

2. Learning process

Learning is a human trait, and since artificial intelligence, as a concept, is about enabling machines to acquire some of the human traits that enable them to achieve their set goals, algorithms have been designed to help computer programs benefit from past experiences.

3. Problem-solving process

It is employed to obtain the necessary solutions from the current circumstance by adopting an alternative strategy. Problem solving can involve identifying alternatives and choosing the best alternative, which is known as decision making.

4. Perception process

It encompasses the selection, acquisition, interpretation, and ultimately the analysis of information.

5. self-correction process

It is designed to continuously refine the algorithm to ascertain the most precise findings.

ARTIFICIAL INTELLIGENCE'S POSITION IN CONTEMPORARY MARKETING

Since the 1980s, conventional marketing has become increasingly fragmented. Marketing processes, client interactions, and stakeholder relationships (e.g., suppliers, channel intermediates, market contacts) are more prioritized (Brodie, 2008). Business marketing was replicated in the field of product and service marketing. The B to B Marketing differed from mass marketing in that it focused on the seller-buyer relationship by delivering a personalized offer to each individual customer (Coviello & Brodie, 2001). Coviello et al (2003) looked into the relation between relationship marketing, which is the contemporary idea of marketing, and e-marketing. According to the study's findings, e-marketing made it possible for businesses to provide a lot of precise data, which helped them tailor the offers they made to clients. Relationship marketing was formerly exclusive to business-to-business (B2B) marketing, but this helped expand it to the retail and commodity industries. Relationship marketing might include internal marketing, personal/social ties, database management, personalized service, loyalty programs, brand loyalty, and strategic alliances (Coviello & Brodie, 1997).

Some computer programs have been employed to aid in marketing decision-making since marketing people are unable to process vast volumes of market data quickly. However, because they depend on human participation for interpretation, analysis, and decision-making, many applications have demonstrated serious limits. Despite its drawbacks and dangers, artificial intelligence offers marketing professionals a chance because it has some traits with human intellect.

One of the primary foundations that has revolutionized the area of digital marketing is artificial intelligence (AI), which has helped to increase client targeting and provide individualized marketing messages with previously unheard-of accuracy. User data on social media, search engines, and e-commerce platforms can be examined to forecast their future requirements and preferences using sophisticated algorithms and machine learning approaches (Chatterjee et al., 2020; Kietzmann et al., 2018). Marketing will become more individualized in a variety of ways thanks to artificial intelligence. AI is already being used by many businesses to better cater to the needs of their clients by personalizing their emails, videos, social media postings, websites, and other content. Making push notifications responsive to mobile devices, for example, is helping e-commerce firm owners achieve better outcomes. When done correctly, push notifications sent through mobile devices attract more customers' attention since they give them a personalized feel (Nalini, 2021).

Systems for recommendation enable the delivery of tailored material or objects to specific users, increasing the likelihood of engagement and acquisition. Other software programs, such as chatbots, are utilized to improve the customer experience by providing quick responses around the clock, increasing customer satisfaction while cutting after-sales service expenses (Syam & Sharma, 2018). Regarding price, AI technologies enable the optimization of dynamic pricing by integrating consumer preferences, rival tactics, and the supply network (Wisetsri et al, 2021). A multiarmed bandit system with artificial intelligence can dynamically change prices in real-time situations. Bayesian approach inference in machine learning algorithms can swiftly modify the price points to match the competitor's price in situations where pricing is constantly changing, such as e-commerce portals (Verma et al, 2021).

Furthermore, AI has improved analytics capabilities for monitoring the digital success of advertising campaigns and modifying strategies in real time to maximise return on investment (Davenport et al., 2020; Kumar et al., 2019). As therefore, artificial intelligence has emerged as a key driver in the creation of digital marketing strategies that combine precision, speed, and efficacy.

The effectiveness of organizations could be greatly increased by integrating artificial intelligence (AI) into customer relationship management (CRM). In order to successfully integrate AI with CRM, businesses must traverse a complicated and challenging environment that is characterized by the unique characteristics of CRM procedures (Ledro et al, 2023). By speeding up the collection and processing of data and turning it into options that enable the creation of a marketing mix suitable for every consumer, technology has aided in the development of models for marketing decision-making.

AI IN RETAIL OUTLETS

Several major retailers began using AI-based robots to do functions previously executed by human client agents (Sharma & Garg, 2021). Additionally, with the help of artificial intelligence (AI), they are able to exploit the vast amount of data more effectively to market their company. A specific system of advancements and its use in computers with human intelligence, visual-audio perception and recognition, and multilingual translation to make the right commercial judgments (Jaheer Mukthar et al, 2022).

New entrants are upsetting conventional retailers' business models by offering more efficient and valuable consumer experiences. According to new research, the old value chain is inefficient and diminishing as manufacturers, third parties, and customers engage directly (Oosthuizen et al, 2021). If businesses want to succeed in the modern era, they need to adapt how they respond to their customers. Digital transformation in retail requires more than just linking items. Its fundamental goal is to transform data into insights that can be utilized to motivate actions that improve company outcomes. Artificial intelligence can analyze big quantities of customers data, updating it over time to offer the optimum marketing mix to each customer (Arachchi & Samarasinghe, 2023).

Through the five processes of artificial intelligence mentioned earlier in this chapter, the use of computer software allows for: predicting consumer behavior, Marketing problem-solving, Marketing learning, Marketing data processing, and Continuous improvement of sales functionality (Sharma & Garg, 2021). AI has an important role in improving customer experience and managing operations in retail establishments, where it is utilized for demand forecasting, inventory management, and tailored marketing. One of the largest American distribution companies, Walmart, for example, uses AI algorithms to predict the most popular products at specific times of year, reducing stockouts and enhancing supply chain efficiency (Huang & Rust, 2021). Additionally, the American convenience store chain "Amazon Go" uses machine learning and computer vision technology to power smart stores that let customers shop without going through conventional checkouts (Grewal et al., 2021). Furthermore, across e-commerce platforms, AI-based data analytics technologies assist in offering clients tailored recommendations, increasing purchase rates and enhancing customer loyalty (Davenport et al., 2020).

Retailers such as Sephora and H&M deploy AI-powered chatbots to provide specialized customer care on digital platforms. (Davenport et al., 2020). Face recognition technology is used in Alibaba's smart stores to expedite checkout and customize offers for customers (Chen et al., 2021). Starbucks uses artificial intelligence (AI) in its app to offer tailored suggestions based on a user's location and previous purchases (Davenport & Ronanki, 2018). One of the forms of using technology in retail trade is Retail 4.0, commonly referred to as omni-channel retail, emerged from the retail sector's adoption of Industry 4.0 technologies (Sakrabani et al., 2019). Retail 4.0 adoption remains delayed in both developing and developed countries (Har et al., 2022). Prior to the introduction of Retail 4.0, merchants and customers had to cope with price disparities, out-of-stock issues, and long wait times.

AI has emerged as one of the most significant technologies in the retail industry. Approximately 89% of retail and consumer products businesses are currently utilizing or testing AI solutions (NVIDIA, 2025). AI apps have also helped to enhance digital sales. During the 2024 holiday season, internet sales in the United States grew to 282 billion$, thanks in part to the deployment of intelligent chatbots, which increased by 42% from the previous year (Reuters, 2025). These figures show how common AI is in retail, even though some developing nations have been slow to adopt it. Chatbots and consumer-facing AI are used to engage with customers, and the internet is used to gather customer data like cookies and process it using computer programs.

The most important applications of artificial intelligence in the field of value creation in retail outlets can be summarized in Table 1.

Table 1. Utilization of Retailers' AI Technology inside the Retail Value Chain

Value chain stage	Retailer	Detail of Technology Use
Design	Adidas	Employing machine learning to assist customers in designing personalized footwear within 24 hours.
sourcing	Simons	Simons employed analytics to gain better insight into predicted demand and provide stock management suggestions that deliver the appropriate product to the right shop proactively.
Manufacturing	Mohammadi Fashion Sweaters	AI-powered sewing tool that makes sweaters
Inventory management& distribution	ThredUp	Scanning almost 100 million distinct inbound items using image recognition, allowing automatic visual labeling of things and providing a unique item code.
Satisfaction	The Home Depot	Using drones and robotics to offer an effective in-store experience that satisfies customers and allows for speedier processing of orders
sales	Sephora	Customers can try things visually using the app's augmented reality feature. The program scans a customer's face, determines where their lips and eyes are, matches colours, and recommends products for them to purchase.
customer service	Ikea	The customer can visually "place" true-to-scale 3D furniture in their home with the aid of augmented reality.

Source: Oosthuizen et al, 2021.

Table 1 illustrates how artificial intelligence helps retail stores manage their supply chains, guarantee customer satisfaction by incorporating customer feedback into product design, lower inventory management cost, and increase the quality of services offered to customers at stores.

THE IMPORTANCE OF AI IN CONSUMER BEHAVIOUR STUDY

Consumer behavior encompasses all of a consumer's decisions about the acquisition and consumption of goods, services, activities, experiences, people, and ideas by decision-making units (Hoyer et al, 2020). Consumer behavior encompasses a wide range of topics, including the study of how people or groups choose, pay for, utilize, or discard goods, services, concepts, or experiences to fulfill needs and wants (Solomon et al, 2012). Researchers primarily concentrate on consumer behavior, purchasing parameters, and satisfaction, which includes the rationale behind a visit to the retail store, the sort of retail format used, and spending trends for various products (Sangvikar & Katole, 2012).

AI has become an essential tool for understanding consumer behavior in retail settings, enabling merchants to collect and analyze vast amounts of data on customer movements, buying trends, and preferences with amazing accuracy. AI is required in order to analyze consumer behavior, purchases, preferences, dislikes, and other aspects. To help determine the most customer-friendly areas of the store and change the layout of the area to boost sales, some merchants, for instance, use cameras driven by computer vision algorithms to analyze movement patterns around the store (Grewal et al., 2021). Machine learning approaches facilitate the examination of historical purchase behavior to forecast future consumer requirements and tailor goods according to their preferences (Davenport et al., 2020). In their discussion of AI advancements, Nazim Sha and Rajeswari (2019) showed off a computer that uses AI to follow the five senses of humans: sight, hearing, taste, smell, and touch. The findings in the e-commerce industry indicated improved associations between consumers and brands as well as between products and brands.

By using data mining, machine learning, and artificial intelligence to evaluate past data and forecast future trends, marketers can use AI to forecast future consumer behavior. Artificial intelligence gathers and examines data on a user's online activity each time they surf the internet. Numerous details are revealed by this data, including the user's brand preferences and frequency of purchases (Nalini, 2021). Artificial intelligence lets the processing of data from social media platforms like as Facebook, TikTok, and others to better understand consumer behavior and preferences for specific products (Wisetsri et al, 2021).

Gkikas & Theodoridis (2021) define user experience as the intersection of AI and consumer behavior. user experience (UX) will help decision makers understand which entity in the entire AI dataflow is the most important and give extra attention to. User experience (UX) refers to how users engage with technologies, such as graphical user interfaces on websites, web applications, software tools, and robots (Gkikas & Theodoridis, 2021).

As reported by Raji et al. (2024), AI-powered personalization has a significant and diverse impact on consumer behavior in e-commerce. It simplifies options, increases trust, stimulates feedback, adapts to unique experiences, and promotes long-term client loyalty. AI-powered personalization plays a crucial role in molding consumer behavior and fostering long-term relationships between businesses and their customers.

Moreover, AI applications like recommendation systems have improved the customer experience by offering real-time ideas during purchasing, informed by consumer behavior both in-store and online (Huang & Rust, 2021). Sephora employs artificial intelligence tools to assess customer preferences via its digital application and deliver tailored cosmetic recommendations. IKEA has adopted AI-driven augmented reality technology to assist customers in seeing things within their residences, hence enhancing the precision of purchasing decisions (Davenport & Ronanki, 2018).

The decision to buy involves five primary processes, according to marketing literature: identifying the need, collecting information, evaluating options, deciding to buy, and the accompanying emotion of the purchase (Panwar et al, 2019). Examples of how artificial intelligence applications contribute at each of these stages are depicted in Figure 1.

Figure 1. The contribution of AI to the purchasing decision-making process

Source: *Petrescu et al, 2024.*

Chatbots, data analysis, natural language processing, real-time customisation, and content development are key tools for meeting client needs and desires. Many retail outlets have used these techniques to investigate the elements driving consumer behavior and acquire precise data on their customers, allowing them to build a product mix that meets their demands.

PREDICTIVE ANALYTICS FOR CONSUMER BEHAVIOR USING AI

Upon comprehending the elements influencing consumer behavior, we can utilize this information to forecast future purchases. In light of customers' demographic information and past purchases, we tackle the challenge of forecasting the time and cost of their subsequent purchases (Kooti et al, 2016). Consumer behavior encompasses all of the choices that consumers make about finding, buying, assessing, choosing, using, and discarding goods and services that meet their needs (Jobanputra et al, 2023).

Predictive analytics is an effective technique that uses statistical algorithms and historical data to estimate future trends or events. Fundamentally, predictive analytics is the process of examining historical data using a variety of methods to find trends that may be used to forecast future events (Okeleke, 2024). By assigning scores, weights, or criteria to forecast future trends or outcomes, this analysis captures the relationship between components to assess risk through a set of conditions. This will help the organization successfully analyze big data to reap the benefits (Lee et al, 2022).

An increasingly useful technology for analyzing and forecasting customer behavior is artificial intelligence (AI). AI can help businesses create more effective and efficient marketing strategies by processing large amounts of data (Nugroho, 2025). Predictive analytics is greatly improved by artificial intelligence (AI), which introduces cutting-edge technologies that can handle and analyze data more efficiently. Three important AI technologies that are essential to predictive analytics are machine learning, natural language processing, and deep learning (Okeleke, 2024).

Numerous challenging issues, like adaptive control, speech recognition from text, and markup estimate in the building sector, have been effectively resolved by machine learning approaches. ML techniques have recently been put out as a substitute method of software effort prediction (Mair et al, 2000). A number of characteristics that support their use in financial and economic applications are integrated into artificial neural networks, which are machine learning techniques. These methods significantly improve corporate operations since they are flexible in handling different kinds of data and have a high degree of prediction accuracy (Badea, 2014). Another essential AI tool for predictive analytics is natural language processing (NLP). NLP focuses on how computers and human language interact, enabling systems to comprehend, interpret, and produce human language. NLP can be utilized in predictive analytics to examine unstructured data, including feedback, social media posts, and consumer evaluations. Businesses can improve the precision of their forecasts of market trends by deriving insights from this textual data about consumer feelings and preferences events (Okeleke, 2024).

Xu and Donata (2024) developed a model to forecast consumer behavior using deep learning, GRU, and resNet-50. They evaluated the model's performance by contrasting its predictions with actual data. Using social media platforms (Twitter, Amazon, Facebook, and Flipkart) as a source of data, Bharti and Dongre (2024) created a framework that integrates deep learning, neural network (GNNS) capabilities, Q-learning, and VARMAX models to create a model for predicting consumer behavior. In order to create precise predictive models for customer purchasing behavior. Azad et al. (2023) employed an innovative strategy that blends machine learning techniques with the theory of planned behavior (TPB). The strategy examined a number of characteristics, including perceived behavioral control, attitude, and social norm. Pretesting and categorizing marketing communications using objective pattern recognition algorithms is made possible by advances in machine learning applied to functional magnetic resonance imaging (FMRI) data (Calvert &

Brammer, 2012).These algorithms can be used to examine how the brain reacts to existing marketing messages, brands, or goods that have either succeeded or failed in the marketplace, and to find the patterns of brain activity that indicate success or failure (Calvert & Brammer, 2012).

Retail outlets spend less time in supply chains when data is analyzed and translated using artificial intelligence tools like deep learning, smart apps, and the Insight Engine (Oosthuizen et al, 2021). The effectiveness of consumer behavior prediction models, especially those based on artificial intelligence, has increased as a result of consumers' growing reliance on the internet for information on purchases (Kooti et al, 2016).

CONCLUISON

The purpose of artificial intelligence (AI), an interdisciplinary field that incorporates computer technology, logic, mathematics, and cognitive science, is to create agents that are capable of perception, learning, and rational behavior. Two criteria—functionality and capabilities—have been used to categorize artificial intelligence. Five steps are involved in the processes of artificial intelligence: self-correction, perception, problem-solving, learning, and reasoning. Applications of artificial intelligence in marketing in general and retail establishments in particular have emerged as a result of the development of information and communications technology and the widespread use of smartphones. Smart applications are being used by major retail firms to monitor satisfaction of customers, analyze client behavior, and display products. Recommendation systems make it possible to send customized content or items to particular consumers, which raises the possibility of engagement and purchase. Other software applications, like chatbots, are used to enhance the customer experience by offering prompt responses 24/7, boosting client satifaction and lowering after-sales care costs.

Nike and Adidas, two rivals in the sportswear market, have used machine learning to let customers customize the product they wish to purchase (Oosthuizen et al, 2021) Virtual assistants, recommendation engines, and chatbots are being used by other businesses to aid customers in precisely identifying their needs (Okeleke, 2024; Petrescu et al, 2024). Customers may now actively choose the product they want in the store thanks to artificial intelligence, which boosts consumer pleasure and guarantees brand loyalty. Additionally, it expedites the collection, analysis, and use of information during the design process. Nowadays, surveillance cameras and individual facial expression analysis can be used to measure customer satisfaction and understand customer motivations. Trend-defining algorithms can also be used to identify customer preferences based on internet browsing habits. This enables precise and quick pricing as well as the creation of advertising messages that motivate targeted individuals to make purchases.

Social media sites such as Facebook, Twitter, Instagram, Snapchat, and others are considered one of the sources of information that companies rely on to obtain consumer data through the use of modern technologies for collection and analysis, which are characterized by effectiveness and speed. In order to provide items that are appropriate and satisfy the wants and wishes of customers, algorithms are also utilized to study consumer trends. In order to influence consumer behavior during the information search phase and help them find and select the best option, robo-shopping assistants, smart shopping carts, pricing algorithms, and web page content engagement optimization are employed.

One of the contributions of artificial intelligence to retail management is its ability to predict market trends and consumer behavior, through its ability to build evaluable and measurable statistical models. The Technology Acceptance Model (TAM) and the theory of planned behavior (TPB), which are based on machine learning and deep learning, are two examples of models that many researchers have created to better understand consumer behavior and identify the product mix that is presented to them at points of sale (Bharti and Dongre, 2024; Okeleke, 2024; Azad et al, 2023; Calvert & Brammer, 2012).

Even though artificial intelligence is widely used to manage points of sale and study consumer behavior, this presents a number of challenges that researchers and businesses must overcome. These challenges include ensuring the security and confidentiality of customer data, boosting customer confidence in these contemporary technologies, and improving the accuracy of artificial intelligence technologies in providing market information. The scope of this investigation was restricted to reviewing a collection of marketing literature that discussed the application of artificial intelligence in distribution channels and consumer behavior research. A quantitative investigation that assessed the connection between the artificial intelligence variable and the consumer behavior research was absent. Future quantitative studies on the role of AI in marketing decision-making, including how AI can be used to build customer loyalty and how confident customers are in its use, as well as qualitative studies like examining the legal framework surrounding AI use in marketing, are made possible by this.

This research is limited to an analysis of artificial intelligence's application in consumer behavior within the retail sector, based solely on a literature assessment of prior studies on the topic. However, the impact of artificial intelligence on this sector was not statistically measured.

REFERENCES

Alam, T. (2021). Cloud Computing and its role in the Information Technology. [ITSDI]. *IAIC Transactions on Sustainable Digital Innovation*, *1*, 108–115.

Arachchi, H. D. M., & Samarasinghe, G. D. (2023). Impulse purchase intention in an AI-mediated retail environment: Extending the TAM with attitudes towards technology and innovativeness. *Global Business Review*, •••, 09721509231197721. DOI: 10.1177/09721509231197721

Babu, S. M., Kumar, P. P., Devi, S., Reddy, K. P., & Satish, M. (2023, October). Predicting consumer behaviour with artificial intelligence. In *2023 IEEE 5th international conference on cybernetics, cognition and machine learning applications (ICCCMLA)* (pp. 698-703). IEEE.

Badea, L. M. (2014). Predicting consumer behavior with artificial neural networks. *Procedia Economics and Finance*, *15*, 238–246. DOI: 10.1016/S2212-5671(14)00492-4

Bharti, J., & Dongre, S. (2024, June). Deep learning for enhanced consumer behavior analysis and predictive accuracy. In *2024 International Conference on Innovations and Challenges in Emerging Technologies (ICICET)* (pp. 1-6). IEEE. DOI: 10.1109/ICICET59348.2024.10616324

Boutaleb, B. (2024). Factors Influencing Smart Phone Buying Behavior of Consumers: Implications for Building a Marketing Strategy. *Business Ethics and Leadership*, *8*(3), 71–81. DOI: 10.61093/bel.8(3).71-81.2024

Boutaleb, B., & Toukabri, M. (2024). Determinants of Consumer's Adoption of Latest Version Smartphones: An Empirical Study of Saudi Consumers. *Engineering, Technology &. Applied Scientific Research*, *14*(6), 18252–18257. DOI: 10.48084/etasr.8914

Brodie, R. J., Coviello, N. E., & Winklhofer, H. (2008). Contemporary Marketing Practices research program: A review of the first decade. *Journal of Business and Industrial Marketing*, *23*(2), 84–94. DOI: 10.1108/08858620810850191

Calvert, G. A., & Brammer, M. J. (2012). Predicting consumer behavior: Using novel mind-reading approaches. *IEEE Pulse*, *3*(3), 38–41. DOI: 10.1109/MPUL.2012.2189167

Çelik, H., Caf, B. B., Geyik, C., Çebi, G., & Tayfun, M. (2024). Enhancing urinalysis with smartphone and AI: A comprehensive review of point-of-care urinalysis and nutritional advice. *Chemicke Zvesti*, *78*(2), 651–664. DOI: 10.1007/s11696-023-03137-z

Chatterjee, S., Rana, N. P., Tamilmani, K., & Sharma, A. (2020). The next frontier of digital marketing: Artificial intelligence. *International Journal of Information Management*, *54*, 102188. DOI: 10.1016/j.ijinfomgt.2020.102188

Chen, J., Xu, H., & Whinston, A. B. (2021). Moderated online communities and quality of user-generated content. *Journal of Management Information Systems*, *38*(1), 11–40. DOI: 10.1080/07421222.2021.1870386

Coviello, N. E., & Brodie, R. J. (2001). Contemporary marketing practices of consumer and business-to-business firms: How different are they? *Journal of Business and Industrial Marketing*, *16*(5), 382–400. DOI: 10.1108/08858620110400223

Coviello, N. E., Brodie, R. J., Brookes, R. W., & Palmer, R. A. (2003). Assessing the role of e-marketing in contemporary marketing practice. *Journal of Marketing Management*, *19*(7-8), 857–881. DOI: 10.1080/0267257X.2003.9728240

Data, I. B. M., & Team, A. I. (2023). Understanding the different types of artificial intelligence. IBM. https://www.ibm.com/think/topics/artificial-intelligence-types

Davenport, T. H., Guha, A., Grewal, D., & Bressgott, T. (2020). How artificial intelligence will change the future of marketing. *Journal of the Academy of Marketing Science*, *48*(1), 24–42. DOI: 10.1007/s11747-019-00696-0

Davenport, T. H., & Ronanki, R. (2018). Artificial intelligence for the real world. *Harvard Business Review*, *96*(1), 108–116.

Gkikas, D. C., & Theodoridis, P. K. (2021). AI in consumer behavior. In *Advances in Artificial Intelligence-based Technologies: Selected Papers in Honour of Professor Nikolaos G. Bourbakis—Vol. 1* (pp. 147–176). Springer International Publishing.

Grewal, D., Noble, S. M., Roggeveen, A. L., & Nordfält, J. (2021). The future of in-store technology. *Journal of the Academy of Marketing Science*, *49*(1), 96–113. DOI: 10.1007/s11747-019-00697-z

Hamet, P., & Tremblay, J. (2017). Artificial intelligence in medicine. *metabolism, 69*, S36-S40.

Har, L. L., Rashid, U. K., Te Chuan, L., Sen, S. C., & Xia, L. Y. (2022). Revolution of Retail Industry: From Perspective of Retail 1.0 to 4.0. *Procedia Computer Science*, *200*, 1615–1625. DOI: 10.1016/j.procs.2022.01.362

Holmes, J., Sacchi, L., & Bellazzi, R. (2004). Artificial intelligence in medicine. *Annals of the Royal College of Surgeons of England*, *86*(86), 334–338.

Hoyer, W. D., MacInnis, D. J., Pieters, R., Chan, E., & Northey, G. (2020). *Consumer behaviour*. Cengage AU.

Huang, M.-H., & Rust, R. T. (2021). Artificial intelligence in service. *Journal of Service Research*, *24*(1), 3–16. DOI: 10.1177/1094670520902266

Jaheer Mukthar, K. P., Sivasubramanian, K., Ramirez Asis, E. H., & Guerra-Munoz, M. E. (2022). Redesigning and reinvention of retail industry through artificial intelligence (AI). In *Future of organizations and work after the 4th industrial revolution: The role of artificial intelligence, big data, automation, and robotics* (pp. 41–56). Springer International Publishing. DOI: 10.1007/978-3-030-99000-8_3

Jin, K., Li, Y., Wu, H., Tham, Y. C., Koh, V., Zhao, Y., Kawasaki, R., Grzybowski, A., & Ye, J. (2024). Integration of smartphone technology and artificial intelligence for advanced ophthalmic care: A systematic review. *Advances in Ophthalmology Practice and Research*, *4*(3), 120–127. DOI: 10.1016/j.aopr.2024.03.003

Jobanputra, R., Kulkarni, P., Marhoon, H. A., & Palloan, H. (2023, September). Role of artificial intelligence in analyzing and predicting consumer behavior. In. AIP Conference Proceedings: Vol. 2736. *No. 1* (p. 060016). AIP Publishing LLC. DOI: 10.1063/5.0170685

Kaplan, A., & Haenlein, M. (2019). Siri, Siri, in my hand: Who's the fairest in the land? On the interpretations, illustrations, and implications of artificial intelligence. *Business Horizons*, *62*(1), 15–25. DOI: 10.1016/j.bushor.2018.08.004

Kietzmann, J., Paschen, J., & Treen, E. (2018). Artificial intelligence in advertising: How marketers can leverage artificial intelligence along the consumer journey. *Journal of Advertising Research*, *58*(3), 263–267. DOI: 10.2501/JAR-2018-035

Kooti, F., Lerman, K., Aiello, L. M., Grbovic, M., Djuric, N., & Radosavljevic, V. (2016, February). Portrait of an online shopper: Understanding and predicting consumer behavior. In *Proceedings of the ninth ACM international conference on web search and data mining* (pp. 205-214). DOI: 10.1145/2835776.2835831

Kumar, V., Dixit, A., Javalgi, R. G., Dass, M., & Dixit, A. (2019). Digital transformation of business-to-business marketing: Framework, evolution, and research directions. *Industrial Marketing Management*, *81*, 12–25. DOI: 10.1016/j.indmarman.2019.02.034

Ledro, C., Nosella, A., & Dalla Pozza, I. (2023). Integration of AI in CRM: Challenges and guidelines. *Journal of Open Innovation*, *9*(4), 100151. DOI: 10.1016/j.joitmc.2023.100151

Lee, C. S., Cheang, P. Y. S., & Moslehpour, M. (2022). Predictive analytics in business analytics: Decision tree. *Advances in Decision Sciences*, *26*(1), 1–29. DOI: 10.47654/v26y2022i1p1-29

Mair, C., Kadoda, G., Lefley, M., Phalp, K., Schofield, C., Shepperd, M., & Webster, S. (2000). An investigation of machine learning based prediction systems. *Journal of Systems and Software*, *53*(1), 23–29. DOI: 10.1016/S0164-1212(00)00005-4

Manovich, L. (2018). *AI aesthetics*. Strelka Press.

Mantena, S., Celi, L. A., Keshavjee, S., & Beratarrechea, A. (2021). Improving community health-care screenings with smartphone-based AI technologies. *The Lancet. Digital Health*, *3*(5), e280–e282. DOI: 10.1016/S2589-7500(21)00054-6

Nalini, M., Radhakrishnan, D. P., Yogi, G., Santhiya, S., & Harivardhini, V. (2021). Impact of artificial intelligence (AI) on marketing. *International Journal of Aquatic Science*, *12*(2), 3159–3167.

Nazim Sha, S., & Rajeswari, M. (2019). Creating a brand value and consumer satisfaction in E-commerce business using artificial intelligence with the help of vosag technology. *International Journal of Innovative Technology and Exploring Engineering*, *8*(8), 1510–1515.

Nilsson, N. J. (2009). *The quest for artificial intelligence: A history of ideas and achievements*. Cambridge University Press. DOI: 10.1017/CBO9780511819346

Nugroho, D. A. (2025). The Role of AI in Predicting Consumer Behaviour and Effective Marketing Strategies. *Return: Study of Management. Economic and Bussines*, *4*(3), 302–312.

NVIDIA. (2025). AI in retail and CPG survey 2025. Retrieved from https://blogs.nvidia.com/blog/ai-in-retail-cpg-survey-2025

Okeleke, P. A., Ajiga, D., Folorunsho, S. O., & Ezeigweneme, C. (2024). Predictive analytics for market trends using AI: A study in consumer behavior. *International Journal of Engineering Research Updates*, *7*(1), 36–49. DOI: 10.53430/ijeru.2024.7.1.0032

Oosthuizen, K., Botha, E., Robertson, J., & Montecchi, M. (2021). Artificial intelligence in retail: The AI-enabled value chain. *Australasian Marketing Journal*, *29*(3), 264–273. DOI: 10.1016/j.ausmj.2020.07.007

Oosthuizen, K., Botha, E., Robertson, J., & Montecchi, M. (2021). Artificial intelligence in retail: The AI-enabled value chain. *Australasian Marketing Journal*, *29*(3), 264–273. DOI: 10.1016/j.ausmj.2020.07.007

Panwar, D., Anand, S., Ali, F., & Singal, K. (2019). Consumer decision making process models and their applications to market strategy. *International Management Review*, *15*(1), 36–44.

Petrescu, M., Krishen, A. S., Gironda, J. T., & Fergurson, J. R. (2024). Exploring AI technology and consumer behavior in retail interactions. *Journal of Consumer Behaviour*, *23*(6), 3132–3151. DOI: 10.1002/cb.2386

Poole, D., & Mackworth, A. (2017). *Artificial intelligence: Foundations of computational agents* (2nd ed.). Cambridge University Press. DOI: 10.1017/9781108164085

Reuters. (2025, January 6). AI-influenced shopping boosts online holiday sales, Salesforce data shows. Retrieved from https://www.reuters.com/business/retail-consumer/ai-influenced-shopping-boosts-online-holiday-sales-salesforce-data-shows-2025-01-06

Russell, S., & Norvig, P. (2021). *Artificial intelligence: A modern approach* (4th ed.). Pearson.

Russell, S., & Norvig, P. (2021). *Artificial intelligence: A modern approach* (4th ed.). Pearson.

Sakrabani, P., Teoh, A. P., & Amran, A. (2019). Strategic impact of retail 4.0 on retailers' performance in Malaysia. *Strategic Direction*, *35*(11), 1–3. DOI: 10.1108/SD-05-2019-0099

Sangvikar, B. V., & Katole, H. J. (2012). A study of consumer purchase behavior in organized retail outlets. *The Journal of Business and Retail Management Research*, *7*(1), 39–47.

Schank, R. C. (1991). Where's the AI? *AI Magazine*, *12*(4), 38–38.

Sharma, L., & Garg, P. K. (2021). *Artificial Intelligence: Technologies, Applications, and Challenges*. Taylor & Francis. DOI: 10.1201/9781003140351

Singh, R., & Gill, S. S. (2023). Edge AI: A survey. *Internet of Things and Cyber-Physical Systems*, *3*, 71–92. DOI: 10.1016/j.iotcps.2023.02.004

Solomon, M., Russell-Bennett, R., & Previte, J. (2012). *Consumer behaviour*. Pearson Higher Education AU.

Stahl, B. C. (2021). Ethical issues of AI. In *Artificial Intelligence for a better future: An ecosystem perspective on the ethics of AI and emerging digital technologies* (pp. 35–53). Springer International Publishing. DOI: 10.1007/978-3-030-69978-9_4

Syam, N., & Sharma, A. (2018). Waiting for a sales renaissance in the fourth industrial revolution: Machine learning and artificial intelligence in sales research and practice. *Industrial Marketing Management*, *69*, 135–146. DOI: 10.1016/j.indmarman.2017.12.019

Verma, S., Sharma, R., Deb, S., & Maitra, D. (2021). Artificial intelligence in marketing: Systematic review and future research direction. *International Journal of Information Management Data Insights*, *1*(1), 100002. DOI: 10.1016/j.jjimei.2020.100002

Watchus, B. (2024). Towards self-aware ai: Embodiment, feedback loops, and the role of the insula in consciousness. DOI: 10.20944/preprints202411.0661.v1

Wisetsri, W., Ragesh, S. T., Aarthy, C. C. J., Thakur, V., Pandey, D., & Gulati, K. (2021). Systematic analysis and future research directions in artificial intelligence for marketing. *Turkish Journal of Computer and Mathematics Education*, *12*(11), 43–55.

Wisetsri, W., Ragesh, S. T., Aarthy, C. C. J., Thakur, V., Pandey, D., & Gulati, K. (2021). Systematic analysis and future research directions in artificial intelligence for marketing. *Turkish Journal of Computer and Mathematics Education*, *12*(11), 43–55.

Xu, A., Li, Y., & Donta, P. K. (2024). Marketing decision model and consumer behavior prediction with deep learning. [JOEUC]. *Journal of Organizational and End User Computing*, *36*(1), 1–25. DOI: 10.4018/JOEUC.336547

Chapter 5
Customer Journey Analysis:
Insights From a Quantitative Approach on Consumer Behavior Across Touch points

Mahima Dogra
Noida Institute of Engineering and Technology, Greater Noida India

Pawan Kumar
https://orcid.org/0000-0003-4892-6374
Graphic Era University, Dehradun, India

Chahat Sahni
https://orcid.org/0009-0008-1771-6095
Graphic Era University, Dehradun, India

ABSTRACT

This study examines the influence of touchpoint frequency, message consistency, and response time on consumer decision-making, offering valuable insights for businesses aiming to enhance customer engagement. A total of 268 respondents were surveyed using a stratified random sampling technique, ensuring demographic diversity. Employing a cross-sectional research design, the data was analyzed using multiple regression analysis to quantify the relationships between the independent variables and customer decisions. The study found that frequent touchpoints, consistent messaging, and prompt responses significantly enhance the likelihood of favorable consumer decisions. These findings have profound implications for

DOI: 10.4018/979-8-3373-4392-1.ch005

businesses seeking to enhance customer experience, underscoring the importance of integrating these factors for more effective marketing strategies and improved customer satisfaction

1.INTRODUCTION

Consumer behavior in the modern age of market explained by growing complex and diversified ways as consumers are highly affecting by the branding pf products and services. This process based on prediction and linear course, have shifted into touchpoints with dynamic and, variety of experiences (Widayat et al., 2025). Such type of shifting is primarily determined by the at large scale adoption of information technologies and the emerging consumers expectations. As the explosion of offline and digital interactions among stakeholders reshaping the interactions among the consumers with branding and customers participation approaches. From center to this shift is the requirement to know the determinants that affecting the buyers decision throughout their experiences and variables like range from the frequency of touchpoints to the consistency of messaging and the speed at which brands retort to customers queries (Ali et al., 2025). The foundation of customers experiences throughout roots in conventional method, has emerged importantly in recent period of time. Formerly, it was understood as a linear categorization of stages, classically moving from awareness to reflection and, eventually, to buy. Whereas the evolution of digital touchpoints such as websites, mobile apps, social media, and email communications has rendered this linear view obsolete. Today's customer journey is non-linear, characterized by constant movement between stages, with consumers looping back and forth across touchpoints at their discretion. The complexities of this journey necessitate that businesses adopt a more fluid and sophisticated approach to understanding consumer behavior (Meng et al., 2025). It is no longer enough to examine a single touchpoint or interaction; the full spectrum of engagement must be considered to understand how consumers navigate the decision-making process. At the heart of this customer journey lie three essential variables: touchpoint frequency, message consistency, and response time. These elements have been identified as pivotal in shaping consumer engagement and decision-making. Each of these factors plays a crucial role in either facilitating or hindering a consumer's progression along the journey and collectively, they contribute to creating a cohesive experience that can lead to successful conversions and sustained brand loyalty (Quan & Han, 2025). And endeavor of businesses to optimize their marketing approaches and increase customer understanding and satisfaction, domination and influence of these factors have become inevitable. (Munap et al., 2025).

1.1. The Power of Engagement and Touch point frequency:

Touch point frequency describes as the frequency at which a consumer engages with a brand at various points in the customers experience. It comprises interactions with consumers via digital platforms, such as websites, social media, and email promotions, as well as physical level interactions in physical market, call centers, facilitates engagement at offline market. Degree of such interactions plays a vital role in shaping the perception of customers towards brands and their cognition regarding offers and buying decisions. Previous literature recommends that frequent touchpoints lead to greater brand recognition and recall (Herzig & Zander, 2025). Customers having various types of interaction touchpoints for a brand are more found themselves familiar with the brand and recognizing this brand with trust. This frequency has increases the preferences of emotional connection that leads the customers loyalty towards. This spectacle is predominantly noteworthy in businesses where several players contend for customer consideration. Recurrent connections with a brand can decrease the perceived risk of a buying by increasing consumer confidence and strengthening brand value (Moradi & Farzaneh, 2025). Studies on the topic highlights that consistent connections, predominantly during critical moments of the customer expedition, such as in the contemplation and decision-making phases, have the likely to push consumers nearer to making a buying. Though, merely growing the number of touchpoints is not sufficient. The excellence and significance of the touchpoints also play a serious role in their success. Investigations have revealed that customers are more prospective to involve with brands that bid adapted, targeted connections. Whether over email operations tailored to past perusing behavior or social media content that reflects individual favorites, the frequency of touchpoints must be sensible with customers' requirements. Consumers who feel that connections are pertinent to their requirements are more possible to sight the brand certainly and involve more recurrently (Essman et al., 2025). Besides, the mastery of these touchpoints is similarly imperative. Moreover, several touchpoints in a short period can overcome the customer, whereas rare can lead to brand obliviousness. Consequently, industries must purposefully accomplish the incidence and timing of touchpoints to exploit their efficacy.

1.2. Message Consistency: The Bedrock of Trust

Communication uniformity diagonally all touchpoints is another central aspect persuading the behavior of customers. Nowadays, customers relate with brands through a varied assortment of networks, and each interface proposals an occasion to strengthen the brand's uniqueness, values, promises and values. Uneven messaging, whether in contents, tone and delivery, can produce mistrust and confusion. Once a customer meets inconsistent messages across different touchpoints, it demoralizes the brand's trustworthiness, possibly leading to a negative perception about the branding of a product (Mennekes & Schramm-Klein, 2025).

Investigate in the arena highlights the status of transmission a comprehensible and incorporated communication that aligns with the core values of brands. Customers suppose brands to connect their value intentions consistently and clearly irrespective of the stage or standard they routine. When industries uphold message constancy, they make a sense of trustworthiness and reliability, which is critical for building long-term associations. Uniformity nurtures a sense of safety, as customers arise to trust that the brand will bring on its potentials across every communication (Savall-Mañó et al., 2025).

Consistency in messaging and communication has significant role evidenced by the literature that also notes that industries must strike a balance between sustaining consistency and familiarizing their messaging to suit the exceptional touchpoints attributes. The manner and style of messaging on social media may vary from that of a email or website, but the main message should have uniformity. Such flexibility allows brands to involve customers in a way that is most suitable for each network though still strengthening their predominant brand description (Shirdastian et al., 2025). Additionally, in a period where customers have more access to evidence than ever before, message uniformity covers out there a business's owned channels to third-party platforms included. These propagation policies of user-generated content, social media conversations and online reviews, means that a brand's message can be shared, modified and understood by their target stakeholders. It's the accountability of brands that must ensure that the messaging consistency has maintained throughout in these external touchpoints as well and fit. Because such external consistency can meaningfully influence the perception of brand as customers gradually trust on third-party suggestions and comments during buying decisions. (Senan et al., 2025).

1.3. Growing Belief of Proximity: Real time

At present in the age of digitalization where customers have become familiar to prompt access to services and information, response time has emerged as a crucial factor influencing customer decision-making and satisfaction of customers. Study constantly demonstrates that swift replies to investigations whether complete conscious chat, or email exchanges and social media interactions, are definitely connected with advanced levels of satisfaction among the customer. Prompt replies carry a customer focus and sense of reliability while interruptions in message can cause of dissatisfaction and hindrance (Lee, 2025).

Significance of timely response has evolved predominantly apparent during the decision making and consideration of consumers expectations and experiences.

Customers those are find out solutions of their queries and questions feel important which leads in enhance a strong emotional attachment with brand. On the other hand, slow process of response can lead likely customers to observe the brand as insensitive or insensible, which may quick them to unrestraint their buying's and can search options of such brands. Researches have confirmed that customers suppose brands to respond rapidly frequently within a few moments depending on the channel of communication (Chen et al., 2025). The increasing reliance on digital platforms has only heightened this expectation, with many consumers now expecting near-instantaneous feedback during their interactions with brands. While industries are gradually turning to automation techniques, such as and AI-driven customer service platforms and chatbots, to discourse the claim for speedy responses, study designates that automation is not sufficient as a single tool. While these technologies can deliver instant responses to common questions, they must be joined with human oversight to confirm that replies remain relevant, meaningful and personalized. The works on this theme highlights the role of optimization of human participation and automation. (Iniesta-Bonillo et al., 2025).

1.4. The association among the frequency of Touchpoint Frequency, response time and consistency of Messages

Current researches have gradually attentive on the connections between real time response, touchpoint frequency, message consistency. This is possible to survive in long period with ignorance of these factors; the collective impact of these factors is what eventually forms the journey of customers. Investigations has revealed that when these factors work in congruence, they generate a unified customer involvement that rises the probability of a promising decision for products and services. Frequency of communications that sustain a consistency in messaging and rapidly answer to question raised by customers have predominantly role to boost satisfaction and participation of customers.(Maione et al., 2025). On the other hand, if any single factor is not properly managed such as delayed responses and inconsistency in messaging the whole customer journey may be interrupted, foremost to lower rates of adaptation and low level of loyalty for a brand. The interdependence among these variables has made it clear that industries must not only accomplish each component effectually but also mix them in a system that improves customers journey and their experiences. This capability to tactically align frequency of touchpoint frequency, response time and message consistency have evolved a crucial differentiator for industries in today's competitive environment. Businesses that leading the art of handling these factors concurrently will be better positioned to generate seamless, an engaging, and satisfying experiences of consumers that drives both long term loyalty as well as short-term conversions (Tang et al., 2025). The customer trip of customers remains to develop in reply to advancements of technologies and shifting of customers' expectations, industries must remain agreed to the factors that affecting the level of process of decision making of buying a product. Message consistency, Touchpoint frequency, and response time have appeared as key factor during the process of decision, with each playing a different yet interrelated role in formative the experience of customers. Thoughtful how these fundamentals relate and impact consumer psychology is vital for industries looking for to improve their customer visit. With approaches handling these touchpoints, industries can generate a customer trip that not only meets but surpasses expectations of consumer, promotion long-term achievement in an gradually competitive environment (Ajekiigbe et al., 2025).

2. LITERATURE REVIEW

Earlier years, the research of customers experiences has emerged as a important aspect for market to know the customers psychology. Businesses adopting technologies continuously for rapid changes of landscape to know the reaction of customer towards brands. Critical moments from Touchpoints for collaboration between traders and consumers varies from digital encounters to physical presence, and their comprehensive influence scores prominently impact on the procedure of decision. The journey of customers once a time perceived as a predictable sequence and linear sequence has accepted as a robust diversified experience that is highly personalized. Nowadays companies have raised engagement with buyers in various platforms, messages consistency, touchpoint frequency and timely response evolved as a important factors affecting the entire process of decision making. Review from previous studies aims to explore recent results and vital role of various factors those are reshaping the customers experiences (Tonin et al., 2025). Earlier the journey of customer has been observed as a upfront sequence of stages: consideration, awareness and buy of products and services. However, as digital media has proliferated, the journey has become increasingly nonlinear. The traditional stages of the customer journey have been replaced by a more fluid model, where consumers may move back and forth between stages based on external influences such as social media, online reviews, and even personal referrals. This evolution reflects the broader shift in consumer behavior, where traditional paths are now punctuated by various touchpoints that influence decision-making. These touchpoints, whether digital or physical, represent critical opportunities for businesses to engage consumers, enhance their experience, and ultimately drive purchasing decisions. Touchpoint frequency refers to the frequency at which a consumer interacts with a brand across multiple platforms, and recent literature underscores its profound influence on consumer behavior. Increased touchpoint frequency has been linked to greater brand familiarity, trust, and, ultimately, purchase intent (Barhoumi et al., 2025). Businesses that strategically increase the frequency of their touchpoints, particularly during the consideration and evaluation stages, create an environment where consumers feel continually engaged, ultimately leading to higher conversion rates. In the digital age, the frequency of touchpoints can significantly affect brand recall and customer satisfaction. Research suggests that frequent touchpoint interactions keep a brand at the forefront of the consumer's mind, reinforcing brand awareness and emotional connection. Digital platforms, including social media, email marketing, and personalized online experiences, provide businesses with a range of tools to engage with customers on a more regular basis. However, it is not just the number of touchpoints that matters, but their strategic placement within the customer journey (Reshma et al., 2024; Tanwar, Aggarwal, et al., 2024). Studies have shown that while frequent interactions can lead to better consumer engagement, the effectiveness of these touchpoints depends heavily on the timing and context of the interaction. In particular, touchpoints that occur during the critical moments of the buying decision—such as the consideration or intent stages—are more likely to influence consumer behavior positively. Moreover, recent findings suggest that the frequency of touchpoints is not merely a quantitative issue but also a qualitative one. The type of touchpoint, the platform used, and the content presented can all significantly impact how consumers perceive the brand. For instance, consumers may appreciate frequent interactions on social media platforms like Instagram or Twitter, but they may expect more personalized communication through email or customer service interactions. Thus, businesses must tailor their touchpoint strategy to reflect not only the frequency but also the content and delivery method that resonates most with their audience (Sharma et al., 2022; Tanwar, Malhan, et al., 2024).

Message consistency has long been recognized as a critical factor in maintaining brand coherence, trust, and overall consumer satisfaction. As the consumer journey has become more fragmented with the rise of omnichannel marketing, message consistency has become even more vital. Recent studies have shown that consumers expect brands to deliver a cohesive message across all touchpoints whether they are interacting with a company through its website, mobile app, or physical store (A. Kaur et al., 2024). The importance of message consistency is underscored by the fact that inconsistent messaging can lead to confusion, reduced trust, and, ultimately, a decline in customer loyalty. A lack of consistency across channels can create dissonance in the consumer's mind, leading to skepticism about the brand's reliability and value proposition. When a business presents a fragmented or contradictory message, consumers may question the authenticity of the brand, which can directly impact their purchasing decisions. However, the literature also highlights that message consistency does not mean rigidity (Kukreti et al., 2024b). While the core brand message must remain uniform, there is flexibility in how that message can be tailored to suit different touchpoints. For example, while a brand may present a core value proposition across various platforms, the way it is communicated might vary depending on the medium. A brand's social media posts may adopt a more casual and engaging tone, while its website may present information in a more formal, informational manner. In both cases, the underlying message remains consistent, but the approach is tailored to suit the consumer's preferences at each touchpoint (R. Kaur et al., 2025). Moreover, with the rise of consumer-generated content and the increased reliance on user reviews and feedback, businesses now face the added challenge of maintaining message consistency in the face of external voices. Consumers often engage with brands not only through official channels but also through third-party platforms, such as review sites, forums, and social media discussions (Gupta et al., 2025). The consistency of the brand's message must, therefore, extend beyond its owned touchpoints and into the broader online discourse. This dynamic shift in the role of message consistency has become a significant focus in recent research; with studies showing that brands that consistently align their messaging across both official and external touchpoints experience higher levels of customer trust and loyalty. In present time fast-paced, digital-first world, response time has become a crucial factor in determining customer satisfaction and decision-making. Consumers now expect swift and efficient responses from brands, especially in the context of online shopping and customer service interactions. Recent literature has examined the direct relationship between response time and customer satisfaction, highlighting that faster responses lead to higher levels of engagement, trust, and conversion (Yadav et al., 2024). In particular, the immediacy of response times during the consideration and purchase stages is critical. Studies have demonstrated that consumers who receive timely responses to inquiries whether through live chat, email, or social media are more likely to complete their purchase. This finding is particularly relevant for industries such as retail, where consumers may have numerous questions about product features, availability, or delivery timelines (Reshma & Singh Attwal, 2024). Slow response times during these critical decision-making moments can lead to frustration, potentially causing customers to abandon their purchase or switch to a competitor. Research highlights the growing role of automation and AI technologies in reducing response times. Chatbots, automated email systems, and AI-driven customer service platforms are becoming increasingly common in providing quick answers to consumer queries (Sehajpal & Sidhu, 2024). However, while automation can address the need for speed, studies suggest that it is essential to strike a balance between efficiency and personalization. Consumers still expect meaningful interactions, and automated responses that lack personalization or relevance can detract from the overall experience. Therefore, businesses must strike a delicate balance between leveraging automation to improve response times and ensuring that interactions remain customer-centric (Kukreti et al., 2024a).

Recent research suggests that the three key variables touchpoint frequency, message consist ency, and response time do not operate in isolation. Instead, they are interdependent and must be strategically integrated to optimize the customer journey. For example, while frequent interactions with a brand can build familiarity and trust, these interactions must be underpinned by consistent messaging to avoid confusion. Additionally, the effectiveness of frequent touchpoints is contingent upon timely responses, as delays in response can negate the positive effects of frequent engagement. Studies have shown that when touchpoint frequency, message consistency, and response time are aligned, businesses can create a seamless and cohesive customer experience. For instance, a consumer who engages with a brand through multiple touchpoints such as social media, email, and customer service while receiving a consistent message and prompt responses is more likely to develop a positive perception of the brand and proceed with a purchase. In contrast, inconsistencies or delays in any of these variables can disrupt the customer experience and lead to dissatisfaction (Kukreti et al., 2024c).

The collaboration among these factors shows the difficulty of handling customer touchpoints in present scenario of competitiveness. Industries must not only optimize each touchpoint but also ensure that their touchpoint strategy is integrated and coordinated across all platforms. The increasing reliance on digital channels has made this integration even more critical, as consumers now expect a seamless transition between online and offline touchpoints. The ability to deliver consistent, timely, and frequent interactions across both digital and physical channels is essential for creating a comprehensive customer experience that drives brand loyalty. The customer journey has evolved into a multifaceted process that requires businesses to understand and effectively manage a variety of touchpoints. Various researches regarding frequency of touchpoint, consistency in messaging and timely response shows the implication of each factor in influencing psychology of customers. Being firms constantly explore gradually competitive marketplace, digital, integration and factors optimization can be key to steer brand loyalty, customer engagement and satisfaction. Enduring study in this zone delivers valuable understandings into the ever-evolving landscape of customers psychology enabling real direction for industries looking for to improve involvement approaches for customers experience.

3. RESIGN DESIGN

This research used a quantitative cross-sectional survey approach to assess how frequency, of touchpoints, consistency in message, and response time influence customer decision-making, employing stratified random sampling of 268 respondents representing varied behavioral profiles and demographic data have been gathered through structured questionnaires and analyzed using multiple regression techniques to measure the strength and significance of relationships among variables, while reliability and validity were ensured through pre-testing and statistical checks, ultimately aiming to generate empirical insights that help businesses refine their customer engagement strategies and enhance decision-making effectiveness across integrated digital and physical marketing touchpoints.

4. PURPOSE OF THE STUDY

The purpose of this study is to empirically investigate how touchpoint frequency, message consistency, and response time collectively and individually influence consumer decision-making, thereby offering actionable insights for businesses to refine their omnichannel engagement strategies, enhance customer satisfaction, and ensure a seamless, cohesive, and conversion-driven experience across diverse digital and physical interaction points.

Table 1. Variables of the empirical study

S. No.	Variable	Definition (with Complex Vocabulary)
1	Touchpoint Frequency	Refers to the quantitative intensity and recurrence of brand–consumer interactions across multiple communication interfaces, signifying the degree of sustained engagement and the regularity with which consumers encounter the brand throughout their decision-making continuum.
2	Message Consistency	Denotes the strategic uniformity and semantic coherence of brand communication disseminated across diverse channels, ensuring alignment of tone, values, and narrative identity to reinforce cognitive association, brand trust, and perceptual stability among consumers.
3	Response Time	Represents the temporal efficiency and immediacy with which a brand acknowledges, addresses, or resolves consumer inquiries and interactions, reflecting operational agility, customer-centric responsiveness, and the brand's commitment to service excellence.
4	Customers' Decision	Encompasses the culmination of cognitive evaluation, affective inclination, and behavioral intention that drives consumers toward a specific choice or purchase action, shaped by their experiential perceptions of brand engagement, consistency, and responsiveness.

Source: Data and information compiled by authors from various related studies

Table 2. Descriptive Statistics

	N	Minimum	Maximum	Mean		Std. Deviation	Skewness		Kurtosis	
	Statistic	Statistic	Statistic	Statistic	Std. Error	Statistic	Statistic	Std. Error	Statistic	Std. Error
Touchpoint_frequency	268	1.00	7.00	4.8246	.07937	1.29932	-.094	.149	-.436	.297
Consistency_Message	268	2.00	7.00	4.8769	.07633	1.24962	.049	.149	-.452	.297
Response_time	268	1.00	7.00	4.7948	.08050	1.31786	-.220	.149	-.266	.297
Customers_decision	268	1.00	7.00	5.0597	.06904	1.13019	-.181	.149	.157	.297
Valid N (listwise)	268									

The statistical matrix revealed by table 2 that across observations, all variables—Touchpoint Frequency, Consistency of Message, Response Time, and Customers' Decision—demonstrate moderate mean values on a seven-point scale, indicating generally favorable perceptions, while the low standard deviations reflect constrained dispersion; slight positive and negative skewness values suggest mild asymmetry without severe deviation from normality, and marginally negative kurtosis values denote relatively flatter distributions, collectively signifying balanced an reliable data patterns with minimal extremities in respondents' evaluations.

Table 3. Model Summary

Model	R	R Square	Adjusted R Square	Std. Error of the Estimate	Change Statistics					Durbin-Watson
					R Square Change	F Change	df1	df2	Sig. F Change	
1	.881[a]	.776	.769	.75081	.564	113.665	3	264	.000	1.554

a. Predictors: (Constant), Response_time, Touchpoint_frequency, Consistency_Message
b. Dependent Variable: Customers_decision
Source: Data compiled by authors

The regression model exhibits in table 3 that a robust explanatory capability, indicating that customers' decision is strongly influenced by the combined impact of response time, touchpoint frequency, and message consistency, while the adjusted reliability measure confirms the model's stability; the significant change statistics affirm its predictive validity, and the diagnostic test for residual independence suggests minimal autocorrelation, collectively demonstrating a highly coherent, statistically sound, and dependable linear association among the independent constructs and the dependent behavioural outcome.

Table 4.Coefficients

Model		Unstandardized Coefficients		Standardized Coefficients	t	Sig.
		B	Std. Error	Beta		
1	(Constant)	1.239	.212		5.839	.000
	Touchpoint_frequency	.288	.044	.331	6.591	.000
	Consistency_Message	.224	.051	.248	4.396	.000
	Response_time	.280	.044	.326	6.325	.000

a. Dependent Variable: Customers_decision
Source: Data compiled by authors

The regression coefficient analysis reveals by table 4 that all predictor variables—touchpoint frequency, consistency of message, and response time—exert a statistically significant and positive influence on customers' decision, indicating that enhancements in these dimensions substantially elevate decision-making outcomes; the standardized coefficients demonstrate comparable yet distinct magnitudes of impact, suggesting a synergistic interplay among communication consistency, interaction frequency, and responsiveness, while the high significance levels authenticate the robustness and reliability of the model in explicating customer behavioural tendencies within the studied framework.

Table 5.Coefficient Correlationsa

Coefficient Correlations[a]					
Model			Response_time	Touchpoint_frequency	Consistency_Message
1	Correlations	Response_time	1.000	-.149	-.476
		Touchpoint_frequency	-.149	1.000	-.427
		Consistency_Message	-.476	-.427	1.000
	Covariances	Response_time	.002	.000	-.001
		Touchpoint_frequency	.000	.002	-.001
		Consistency_Message	-.001	-.001	.003

a. Dependent Variable: Customers_decision
Source: Data compiled by authors

The coefficient correlation matrix demonstrates in table 5 moderate negative associations among the predictor constructs—response time, touchpoint frequency, and message consistency—indicating partial interdependence without severe multicollinearity; the covariance configuration substantiates minimal overlapping variance, signifying that each independent variable retains distinct predictive potency, thereby ensuring analytical precision, conceptual exclusivity, and structural soundness in explicating variations in customers' decision-making behaviour within the regression framework.

Table 6. Casewise Diagnostics

Case Number	Std. Residual	Customers_decision	Predicted Value	Residual
23	-5.566	1.00	5.1793	-4.17934
55	3.075	7.00	4.6914	2.30864
58	3.085	7.00	4.6835	2.31652
60	3.075	7.00	4.6914	2.30864
169	3.159	7.00	4.6280	2.37201
253	4.427	7.00	3.6760	3.32401

a. Dependent Variable: Customers_decision
Source: Data compiled by authors

The casewise diagnostic outcomes reveal in table 6 the existence of a few influential outliers, as indicated by extreme standardized residuals, suggesting sporadic deviations between observed and predicted customer decision scores; nevertheless, such anomalies appear statistically manageable, signifying that the regression equation maintains overall predictive reliability, stability, and robustness despite marginal cases exhibiting higher variance, thus confirming that model performance remains within acceptable empirical thresholds for behavioural interpretation.

Table 7.

Residuals Statistics					
	Minimum	Maximum	Mean	Std. Deviation	N
Predicted Value	2.4784	6.7776	5.0597	.84849	268
Residual	-4.17934	3.32401	.00000	.74658	268
Std. Predicted Value	-3.042	2.025	.000	1.000	268
Std. Residual	-5.566	4.427	.000	.994	268

a. Dependent Variable: Customers_decision
Source: Data compiled by authors

The residual statistics indicate in table 7 symmetrical data dispersion around the mean with limited deviation, implying minimal systematic error and satisfactory model fit; the standardized values demonstrate that most residuals lie within acceptable statistical bounds, confirming the absence of heteroscedasticity or distortion, while the balanced mean and consistent spread authenticate the model's precision, validating that the predictive framework effectively captures the behavioral tendencies underlying customer decision patterns with analytical reliability. And high empirical coherence.

6. OUTCOMES AND RESULTS OF THE STUDY

This investigation explores the impact of various factors like touchpoint frequency, message consistency, and response time collectively exert a profound and statistically significant influence on consumer decision-making, with touchpoint frequency emerging as the strongest predictor of favorable purchase intent, followed by response time and message consistency, each reinforcing customer trust, loyalty, and engagement; the high explanatory power of the model confirms its robustness, while the observed inter-variable correlations reveal operational trade-offs between engagement intensity, communication coherence, and responsiveness, ultimately demonstrating that effective management of these interconnected dimensions is crucial for optimizing brand perception, enhancing customer satisfaction, and loyalty-oriented consumer decisions across multi-channel dimensions and driving more consistent.

7. IMPLICATIONS OF THE RESEARCH CHAPTER

The study's findings bear profound social and practical significance by emphasizing that frequent, consistent, and timely brand interactions are central to shaping positive consumer experiences, strengthening trust, and fostering loyalty; socially, they highlight the rising demand for authenticity, coherence, and responsiveness in digital consumer relationships, while practically, they guide businesses to strategically integrate touchpoint management, message uniformity, and prompt responsiveness into their marketing frameworks through advanced customer relationship systems and automated tools, ensuring that rapid engagement does not compromise communication quality, thereby enabling brands to cultivate deeper connections, enhance satisfaction, and maintain competitive advantage in an increasingly consumer-driven marketplace and with dynamism.

8. DISCUSSION OF THE STUDY

This empirical research offers evidence that decision taken by the buyers on digital platforms influencing y the frequency of touchpoints, consistency in messaging and real time response. The prediction revealed from statistical inference underlines that high degree of frequency for interaction intensifies the brand resilience and perceptive recall: while such type of participation should be strategically curated to avoid perceptual saturation and fatigues. Correspondingly, the research strengthens that a comprehensible and semantically stable brand description diagonally omni-channel interfaces works as the pivot of trust formation, and enhancing credibility and vindicating cognitive conflict. Additionally, the essential role of temporal responsiveness clarifies consumers' mounting expectation for imminence, wherein overdue brand responses can prompt derail buying purposes. The vigorous explanatory influence of the statistical design regression model proves that these variables do not function in isolation but converge to generate a synergistic effect, and frictionless decision environment and nurturing a more influential. Particularly, frequency of touchpoint emerged as the most influential predictor, suggesting that continuous yet expressive brand presence remains crucial in extremely competitive environment in today's market. Mutually, the conclusions emphasize the need for organizations to compose a harmonized engagement ecosystem balancing exposure, agility to optimize experiential value, coherence, safe continuous competitive benefit and excite trustworthy behavioural intents.

9. LIMITATIONS OF THE RESEARCH STUDY

Notwithstanding its observed robust and rigor research design based empirical study, investigation is not free from limitations in context of contextual and methodological that restrict the generalizability of its verdicts. Initially, the cross-sectional design working limits underlying implication, as the data apprehension perception of consumer at a single temporal interval rather than exemplifying behavioural progress across the period. Subsequently, longitudinal differences in customer participation or engagement dynamics persist unexplored. Then, the dependence on self-reported trials through structured surveys may have engendered response prejudices mainly cognitive distortion and social prestige thus prompting the genuineness of documented insights. Moreover, the composition of sample though stratified have been demographically and geographically incomplete, which may not present holistically denote the heterogeneity of digital consumers working across different socio-economic scales. This investigation concentrates on three key factors frequency of touchpoint, consistency of message and real time response whereas supposedly noteworthy, overlooks other latent factors like the contextual and psychographic attributes like the emotional resonance, perceived value and brand trust, that may mediate the findings of the influencing behaviour. Constraints from Statistical points of view including unobserved endogeneity and latent multicollinearity, additional compel revealing accuracy. At last, the growing advance technological ecosystem manifest by predictive analytics and AI-driven personalization extracts consumer behaviour highly instable, inferring that the relations outlined herein may vary with swings in digital communication paradigms and algorithmic visit symbols. Since such limits collectively require carefulness in extrapolating conclusions across businesses or cultural settings without extra empirical validation.

10.FUTURE SCOPE OF THE STUDY

This research may extend the present study across interdisciplinary and longitudinal mechanism that apprehension the chronological progress of behavioural consequences and its consumer engagement. Growing the analytical outline to integrate moderating and mediating variables such as trust orientation, emotional intelligence, cultural cognition and perceived personalization, could bid a more nuanced conception of decision procedure and style. Engaging combines methods that cartel quantitative modelling with qualitative explanatory examines may also expose deeper psychographic undercurrents persuading digital decision-making routes. Besides, relative cross-cultural investigations could outline how technological, socio-economic, and cultural heterogeneousness forms the interaction among frequency of touchpoint, consistency in messages and response at time. Mixing advanced computational methods such as SEM (structural equation modelling), and sentiment analytics and machine learning algorithms could extra improve predictive correctness and enable real-time recording of customer involvements. Upcoming study might also discover the role of AI, metaverse-based contact atmospheres, and immersive skills like virtual reality and augmented in redefining brand lines for consumers. In context of management points of view researchers may conduct research survey to investigate the ecosystem of omni channel optimization, balancing of automation with atheneite along with human to customers connection with brands. Lastly, integrating ethical dimensions and environmental into forthcoming researches could brighten how sustainability awareness interconnects with brand coherence and digital responsiveness. With advancement the lines of investigations the future researches can develop an advanced academic style that glasses the energy in the 21st centuries customer, contributing both to practical novelties in marketing intelligence and academic enrichment.Bottom of Form

11. CONCLUSION

In the summary of this research findings it underlines that touchpoint frequency, message consistency, and response time collectively serve as critical determinants of customer decision-making, revealing that frequent and coherent brand interactions, coupled with timely responses, substantially enhance consumer trust, loyalty, and purchase intent; it underscores the necessity for businesses to balance engagement intensity with communication quality and operational efficiency, ensuring responsiveness without compromising message integrity, thereby promoting a cohesive and customer-centric engagement strategy that strengthens brand credibility, sustains satisfaction, and drives competitive advantage within today's dynamic digital marketplace where consumer expectations demand authenticity, immediacy, and consistent experiential value throughout the domain of channels. The outcomes of this research surpass the limits of customers behavior by enlightens the pure dependencies that controls decision making process within digital network ecosystem. Nowadays in the contemporary world markets symbolized by experimental proximity and algorithm mediation, the customer no longer lodges a in active role but works as a co-generator of brand values. The model changes required that firms nurture not simply transactional associations but epistemological familiarity a profound cognitive knowledge, impactful and behavioral instincts that shifting the customers perception for judgements. Subsequently, the link between messages consistency, engagement frequency, and timely replies with good responsiveness must be redesigned as a dynamic triangle that endlessly grows in retort to behavioral plasticity and technological acceleration. In the context of strategical point, the research underscores the rising indispensableness of cardinal agility and data-driven personalization as the fundamental's sustainable competitive environment. Brands that positively mix and AI-augmented decision systems and predictive analytics into their customer relationship design will direct adaptability in present smart markets. Though, this integration must be escorted by semantic coherence and ethical governance to avoid erosion of consumer trust and algorithmic overreach. Capability to improve technology guaranteeing that automation intensifies considerate rather than weakens it will outline the future prospects of differentiation in present super market. Also, the conclusions bid convincing indication for the academic reconceptualization of "consumer touchpoints" as not simply transactional incidents but as places of symbolic meanings of exchange and construction. Respectively communication backs to a collective semiotic embroidery that regulates how consumers observe genuineness and worth. Rationality of this story is deeply prejudiced by message constancy, which works as the semantic anchor alleviating identity of brand identity amid mutable market incentives. Henceforth, upholding ethical uniformity and linguistic, tonal, across stages is not only a marketing imperious but a logical one an appearance of corporate honor in a fragmented messaging and communication atmosphere. Furthermore, the empirical design outlines in this research improves the discourse on buyers' decision making through enabling quantifiable authentication of academic constructs frequently preserved as intangible or abstract. The strength of the statistical relations not merely strengthens the consistency of the concepts but also covers the way for extrapolative behavioral model. Like Such type of quantitative analysis, the consumer mindset from a expressive science into a rigid castigation, permitting governments to pre-empt behavioral changes with extraordinary accuracy. Such advance design assists as a critical walking stone toward emerging adaptive advertising architectures accomplished of replying to instability in real period-based response. Eventually, the investigation invitations a re-assessment of what establishes "engagement" in the time highly connectivity in market. Meeting must be redefined beyond simple collaboration metrics to summarize cognitive involvement, and relational continuity and emotional resonance. Brands that leading this multi-dimensional appointment will transcend transactional trustworthiness, attaining in its place a method of affective commitment stuck in trust, experiential genuineness and consistency. In deed so, they will not only enhance financial performance but also contribute to the formation of a digital market place known as pro humanize which one that joy linking over and meaning over metrics and adaptation.

REFERENCES

Ajekiigbe, V. O., Ogieuhi, I. J., Anthony, C. S., Bakare, I. S., Anyacho, S., Ogunleke, P. O., Fatokun, D. I., Akinmeji, O., Ruth, O. T., Olaore, A. K., Amusa, O., & Agbo, C. E. (2025). Consumer behavior and its role in E. coli outbreaks: The impact of fast-food preparation practices and hygiene awareness. *Tropical Medicine and Health, 53*(1), 27. Advance online publication. DOI: 10.1186/s41182-025-00710-y

Ali, L., Ali, F., Abdalla, M. J., & Alotaibi, S. (2025). Beyond the hype: Evaluating the impact of generative AI on brand authenticity, image, and consumer behavior in the restaurant industry. *International Journal of Hospitality Management, 131*, 104318. Advance online publication. DOI: 10.1016/j.ijhm.2025.104318

Barhoumi, L., Rached, Z., & Boudiche, S. (2025). Tunisian Consumer Behavior and Acceptance of Farmed Fish Versus Wild Fish and Its Determinants Factors. *Aquaculture Studies, 25*(4), 173–181. DOI: 10.4194/AQUAST2236

Chen, Z., Wu, J., Tian, C., & Liu, Z. (2025). Gray market speculation: Analyzing retailer behavior and manufacturer strategies in the context of strategic consumer behavior. *International Journal of Production Economics, 284*, 109607. Advance online publication. DOI: 10.1016/j.ijpe.2025.109607

Essman, M., Burgoine, T., Jones, A., Polden, M., Robinson, E., Sacks, G., Sharp, S. J., Smith, R., Vanderlee, L., White, C. M., White, M., Hammond, D., & Adams, J. (2025). Assessing the impact of a mandatory calorie labelling policy in out-of-home food outlets in England on consumer behaviour: A natural experimental study. *BMC Public Health, 25*(1), 955. Advance online publication. DOI: 10.1186/s12889-025-22150-3

Gupta, S. T., Joshi, P., Kaur, A., & Kumar, P. (2025). Digital tools and technologies: Enabling knowledge sharing and collaborative business culture. In *Knowledge Sharing and Fostering Collaborative Business Culture*. IGI Global., DOI: 10.4018/979-8-3373-0710-7.ch016

Herzig, J., & Zander, K. (2025). Determinants of consumer behavior in short food supply chains: A systematic literature review. *Agricultural and Food Economics, 13*(1), 21. Advance online publication. DOI: 10.1186/s40100-025-00370-w

Iniesta-Bonillo, M.-A., Pompeu-Queiros, A., Capobianco Uriarte, M. M., & Alves, H. (2025). Mindfulness and consumer behavior: A bibliometric analysis of themes and trends over 20 years. *Humanities & Social Sciences Communications, 12*(1), 93. Advance online publication. DOI: 10.1057/s41599-025-04367-0

Kaur, A., Bhatnagar, D., & Singh, G. (2024). Exploring the machine learning-based decision tree technique in assessing credit risk likelihood of P2P Fintech lending for effective marketing. In *Neuromarketing's Role in Sustainable Finance*. IGI Global. DOI: 10.4018/979-8-3693-9117-4.ch019

Kaur, R., Kaur, S., & Kaur, A. (2025). Fintech and Financial Inclusion: Trends and Challenges. In *FinTech and Financial Inclusion: Leveraging Digital Finance for Economic Empowerment and Sustainable Growth*. Taylor and Francis., DOI: 10.4324/9781003514114-6

Kukreti, M., Sehajpal, S., Tiwari, R., & Sood, K. (2024a). Driving global health and sustainable development goals with smart technology. In *Driving Global Health and Sustainable Development Goals With Smart Technology*. IGI Global., DOI: 10.4018/979-8-3373-0240-9

Kukreti, M., Sehajpal, S., Tiwari, R., & Sood, K. (2024b). Introduction. In *Driving Global Health and Sustainable Development Goals With Smart Technology*. IGI Global. DOI: 10.4018/979-8-3373-0240-9

Kukreti, M., Sehajpal, S., Tiwari, R., & Sood, K. (2024c). Preface. In *Driving Global Health and Sustainable Development Goals With Smart Technology*. IGI Global. DOI: 10.4018/979-8-3373-0240-9

Lee, H.-S. (2025). Defining core science of 'sensory and consumer science': Understanding human sensory perception, foods/materials interaction, and their influence on consumer behavior, health, and well-being. *Food Quality and Preference*, *129*, 105492. Advance online publication. DOI: 10.1016/j.foodqual.2025.105492

Maione, G., Supino, S., Grimaldi, M., & Troisi, O. (2025). Exploring the political-institutional perspective of sustainable consumer behavior within the circular economy: A structural equation modeling approach from nudge theory. *Socio-Economic Planning Sciences*, *100*, 102254. Advance online publication. DOI: 10.1016/j.seps.2025.102254

Meng, H., Xu, X., & Tian, T. (2025). Empirical study of Neo-Chinese fashion consumer behaviour from the perspectives of cultural identity and emotional self-regulation mechanism. *Asia Pacific Journal of Marketing and Logistics*, *37*(6), 1591–1607. DOI: 10.1108/APJML-07-2024-1004

Mennekes, T., & Schramm-Klein, H. (2025). Effects of crisis-induced inflation on purchasing and consumer behavior in Germany. *Journal of Retailing and Consumer Services*, *85*, 104295. Advance online publication. DOI: 10.1016/j.jretconser.2025.104295

Moradi, M., & Farzaneh, H. (2025). Hybrid local energy markets in Japan: Assessing the impact of regional renewable energy integration, demand flexibility, and consumer behavior. *Energy Conversion and Management, X*, 27. DOI: 10.1016/j.ecmx.2025.101075

Munap, R. B., Obeto, M. N., Salean, S. A. P., Hamid, S. N. B. A., & Salleh, S. N. A. B. M. (2025). TikTok Shopping Surge: Impact on Consumer Behaviour in Klang Valley, Malaysia. *International Review of Management and Marketing, 15*(1), 204–213. DOI: 10.32479/irmm.17441

Quan, L., & Han, H. (2025). Consumer behavior toward cultured meat in the foodservice industry: Insights from IPA and fsQCA analysis on shifting trends. *Journal of Retailing and Consumer Services, 85*, 104307. Advance online publication. DOI: 10.1016/j.jretconser.2025.104307

Reshma, S., T., Pareek, S., & Kuhar, S. (2024). House Price Prediction using Machine Learning Approaches. *2024 OPJU International Technology Conference on Smart Computing for Innovation and Advancement in Industry 4.0, OTCON 2024*. DOI: 10.1109/OTCON60325.2024.10687534

Reshma, & Singh Attwal, K. P. (2024). A Review on Medicinal Plant identification through Leaf Image. In M. H. (Ed.), *Proceedings - 2024 6th International Conference on Computational Intelligence and Communication Technologies, CCICT 2024* (pp. 27 – 33). Institute of Electrical and Electronics Engineers Inc. DOI: 10.1109/CCICT62777.2024.00015

Savall-Mañó, M., Hook, H., & Abouelela, M. (2025). Can higher delivery costs promote greener practices? Consumer behaviour insights from Barcelona. *Journal of Retailing and Consumer Services, 86*, 104343. Advance online publication. DOI: 10.1016/j.jretconser.2025.104343

Sehajpal, S., & Sidhu, N. K. (2024). Neuroscience, nursing, and financial innovation: A synergistic approach to optimized patient care and economic well-being. In *Neuromarketing's Role in Sustainable Finance*. IGI Global., DOI: 10.4018/979-8-3693-9117-4.ch008

Senan, N. A. M., Al-Kahtani, S. M., Alanazi, I. D., AbdAlatti, A., Alshadadi, M. A., Alhebri, A., & Mohammad, R. A. (2025). Unveiling the linkages between greenwashing, brand hate, and negative consumer behavior: The moderating effect of environmental concern. *Discover Sustainability, 6*(1), 446. Advance online publication. DOI: 10.1007/s43621-025-01179-9

Sharma, K. K., Mmdu, A. B., & Reshma. (2022). Biological Impacts of MRI Examinations of Different Ratings on Human Tissue. *Proceedings - 2022 International Conference on Computing, Communication and Power Technology, IC3P 2022*, 172 – 175. DOI: 10.1109/IC3P52835.2022.00043

Shirdastian, H., Bartikowski, B., Laroche, M., & Richard, M.-O. (2025). Mobile app localization-based advertising: Effects of spatial and social-cultural distances on consumer behavior. *International Journal of Information Management*, *84*, 102929. Advance online publication. DOI: 10.1016/j.ijinfomgt.2025.102929

Tang, C.-H. H., Fan, A., & Park, J. E. (2025). Mass customization and consumer behaviors: Exploring the roles of perceived value, perceived cost, and time pressure. *International Journal of Hospitality Management*, *130*, 104278. Advance online publication. DOI: 10.1016/j.ijhm.2025.104278

Tanwar, A., Aggarwal, R., & Kaur, A. (2024). Explainability of AI in Improving the Quality of Service in the Actuarial Industry. In *Artificial Intelligence and Actuarial Science: Applications and Case Studies from Finance and Insurance*. CRC Press., DOI: 10.1201/9781003472551-7

Tanwar, A., Malhan, S., Punj, N., & Kaur, A. (2024). Integration of Artificial Intelligence and Internet of Things in the Banking Sector: A Convergence of Frontiers. In *Integration of Cloud Computing and IoT: Trends, Case Studies and Applications*. CRC Press., DOI: 10.1201/9781032656694-25

Tonin, P. E. H., Nickel, E. M., & dos Santos, F. A. V. (2025). The Impact of Sensory Branding and Technology on Consumer Behavior in Physical Retail Experience Design: A Multi-generational Experimental Study. *International Journal of Design Management and Professional Practice*, *19*(1), 87–110. DOI: 10.18848/2325-162X/CGP/v19i01/87-110

Widayat, H., Handayanto, E., Irfani, A. D., & Masudin, I. (2025). A systematic literature review and future research agenda on the dynamics of food waste in the context of consumer behavior. *Sustainable Futures : An Applied Journal of Technology, Environment and Society*, *9*, 100491. Advance online publication. DOI: 10.1016/j.sftr.2025.100491

Yadav, B. K., Keyal, P. K., Khan, R., Chaube, N., Chaudhary, P., & Chaurasiya, P. (2024). Advanced Threat Detection: Leveraging Data Analytics for Cybersecurity Enhancement. *Proceedings of International Conference on Emerging Technologies and Innovation for Sustainability,* EmergIN 2024, 62 – 67. DOI: 10.1109/EmergIN63207.2024.10961019

Chapter 6

Impact of Artificial Intelligence on Luxury Consumer Behavior and Experience

Guruprasanna G. Hegde
Dayananda Sagar College of Engineering, Yellapur, India

K.S. Ganesha
https://orcid.org/0000-0001-8181-2411
Dayananda Sagar College of Engineering, India

ABSTRACT

The luxury industry is undergoing a profound transformation driven by Artificial Intelligence (AI), which is redefining consumer expectations, brand interactions, and value creation. This chapter examines the impact of AI on luxury consumer behaviour and experience by integrating theoretical insights with illustrative case studies from global luxury brands. The study begins by introducing the growing role of AI in the luxury sector and outlining its significance for personalization, exclusivity, and consumer engagement. The conceptual background explores key frameworks that link AI-driven innovations such recommendation systems, chatbots, virtual try-ons, and predictive analytics with shifts in consumer attitudes, purchase intentions, and loyalty.Selected case studies highlight how leading luxury brands leverage AI to strengthen brand equity while navigating challenges of authenticity and data ethics. The analysis discusses the dual dimensions of AI adoption: the benefits of enhanced personalization, efficiency, and predictive value, as well as the challenges of over-automation.

DOI: 10.4018/979-8-3373-4392-1.ch006

1. INTRODUCTION

The luxury industry has long been defined by its emphasis on exclusivity, personalization, and exceptional customer experiences. However, in the last decade, the rapid evolution of digital technologies particularly Artificial Intelligence (AI) has begun to transform how luxury brands engage with their customers. AI is no longer confined to operational efficiency or data processing; it has emerged as a strategic tool that reshapes consumer behavior, redefines brand–customer interactions, and elevates the meaning of luxury in the digital age.

In the luxury market, customers seek not only superior products but also highly curated and emotionally engaging experiences. AI enables brands to deliver on these expectations by offering hyper-personalized recommendations, predictive insights into consumer preferences, immersive virtual experiences, and AI-powered customer service through chatbots and virtual assistants. This convergence of advanced technology with traditional luxury values creates both opportunities and obstacles: while it enhances exclusivity and engagement, it also raises concerns around authenticity, human touch, and data privacy.

The academic and managerial relevance of this study lies in understanding how AI influences luxury consumer behavior and experience, both conceptually and in practice. For scholars, it provides insights into evolving theories of consumer psychology, technology adoption, and experiential marketing in high-end markets. For practitioners, it offers actionable implications for sustaining brand equity while embracing digital transformation. By analyzing conceptual foundations and real-world case studies, this paper seeks to explore the benefits, limitations, and future trajectory of AI in shaping luxury consumer dynamics.

Thus, the introduction of AI into the luxury sector is not merely a technological shift it represents a paradigm change in how exclusivity, personalization, and brand value are perceived and delivered. This paper sets the stage for a deeper exploration of AI's role in redefining luxury experiences, offering both academic and practical contributions to the discourse.

2. CONCEPTUAL BACKGROUND OF STUDY

The luxury industry has historically been characterized by exclusivity, craftsmanship, heritage, and symbolic value creation (Kapferer & Bastien, 2012). Unlike mass-market consumption, luxury purchases are driven not only by functional utility but also by social signaling, emotional satisfaction, and self-expression (Han, Nunes, & Drèze, 2010). Consumers in the luxury market expect curated, personalized, and memorable experiences that enhance their sense of uniqueness and status. With the rapid integration of Artificial Intelligence (AI), these dynamics are evolving in unprecedented ways.

1. Luxury Consumer Behavior

Luxury consumer behavior is distinct from mass-market consumption due to the symbolic, hedonic, and experiential value attached to luxury products and services. Key characteristics include:

- Emotional and Experiential Motivation: Luxury consumers often seek experiences that reflect prestige, self-expression, and exclusivity rather than mere functionality. This includes desire for status signaling, aesthetic appreciation, and sensory gratification (Kapferer & Bastien, 2012).
- High Involvement Decision-Making: Luxury purchases are characterized by extended information search, evaluation of alternatives, and deliberation, influenced by brand reputation, craftsmanship, and social influence.
- Selective Consumption: Luxury buyers value rarity, scarcity, and bespoke experiences. Their purchasing decisions are influenced by the alignment between brand values and personal identity.

Understanding these behavioural characteristics is critical because AI interventions in luxury must go beyond functional efficiency they must enhance emotional connection, personalization, and exclusivity.

2. Artificial Intelligence in Luxury

Artificial Intelligence encompasses technologies that enable machines to mimic human intelligence, including machine learning, natural language processing (NLP), computer vision, and predictive analytics. In luxury contexts, AI is applied in multiple dimensions:

1. Personalization: AI enables brands to tailor offerings to individual consumer preferences. Examples include Burberry's AI-driven customer profiles and Prada's omnichannel recommendation engines.
2. Predictive Analytics: AI analyzes historical and behavioural data to forecast trends, optimize inventory, and anticipate consumer demand, as seen in Gucci's trend-forecasting initiatives.
3. Conversational AI and Chatbots: AI-powered chatbots, such as Louis Vuitton's LV Virtual Advisor, provide real-time, personalized interactions that replicate high-touch boutique services.

4. Immersive and Experiential Technologies: AR and AI integrations, such as Dior's Virtual Try-On, create engaging digital experiences that replicate sensory interactions of physical luxury shopping.
5. Operational Efficiency: AI optimizes supply chains, fraud detection, and customer relationship management, enabling luxury brands to deliver superior service at scale.

AI in luxury not only enhances operational efficiency but also reinforces brand identity, personalization, and consumer engagement, bridging the gap between heritage and modern digital expectations.

2.1 Luxury Consumer Behaviour

Luxury consumption has long been associated with prestige-seeking, hedonic pleasure, and symbolic differentiation Consumers perceive luxury brands as extensions of identity and social belonging. The demand for exclusivity and personalization distinguishes luxury consumer behavior from mainstream markets. In this context, AI emerges as a powerful tool to enhance personalization, predict behavior, and strengthen brand–consumer relationships.

2.2 Artificial Intelligence in Consumer Markets

AI refers to machine-based systems that simulate human intelligence to perform tasks such as learning, reasoning, and decision-making (Russell & Norvig, 2020). In consumer markets, AI applications range from recommendation systems and natural language processing to predictive analytics and virtual assistants (Davenport, Guha, Grewal, & Bressgott, 2020). These technologies allow firms to analyze large-scale consumer data, identify behavioral patterns, and deliver tailored offerings that align with consumer preferences.

2.3 AI and the Luxury Experience

In the luxury sector, AI is not simply a tool for efficiency but a mechanism to reinforce exclusivity and engagement (Hoffmann & Coste-Manière, 2012).

Personalization: Algorithms provide unique product recommendations, mirroring the bespoke nature of traditional luxury.

Immersive Experiences: AI-driven AR/VR platforms create digital experiences that replicate or enhance in-store encounters (Jain, Kumar, & Mishra, 2021).

Service Augmentation: Virtual stylists and AI chatbots extend concierge-like services to a global clientele, enabling 24/7 engagement without undermining exclusivity.

Consumer Insights: Predictive analytics anticipate shifts in luxury consumer sentiment, allowing brands to remain agile in fast-changing markets (Shankar, 2018).

2.4 Theoretical Underpinnings

This study draws on several conceptual frameworks:

Technology Acceptance Model (TAM): Explains how perceived usefulness and ease of use influence consumer adoption of AI-enabled luxury services (Davis, 1989).

Experiential Marketing Theory: Suggests that AI enhances sensory, affective, and cognitive engagement in luxury consumption (Schmitt, 1999).

Consumer–Brand Relationship Theory: Provides insights into how AI-driven personalization may either strengthen or weaken trust, authenticity, and emotional connection (Fournier, 1998).

1. Maslow's Hierarchy of Needs and Luxury Consumption

Maslow's Hierarchy of Needs (Maslow, 1943) posits that human behavior is guided by a progression of needs, from physiological to self-actualization. In luxury consumer behavior, AI technologies cater primarily to the higher-order needs:

- **Esteem Needs:** Luxury goods satisfy consumers' desires for status, recognition, and prestige. AI-driven personalization (e.g., Burberry's unified customer profiles) enhances these needs by delivering exclusive, tailored experiences.
- **Self-Actualization:** Luxury consumption often enables self-expression and identity creation. AI technologies, such as Gucci's digital sneakers or Dior's AR beauty experiences, allow consumers to experiment creatively in both physical and digital spaces, supporting self-actualization.

By aligning AI-driven personalization with the emotional and psychological dimensions of luxury consumption, brands strengthen consumer loyalty and perceived value.

2. Consumer Experience Theory

The **Consumer Experience Theory** (Schmitt, 1999) emphasizes that consumption is not solely transactional but experiential. Luxury consumption, in particular, revolves around multi-sensory, emotional, and cognitive experiences:

- **Sensory Experiences:** AR and AI applications, like Dior's Virtual Try-On, allow consumers to engage visually and interactively with products.
- **Emotional Engagement:** AI-driven chatbots (e.g., Louis Vuitton's LV Virtual Advisor) create conversational, human-like interactions, fostering emotional connection.
- **Cognitive Processing:** Predictive analytics and personalized recommendations engage consumers intellectually by offering relevant, curated choices that enhance decision-making efficiency.

Luxury brands leverage AI to deliver experiential differentiation, making the consumer journey as memorable and personalized as the product itself.

3. Technology Acceptance Model (TAM)

The Technology Acceptance Model (Davis, 1989) explains consumer adoption of technology through two primary determinants:

- Perceived Usefulness (PU): The extent to which AI-enabled tools improve the shopping experience. For instance, AI-driven product recommendations or digital try-ons simplify decision-making and enhance convenience.
- Perceived Ease of Use (PEOU): The ease with which consumers interact with AI tools. Intuitive chatbots, user-friendly virtual reality interfaces, and mobile apps increase adoption by reducing cognitive load.

In luxury contexts, TAM is particularly relevant because AI adoption must not only be functional but also maintain the sense of exclusivity and premium service. High PU and PEOU support positive attitudes toward AI adoption without undermining the luxury brand aura.

4. Personalization and Relationship Marketing Theory

Relationship Marketing Theory (Berry, 1983) emphasizes long-term customer engagement rather than transactional exchanges. AI enables personalized interactions that align with this theory:

- Data-Driven Personalization: Burberry and Prada use AI to analyze customer behavior across channels, tailoring product recommendations, communications, and experiences.

- Enhanced Loyalty: AI-supported customization increases perceived value and strengthens consumer-brand relationships, encouraging repeat purchases and advocacy.
- Predictive Relationship Management: AI predicts preferences and identifies opportunities to delight consumers proactively, reinforcing emotional bonds and loyalty.

In luxury sectors, relationship marketing powered by AI strengthens brand equity and ensures consumers feel uniquely valued.

5. Experiential Marketing and Hedonic Consumption

Luxury consumption is predominantly hedonic, emphasizing pleasure, fantasy, and sensory gratification. Experiential marketing theory (Pine & Gilmore, 1998) highlights that experiences, rather than products alone, drive consumer engagement:

- Immersive Digital Experiences: AR and AI-driven experiences (Dior Virtual Try-On, Gucci digital sneakers) provide playful and novel interactions, enhancing hedonic satisfaction.
- Multi-Sensory Engagement: AI augments visual, tactile, and interactive dimensions of luxury retail, enriching sensory pleasure.
- Emotional Connection: Personalized AI-driven interactions evoke emotions of exclusivity, delight, and personal recognition.

Hedonic consumption theory explains why luxury consumers are willing to engage with AI-driven experiences that replicate or enhance in-store pleasures in digital formats.

6. Consumer Decision-Making and Predictive Analytics

The Consumer Decision-Making Theory (Engel, Blackwell, & Miniard, 1995) suggests that consumers move through stages problem recognition, information search, evaluation, purchase, and post-purchase behavior. AI interventions can influence every stage:

- Problem Recognition: AI identifies consumer needs by analyzing browsing patterns or social media sentiment.
- Information Search: Chatbots and recommendation engines reduce search costs by presenting curated options.

- Evaluation: Predictive analytics provide insights into trending products, helping consumers make informed choices.
- Purchase & Post-Purchase: Personalized follow-ups and virtual customization ensure satisfaction and repeat engagement.

Luxury brands use AI to streamline decision-making while maintaining the exclusivity and deliberative nature of high-involvement purchases.

7. Diffusion of Innovations Theory

Rogers' Diffusion of Innovations Theory (1962) explains how new technologies spread through populations. In luxury contexts:

- Innovators and Early Adopters: Tech-savvy consumers (especially Gen Z and Millennials) are drawn to AI innovations like Gucci's digital sneakers or Tesla's autonomous features.
- Social Influence: AI adoption signals status and modernity, creating aspirational appeal.
- Observability: Visible AI-driven experiences, such as AR try-ons or digital fashion items, encourage broader adoption by demonstrating benefits clearly.

Understanding adoption patterns helps luxury brands manage AI rollouts while preserving exclusivity for early adopters.

8. Service-Dominant Logic (SDL)

Service-Dominant Logic (Vargo & Lusch, 2004) proposes that value is co-created through interactions between consumers and brands. AI in luxury:

- Co-Creation: Digital customization (Cartier's AI jewellery tools) allows consumers to participate in the design process.
- Enhanced Service Quality: Chatbots, recommendation engines, and AR experiences contribute to value creation beyond the tangible product.
- Integration Across Touchpoints: AI enables consistent, high-value experiences across digital and physical channels.

SDL underscores the shift from product-centric to experience- and relationship-centric luxury consumption.

9. Summary of Theoretical Implications

The theoretical underpinnings demonstrate that AI impacts luxury consumer behavior across multiple dimensions:

1. Psychological Needs: AI addresses esteem and self-actualization needs (Maslow).
2. Experience and Hedonics: AI enhances experiential consumption (Schmitt; Pine & Gilmore).
3. Decision-Making: AI influences search, evaluation, and post-purchase satisfaction (Engel et al.).
4. Technology Adoption: AI acceptance depends on usefulness, ease of use, and social diffusion (TAM; Rogers).
5. Relationship and Co-Creation: AI strengthens customer relationships and co-creation opportunities (Berry; Vargo & Lusch).

Collectively, these frameworks explain why AI is not merely a tool but a transformative driver in luxury consumer behavior, enhancing personalization, engagement, and brand equity while respecting heritage and exclusivity.

2.5 Research Gap

Although AI adoption in mainstream retail has been extensively explored (Davenport et al., 2020), limited research addresses its implications for luxury consumption, which is deeply rooted in heritage, craftsmanship, and symbolic value. Key unanswered questions include: Can AI sustain the aura of exclusivity while scaling personalization? How do customers perceive authenticity when their interactions are mediated by algorithms? Addressing these gaps is essential for both academics and practitioners to understand the evolving intersection of AI and luxury.

1. Limited Focus on Luxury Consumer Psychology

Most studies on AI adoption focus on functional benefits such as efficiency, personalization, and sales optimization (Davenport et al., 2020; Bughin & Van Zeebroeck, 2018). However, luxury consumption is fundamentally experiential, hedonic, and symbolic. There is limited research examining:

- How AI affects emotional and psychological drivers of luxury consumption, such as status signaling, self-expression, and exclusivity.
- The influence of AI on consumer perceptions of luxury brand authenticity, given that over-automation may dilute artisanal or heritage appeal.

This gap is critical because luxury consumers evaluate digital interactions differently from mass-market shoppers; the perceived value of AI-driven experiences may vary significantly based on brand heritage and consumer expectations.

2. Inadequate Analysis of Brand-Specific AI Strategies

While studies examine AI applications in retail broadly, few provide comparative analyses across different luxury brands. Brands vary widely in their heritage, positioning, and target demographics:

- Heritage-focused brands like Hermès are conservative in AI adoption.
- Innovation-driven brands like Gucci and Burberry integrate AI extensively.
- The effectiveness of AI strategies across these different approaches remains underexplored.

Research is lacking on how brand DNA influences AI implementation, the balance between digital innovation and traditional luxury values, and the outcomes on consumer loyalty and engagement.

3. Sparse Research on Experiential and Immersive Technologies

Luxury consumer engagement increasingly leverages AI-enabled AR, VR, and digital-only products:

- Examples include Dior's virtual try-ons, Gucci's digital sneakers, and Louis Vuitton's AI chatbots.
- Most studies have not examined how immersive AI-driven experiences influence perceived value, purchase intention, or brand loyalty in luxury contexts.

Additionally, the long-term impact of virtual luxury consumption on consumer behavior and emotional attachment remains under-researched.

4. Insufficient Understanding of Omnichannel Integration

AI in luxury often spans both digital and physical channels. Although omnichannel retail is well-documented in general markets, there is limited literature on:

- How AI enhances consistency and personalization across online, mobile, and in-store interactions for luxury consumers.

- The role of AI in creating seamless, high-touch experiences without eroding brand exclusivity.

Given the high expectations of luxury consumers for curated experiences, understanding the interplay between AI and omnichannel strategies is crucial.

5. Gap in Measuring ROI and Consumer Perceptions

While operational benefits of AI (e.g., supply chain optimization, predictive analytics) are often discussed, few studies measure consumer-perceived ROI:

- How do consumers perceive AI-driven personalization in terms of luxury value?
- Does AI enhance perceived exclusivity, trust, and emotional connection?
- What metrics best capture both business performance and consumer satisfaction in luxury AI adoption?

Addressing this gap is essential for brands seeking to justify AI investments while preserving premium positioning.

6. Limited Cross-Cultural Insights

Luxury consumption varies across geographies, cultures, and demographics. Current research on AI in luxury is primarily Western-centric, with little focus on emerging markets like Asia-Pacific or the Middle East, which are growing luxury markets:

- Consumer attitudes toward AI, privacy, and digital interactions may differ across regions.
- The effectiveness of AI-driven personalization, immersive experiences, and chatbots may vary culturally.

Understanding cross-cultural responses is necessary for brands with global presence, such as LVMH, Prada, and Burberry.

7. Need for Integration of Theoretical and Practical Insights

Existing literature is often fragmented:

- Theoretical frameworks (TAM, Consumer Experience Theory, Relationship Marketing) provide insights on adoption but rarely connect directly to luxury-specific case studies.
- Practical applications (AR try-ons, AI chatbots, predictive analytics) are discussed descriptively but lack empirical testing of theoretical propositions.

There is a need for research that bridges theory and practice, linking AI interventions to behavioural outcomes, brand equity, and consumer perceptions.

Summary

Despite the growing adoption of AI by luxury brands, there is a clear research gap in understanding:

1. The psychological and emotional impact of AI on luxury consumers.
2. How brand heritage and identity mediate AI effectiveness.
3. The role of immersive and digital experiences in shaping consumer behavior.
4. Effective strategies for omnichannel integration while preserving exclusivity.
5. Metrics for assessing consumer-perceived value and ROI of AI initiatives.
6. Cross-cultural perspectives on luxury AI adoption.
7. A coherent integration of theoretical frameworks with empirical luxury applications.

Addressing these gaps will enable luxury brands to deploy AI not only as a technological innovation but as a strategic tool that enhances experiential value, brand authenticity, and consumer engagement.

3. CASE STUDIES

Luxury brands are increasingly leveraging Artificial Intelligence (AI) to redefine consumer engagement, personalization, and experiential marketing. The following case studies illustrate how leading luxury brands have adopted AI, highlighting practical implementations, consumer responses, and broader implications for luxury consumption.

1. Burberry: AI-Driven Personalization and Data Integration

Burberry, a British luxury fashion house renowned for its iconic trench coats and timeless designs, has positioned itself as a pioneer in integrating artificial intelligence into its luxury retail strategy. With a history rooted in craftsmanship and British heritage, the brand faced a strategic challenge: how to maintain its reputation for exclusivity while adapting to the digital-first behaviours of modern luxury consumers. Burberry recognized that AI could provide a bridge between heritage and innovation, enabling highly personalized consumer experiences without diluting brand identity.

AI Initiatives and Strategic Integration

To achieve this, Burberry partnered with leading AI and cloud-based platforms such as Salesforce, allowing it to aggregate customer data from multiple touchpoints. These include online browsing behavior, in-store interactions, social media engagement, and mobile app usage. By integrating these diverse data sources, Burberry can construct comprehensive, unified customer profiles that inform targeted marketing campaigns and drive personalized experiences.

The brand leverages AI-powered analytics to track individual consumer journeys. This allows marketing teams to design campaigns tailored to the needs and preferences of each consumer. For example, predictive algorithms analyze purchasing behavior to recommend products likely to appeal to a given customer, even anticipating preferences before they are explicitly expressed. AI also aids in segmenting the customer base for more precise targeting, differentiating between high-value loyal clients and occasional buyers.

In-Store AI Application

In physical stores, Burberry equips sales associates with tablets providing real-time AI insights. These insights include past purchases, style preferences, and browsing history. This empowers sales staff to make personalized recommendations, creating an in-store experience that mirrors the individualization commonly associated with digital commerce. The result is a seamless integration of online and offline experiences, reinforcing the brand's reputation for attentive, customer-centric service.

Operational Impact

Beyond enhancing customer experience, AI contributes to Burberry's operational efficiency. Predictive analytics are employed to forecast product demand, enabling better inventory management and reducing the risk of overproduction or stockouts. By aligning production with anticipated consumer needs, Burberry ensures that supply chain operations are responsive, sustainable, and cost-effective.

Consumer Outcomes

The outcomes of Burberry's AI adoption have been substantial. Consumers feel valued and recognized, reinforcing loyalty and encouraging repeat purchases. By combining heritage with technological sophistication, Burberry demonstrates that AI can augment rather than undermine the perceived value of luxury. Personalized experiences are no longer limited to physical interactions; they extend to online platforms, social media, and mobile applications, creating a holistic, digitally enhanced brand experience.

2. Louis Vuitton: AI-Powered Chatbots and Virtual Assistants

Louis Vuitton, the French luxury powerhouse known for its leather goods and high-fashion collections, has been exploring AI to transform customer service and engagement. The brand's approach reflects an understanding that luxury consumers increasingly seek both exclusivity and convenience, particularly through digital channels.

The LV Virtual Advisor

Louis Vuitton introduced the **LV Virtual Advisor**, an AI-powered chatbot integrated with platforms such as Facebook Messenger and its own website. This tool leverages natural language processing (NLP) to simulate the conversational interactions typically offered in high-end boutiques. Through the chatbot, consumers can receive product recommendations, styling advice, and guidance on completing purchases.

The AI engine powering the Virtual Advisor personalizes its responses based on the consumer's previous interactions with the brand, their browsing history, and purchase behavior. This creates a tailored dialogue that preserves the sense of individual attention and care emblematic of Louis Vuitton boutiques.

Advantages of AI Integration

The chatbot offers several benefits: it provides round-the-clock availability, extending luxury accessibility beyond traditional store hours; it reduces response times, enhancing convenience; and it collects data that informs future marketing campaigns. By combining personalization with automation, Louis Vuitton can maintain high-touch service standards while scaling interactions across global markets.

Challenges and Considerations

Despite these advantages, the integration of AI also poses challenges. Some consumers express concerns that automation may diminish the human-centric nature of luxury retail. The brand must carefully balance technological innovation with the preservation of artisanal, heritage-based values. Maintaining this equilibrium is critical for sustaining brand authenticity and customer trust.

Consumer and Brand Impact

The LV Virtual Advisor has strengthened customer engagement, providing seamless and personalized digital interactions. By offering a high-quality virtual luxury experience, Louis Vuitton reinforces its brand promise while responding to the evolving expectations of tech-savvy consumers.

3. Dior: Augmented Reality (AR) and AI in Beauty

Christian Dior, a brand synonymous with haute couture and premium beauty products, has embraced a combination of AI and augmented reality (AR) to transform digital beauty experiences. Dior's focus has been on enabling immersive, interactive experiences that replicate the sensory engagement of physical stores in a digital environment.

Virtual Try-On Platform

Dior's **Virtual Try-On platform** employs AI-driven facial recognition to allow customers to experiment with makeup products digitally. By accurately mapping facial features in real time, consumers can try different shades of lipstick, eye shadow, and other cosmetics via smartphones or tablets. This innovation became particularly significant during the COVID-19 pandemic, when physical store visits were limited, and digital engagement surged.

Data-Driven Personalization

Every interaction on the platform generates valuable data. Dior collects this information to refine marketing campaigns and provide personalized recommendations. This not only enhances consumer engagement but also allows Dior to tailor communications based on individual preferences, purchase histories, and trends observed in virtual trials.

Impact on Customer Experience

The integration of AR and AI bridges the gap between digital convenience and luxury sensorial richness. Consumers gain the ability to experiment freely without compromising the exclusivity of the brand experience. Dior's approach demonstrates how AI can extend experiential marketing strategies into the digital domain, creating unique, memorable interactions that strengthen brand loyalty.

Broader Implications

By leveraging AI for both personalization and immersive experiences, Dior illustrates a forward-looking model for luxury beauty. The brand showcases how technology can enhance traditional retail while respecting the luxury principles of exclusivity and high-quality service.

4. Gucci: Predictive Analytics, Digital Sneakers, and Trend Forecasting

Gucci, an Italian luxury fashion brand renowned for its bold designs and cultural influence, has strategically positioned AI at the heart of its innovation strategy. The brand's goal is to combine heritage with forward-looking digital practices to engage younger, tech-savvy consumers.

Predictive Analytics and Trend Insights

Gucci employs AI-driven predictive analytics to anticipate fashion trends. By analyzing social media trends, cultural discourse, and consumer behavior data, Gucci identifies emerging preferences and adapts collections accordingly. This proactive approach allows the brand to remain culturally relevant, particularly among Gen Z consumers who value both innovation and self-expression.

Digital-Only Products

One of Gucci's pioneering AI initiatives is the creation of digital-only sneakers, designed for use in virtual environments such as social media, gaming platforms, and augmented reality applications. These digital products allow consumers to showcase luxury identity in online spaces, reflecting the increasing value of virtual ownership and digital self-expression.

Operational Efficiencies

AI also supports Gucci's supply chain optimization. By forecasting product demand accurately, the brand reduces overproduction, limits waste, and aligns production volumes with consumer needs. This efficiency preserves brand exclusivity while addressing sustainability concerns.

Consumer Impact

The integration of AI reinforces Gucci's reputation as a trendsetter and innovator. Consumers experience a seamless blend of physical and digital luxury, engaging with the brand across multiple touchpoints. Gucci's approach demonstrates that luxury brands can leverage AI to maintain cultural relevance while safeguarding heritage values.

5. LVMH Group: AI in Customer Experience and Operations

LVMH, the French conglomerate overseeing brands such as Louis Vuitton, Dior, Fendi, and Givenchy, has strategically integrated AI across its luxury portfolio. The group recognizes AI as a tool to enhance operational efficiency and deliver superior customer experiences at scale.

Investments and Innovation

Through the **LVMH Innovation Award**, the conglomerate invests in AI startups to explore cutting-edge solutions. These investments target applications in customer profiling, supply chain optimization, and fraud detection, ensuring that AI adoption aligns with the group's commitment to craftsmanship and authenticity.

Applications Across Brands

AI facilitates enhanced customer segmentation and personalized interactions, enabling LVMH brands to scale luxury services without compromising exclusivity. Smart algorithms optimize supply chains, while AI-driven fraud detection safeguards against counterfeiting, reinforcing consumer trust in the brand.

Strategic Outcomes

LVMH exemplifies a balanced approach to AI: the group integrates innovative technology while respecting heritage and artisanal values. This alignment ensures that AI amplifies rather than undermines brand identity, creating a model for other conglomerates navigating the digital transformation of luxury.

6. Hermès: Balancing Heritage with Digital Innovation

Hermès, synonymous with timeless craftsmanship and scarcity-driven exclusivity, has traditionally been cautious in adopting digital tools. The brand's strategy illustrates a conservative yet strategic integration of AI, ensuring that technological enhancements support rather than replace human expertise.

AI in Operations

Hermès employs AI for back-end logistics, managing global inventory distribution to maintain scarcity for highly coveted products such as Birkin and Kelly bags. By accurately predicting demand and allocating stock strategically, the brand preserves the perceived value of rarity while satisfying client expectations.

Digital Personalization

Hermès also experiments with subtle e-commerce personalization. AI provides gentle recommendations without overwhelming consumers, maintaining the aura of exclusivity associated with Hermès boutiques. This measured approach highlights how AI adoption in luxury is heavily influenced by brand DNA and heritage.

Consumer Outcomes

Consumers benefit from improved service and availability without compromising the artisanal, heritage-driven experience. Hermès demonstrates that conservative AI adoption can still create meaningful enhancements in customer satisfaction and operational efficiency.

7. Cartier: AI in High-End Jewellery Customization

Cartier, a leader in high-end jewellery and horology, integrates AI to modernize bespoke services and enhance client engagement.

AI-Enhanced Customization

AI-powered visualization tools allow clients to explore custom jewelry designs digitally, adjusting gemstones, settings, and materials in real time. This mirrors the hands-on craftsmanship of Cartier's ateliers, offering flexibility and interactivity while retaining exclusivity.

Personalized Client Engagement

AI analyzes the preferences of high-net-worth clients, tailoring communications, invitations to private events, and after-sales services. This targeted personalization ensures that Cartier strengthens its relationships with clients while maintaining the luxury experience.

Impact

By combining digital tools with artisanal expertise, Cartier enhances accessibility without diluting the brand's prestige. Consumers experience the bespoke nature of luxury in an innovative, technologically enriched environment.

8. Prada: AI for Omnichannel Luxury

Prada, an Italian luxury house with a strong global presence, has embraced AI to integrate omnichannel retail experiences.

Seamless Omnichannel Integration

AI algorithms track consumer behavior across online, mobile, and physical store channels. This ensures consistent personalization and recommendations regardless of the shopping medium. AI-powered recommendation engines enhance product discovery, enabling cross-selling opportunities that align with consumer preferences.

Strategic Implications

Prada demonstrates that mid-to-large luxury houses can leverage AI strategically to compete with conglomerates. By harmonizing digital and physical experiences, the brand strengthens customer engagement and reinforces its modern luxury positioning.

9. Tesla: Redefining Luxury through AI and Technology

Although Tesla is an automotive technology company, its positioning blurs the line between technology and luxury.

AI in Products

Tesla employs AI in autonomous driving, predictive maintenance, and personalized in-car experiences. Consumers perceive the brand as a symbol of technological sophistication, environmental consciousness, and prestige.

Impact on Luxury Definition

Tesla illustrates how AI can redefine luxury, shifting emphasis from traditional markers like craftsmanship to intelligence, sustainability, and innovation. The brand exemplifies the convergence of technology and status in modern luxury consumption.

Cross-Case Insights

Several key insights emerge from these case studies:

1. Personalization: AI enables precise consumer segmentation, personalized marketing, and tailored recommendations, enhancing perceived exclusivity.
2. Operational Efficiency: Predictive analytics, inventory management, and supply chain optimization ensure brands maintain luxury standards while reducing waste.
3. Digital Immersion: AR, VR, and digital-only products create immersive experiences that complement physical retail.
4. Brand-Specific Adoption: Heritage-driven brands like Hermès adopt AI cautiously, while others such as Burberry and Gucci integrate it fully as a differentiator.
5. Redefinition of Luxury: Brands like Tesla highlight that technological sophistication is increasingly seen as a component of modern luxury.

Conclusion

AI is reshaping the luxury sector, enhancing personalization, operational excellence, and digital engagement. However, adoption strategies must align with brand identity, heritage, and consumer expectations. Successful luxury AI implementation requires balancing innovation with tradition, ensuring that technology amplifies exclusivity, authenticity, and craftsmanship rather than diminishing them. These case studies collectively illustrate that AI is a transformative force in luxury, but its impact is mediated by culture, brand positioning, and strategic vision.

4. BENEFITS AND CHALLENGES

The integration of Artificial Intelligence (AI) into luxury brand management represents a double-edged transformation. On one side, AI enhances personalization, operational efficiency, and consumer engagement, allowing luxury brands to stay competitive in an increasingly digital environment. On the other side, it raises obstacles concerning authenticity, privacy, ethics, and the preservation of the "human touch" that defines luxury consumption. This section critically explores both benefits and obstacles to provide a holistic view of AI's role in shaping luxury consumer behavior and experience.

4.1 Benefits of AI in Luxury Consumer Experience:

4.1.1 Hyper-Personalization and Bespoke Services:

Luxury customers value exclusivity and individuality. AI enables hyper-personalization by analyzing consumer purchase history, browsing behavior, and social media interactions to create tailored product recommendations and experiences (Davenport et al., 2020). For example, Burberry employs AI-driven customer data platforms to equip sales associates with individual consumer profiles, allowing them to provide highly bespoke services both online and offline. This enhances consumer satisfaction and reinforces the symbolic value of luxury consumption.

Analysis: Personalization supported by AI extends the craftsmanship ethos of luxury into the digital age. Instead of mass customization, AI enables micro-level tailoring, aligning with the consumer desire for uniqueness.

4.1.2 Enhanced Customer Engagement Through Immersive Experiences:

AI empowers immersive brand interactions through augmented reality (AR), virtual try-ons, and intelligent chatbots. Dior's Virtual Try-On service, powered by AI-driven facial recognition, allows customers to digitally test products, replicating in-store sensory experiences (Jain, Kumar, & Mishra, 2021). Similarly, Louis Vuitton's AI chatbot provides concierge-like assistance globally, democratizing access to luxury while maintaining exclusivity.

Analysis: These tools bridge physical and digital luxury experiences, expanding reach while preserving emotional engagement. The use of AI here does not dilute luxury's aura; rather, it translates its exclusivity into new technological contexts.

4.1.3 Predictive Analytics and Market Forecasting:

Analysis: Predictive analytics provides a competitive edge by aligning production with anticipated consumer demand. In luxury, where scarcity is a value driver, AI helps balance exclusivity with efficiency.

4.1.4 Operational Efficiency and Fraud Prevention:

AI also adds to backend operations such as supply chain optimization, logistics, and counterfeit detection. LVMH employs AI to monitor product authenticity and detect counterfeits, thereby protecting brand equity. AI-driven supply chain tools also improve inventory management, ensuring availability of products without compromising exclusivity.

Analysis: Operational benefits indirectly enhance consumer trust and loyalty. A luxury purchase is not only about consumption but also about authenticity and heritage—AI safeguards these dimensions while streamlining operations.

4.2 Challenges of AI in Luxury Consumer Experience

4.2.1 Threat to Authenticity and Human Touch:

Luxury consumption is deeply rooted in heritage, craftsmanship, and human artistry (Kapferer & Bastien, 2012). Overreliance on AI risks diminishing these values. For instance, while Louis Vuitton's chatbot enhances convenience, some customers may perceive AI-driven interactions as less authentic than human-led services.

Analysis: The challenge lies in balancing automation with the emotional and artisanal essence of luxury. If AI replaces too much of the human element, it could undermine brand identity.

4.2.2 Data Privacy and Ethical Concerns

AI-driven personalization requires vast amounts of consumer data, raising concerns over privacy and security. Consumers in the luxury segment are often high-net-worth individuals (HNWIs), making data breaches particularly damaging. A 2020 survey by Deloitte revealed that luxury customers are more sensitive to data misuse compared to mass-market customers (Deloitte, 2023).

Analysis: While data enables personalization, misuse could damage trust—an asset central to luxury brands. Brands must therefore prioritize transparency and compliance with regulations such as GDPR.

4.2.3 Risk of Over-Digitization

While AI enables scalability, excessive digitization may erode the sense of exclusivity. Gucci's virtual sneakers, though innovative, received mixed responses; some critics argued that digital-only products dilute the tangible craftsmanship traditionally associated with luxury.

Analysis: The paradox is that while digital products appeal to Gen Z, they may alienate traditional customers who associate luxury with material artistry. Balancing physical and digital luxury offerings is thus essential.

4.2.4 High Implementation Costs and Inequality of Adoption

AI systems require significant investment in infrastructure, training, and talent. Large conglomerates like LVMH can afford such investments, but smaller luxury houses may struggle to adopt AI effectively. This creates a digital divide in the luxury sector.

Analysis: If only large players integrate AI successfully, smaller heritage brands may lose competitive relevance, leading to consolidation in the industry.

4.2.5 Consumer Resistance and Trust Issues

Not all customers are comfortable with AI-driven luxury experiences. Research shows that luxury customers often prioritize discretion, privacy, and exclusivity, which may conflict with the transparency of AI-driven personalization.

Analysis: Consumers may view AI with suspicion, questioning whether algorithmic curation truly reflects their individuality or whether it homogenizes experiences. Over-reliance on AI risks commodifying luxury.

4.3 Analytical Insights

- The benefits and obstacles of AI in luxury reveal a paradoxical dynamic:
- AI enhances exclusivity (through personalization, predictive analytics, and fraud detection), yet also risks diluting authenticity if over-applied.
- AI extends accessibility through global digital engagement, yet may undermine the scarcity that defines luxury value.
- AI improves operational efficiency, but raises privacy and ethical concerns in handling sensitive consumer data.

Ultimately, the success of AI in luxury depends on its ability to complement rather than replace traditional values. Luxury brands must carefully balance innovation with heritage, ensuring that technology amplifies rather than diminishes their core identity.

5. FUTURE DIRECTIONS

As Artificial Intelligence (AI) continues to evolve, its role in the luxury sector will expand from an auxiliary tool to a core driver of value creation. Future applications will not only enhance personalization and operational efficiency but also redefine the boundaries of luxury through immersive digital ecosystems, ethical AI practices, and human–AI collaboration. This chapter explores the potential directions in which AI is likely to transform luxury consumer behavior and experiences, while critically analyzing the implications for brands and customers.

5.1 Deeper Personalization through Emotional AI:

The next frontier of luxury personalization lies in emotional AI, where algorithms can interpret consumer emotions through facial recognition, voice tone, and biometric signals. This would allow brands to offer not just customized products, but emotionally resonant experiences. For example, luxury fashion houses could deploy AI to detect a consumer's mood and suggest outfits that match their psychological state (McStay, 2018).

Analytical Insight: Emotional AI could enhance consumer–brand intimacy, but raises ethical concerns regarding surveillance and privacy. Luxury brands, which depend on consumer trust, will need to implement emotional AI carefully to avoid perceptions of intrusion.

5.2 Expansion into the Metaverse and Web3:

Luxury brands are increasingly experimenting with virtual goods, NFTs, and metaverse experiences. AI will play a crucial role in creating intelligent virtual assistants, digital twins, and personalized metaverse experiences (Dwivedi et al., 2022). For instance, Gucci's digital sneakers and Louis Vuitton's NFT-based video game skins illustrate how luxury is expanding into the digital realm.

Analytical Insight: The metaverse offers opportunities to engage digitally native Gen Z and Gen Alpha customers who view digital possessions as status symbols. However, this expansion obstacles traditional notions of craftsmanship and materiality that underpin luxury. AI-driven virtual luxury must therefore balance digital innovation with symbolic authenticity.

5.3 AI for Sustainable Luxury

Sustainability is becoming a defining factor for luxury customers (Kapferer & Michaut-Denizeau, 2020). AI will enable luxury brands to optimize production, reduce waste, and develop circular economy models. For example, predictive analytics can prevent overproduction, while AI-driven supply chain tools can enhance transparency in sourcing.

Analytical Insight: Aligning AI with sustainability reinforces the luxury ethos of timeless value. However, brands must communicate these practices authentically; otherwise, customers may dismiss them as "greenwashing."

5.4 Hybrid Human–AI Experiences

While automation is accelerating, luxury will continue to require a human–AI hybrid model. For instance, AI can handle data-driven personalization, while human sales associates provide emotional storytelling and artisanal expertise (Fournier & Alvarez, 2012). The future lies in blending AI efficiency with the craftsmanship and empathy that define luxury heritage.

Analytical Insight: The balance between human artistry and AI automation will differentiate successful luxury brands. Over-reliance on AI risks commodification, while resistance to AI risks irrelevance.

5.5 Ethical and Responsible AI in Luxury

As AI adoption accelerates, issues of ethics, fairness, and transparency will become central. Luxury customers, who often prioritize discretion and exclusivity, are likely to be particularly sensitive to misuse of personal data (Deloitte, 2020). The future will require brands to integrate responsible AI frameworks that ensure data privacy, algorithmic transparency, and inclusivity.

Analytical Insight: Trust will be the currency of future luxury experiences. Brands that embed responsible AI will not only comply with regulations but also strengthen their reputation as custodians of exclusivity and integrity.

5.6 Collaborative AI Ecosystems

The future will also see luxury brands collaborating with technology firms, startups, and even customers to co-create AI-driven experiences. LVMH's "Innovation Award" already reflects this trajectory, supporting AI startups to integrate cutting-edge solutions into luxury operations.

Analytical Insight: Such collaborations will democratize access to innovation, but also risk diluting brand control. Luxury brands must strategically curate partnerships to ensure alignment with their heritage and identity.

5.7 Synthesis of Future Trajectories

- The future of AI in luxury will be defined by paradoxes:
- Personalization vs. Privacy → AI offers deeper insights but risks overstepping consumer boundaries.
- Digital Luxury vs. Craftsmanship → Virtual goods expand reach but may challenge heritage-based value.
- Automation vs. Human Touch → Efficiency is maximized, but emotional resonance requires humans.
- Innovation vs. Exclusivity → AI enables mass personalization, but luxury thrives on scarcity.

Luxury brands must navigate these tensions carefully. The most successful will be those that use AI not as a substitute for heritage but as an amplifier of the core values of exclusivity, authenticity, and emotional engagement.

6. CONCLUSION

The integration of Artificial Intelligence (AI) into the luxury industry represents a profound shift in how customers experience, interact with, and perceive luxury brands. This conceptual paper has examined the impact of AI on luxury consumer behavior and experience through theoretical grounding, case study analysis, and exploration of benefits, obstacles, and future trajectories.

6.1 Key Insights from the Study

Redefining Consumer Experience:

AI enhances luxury by enabling hyper-personalization, predictive analytics, and immersive digital engagement. Consumers are no longer passive recipients but co-creators of luxury value, interacting with AI-powered chatbots, virtual stylists, and recommendation systems that anticipate desires and emotions.

Balancing Tradition and Innovation:

Luxury thrives on heritage, craftsmanship, and exclusivity, yet AI stresses efficiency, automation, and scalability. Case studies such as Louis Vuitton, Gucci, and Burberry illustrate how successful brands use AI not to replace tradition but to augment human creativity and brand storytelling, reinforcing emotional bonds while modernizing delivery.

Duality of Benefits and Challenges:

While AI empowers brands with customer insights, operational efficiency, and new revenue streams, it simultaneously introduces risks related to privacy, authenticity, and over-automation. Luxury brands must manage this paradox carefully, ensuring that AI strengthens exclusivity rather than diluting it.

Future-Oriented Shifts:

The trajectory of AI in luxury points toward emotional AI, metaverse integration, sustainable luxury, hybrid human–AI service models, and ethical frameworks. These emerging pathways will redefine the consumer–brand relationship, especially for digitally native generations who perceive luxury as both material and digital status symbols.

6.2 Theoretical Contributions

This paper advances understanding of how technology and consumer psychology intersect in the luxury domain. By conceptualizing AI as both a tool of personalization and a disruptor of exclusivity, it adds to ongoing debates in consumer behavior theory, experiential marketing, and digital transformation literature. The integration of emotional AI, metaverse luxury, and sustainability further extends theoretical discussions of how luxury consumption evolves in the age of intelligent technologies.

6.3 Managerial Implications:

- For practitioners, the findings emphasize that AI adoption in luxury is not merely a technological choice but a strategic imperative:
- Brand Managers must design AI-driven personalization that respects consumer privacy and cultural sensitivities.
- Retail Strategists should leverage AI–human hybrid service models, blending efficiency with storytelling.

- Sustainability Leaders can harness AI to implement responsible sourcing, waste reduction, and transparency as part of luxury's long-term value proposition.
- Executives must invest in responsible and ethical AI frameworks, safeguarding exclusivity, discretion, and trust core attributes of luxury.

6.4 Concluding Perspective

AI in luxury presents a paradox: it democratizes access to personalized experiences while challenging the scarcity and craftsmanship that define luxury's essence. The future of luxury will depend on how effectively brands navigate this tension using AI not as a substitute for human artistry but as an amplifier of authenticity, exclusivity, and emotional engagement.

Ultimately, the impact of AI on luxury consumer behavior and experience lies not in technology alone, but in the ability of brands to merge innovation with heritage, creating a new form of luxury that is intelligent, immersive, sustainable, and human-centric.

REFERENCES

Bughin, J., & Van Zeebroeck, N. (2018). Artificial intelligence: The next digital frontier? McKinsey Global Institute. https://www.mckinsey.com

Davenport, T. H., Guha, A., Grewal, D., & Bressgott, T. (2020). How artificial intelligence will change the future of marketing. *Journal of the Academy of Marketing Science*, *48*(1), 24–42. DOI: 10.1007/s11747-019-00696-0

Deloitte. (2023). Global powers of luxury goods 2023. Deloitte. https://www.deloitte.com

Dwivedi, Y. K., Hughes, L., Baabdullah, A. M., Ribeiro-Navarrete, S., Giannakis, M., Al-Debei, M. M., Dennehy, D., Metri, B., Buhalis, D., Cheung, C. M. K., Conboy, K., Doyle, R., Dubey, R., Dutot, V., Felix, R., Goyal, D. P., Gustafsson, A., Hinsch, C., Jebabli, I., & Wamba, S. F. (2022). Metaverse beyond the hype: Multidisciplinary perspectives on emerging challenges, opportunities, and agenda for research, practice and policy. *International Journal of Information Management*, *66*, 102542. Advance online publication. DOI: 10.1016/j.ijinfomgt.2022.102542

Engel, J. F., Blackwell, R. D., & Miniard, P. W. (1995). *Consumer behavior* (8th ed.). Dryden Press.

Fournier, S. (1998). Consumers and their brands: Developing relationship theory in consumer research. *The Journal of Consumer Research*, *24*(4), 343–373. DOI: 10.1086/209515

Fournier, S., & Alvarez, C. (2012). Brands as relationship partners: Warmth, competence, and in-between. *Journal of Consumer Psychology*, *22*(2), 152–163. DOI: 10.1016/j.jcps.2011.10.003

Kapferer, J. N., & Bastien, V. (2012). *The luxury strategy: Break the rules of marketing to build luxury brands* (2nd ed.). Kogan Page.

Maslow, A. H. (1943). A theory of human motivation. *Psychological Review*, *50*(4), 370–396. DOI: 10.1037/h0054346

McStay, A. (2018). *Emotional AI: The rise of empathic media*. SAGE Publications Ltd. DOI: 10.4135/9781526451293

Pine, B. J., & Gilmore, J. H. (1998). The experience economy. *Harvard Business Review*, *76*(6), 18–23.

Schmitt, B. (1999). *Experiential marketing: How to get customers to sense, feel, think, act, and relate to your company and brands*. Free Press.

Shankar, V. (2018). How artificial intelligence (AI) is reshaping retailing. *Journal of Retailing*, *94*(4), vi–xi. DOI: 10.1016/S0022-4359(18)30076-9

Tynan, C., McKechnie, S., & Chhuon, C. (2010). Co-creating value for luxury brands. *Journal of Business Research*, *63*(11), 1156–1163. DOI: 10.1016/j.jbusres.2009.10.012

Chapter 7
Leveraging AI for Promotional Campaigns

J R Ashlin Nimo
https://orcid.org/0000-0002-3035-581X
Villa College, Male, Maldives

S. Pradeep Kumar
Rajalakshmi Engineering College, India

ABSTRACT

The marketing environment is promoted with the implementation of Artificial Intelligence (AI), which transforms the way promotional campaigns are planned, implemented, and, ultimately, fine-tuned. This chapter discuss how AI has revolutionized up-to-date marketing strategies, how it is gradually taking over different activities in promotional campaigns. Starting with the overview of the emergence of AI in marketing, this chapter defines major AI technologies and machine learning applications that allow making smarter and data-driven decisions. This chapter also talks about the techniques of AI that are used to personalize campaigns based on the behavior of consumers and to make campaigns efficient and to delight customers. As a result, it acknowledges the effectiveness of promoting campaigns driven by AI and includes measurable outcomes through case studies of real-life situations. Through this thorough analysis, it is important to note that AI can transform the promotional efforts, with companies getting a competitive advantage in this digital age.

INTRODUCTION

"Next-gen marketers know that in order to deliver the personalization and experiences modern consumers expect, marketing must become smarter. It must become

DOI: 10.4018/979-8-3373-4392-1.ch007

marketer + machine." In the last few years, AI started to be a key factor in rethinking and running marketing events using automation and data instead of manual processes. With the help of AI, promotional campaigns can have better automation, more accurate predictions and improve both targeting and personalized messages. As a result, using AI in business strategies, companies boost their marketing campaigns and ensure they run appropriately.

Traditionally, marketing has been accomplished offline by displaying ads on billboards, newspapers, radio and television. Marketing became very different at the start of the millennia when companies started to take advantage of the internet for their operations. With the digital environment, businesses had the chance to increase their activities and make use of the internet to bring their products to more people speedily. With the arrival of digital media, companies could now design business models that make online platforms the key element(Kannan & Li, 2016a). As a result of viewing the internet as a new business avenue, companies had to change their strategies and search for fresh approaches to reach their customers on the web. With today's large availability of the internet on mobile devices, marketers can use it to reach potential buyers in places and times that were not practical before. It is also useful for marketers that digital platforms enable them to gather and process important customer data. Using this data, businesses can market better by understanding what their customers like and hope to find in ads(Ellis-Chadwick & Chaffey, 2012).

AI is getting better and going into new areas of digital marketing and promotions. Running campaigns with artificial intelligence in digital marketing helps both marketers and their customers. The reason marketers use AI is that it helps automate data-driven tasks involved in their promotional strategies. Using artificial intelligence can mean developing chatbots, recommendation engines, programmatic advertising and tools for analytics. Marketers benefit from being able to improve their marketing routines with automation and analyzing large customer data sets to take marketing actions. What is gained because of artificial intelligence, companies have the ability to offer customers a better and more personal experience when interacting. With artificial intelligence, we can look at what customers are saying. To learn about consumers' needs, companies use historical data and what consumers do on the internet. The combination of better understanding and automation allows the marketer to make advertising more personal for individuals, resulting in more customized experiences that please customers and make ads more successful.

Artificial intelligence (AI) has for the last few years had a strong impact on transforming both digital marketing and promotional campaigns. Artificial intelligence has existed as a technology for some years, but the progress in technology has made AI tools simpler for marketers to use. While they get better, these tools are set to reshape digital marketing by making it easier and more powerful for marketers and customers. Currently, companies mostly use artificial intelligence tools to automate marketing tasks and processes such as looking at analytics, choosing who to target, placing ads, offering customer service and writing content(Hall, 2019a). Digital marketing is now discovering artificial intelligence and because tools are constantly improving, marketers can always find additional ways to apply AI in marketing efforts. Because marketing and promotional campaigns are always developing, the use of technology by companies varies widely. The use of artificial intelligence in marketing can help produce better promotional campaigns and place ahead of companies that have not yet embraced AI. These advancements and the openings they create, industry leaders are encouraged to try artificial intelligence in their promotional campaigns(Shaik, 2023a).

Companies can improve their personalized marketing by using better ways to segment customers, get predictive insights and customize content. Financial professionals benefit from AI which can spot meaningful patterns and information that humans cannot find in huge data sets. Marketers are able to target their campaigns strongly to specific consumer groups which helps engagement and leads to more conversions. As an example, sites like Netflix and Amazon use AI to recommend things users might want which leads to increased user interaction and more sales. Unlike the usual marketing, personalized campaigns consider and address the tastes and actions of individual clients. The increasing need for personalized experiences among customers means companies must use new approaches. The use of AI allows us to handle big data, train computers to make predictions and use machine learning to meet these demands. Because AI looks at huge amounts of data, marketers can aim campaigns at specific individuals by understanding their interests better. AI helps personalized marketing largely by analyzing information about customers. AI enables marketers to go through a wide range of data to recognize what customers like, so marketers can better group their audience.

AI technology is able to study a customer's actions, what they buy online, what pages they visit and what they share through social media to build detailed profiles. Based on these profiles, companies can create content and offers intended services for those visitors. AI improves personalized marketing by using dynamic pricing. The use of AI makes it possible to look at shifts in demand, competitors' actions and behavior of customers to help decide on the best pricing quickly. Using this method, businesses can make prices more fitting for each customer and boost profit. AI being used in personalized marketing campaigns is a major improvement for the marketing world. Applying AI for data analysis, predictions, automating tasks, NLP and dynamic pricing helps businesses create marketing plans that increase how much customers engage with the business. Using AI in marketing increases the performance of campaigns and guarantees that customers get experiences customized to their needs that what individuals need and prefer.

THE EMERGENCE OF AI IN MARKETING

The world of marketing is highly dynamic and it is not slowing down; hence, in the world of marketing we are always going to have changes in technologies, methodologies, channel and mediums. Marketing has conventionally been accomplished via various forms of offline media such as billboard advertising, newspaper advertisements, radios, and television. One of the most radical changes in the field of marketing occurred at the beginning of the millennia when commercial application of the internet was starting to grow, and available to the companies to be a part of their business model. The online space produced new possibilities of business expansion and using the internet as an accessory to attract the potential customers more effectively. The new digital medium also enabled business organizations to develop new business model where Internet hosting forms the most important element(Kannan & Li, 2016b).

In marketing this adaptation of the internet as a new business medium has meant that they will have to adjust to this new climate and will have to figure out new methods of contacting their possible audience on the internet. The internet today can be accessed using mobile phones almost anywhere at any time and this implies that it provides marketers with a means of reaching their potential customers far much easily than they could do via the traditional systems. The second valuable opportunity of the digital environment which the marketer can offer is customer data collection and utilization. One can also utilize marketing with this collected data to learn more about the needs and preferences of customers in order to promote them even more personal and relevant advertising.

Implementation of artificial intelligence (AI) can be discussed as one of the most powerful factors changing the domain of digital marketing and promotional campaigns in recent years. The theory behind artificial intelligence as a technology is not new but the changes in the technologies implies that tools based on artificial intelligence have become more accessible to the marketers. These tools continue to get better and in the future, they can transform how digital marketing is handled and provide better efficiency and effectiveness to the marketers and the promotional experience to the customers. But as things stand now, tools with artificial intelligence mainly used offer to enhance the efficiency of marketing through automating various tasks and processes including the analytics process, targeting, placing advertisements, customer support and creation of content(Hall, 2019b).

Integrated feature of long-term impact of Artificial Intelligence (AI) on all the commercial entities of the world will be the outcome. The new directions of AI-based automation indicate the tremendous changes in the landscape of AI. It has been manifested as rearranged thoughts, preferences, and circulation of investments in the domain of AI implementation within the enterprise. This technology is highly advanced to the extent of facial and object recognition which has gigantic business implication in a wide range of application. Facial recognition can be employed to differentiate between persons due to security reasons; on the other hand, one can differentiate as well as analyse images using object detection. AI processes human pictures as cookies that make it possible to offer more personalised services depending on the preferences of customers. There are some companies which are testing facial recognition to solve the mood of their customers and in the process give them the right product to purchase.

In digital marketing, AI is mainly interested in retaining the user base and converting leads. It can guide the user towards that path that conforms to the objectives of the enterprise using the aid of intelligent AI chatbots, intelligent email marketing, interactive web design among other digital marketing services. The impact of AI on online marketing is determined by a number of issues. ML is a subclass of AI and concerns itself with computer programmes that have access to data and learn on the basis of the latter. It combines data in other places such as social media accounts, menus, online reviews and the web. At this point, AI analysis takes into account information and generates and delivers the inputs of the kind that is relevant to the listeners. As a hypothetical scenario, the AI software allows the analysis of online restaurants and their customers in depth. This will be possible as businesses will get to use the information they have by employing the AI in the marketing plan to reach out to the potential buyers with appealing commercials during hours that they find it convenient.

Along with the concept of AI in advertising on the social media and other digital networks such as Facebook and Instagram, the digital marketing offers an evidently comfortable experience, which is perceived by the customers. These sites allow the data pertaining to the users to be majorly analyzed and then forwarded to the offers that they desire. It is also the role of AI to help marketers to identify and predict trends. It saves the company the hassle of over-committing with digital ads and investing good money in unnecessary marketing. Computer vision is the proficiency that affects a computer to interpret things, scenes and actions in an image. Examples used are medical analysis of images, face recognition, security monitoring, and the security of the population. By appending computer vision and AI to it, it will then predetermine the events to take place and react to the same depending on the developments that are likely to take place in the future.

The development of profiles of clients and getting insight into the process of the customers journey has been made easy by artificial intelligence. It allows the efficient and painless transmission of useful context-specific material to the various client segments at any point of the marketing funnel and at every marketing channel. Based on facts available about the usage of AI in digital marketing, it is capable of forecasting which content is most likely to secure the customers to the site once more. AI can identify the most likely customers who may no longer want to use a certain service and investigate what is common among subscribers who haven no longer want to use a certain service. The marketers will be in a position to know what their future campaigning and practices will be as a result of the given analytics so that people will be here (Haleem et al., 2022).

AI TECHNOLOGIES USED IN MARKETING

Today the most promising new technology in the world is artificial intelligence and suggests programs, algorithms, systems and machines reproducing the intelligent behaviour of the human. They are usually machine learning, natural language processing, and neural networking and allow the machine to sense, comprehend, perform, and learn in the context of Human Machine Interaction(HMI).

Human-Machine interaction (HMI)

Human-Machine Interaction (HMI) is the type of interaction and communication between people and automated systems, which occurs through touch, gestures, voice and sensors. The use of man and machine as a robot machine to assist man is incorporated in the AI based applications that depend on HMI(Wilson & Daugherty, 2018).

Cognitive technologies such as computer vision, machine learning, natural language processing, speech recognition technologies and robotics allows people to communicate with machines and it is being capable of performing the job of humans. Besides, AI-enhanced machines are able to supplement human capacities in terms of enhancing their cognitive performance and expanding their physical capacity. (Kaplan & Haenlein, 2019a) have stated, AI and human beings can exist in a symbiotic relationship: Humans may delegate the tasks they feel to AI and use it as an instrument to make decisions that are more beneficial to humans. An example of such symbiotic relationship can be seen in (Huang et al., 2019) approach when they consider how firms should make decisions of assigning tasks to humans or machines and how AI is likely to replace mechanical tasks in the short-term, analytical task in the medium term and finally in the long-term, they will replace intuitive and empathetic tasks.

In the light of the growing ability of AI to perform at the same level as a human being or even, with time, replace human, more marketing scholars now turn to the idea of AI as an alternative to human raise issues about its potential deficiencies. On a recent case, some scientists assert that though in nations such as the United States, China and India, etc. the machine learning methods are actually very powerful as regards to the processing of large-scale unstructured data, and with high predictive accuracies, such type of technologies lacks in transparency and interpretability. In the same tone, several scholars debate on the importance of human synthesis and knowledge in AI applications. Both (Kopalle et al., 2022) and (Davenport et al., 2020) believe that AI might be made even more effective through increased efficiency of human managers (rather than replacing them). Speaking of such augmentation, as one of the examples, (Chintagunta et al., 2016) write about how big data and analytics may be employed to make customers relevant product recommendations, hence the worth of HMI. As an example, North Face and IBM Watson have come up with a personalized online experience in which an Artificial Intelligent-powered-online quiz suggests specific ''high-match" and ''low-match clothes'' according to customer preferences. As the given example may demonstrate, the retailing industry possesses some of the attractive qualities, the large volume and the abundance of data among them, which allows developing superior HMI applications.

It is also possible that HMI enables firms to provide personal, two walks communication with customers in real-time by using chat bots. As an example, chatbots like the 1-800-Flowers Facebook Messenger bot has revolutionized the process of delivering the customer service, and conversational chatbots like eBay bot tailored towards Google Assistant, facilitates quick search of the customer across the various categories of products. According to a recent field experiment conducted, AI chatbots perform equally well compared to experienced workers in making their customers purchase. HMI-relevant studies of other interest focus on a wide range of applications covering internet-of-things (IoT) and smart objects, collaborative decision systems, virtual and augmented reality, personalization, virtual reality experiences and facial recognition (e.g. Amazon cashierless Go stores).

Studies that have been carried out in the past also deliberated on how HMI makes complex decisions in the buying sector, provided recommendation on how to improve a computerized mediated behaviour between buyers and sellers and how HMI affects the decision-making process of the consumers via the voice assistants and how it alters the behaviour of the buyers in making the shopping as well as the real time response that the consumers may acquire in regards with the expenses. Behavioral research design, data-based automation of marketing, B2B marketing and HMI have also been used to enhance sales forecasts. The same can be seen in such use cases as described by (Kaplan & Haenlein, 2019b) regarding HMI in organizations and (Di Vaio et al., 2020)in terms of its effect on resource management.

Automated analysis of text, audio, images, and video

The marketing professionals and researchers have traditionally derived the data that they usually analyze through the primary data, observation, surveys and collections in the form of experiments. Although such lines of investigation delivered outstanding results, there are some of the limitations of insights. To give an example, a survey in most cases is very unlikely to find a causality and a possible limitation of an experiment is its generalizability. Automated analysis promises to offset part of the expenses of the drawbacks of the traditional forms of inquiry and for at least three significant reasons. To begin with, digital revolution means that the access to primary data has a major scale and scope today in most firms. As an example, Amazon and other businesses with operations in India can access millions of Amazon U.S. consumer reviews and get informed about it. Second, AI-related methods of collection tend to be less obtrusive as compared to other forms of investigation, thus minimising potential biases, such as the observation effect. Thus, the days of researchers and practitioners bothering customers to complete an ordering of survey questions or exposing study subjects to (artificial) laboratory conditions are over, and they now can get their hands on big data volumes of behavior based information that is recorded unobtrusively in the real time. Third, AI has enabled convenient gathering of the primary information in resources that were not used before and that can be gathered automatically and auto-assembled across different digital sites. To give an example, gathering (and often analysis) of the customer conversations on various social media platforms was automatized through AI-based technologies.

These days, the artificial intelligence (AI) is represented by automated features like language processing, independent Web scraping, and computer vision which is able to glean valuable information out of raw data in non-numeric (e.g. text, audio, images, video) sources. Text- The type of data available on a base is not only data produced by consumers through social media postings and customer reviews but also data produced by the firm. These types of data included advertising copy and financial reports which were originated (Berger et al., 2020). The examples of audio-based data and non-text (voice, music and sounds) are spoken words. Finally, data in the form of pictures also consist of a broad scope of stationary images and video materials. One of the examples of the automated analysis can be in the form of the virtual assistant available at the stores known as Millie which detects the consumer emotion by studying words and body gestures of individuals who come to the stores in order to organize a better customer experience since of such a kind.

Prospectively, scientists foresee that the processing, usage and collection of information might be fully automated through the advent of what scientists refer to as an autonomy intelligence. Thus, firms one day also can be changed into automated analysis-based organizations that are full of highly nuanced understandings of they have clients around the world and can mass customize solutions that understand and take action on data-generated insights with minimal, if any, any, human supervision. Even though an automated analysis can yield a set of diverse benefits, the use of this technology begs a question pertaining to the number of data-related issues. As an example, items to be completed in a survey could be filled automatically (e.g.

by a robot) and thus provide data twisting and predisposed conclusions. Similarly, such algorithm types have also been even blamed to (automatically) generate data such as social media trolling or demonstrating reviews. To curb this vice, firms like Amazon are hiring the help of natural language processing to recognize and rectify possible distortion of data. Additionally, there is limited information on the implication of these automated analysis as regards to the world. So in this regard we believe how far automated analysis of text, audio, image and video might cause these complications in the shapes of inequality, glocalization and global ethical and privacy concerns.

EVOLUTION OF PROMOTIONAL CAMPAIGNS

The transformation of the promotional campaigns indicates the way the companies have been developing their marketing strategy throughout history with the changing technology, consumer behavior and the media capabilities.

Traditional Era (Pre-1990s): Mass Marketing

Mass marketing techniques were used in the Traditional Era of promotional campaigns that preceded the 1990s. Print adverts, radio, television, billboards and direct mails were some of the main ways business reached the consumers. This was mostly a one way communication that involved sending of messages via broadcasting to a large number of people where the type of interaction and feedback with these people was minimal. Its primary role was related to the creation of brand awareness and the data on goods or services. A typical sample of this period involves the television and newspaper advertisement of the Coca-Cola by the local retailers as a means of securing patrons.

Digital Emergence (1990s–2000s): The Internet Boom

Internet powered promotions began in the Digital Emergence period that began in the 1990s and continued until the 2000s. Companies started using the web, email promotions, banners and simple search optimization (SEO) to access Internet users. It is during this time that interactive marketing came into existence because businesses began to gather simple user data to have a more effective idea of what people were like. It started focusing on traffic, bringing accounts to websites, attracting people to subscribe to email as the methods to direct relationships with customers. An exemplary case during this period is when Amazon launched its initial marketing communications via email, when it would personalize the products stock and laid the basis of data-driven messages.

Social Media Rise (2005–2015): Two-Way Engagement

Social Media Rise period (2005 2015) changed the nature of promotional campaigns by creating platforms such as Facebook, Twitter, Youtube and Instagram. As opposed to the previous one-way communication services, this era focused on the two-way communication strategy where consumers communicated directly with brands. It became all about producing content that evoked interest and story-telling that endorsed likes, sharing, comments as well as formation of loyal brand communities. Campaigns were more interactive, invitational and user built, and the users were building the brand message. One of the most prominent examples of the time is the viral campaign, the Old Spice Man Your Man Could Smell Like that became extremely popular with the use of humor and creativity as well as interactivity between the brand and the audience.

Data-Driven & Personalization Era (2015–2020): Precision Marketing

The era between 2015 and 2020, known as the Data-Driven and Personalization Era is the period that contributed to a change in direction to precision marketing and based on technology and analytics. More channels such as programmatic advertising, CRM tools, marketing automation and influencer marketing were also used by businesses to create very specific and personalized messages. Depending on the consumer behavior, demographics and individual preference, each campaign was customized to target specific user in the customer journey, as marketers approached them at various customer journey steps. It focused on lead nurturing, better customer experience, and return on investment (ROI). One memorable one was the Special Spotify Wrapped, where listeners were given individual summaries based on their yearly listening habits that were made into an emotional, sharable and promotion piece based purely on statistics.

AI & Experience-Driven Era (2020–Present): Immersive & Predictive Marketing

A new era of immersive and predictive marketing described as AI and Experience-Driven Era (2020-onwards) is a new frontier of promotional campaigns. The high-level channels have been entered into businesses, where the use of chatbots, augmented and virtual reality (AR/VR), TikTok, voice assistants, and dynamic video ads are employed as methods of the delivery of engaging and personalized experiences. It is based on the predictive analytics and user-generated content and allows real-time communication and stronger connections with the consumers on an emotional level. The campaigns are structured to be very agile and personalised to scale, and are both more relevant and more engaging. Examples such as Nike AR try-on capabilities that allow trying out products and brands with chatbots including ChatGPT being used to provide marketing experience through chatting and interactions.

CHALLENGES IN TRADITIONAL PROMOTIONAL CAMPAIGNS

Although the traditional marketing campaigns remain to be the pillars of history in business promotions, many dynamics in the modern marketplace continue to present daunting challenges to the traditional marketing campaigns. The development of consumer behavior and the emergence of new technologies has demonstrated the inefficiency of common marketing tools, which requires a change of approach to more creative and attentive strategy. This is one of the major costs of traditional marketing campaigns which lack definite targeting. Most established ways, which include television, print advertisement, and radio, tend to use general demography profiles to attract a potential list of customers. Although this is a good method of building mass awareness about the brand, the action is likely to lead to generic communications that do not appeal to certain categories of consumers. This leads to poor marketing effectiveness to fuel interest and conversions. The lack of custom ability to meet different needs with messages would make the marketing funds go to waste since the advertisement would be targeting audiences that might not be in need of the product or service communicated.

Moreover, conventional marketing campaigns tend to have no defining measurability and live feedback. In contrast to digital marketing, where one can specify the interaction with the consumer and see the success of the campaign, traditional marketing techniques give a few hints about the efficiency of the marketing activity. An example is that without doing a research it is difficult to know the extent to which a billboard advertisement or a television commercial establishes an influence on consumer behavior. Such absence of data reduces the capacity of marketers to act on evidence and to maximize their strategies by using the real-time responses to their actions. High cost of traditional marketing campaigns is another major problem. Running advertising programs using conventional media options like television, radio, and print may be too costly, particularly on small and medium-sized businesses (SMEs). All these expenses may restrict frequency and spread of the marketing messages thus diminishing the efficiency of the whole campaign. Also, the ROI of the traditional marketing campaigns can be quite complicated to calculate and in that case, the businesses may not find it easy to justify high costs of such programs.

The traditional marketing campaigns are also characterized by stiffness and lack of flexibility that challenges the same significantly. The traditional advertise campaigns are usually developed and implemented over long durations and therefore it becomes hard to respond fast to the dynamics of the market and consumer behaviour. Such rigidity may lead to a loss of opportunity and decline in competitiveness in an environment that is fast changing. Alternatively, digital marketing campaigns are adaptable in real-time with the help of performance records and real-time trends so that a business can remain nimble and responsive to consumer demand. Furthermore, the conventional marketing campaigns cannot attract modern consumers as effectively as they are expected to emerge, the interaction and customization being the critical markers of their preferences. The emergence of digital technologies has altered consumer expectations quite significantly, as nowadays even a significant proportion of people want to receive customised content meaning something that resonates with the needs and the interests that the consumers might have. The methods of customized marketing simply fail to hon its expectations, and so there is reduced levels of engagement and satisfaction in marketing in general. Nowadays people are overwhelmed with marketing messages (especially in the online environment) and to be able to stand out one has to be more personal and precise.

The problems are also aggravated by the decrease in the number of users of traditional media. As the use of digital media becomes increasingly popular, via sources like social media, streaming services, and online news media, the traditional media sources are losing audiences in both viewership and readership. Such a shift in the media consumption habit decreases the scope and impact of the conventional marketing campaigns, since not all consumers view the adverts through such mediums. Therefore, companies, which use the conventional methods of marketing extensively, might not be able to reach their target audiences as easily as before. The conventional marketing campaign has so many problems that constrain its usefulness in the contemporary brisk and online-oriented marketplace. Creativity, imprecise targeting, measurability and absence of real time feedback, when coupled to high costs and rigidity does not allow the traditional marketing to be able to give desirable results. In addition, the increasing preference to more personalized experiences and the decreasing tendency to use the traditional media also weaken the influence of ordinary marketing techniques. There is an evident emergence of more creative and dynamic marketing solutions that would incorporate the influence of digital technologies and data-driven ideas on reaching modern consumers in the effort to overcome such challenges to business(Ignatius Ijomah et al., 2024).

ROLE OF AI IN DIFFERENT STAGES OF THE PROMOTIONAL CAMPAIGN

According to the study of (Shaik, 2023b), although the implementation of AI is used in the majority of companies, in several situations, the high implementation level continues to be absent. This trend was evident since it was possible to observe this trend in the lines of the expert interview as most of the interviewees cited the implementation of AI in their customer companies as an example. The case companies were industry professionals in the sphere of digital marketing and advertising and hence had a lot of knowledge in artificial intelligence and how to apply with this and their customers were different companies in all the spheres and in most of the cases there was no artificial intelligence applied. The majority of businesses are only beginning to realize the possibility of utilizing AI which is made available to them by the introduction of new implementations and improvements. It is because of this that AI is a very new tool of some firms and this poor level of implementation is assumed to be occasioned to a greater extent by the lack of AI expertise within the firm. The arrival of AI technologies in the world in the future is likely to make the general level of AI implementation better as it gets more accessible and simpler to use without the knowledge of experts.

(Jain & Aggarwal, 2020) analyzed and pointed out that the major advantages that companies which apply artificial intelligence possess are efficiency and enhanced customer experience and satisfaction that contributes to developing better relationships with clients. The principle advantages to customers are founded on a more customized and personal experience with the customer. (Kivistö Arttu, 2024) pays more attention to the power of the analytical aspect of artificial intelligence and informs that artificial intelligence can deliver analytical information and forecast to assist in the decision-making process. Many of the experts emphasized such analytical advantages and said that they play a crucial role in the decision-making part of the process. To the majority of the case companies still those analytical benefits that artificial intelligence provides were the most valuable contribution that AI makes to their promotional campaign despite the growing popularity of generative language models. Tools based on AI played an extremely different role in various phases of promotional campaigns depicted in Figure 1. In the implementation of AI-based tools companies evaluated the value and benefits, which it generates against the costs but do not have criteria in its implementation.

It was evident that the purposes of AI use followed the same three-stage framework, as it was described by (Huang & Rust, 2021), in their work. On the interviews of the designing phases of the promotional campaigns, they adds its primary emphasis on the mechanical AI and its potential to automate various records of analysis. The major tools/equipment utilized were the data analysis tools and the prediction tools which were utilized to plan the campaign and the outcomes and assisted in decision-making. When developing the campaign overview strategy, it undergoes a process. It entails developing the strategy, the promotional channels, the targeted target audiences and the budget. The campaign automatically applies factors such as AB testing, campaign adjustment and optimizing the bidding through the use of mechanical AI. Mechanical AI is also applied during and subsequent to the campaign to furnish input data analysis and make reports regarding the performance as well as the outcomes of the campaigns. The primary purpose of using feeling AI is that it is mostly employed in testing customer emotions and evaluating customer emotions and perceptions regarding the promotion and brand. The AI is applied during the planning and execution of the campaign to create material and design the offerings of various promotional advertisements.

Since the application of AI-based tools in the frames of the promotion campaign activities has become more widespread their influence on the process of decision-making has become dominant. During the process of decision-making AI helps human decision-makers when it comes to promotional campaigns, but also makes decisions of its own as depicted in the Figure 2.

AI is beneficial as it offers rich information, analytics and projections and in this manner, it helps human decision makers by aiding their decision making capability with information-based analysis. The AI-generated content is another type of decision-making, in which the AI aids and works with decision-making. In case of utilizing AI content the content is produced as per descriptions or rules established by humans and the given content is created by AI after it is reviewed it is edited by humans. The artificial intelligence is also in the position to automate most of those manual and creative duties that had involved human decisions. According to the experts, the decisions, which can be attained purely using data, are usually fully attributable to the AI. Such types of decisions involve targeting, segmentation, setting bids, and A/B testing various ad copies. The experts were in consensus that what will remain the concern of a human decision-maker and is likely to remain so in the future are the more important decisions which had a large impact on the company or on the strategy whereas those which are less important and part of a day to day activity would be even more automated by the AI in the future. These are crucial decisions which were believed to remain part of the scope of a human decision-maker such as the strategy, goals, campaign budget, factors involved in brands and campaign objectives. At some point, as more technology developed, the experts had hoped that AI would gain control of the between-platform decisions and, in the process, would be able to ensure the entire campaign was run automatically. This would allow release of less time that has to be allotted to the human decision-makers on the other parts of the campaign.

Although much attention is devoted to artificial intelligence by corporations as mentioned by (Shaik, 2023c) there remains in numerous businesses little implementation of such advanced technologies at the high level. According to the interviews, it is primarily caused by the lack of technological knowledge, the difficulty of using such programs that have AI as their base, and the absence of available resources. The experts predict that its adoption among the businesses would skyrocket in the future with its accessibility being enhanced. The enhanced user interfaces will enhance usability and open the use of such tools to marketers who are not that much up to date with the technology. This would greatly increase the easiness of AI-based tools to most companies that are not already using AI and the future adoption of AI-based tools. Such increase in usability may further have an impact to the area where marketing and advertising agencies work because it may reduce the need of such customers to seek expert familiarity and they may consequently use such programs on their own.

Considering the prospects that AI will bring to the future promotional campaigns the experts that have been talked to regard the greater incorporation of AI factors as the next huge advancement. Most AI programs now tend to perform a predetermined task or channel of promotion. Connection of all of these tools in such a manner that any promotional campaign the company will conduct could be run respectively by the last mile with the help of only one tool would be a giant leap in the seamless artificial intelligence implementation process. One of the opportunities that the professionals examined is how generative AI models could be used in combination with a set of collected data and have much potential. It would enable the marketers to train the generative algorithm so that the latter would produce the content that would be even more specific and fine-tuned to address specific requirements during the promotional campaigns.

Artificial intelligence also has various technical and ethical interactions that place a constraint on its application. Among the technological limitations, it is stated that lack of human-like context and other nuances is considered to be one of the most important ones. This is most evident in generative AI models and it is what makes it hard for such models to create content intended towards a particular purpose that fits within the general tone and image of a brand. Processing power is one aspect that has been slowing things down in the past but with technical advances in place today the restrictions that it puts in place are minimal.

The professionals differed greatly in their viewpoints of ethical factors constraining implementation but the most common issues were that of job displacement, various misleading content, prejudices, and environmental issues because of consumption of more energy and requirements of hardware. The experts who studied this topic feel that transparency of its use, data integrity, evaluating its ethical impact, and applying AI ethically appropriate would be the most significant tools in fighting these factors and using AI responsibly.

MACHINE LEARNING TECHNOLOGIES FOR PROMOTIONAL CAMPAIGNS

Machine learning is a branch of computer sciences, as a field of study it is considered as a branch of artificial intelligence. One of the major areas of study that redefines how computers learn trends and make choices based on data and algorithms is machine learning. These machine learning algorithms endow the computers with the capability to make proper predictions of the outcomes on the basis of the input data and enhance the accuracy of its prediction as it is being presented with new data. Such machine learning algorithms enable marketers to automate such complicated tasks such as analytics, calculations, and optimization.

Machine learning is based on the simple principle that a computer is given some sample data sets. On this basis, the software tries to find pattern and relationships and how they affect the results. Through it, it is possible to forecast what a customer will do using past records of other individuals. The machine learning algorithm is also altered depending on the new data and the results of it to make it more accurate and work better and in that way the software is able to learn on its own without human intervention. Thus, basically the key objective of machine learning is that it has to eventually enable the computers to learn by themselves hence without any further programming or other human assistance.

There are numerous purposes of the use of machine learning technologies in the promotional campaigns depending on the needs and aims of the campaign. In this section, a couple of examples of promotional campaign processes that may be enhanced with the use of such technologies are presented.

AI-Chatbots

The online world has granted the customers the opportunity to access the websites of businesses and shop in online stores 24 hours a day and this translates to the fact that right now there exists a demand that customer service should provide customer service when ever the customer requires it. Customer service in the past depended upon phone lines, e-mails and chats. A big disadvantage of these processes, however, is that they require human labor at all times and therefore it is costly to run which is a challenge particularly to small companies. Companies are addressing such issues by putting chatbots powered by artificial intelligence on the websites.

Artificial intelligence-based bots that are provided with data and patterns and trained to recognize and respond to the commonly asked questions of the customers and assist them with different customer problems by merely reading data about the customers without any human interaction of the prior business. With the help of natural language processing, chatbots are able to interpret the questions of users and, through that, obtain the information of interest. With these queries, deep and machine-learning algorithms are employed to give answers to customers and enhance the performance of bots with time as it gathers more data. It takes this feedback of old queries to modify and optimize the algorithm and as a result it adapts to it and spits out better answers later. Another danger of this learning practice is affecting the performance of the chatbot adversely in case the feedback it is given is flawed.

By adopting the use of chatbots based on artificial intelligence, it is possible to reduce the expenses, and the amount of work that customer service has to do since the chatbots can automatically have the answer to the most frequent and simple problems and complex problems can only be referred to a real customer service worker in case the chatbots is unable to offer a solution to a problem. Chatbots also operate on the 24-hour basis such that it can offer the customer service of the commonest of problems even when the customer service representative is unavailable. One more advantage of chatbots is that they nearly immediately answer the questions of their customers thus making the customer experience better by occupying less time that is usually spent by customers in wait queues before having their problems solved by actual customer service agents(Shaik, 2023b).

Recommendation Engines

Recommendation engines have turned out to be one of the most important aspects of any online store or platform since it offers its customers personal and targeted suggestions. Recommendation engines utilize artificial intelligence and deep learning algorithms to enable their customers to have personalized contents, product suggestions, and experiences. Using recommendation engines to enhance customer experience and increase upselling and cross-selling using product as well as content recommendations that a customer might be interested in is the most common objective of the usage of the recommendation engines. E-commerce and recommendation of products based on browsing and purchasing data, and entertainment such as entertainment streaming services and news websites to recommend items or services based on what the customer has already viewed or read are among the most commonly used methodologies of recommendation engines.

The recommendation engines employ two primary methods and algorithms that include Collaborative Filtering and Content-Based Filtering. In Collaborative Filtering a shared user experience is used to obtain relevant recommendations. Collaborative filtering examines past associations and preferences of past customers so as to arrive at a forecast on what would be of interest to the particular user. On the basis of these past interactions, it suggests content that was of interest to other people of comparable demographics, interests or browsing and purchase patterns. This may be an excellent way of doing cross selling because it may also recommend other products which in some way or the other are linked to the one in question by using collaborative filtering. It goes by the thought of people who purchased this also purchased and therefore when purchasing a printer, it may also suggest printing paper and ink. Probably one of the main applications of collaborative filtering is the so-called cold-start problem. It occurs when initiating the usage of collaborative filtering in the absence or having limited numbers of user data. It (collaborative filtering) does not make relevant suggestions when presented with small historical data. There is more accuracy the more data is collected in the case of collaborative filtering.

The other method is the content-based filtering, and unlike the shared experiences, the recommendations are made on the basis of the content. Content-based filtering is based on recommendations of products or content depending on the qualities of the items themselves and preferences of the user in the past. The item representations and the user profiles are the primary features of content-based filtering. In content based filtering products or content is characterized, based on a set of characteristics and attributes of the actual product and it is on this criteria that the type of product or content in hand will be defined. The user profile is utilized to establish the kind of content according to the interests of a particular user. The user profile is assembled depending on information on the past activity and inclination of the users together with the reviews, likes, and ratings. Content based filtering is following the notion that, since you are interested in this product, then you would also be interested in similar products. This implies that the recommendation engine would propose similar products, so in the case of purchasing a printer, the engine may propose on purchasing several alternatives of printers which are similar in terms of their characteristics. The advertiser can as well determine who he can reach and whom he should reach through this method using those who are very similar to his own main audience or target. This helps to solve the cold start problem since the products are recommended according to the level to which their attributes fit the user profile that is, it does not need such high volume of information to operate as collaborative filtering.

Targeting and segmentation

To make the marketing work more precise, marketers employ the means of segmentation and targeting, which also help to narrow down promotional activities to the particular customer groups. Segmentation is aimed at recognizing various categories of customers in a firm and targeting is a way of channeling certain marketing messages and promoting activities to particular people. Artificial intelligence enabled businesses to enhance their segmentation and targeting by providing the businesses with the data driven and automated process of segmenting customers in various segments and reaching them accordingly to deliver tailor-made message to each segment.

One of the basic marketing practices is customer segmentation, which entails breaking the customers of any company into groups based on certain set characteristics at the individual levels, and behavioral terms. The first goal of the segmentation is to segment the customers depending on their behaviour and preferences to enable the businesses cut their advertising to meet each segment well. Performed properly, the process of segmentation can substantially improve the efficiency of marketing, because with its help, advertisements will be relevant to the individual groups of customers and have a higher chance of being considered. Artificial intelligence has also enabled the advertisers to streamline the segmentation exercise and prepare very specific micro-segments that can be addressed with some customized content. It also provides the advertiser with the power to possess dynamic customer segments that can bring customers in and out of its segments depending on movements in the data and behavior of the customers i.e. whether he or she shows interest in a particular product or goes ahead to do a particular thing i.e. subscribes to a postal list.

Targeting is the act of directing the promotional efforts towards a given target group by relying on a set of given characteristics, behavior, interests or a given factor. Targeting is so as to improve the accuracy of the promotion activities achieve better outcomes since the marketers will have an opportunity to target their efforts on the preferences and the features of a particular target group.

A form of using artificial intelligence in the targeting that is one of the most widely used is referred to as predictive targeting. With the help of artificial intelligence and machine learning algorithms, predictive targeting uses big masses of demographic, and behavioral consumer data to determine the relation between them and the buying behavior of individuals. The objective is that artificial intelligence should recognize the most dominant features and tendencies affecting the purchasing behavior based on the data and direct advertisement campaigns in relation to these factors to the audiences with the same tendencies. An example is when a company knows that the segment that is most profitable to sell a particular product is men, in the age group of 18-25 years old, in Helsinki and interested in sports, the company can then make use of the predictive targeting to reach more of that kind of people.

AI FOR PERSONALIZED PROMOTIONAL CAMPAIGNS

The direction of personalized marketing that has been employed to tail the marketing messages and offers to individual consumers based on their preferences and behaviours has acquired a lot of profile in the modern business environment. The growth of digital technologies and the tremendous volumes of information people create have enabled the businesses to know and predict customer requirements with a higher degree of precision than ever before. What makes the given ability significant is the fact that it enables businesses to provide the experiences that are the most relevant and interesting, consequently, resulting in the better customer relationship and conversion rates.

Personalized marketing has changed with the advent of Artificial Intelligence (AI) since it offers highly refined techniques that highly spur the interaction of customers and the conversion rate.

Machine learning, which is a branch of AI, plays an essential role in personalized marketing because this machine can analyze a large volume of data and detect relationships in consumer behaviour. Machine learning systems are able to access a huge mass of data to segment the customers according to their preferences and behavior. This segmentation gives marketers a chance to focus messages on targeted and specific consumer segments thus giving the marketing campaign more relevancy and efficiency. As an illustration, using clustering algorithms, businesses can cluster together customers subscribing to similar shopping patterns, that is, the businesses can devise marketing plans that accommodate the peculiarities of each cluster.

Natural language processing (NLP) is the next important AI method as far as personalized marketing is concerned. NLP also allows computers to read, interpret, and create human language to make interactions with a customer more personal and stimulating. With the knowledge of the language or emotional needs of their customers, a business can have a more effective advertising message by using the language, or desires, of their customers. NLP chatbots are also gaining popularity as the means of personalized customer service and recommendations in real-time.

Artificial intelligence, and in particular predictive analytics based on machine learning tools and statistical analyses, is essential in predicting the behaviours and trends of customers in the future. The new AI method can help companies foresee the demands and interests of the customers, which will make it possible to conduct proactive marketing. As an example, predictive models may examine the previous buying patterns to forecast future buying so that businesses can make product recommendations to their customers in time and so that such recommendations will be really relevant. Understanding the need of the customer, the business will bring in a better customer experience, and chances of making a conversion.

One of the primary ways personalization in marketing is achieved with the help of recommendation system, and this is a direct application of machine learning and predictive analytics. Recommendation systems utilise its analysis of customer data by providing a suggestion of a product or service that will be of interest to an individual customer. Examples of such companies that have effectively applied the concept of recommendation system so it can maximize customer appeal and increased sales include Netflix and Amazon(Gomez-Uribe & Hunt, 2015). Being a part of them, the collaborative filtering and content-based filtering are used to make it possible to provide customers with the list of custom recommendations, which is why the customers receive the list of options matching their preferences and browser history.

Moreover, there is also dynamic pricing that is based on using personalization through AI since the use of machine learning is implemented to set the price according to the actual demands, market situation, and customer behavior. The method enables companies to develop the best pricing policies to maximize their revenues and enhance client satisfaction. AI can be useful in dynamic pricing models since it can look at variables like rival prices, stock and customer price willingness leading to better price competitive and compelling pricing to consumers.

CASE STUDIES OF AI DRIVEN PROMOTIONAL CAMPAIGNS

AI is changing how promotional campaigns are conducted and it supports expansion in personalization, efficiency and creativity. The first successful example of voice AI usage in case studies is the one by Coca- Cola called the Share a Coke campaign, the second one is the case study of Heinz called the AI Ketchup, and the third case study is the one by Burger King called the Mouldy Whopper. These examples indicate that artificial intelligence can improve customer feedback, increases brand awareness and leads to high performance.

Coca-Cola's Share a Coke

Coca-Cola applied voice processing and recognition as a means of letting customers speak into their phones in order to have their own wordings printed on the bottles of Coke. This generated superior customer interaction and a new personalized product.

Heinz's AI Ketchup

Heinz used text-to-image AI to create ketchup images in different situations, demonstrating the iconic position of the brand and causing a lot of media heat. The campaign possessed over 1.15 billion earned impressions as well as engagement rate which was 38 percent greater than that of the previous campaigns.

Burger King's Mouldy Whopper

Burger king used AI to analyse the sentiment and search pattern of users on the social media about the idea behind the campaign and this gave them a chance to evaluate the potential among people about how they may react and what the risks of the idea could have been prior to the launch. This campaign is at the edge of provoking worldwide discussion and brought the brand credit as exceptionally creative.

Nutella's AI-Generated Labels

Each jar sold features a different label with the help of AI, and Nutella managed to make 7 million different ones. This promotional campaign shows the AI powered product marketing and differentiation.

L'Oreal's ModiFace and SkinConsult AI

Online shopping experience was enhanced with the help of AI and ModiFace by Loreal offers a virtually try makeup, and SkinConsult AI provided personalized skincare analysis and recommendations. The ModiFace and SkinConsult AI of L Oreal enhanced the conversion rates and customer engagement to a great extent.

CHALLENGES IN IMPLEMENTING AI DRIVEN PROMOTIONAL CAMPAIGNS

An organization undergoes several challenges from data management issues to organizational resistance to change in order to implement AI driven promotional campaigns. These challenges must be addressed with thoughtful solutions and best practices for successful implementation of AI in campaigns. For the successful implementation, challenges related to data must be addressed first. The quality and comprehensiveness of data are essential for the effectiveness of AI driven promotional campaign. Gathering data from multiple sources is one of the challenge organizations face. To overcome this specific challenge, organizations must use a centralized system using ERP or Management Information Systems for integrating data from multiple sources. This technique improves data quality and consistency while also enhances data accessibility.

Managing organizational transformation is another biggest challenge organizations face when it comes to adoption of new technologies. Employees resist to adopt new technologies as they fail to understand the benefits of AI or have concerns of compromising their jobs. Change management techniques like insisting employee involvement, training and clear communication regarding the benefits of using artificial intelligence and how it boosts performance must be addressed. Employees must also be helped to mitigate fear on the usage of new technologies. Additionally, offering rigorous training programs can provide employees the skills they need to engage with AI tools, fostering a sense of empowerment and ownership.

Additionally, a vital problem that must be addressed is ensuring ethical use of AI in marketing. Concerns regarding data privacy, security, and ethical use are aggravated by the fact that AI powered personalized marketing often requires significant data collection and usage. Organizations should set clear ethical standards and procedures for employing AI in marketing to overcome these barriers. This means setting strong data security procedures in place to secure to consumer data, like encryption and anonymous access. Organizations can also encourage transparency in AI operations by explicitly stating how customer data is used and how AI algorithms perform (Iyelolu et al., 2024).

CONCLUSION

The way how AI can be discussed in the case of promotional campaigns can provide an idea about the possibility of the transforming nature of the artificial intelligence in the growth of the marketing strategies and the enhancement of businesses. Application of AI technologies in marketing campaigns has been found to have a massive potential in attaining customized customer experience, optimisation of residential marketing campaign, and conversion rates. AI and machine learning are relatively old technologies but over the past few years, these technologies have acquired a lot of new applications that can appropriately be applied in digital marketing and promotion campaigns. Artificial intelligence and other more recent functions are gaining ground to advance technology that can be used to transform the industry of promotional campaigns which is why it is important to assess the manner in which the artificial intelligence is to be applied presently based on the terms of the promotional campaigns and how the professionals see the aspect of accessory of the artificial intelligence as of yet and in the future.

REFERENCES

Berger, J., Humphreys, A., Ludwig, S., Moe, W. W., Netzer, O., & Schweidel, D. A. (2020). Uniting the Tribes: Using Text for Marketing Insight. *Journal of Marketing*, *84*(1), 1–25. DOI: 10.1177/0022242919873106

Chintagunta, P., Hanssens, D. M., & Hauser, J. R. (2016). Marketing and Data Science: Together the Future is Ours. *GfK Marketing Intelligence Review*, *8*(2), 18–23. DOI: 10.1515/gfkmir-2016-0011

Davenport, T., Guha, A., Grewal, D., & Bressgott, T. (2020). How artificial intelligence will change the future of marketing. *Journal of the Academy of Marketing Science*, *48*(1), 24–42. DOI: 10.1007/s11747-019-00696-0

Di Vaio, A., Palladino, R., Hassan, R., & Escobar, O. (2020). Artificial intelligence and business models in the sustainable development goals perspective: A systematic literature review. *Journal of Business Research*, *32*, 283–314. Advance online publication. DOI: 10.1016/j.jbusres.2020.08.019

Ellis-Chadwick, F., & Chaffey, D. (2012). *Digital marketing: strategy, implementation and practice*. Pearson.

Gomez-Uribe, C. A., & Hunt, N. (2015). The netflix recommender system: Algorithms, business value, and innovation. *ACM Transactions on Management Information Systems*, *6*(4), 1–19. Advance online publication. DOI: 10.1145/2843948

Haleem, A., Javaid, M., Asim Qadri, M., Pratap Singh, R., & Suman, R. (2022). Artificial intelligence (AI) applications for marketing: A literature-based study. In *International Journal of Intelligent Networks* (Vol. 3, pp. 119–132). KeAi Communications Co., DOI: 10.1016/j.ijin.2022.08.005

Hall, J. (2019a). How artificial intelligence is transforming digital marketing. *Hg. v. Forbes. Online Verfugbar Unter* Https://Www. Forbes. Com/Sites/Forbesagencycouncil/2019/08/21/How-Artificial-Intelligence-Istransforming-Digital-Marketing

Hall, J. (2019b). How artificial intelligence is transforming digital marketing. *Hg. v. Forbes. Online Verfugbar Unter* Https://Www. Forbes. Com/Sites/Forbesagencycouncil/2019/08/21/How-Artificial-Intelligence-Istransforming-Digital-Marketing

Huang, M.-H., Rust, R., & Maksimovic, V. (2019). The feeling economy: Managing in the next generation of artificial intelligence (AI). *California Management Review*, *61*(4), 43–65. DOI: 10.1177/0008125619863436

Huang, M.-H., & Rust, R. T. (2021). A strategic framework for artificial intelligence in marketing. *Journal of the Academy of Marketing Science*, *49*(1), 30–50. DOI: 10.1007/s11747-020-00749-9

Ignatius Ijomah, T., Vanessa Iyelolu, T., Ebele Agu, E., & Idemudia, C. (2024). Leveraging Artificial Intelligence for Personalized Marketing Campaigns to Improve Conversion Rates. In *International Journal Of Engineering* [). www.ijerd.com]. *Research for Development*, *20*(8), •••.

Iyelolu, T. V., Agu, E. E., Idemudia, C., & Ijomah, T. I. (2024). Leveraging artificial intelligence for personalized marketing campaigns to improve conversion rates. *International Journal of Engineering Research and Development*, *20*(8), 253–270.

Jain, P., & Aggarwal, K. (2020). *Transforming Marketing with Artificial Intelligence*. DOI: 10.13140/RG.2.2.25848.67844

Kannan, P. K., & Li, H. (2016a). *Digital Marketing: A Framework, Review and Research Agenda*. https://ssrn.com/abstract=3000712Electroniccopyavailableat: https://ssrn.com/abstract=3000712Electroniccopyavailableat:https://ssrn.com/abstract=3000712

Kannan, P. K., & Li, H. (2016b). *Digital Marketing: A Framework, Review and Research Agenda*. https://ssrn.com/abstract=3000712Electroniccopyavailableat: https://ssrn.com/abstract=3000712Electroniccopyavailableat:https://ssrn.com/abstract=3000712

Kaplan, A., & Haenlein, M. (2019a). Siri, Siri, in my hand: Who's the fairest in the land? On the interpretations, illustrations, and implications of artificial intelligence. *Business Horizons*, *62*(1), 15–25. DOI: 10.1016/j.bushor.2018.08.004

Kaplan, A., & Haenlein, M. (2019b). Siri, Siri, in my hand: Who's the fairest in the land? On the interpretations, illustrations, and implications of artificial intelligence. *Business Horizons*, *62*(1), 15–25. DOI: 10.1016/j.bushor.2018.08.004

Kivistö Arttu. (2024). *ROLE OF ARTIFICIAL INTELLIGENCE IN PROMOTIONAL CAMPAIGNS*. https://doi.org/https://urn.fi/URN:NBN:fi:jyu-202409055830

Kopalle, P. K., Gangwar, M., Kaplan, A., Ramachandran, D., Reinartz, W., & Rindfleisch, A. (2022). Examining artificial intelligence (AI) technologies in marketing via a global lens: Current trends and future research opportunities. *International Journal of Research in Marketing*, *39*(2), 522–540. DOI: 10.1016/j.ijresmar.2021.11.002

Shaik, M. (2023a). Impact of artificial intelligence on marketing. *East Asian Journal of Multidisciplinary Research*, *2*(3), 993–1004. DOI: 10.55927/eajmr.v2i3.3112

Shaik, M. (2023b). Impact of artificial intelligence on marketing. *East Asian Journal of Multidisciplinary Research, 2*(3), 993–1004. DOI: 10.55927/eajmr.v2i3.3112

Shaik, M. (2023c). Impact of artificial intelligence on marketing. *East Asian Journal of Multidisciplinary Research, 2*(3), 993–1004. DOI: 10.55927/eajmr.v2i3.3112

Shao, C., Ciampaglia, G. L., Varol, O., Yang, K.-C., Flammini, A., & Menczer, F. (2018). The spread of low-credibility content by social bots. *Nature Communications, 9*(1), 4787. DOI: 10.1038/s41467-018-06930-7 PMID: 30459415

Wilson, H. J., & Daugherty, P. R. (2018). Collaborative intelligence: Humans and AI are joining forces. *Harvard Business Review, 96*(4), 114–123.

Chapter 8
Leveraging AI on Sales Management:
A Data-Driven Strategy

Roshan Kumar Shiva
SR University, Hanumakonda, India

Geetha Manoharan
https://orcid.org/0000-0002-8644-8871
SR University, India

ABSTRACT

Using data-driven tactics that improve decision-making, forecasting, and overall sales performance, this chapter examines how artificial intelligence (AI) confers authority onto sales management. In order to improve pipeline management, identify high-potential prospects, and design tailored outreach, sales managers may take use of the capabilities of artificial intelligence in the areas of predictive analytics, lead scoring, customer behavior analysis, and real-time insights respectively. With the use of artificial intelligence, workloads may be simplified by automating common processes and generating suggestions that can be implemented. This enables sales teams to concentrate on high-value activities and maximize win rates. In addition, coaching tools that are powered by artificial intelligence will assist managers in cultivating talent and enhancing the efficiency of their teams. By continually improving tactics based on emerging data patterns, integrating AI into sales management supports agility, precision, and sustained revenue development.

DOI: 10.4018/979-8-3373-4392-1.ch008

1. INTRODUCTION

Artificial intelligence in sales management refers specifically to the use of AI to enhance the preparation, equipping, coaching, and support of sales teams in the execution of their functions. It combines conventional sales management with cutting-edge technologies such as machine learning, natural language processing, predictive analytics, and generative AI. AI sales management solutions go beyond mere task automation. They furnish a management system that synchronizes sales materials, processes, and customer behavioral data. This congruence allows sales people to fully comprehend buyer needs, anticipate buyer behavior, and accurately deliver the appropriate message at an opportune moment. Currently, 81% of sales teams' report use of AI. Predictive analytics is AI's most powerful attribute in sales management. Predictive sales analytics establishes which prospects are most likely to close, when they are most likely to engage, and which sales messages are likely most effective, thus allowing AI to prioritize high value sales opportunities to sales reps. AI rapidly detects buyer intent and market fluctuations. Sales executives who use AI in lead generation and scoring report 25% higher revenue growth than their peers. AI empowered sales management augments not replace existing practices.

It optimizes the sales process, reduces cycles, and enhances the pertinence of every interaction, thus fostering increased engagement. Sales personnel appreciate the opportunity to devote more time to customer interactions rather than auxiliary manual work. Sales managers appreciate the ability to better track their teams' activities and measure their performance against established criteria, including productivity, pipeline velocity, and win rates. The growing adoption of AI in sales empowerment is solidifying its position as a fundamental component of contemporary sales approaches.

1.1 Contextual Background

Artificial Intelligence (AI) is a phenomenon in the contemporary business. It alters the manner in which organizations gather information, how they process and use it. AI will help in faster and accurate decision-making in sales and marketing (Onifade et al., 2025). And algorithms are being used by companies to make patterns of their customer data. This shift enables businesses to scale the forecast of demand and strategies that respond to the real time market. In the current competitive world, companies must be quick. The conventional sales modes were founded on a first-hand experience, paperwork and little prediction. Most of the time these techniques were time consuming and prone to human error. Instead, the contemporary market demands accuracy. The prevalent systems are now the data driven systems. To transform raw data into insights to help in strategy and execution, this is AI.

Over the past ten years, marketing and sales ecosystems have evolved at a very fast pace. These technologies incorporate the consumer interactions of the websites, mobile applications, and social media. They determine what the customers desire and at what time they are likely to make a purchase. The sales process is no longer linear. It will evolve dynamically with regards to fluctuating consumer signals. The integration of machine learning and predictive analytics has changed the model of work of sales teams. Machine learning models utilize data that is acquired in different sources and forecast the sales outcome (Tariq, 2025). They find the potential leads, calculate the conversion rates, and suggest pricing policies. Predictive analytics helps managers to anticipate what their customers require even before they anticipate it. This proactive nature renders the checking more efficient and accurate as well.

AI is also transforming the way we carry out marketing communications (Raju et al., 2025). Companies can now afford to create customized campaigns towards individual customers (Li & Hingoro, 2025). Adjustments through automated systems are done depending on the behavior and desirability of advertisements and promotion. This leads to marketing being more pertinent and cost effective. All this is acquired by salespeople when they consider ways of negotiating or allocating resources. This transformation is founded on data. Each move made by a consumer creates information. The latter is then converted to acted knowledge by AI. It reveals patterns which are not discernible by human analysts. As a result of constant learning, AI progressively becomes more effective in learning with each interaction. This is a never-ending improvement that has led to the creation of adaptive sales models. They are models that react fast to dynamic markets and shifting consumer expectations.

1.2 Problem Statement

In spite of this development, there are issues that businesses face in comprehending the purchasing behavior of consumers. The online market is a complicated one. There are various channels that consumers use simultaneously. They use price comparisons, review and recommend before buying. Such a behavior leads to discontinuous information that is difficult to analyse (Govindaraj et al., 2025). This is too complicated to be taken care of by human judgment alone. The conventional type of analysis fails to include emotional and psychological rationale of online decision. The influencing factors on consumers are context, peer behavior and digital content. These influences change rapidly. The result is uncertainty in making it predictable to forecast what drives the purchase.

Sales managers are faced with another problem - data overload. Companies gather huge amounts of information from customer relationship management systems, social media, and web analytics. Without the proper analytical implementation, a large part of this data is not used properly. Many organizations are still using static dashboards or spreadsheets. These tools have no ability to detect the hidden patterns that tell true customer intent. Consumer privacy and ethical issues also make data use more complicated. Regulations such as GDPR and data protection laws limit the way of processing of personal data. Firms need to compromise between personalization and privacy respect. Misuse of data can damage to reputation and trust. AI systems must therefore be transparent and fair. In many organizations' integration between marketing, analytics and sales remains weak. Departments operate in silos, and the potential of AI is limited (Mtengwa et al., 2025).

1.3 Methodology, Purpose and Scope

The research methodology outlines the systematic approach adopted to achieve the study's purpose. The chapter is dedicated to the development of AI in sales management to be able to obtain a data-based understanding of consumer purchasing patterns. It is more concerned with how the organizations can utilize AI tools to come up with something that can be acted on. The AI technologies discussed are machine learning, natural language processing and predictive analytics. These are used in customer segmentation, demand forecasting and sales optimization. The chapter also looks at the transformation of AI on the way sales process is made. It underlines the importance of data in the forecast pricing appeal or personalised communication (Ofosu-Ampong et al., 2025). It describes the role of AI in assisting in making decisions in various phases of the sales funnel such as the lead generation phase to the after-sales service phase.

Moreover, the concept of consumer psychology is also improved in this chapter as it talks of how AI can be used to comprehend consumer psychology. It analyses the effect of emotional cues, search history and online behaviour in shaping buying behaviour. It also talks about the ways the companies can integrate those insights into marketing campaigns. The other area is on the strategic implications to the managers. The application of AI, necessary skills The chapter explains the skills that are needed to implement AI successfully. It considers issues, including system integration, data management, and ethical issues (Mohapatra et al., 2025). It focuses on the way in which firms are able to create a culture of data-driven decision making. The general objective is to ensure that AI is a strategic enabler in the context of sales management in the present day. Moreover, the organizations, which implement the data-driven insights, may grow their European business, build a better relationship with customers, increase the sales efficiency, and secure the competitive position in the long-term perspective.

2. CONCEPTUAL AND THEORETICAL FOUNDATIONS

2.1 Artificial Intelligence in Business Context

Artificial intelligence (AI) is the ability of machines to mimic the intelligence exhibited by humans. It is a process of learning, reasoning and problem solving. In business, Artificial intelligence (AI) systems is used to take data and analyze it to find patterns in data, and make recommendations. These capabilities of firms are useful to aid their decision-making and decision approaching on time with informed decision. AI is applied to technologies such as machine learning (ML), natural language processing (NLP) and visual computing. Machine learning enables machine systems to improve through experience. NLP helps machines comprehend and act accordingly to human language. Computer vision assists systems in understanding visual information from the visual image or video. Together these tools form a suite of tools for powering a variety of business applications (Jeyaprabha et al., 2025).

In marketing, as well as sales, AI aids in automation, personalization and prediction. It can be used to help with tasks such as customer segmentation, demand forecasting, and lead prioritization. AI-based tools also analyse customers' online behaviour and sentiments. As a consequence, businesses get more in-depth knowledge of their targeted audiences. AI has changed business strategy from reactive to proactive. Rather, companies no longer react to what customers say; they predict actions before they happen. Predictive models can predict potential customers and recommend them appropriate offers (Mamun, 2025). In other words, AI helps to fortify the relationship between customer understanding and business performance.

2.2 Knowledge of Sales Management

Sales management is concerned with the planning, directing, and controlling of sales. Its objective is to attain sales objectives with an approach of customer satisfaction. The process includes prospecting, lead generation, negotiation, and relationship management. Sales management is the alignment of marketing objectives and customer needs. Traditionally, sales management used to depend very much on personal skills and intuition. Managers took decisions on the basis of experience or observation. While perfect in static environments, the latter approach fails in the dynamic setting of markets. Today's digital age demand for accuracy, efficiency, and measurable results.

AI automates repetitive tasks and improves accuracy. It helps sales teams develop strategy rather than data input. Examples of these are CRM automation, predictive scoring and chatbots using which day to day activities become easier. AI analytics enables performance monitoring. Customer Success Managers can track crucial metrics like conversion rate, response time, and customer lifetime value. Sales forecasting also has changed. Machine Learning algorithms are used to analyze past data and market signals in order to forecast future sales patterns. This ensures that firms can distribute resources effectively. Demand-based Dynamic pricing - Dynamic pricing systems automatically update the price based on competition and demand. Thus, using AI in sales management improves both qualitative and quantitative aspects of business. AI-based systems also create ongoing learning (Hautamäki & Heikinheimo, 2025). They record new sales and analyze results and adjust their models. It is this feedback loop that allows continuous improvement. Hence, the expectations from customers would align better with a business (Wang et al., 2025).

2.3 Consumer Buying Behaviour: Theory Review

Buying behavior of consumers refers to how consumers make their purchasing decisions. It has psychological, social, cultural, economic factors. The process starts with need identification and ends with post-purchase assessment. There are many classical models of this process. The Engel Kollat Blackwell (EKB) model considers the buying as a problem-solving activity. The Howard Sheth model is focused on the input, perception and learning of information. Both emphasize the significance of both internal and external factors on consumer choice. In the digital market, conventional behavior patterns have changed. Consumers are more educated and connected. Online reviews, social media and digital advertisements help them weigh options. They expect speedy and personalized deals. The buying journey has been transformed to multi-channel and omni-channel. A.I. is extremely important to understanding this complexity. It tracks and scans for behavioural indicators like clicks, search queries, and browsing visits (Sarin, 2025). Sentiment analysis tools cover the emotional variables under customer's feedback. Predictive algorithms - used to predict purchase intent. Through these functions, AI builds an entire image of every consumer. This behavioral insight is useful to companies to improve their marketing and their sales strategies. For example, AI can recommend products according to previous purchases. Additionally, it can predict when a customer is likely to switch brands. These insights fuel engagement and loyalty (Rosario & Casaca, 2025).

2.4 Interlinkages Between AI, Sales, and Consumer Behaviour

AI develops a direct connection between sales management and consumer psychology. It makes subjective decision-making evidence-based action. By analysing data of consumer behaviour, AI determines which factors influence the buying (Alipour et al., 2025). It defines the factors that contribute to the satisfaction, trust and loyalty.

One of the ways in which sales organizations can take advantage of these insights is to make modifications of the communication and negotiation styles. AI-based systems recommend when to reach out to the leads and through what channels to do it through. They can even recommend language tones that are congruent with customer sentiment. AI insertion inside the systems of sales provides a continuous atmosphere of learning. In each interaction we have with a patient we are generating data (Zaki et al., 2025). These statistics are used in order to improve subsequent interaction. With time, the system gets better in its accuracy and sensitivity.

Moreover, the use AI for planning strategically. The top-down view is used to show the business manager as it allows them to analyse the performance of products, regional trends and market opportunities. Investments and resource allocation choices are directed by predictive analytics (Hrr, 2025). And these strategies help in the competitiveness of the organization. From the behavioral point of view, AI enhances personalization. It matches company services with individual needs. This personalization helps build an emotional connection between the customer and brand. As the level of satisfaction increases, so does loyalty. However, such successful implementation involves close management. Sales individuals need to understand technology, but also know human behavior. Without this balance, AI insights can be misinterpretation or misapplied. Trust is also built on data that is ethical and transparent.

3. THE POWER OF DATA IN AI-POWERED SALES MANAGEMENT

Data is the backbone of each AI system. AI cannot learn, predict, or make decisions in the absence of data. In sales management, data is the input for analysis and strategy. It turns routine sales operations into smart and adaptable systems.

3.1 Data as the Central Reference of AI Applications.

AI is based on volume and variety of data. These are both structured and unstructured data. Structured data comes from sales, invoices, CRM systems, etc. Unstructured data: This type of data comprises emails, customer feedback, and social media content (Grover et al., 2025). Taken together, these sources paint a full picture of the customer. Data is used to train AI to recognize patterns and trends. These statistics are then used with algorithms to predict the future. For example, AI can predict which customers will buy or churn. It can also be used to predict demand for particular products or geographical areas. These kinds of predictions help to guide managers in implementing proactive sales strategies. The accuracy of the AI is directly related to the quality of data. Unfilled or unbalanced data may suggest false results. Therefore, data integrity is something that any firm should take care of. All records require constant cleansing, validation, and updating.

3.2 Data Collection: Sources of Information in Sales and Marketing

Sales information is from various channels Traditional sources for data include CRM systems, billing sources and call logs. Digital transformation has led to the development of new sources such as websites, mobile apps, social media, etc. Every interaction leaves an imprint of the behavior of the consumer. Websites are able to record clickstream, search history and purchase frequency. Social media reveals opinion, interests and sentiments. Email campaigns indicate how much people engage in emails, and how quickly they respond. When taken together, these inputs create a 360-degree view of the customer (Zang et al., 2025). Importance of making use of various data sources It makes sure that there is consistency between systems and departments. Tools for data integration and cloud storage ease this process. They provide the opportunity for real-time transfer of insights across sales, marketing and customer service teams.

3.3 Processing of Data and Predictive Analytics

Data is no good in its raw state. AI involves data preprocessing and cleaning. This includes deduplication, error fixing and standardisation of formats. Once cleaned, data is ready to be used for machine learning models. Predictive analytics is among the strongest effects of this process (Thandapani & Karthika, 2025). It applies prior behavior to predict future behavior. In sales - predictive models are used to forecast conversion rate, product demand, and customer lifetime value (Venkataramanan et al., 2024). Managers can use the insights to prioritize leads and allocate resources. AI-based analytics also help in customer segmentation. By grouping together like-minded buyers, firms can better target messages. Recommendation engines are based on the same principle to recommend products that are compatible with the preferences of customers. This level of personalization drives engagement and selling power. Real-time analytics also further improves decision-making. Dashboards provide real-time sales performance and customer interactions. Managers would also be able to change campaigns on the fly. Quick results provide a fast adjustment to market alterations.

3.4 Ethical aspects and data privacy

Sales systems that use data get messy very quickly in terms of ethics. Data collection and data analysis of customers require transparency and permission. Many countries have laws such as GDPR for the protection of the data. Organizations must offer this regulation in order to retain the trust. Customers are entitled to privacy and equality. Use of personal information in any negative way could have a negative reputation, and lead to fines. It is thus crucial to get data management right ethically. AI models should be made to prevent bias and discrimination. Due to the constant monitoring, systems are fair and reliable. Explainability is another challenge as well. AI systems are often so-called black boxes. Managers may not have a complete understanding of the decision-making process involved by a model. This can result in confusion and accountability. To address that, companies should put in place models of AI that can be interpreted. Documentation and human supervision is also required. Security should also be considered. Data breaches have the power to leak the private data of customers. Companies must have the encryption and access controls in place as well as frequent audits. We protect customers and organizations by defining and creating a culture of responsible data usage.

3.5 Strategic Value of Data

Data makes sales teams strategic. It helps them to see opportunities before their rivals. This leaves an environment for continuous improvement through the learning and feedback. The reason why AI systems get smarter is that as more data is used to train the AI system. This constant process of education allows and establishes sustainable achievement (Michael et al., 2024). In addition, insights that are generated through data allow for innovation. Companies can embrace new product and pricing models according to customer trends. For them, they can experiment with at least real-time feedback. AI coupled with data makes the environment of sales a dynamic and adaptive environment. In other words, the role of data is not limited to an input; data is the source of power behind AI-driven sales management. Organisations who manage to effectively collect, store and interpret data can make transformations in decision making. 2.1.5 Data science and its applications Data science play a vital role in everyday life and encompasses numerous facets of human activities such as communication, business operations, engineering, and science, yet, for the purposes of this paper we will examine data science and its technologies within the digital context. They are moving away from reactive approaches to predictive and proactive approaches (Rane et al., 2024).

4. APPLICATIONS OF AI IN SALES MANAGEMENT

Artificial Intelligence (AI) is changing sales management by the way it is structured and its role in sales management. It helps in the decision-making process, automation, and people relationships. Through AI tools sales manager could predict trends, identify opportunities, and drive performance.

4.1 AI- Enhanced Customer Relationship Management (CRM)

CRM systems are the backbone of the sales operations. They contain customer information, lead supervision, as well as communication tracking. When these systems are combined with A.I. they become smarter and predictive. AI enabled CRM platforms analyse the interaction with customers in real-time. They derive the purchasing intention from emails, chat and calls. This analysis allows the sales team to target the leads that have high potential (Magableh et al., 2024). AI also is prioritizing prospects based on predictive scoring models. These models are applied to measuring past behavior, engagement and purchase likeness. Popular CRM systems such as Salesforce Einstein and Zoho Zia, use AI in automation. They recommend the best time to contact customers, recommend the next steps to be taken and predict the results. This support reduces human error and also makes things more efficient. CRM with AI also helps to retain customers better. It observes the early signs of dissatisfaction by being able to observe feedback and sentiment. Managers can intervene, fast to retain customers. The combination of automation and analytics helps strengthen long term relationships.

4.2 Sales Forecasting and Demand Prediction

Forecasting is very important in sales planning. Traditional forecasting tended to make use of historic data and estimations made by hand. These methods were frequently slow and inaccurate. AI has revolutionized this process. Machine learning algorithms are now used to process a massive set of data from multiple sources. They include past sales, market conditions and even factors outside of the corporation such as seasonality. AI models are able to identify complex patterns that humans can miss. The outcome is accurate and timely forecasts (Singh et al., 2024). Predictive forecasting helps the firms in an efficient approach to manage the inventory and supply chains. It minimizes overstocking and stockouts. Sales managers can plan marketing campaigns and promotional activities on the basis of demand predictions. AI driven forecasting tools are also learning on a continuous basis. Each round of the sales data adds to the precision of the model. This adaptability provides sustainable competitive advantage to the firms operating in fast changing markets.

4.3 Personalization as well as Recommender Systems

Personalization: Personalization is one of the best contributions of AI to sales management. Customers nowadays demand experiences that fit their likes and needs. AI allows firms to provide this on a large scale. Recommendation systems are based on browsing history, past purchases and customer profiles. They recommend applicable products or services to each user (Theodorakopoulos & Theodoropoulou, 2024). Companies such as Amazon and Netflix have demonstrated the potency of such systems. Similar models are now used in the B2B and B2C sales. Personalization is more than just product recommendations. AI is used to adjust emails, web layouts and advertisements depending on user behaviour. It ensures that each interaction gets a personal touch. This way the engagement, trust and conversion rate increases. Cross-selling and up-selling opportunities are also identified using AI. By analysing the transaction data, it recommends complementary or premium products. This strategy creates a higher average order value and customer satisfaction.

4.4 Chatbots and Virtual Assistants

AI-driven chatbots have become an integral part of customer engagement. They answer routine questions, screen leads, and manage users through the buying process. These tools are 24/7, so they provide immediate support. Chatbots lower the response time and enhance the customer experience (Shiva & Manoharan, 2026). They can schedule meetings, receive feedback and pass complicated problems on to human agents. Additional-Advanced bots have the capability to respond to tone and intent using natural language processing (NLP). Virtual assistants bring these capacities down to an internal sales team. They remind managers of deadlines, summarize the notes from meetings and create reports. Such an automation saves us time and helps in raising the productivity. Chatbots also gather data from all of the interactions. This information is provided back to the AI systems for further analysis. As time passes by, the system learns from the conversations, and grows more accurate.

4.5 Dynamic Pricing Models

A price is the biggest factor that determines profitability. Traditional pricing strategies were based on a manual analysis or a hard rule. Indeed, AI provides flexibility in the form of dynamic pricing. Dynamic pricing algorithms track the real-time demand, competition and customer behaviour. Consumers change price at will to get the maximum revenue. For instance, AI is applied by airlines, hotels, and e-commerce companies to change prices based on market conditions. In sales management, dynamic pricing is useful to bring balance between profit and customer satisfaction. Strategically used, it ensures competitive price and economical margins. AI considers such factors as location, season and disposable income. These systems also experiment with different pricing scenarios. They rely on the measurement of customers' response to discounts or the value-added offers. This information gained has been used to improve pricing strategies.

5. DISCUSSIONS: UNDERSTANDING CONSUMER BUYING BEHAVIOUR USING AI

Consumer buying behaviour represents a study on the purchase decision. This encompasses what they buy, why they buy and their response to marketing campaigns. In cyber space this is a complex and active behaviour. Artificial Intelligence (AI) helps organisations get a better sense of these patterns through analysis of data.

5.1 AI and Consumer Psychology

AI provides information about the psychological aspects that affect consumer decisions. It studies feelings, likes and motivations. Traditional methods of research (such as surveys and interviews) offer partial insight. AI however, needs and processes a huge amount of behavioural data in real-time. The following are some of the most popular sentiment analyses and tools: Sentiment analysis tools read feedback, social media posts, and customer reviews. It is these systems that create positive or negative emotions for brands. Machine learning models then link these emotions with buying decisions. For example, increase of positive sentiment can be used to predict increase of purchase intent (Onesi-Ozigagun et al., 2024).

Emotional AI goes deeper. It reads tone, facial expressions and text cues. This helps marketers to know the emotional state of the consumers at the time of interactions. Companies use these insights to customise communication and enhance satisfaction. AI is also behind the support of cognitive analysis. It monitors attention span and engagement level, and decision fatigue. This information helps firms to design more effective advertisement and sales messages. Understanding how consumers think and how they feel helps brands to influence how they feel or think more precisely about brands in the purchase process.

5.2 Customer Journey Mapping

Customer journey is all the phases that the buyer passed through before and after buying. These stages are awareness, consideration, purchase and loyalty. AI is useful in visualizing and optimizing this journey with data. AI systems gather behavioural signals across various touchpoints - to websites, emails and chatbot interactions and to stores. They determine which channels are driving engagement and conversion. This mapping will expose gaps in the sales process and identify how they can improve. Predictive journey analytics anticipates what the customer will do. It decides when a consumer is likely to give up on a cart or a transaction. Sales teams can then intervene with personalised offers or messages (Okeke et al., 2024). Customer journey mapping is also a good idea for retaining better. By monitoring post-purchase behaviour AI picks up early signs of dissatisfaction. Firms can address problems fast, with loyalty increasing.

5.3 Predicting Purchase Intent

Purchase intent prediction is one of the greatest applications of AI in sales management. It is an estimate of how likely a consumer will make a purchase. This is useful to prioritize leads and use marketing resources effectively. AI models feature data such as browsing history, click patterns and product views. They are engagement time, engagement frequency and engagement recency. Thus, in sum, these cues, to put it simply, are readied to buy (Tadimarri et al., 2024). The Machine learning algorithms improve their predictions. As new data is entered in the system, the amount of accuracy gets more. These models also can be used to find customers at risk of churn. Early detection can allow the firms to form retention plans. For example, e-commerce companies use AI to remind their undecided buyers to make a purchase, or to offer them a discount. In B2B sales, AI knows who to target as potential customers who are searching for solutions similar to yours. This far-sighted approach can be used to increase conversion rates and efficiencies by driving sales.

5.4 AI in Market Segmentation

Market segmentation is a process of dividing the consumers into targetable groups based on the similarity of characteristics. Older segmentation was based on demographics: age, gender and income. AI goes further and adds the behavioural and psychographic data. AI makes use of algorithms called clustering to look for hidden patterns in customer data. These typologies refer to the way groups differ in terms of preferences, motivations, and decision styles. For instance, in one segment, discounts can be effective, whereas in another, premium quality is the key selling point. Dynamic segmentation is a method that is changing dynamically based on the availability of its additional data. This allows firms to adapt to the variation in the behavior of consumers. AI also enables hyper-segmentation - in which marketing is made more personalised and targeted at an individual level. AI-powered segmentation better targeting - it identifies messages and audience needs and expectations As a consequence, the efficiency of marketing is enhanced, and the relationship with the customer is improved (Upadhyay et al., 2024).

5.5 Benefits and Strategic Implications

There are some obvious benefits associated with AI's role in analysing consumer buying behaviour. It helps you predict better; personalization is also better and decision making is better. Managers can respond strategically and with rapid speed to the future market outlook. Firms can invent more meaningful experiences with the assistance of getting understanding of consumer psychology. Predictive analytics gives the power to act in time and avert defection. Personalization is a trust and potentially a loyalty booster. AI insights also affect the development of the product. Companies are able to design features based on actual customer feedback. This helps to decrease risk, and increase satisfaction. However, AI usage has to be ethical data handling, for it to be effective. Transparency and fairness should determine all processes. Consumers are more likely to share data when they trust what data will be done with it. Responsible AI practices bring credibility to the brand over time.

6. STRATEGIC IMPLICATIONS FOR SALES MANAGERS

Sales managers have acknowledged the way AI has revolutionized the method of arranging, carrying out, and surveying strategies. It provides tools for efficiency optimisation, trend prediction and consumer behaviour insights. However, the integration of AI must be well-planned and aligned with organizational objectives.

6.1 Incorporating AI in Selling Strategies.

Sales managers will need to implement AI on a daily basis. These include CRM systems, predictive analytics, chatbots, and marketing automation. Integration helps make information flow easily across teams. AI assists in making strategic decisions. Sales reps will be able to sort leads, allocate resources and structure campaigns according to data-driven predictions. It removes the guess-work and increases the accuracy. Implementation starts with the discovery of vital business issues. Clear AI adoption goals for managers: This helps align the AI adoption goals with those of the organization. There is also a need to seek the support of stakeholders. Marketing and sales need to coordinate with IT. Information sharing and communication is one such technique that makes AI applications efficient (Moniz et al., 2024).

6.2 Human-AI Collaboration

The purpose of AI is not to substitute the human decision but to enhance it. Managers are still an important aspect of the relationship building and decision-making process. What is important to remember is that AI provides insights, and humans use and understand it. Productivity is enhanced with Human-AI collaboration. AI is used to automate tasks that are of low value, such as data entry or lead scoring. Managers are on strategy, negotiation and customer engagement. This combination is more efficient and preserves the need for human interference. Training is a key ingredient as there can't be collaboration without it. For sales pros, it is important to be able to understand how to analyze data and use AI tools to interpret the insights (Brunner et al., 2024). Learning programs are critical to bridge technological divides.

6.3 Challenges and Limitations

For all the advantages of AI adoption, there is a negative side to it. Data quality is a major issue. If the data is incomplete or poor, the predictions are also inaccurate. The managers will ensure that the data is cleaned, checked and updated. Also, of course, there is the issue of system integration being complicated. Legacy sales systems are usually not able to communicate with AI platforms. Such developments call for investments in the related infrastructure. The ethical issues in it are very important to keep under control. We are putting implicit bias into AI models. All of the interactions can be automated in order to let customers become more impersonal in their interactions. In addition, systems managers must maintain the fairness and transparency of systems. Another weakness is the lack of explainability. Many AI algorithms are still like black boxes. Managers are not clear on what is involved in the decision-making process. AI models need to be clear and justifiable to guarantee accountability.

6.4 Key Performance Metrics

AI enables the sales performance to be accurately measured. Metrics include customer travel time, lead to response time, lead to conversion, CLV and customer retention Forecasting - Predictive modelling is also used to anticipate possible increases and decreases in revenue and demand. Data-driven dashboards also provide real-time insight into team performance. Management is able to identify areas of underperformance and corrective action can be taken immediately. This constant feedback cycle makes things overall more efficient. Other more customer-centric measures are also equally important (Madanchian, 2024). Engagement scores, sentiment analysis and personalization effectiveness are only some ways in which AI aids the comprehension of consumer behavior. These understandings are influential when it comes to future strategy and learning to make better decisions.

7. FUTURE TRENDS AND RESEARCH DIRECTIONS

AI is a fast-changing field that is revolutionizing sales management. Emerging technologies can offer new opportunities to understand consumers, optimize processes and make better decisions.

7.1 Emerging AI Technologies

Generative AI is gaining popularity in the field of marketing and sales. As a consequence, it's quite capable of generating personalised content, proposals are automated, and customer interactions are simulated. Customers receive assistance in communication, reporting and predictive insights with ChatGPT like tools. The technology of artificial intelligence (AI) combined with human intelligence is called cognitive computing. It reads complicated patterns, considers the context and facilitates strategic decision-making. These systems can analyze ambiguous data and provide actionable insights in the form of recommendations. Hyper-personlization is considered one of the trends, too. AI's role in personalization AI can enable one-to-one personalization (Manoharan et al., 2025). Each message, product recommendation or promotional offer is presented according to the behaviour and preferences of consumers. This makes for better engagement, satisfaction and loyalty.

7.2 Changing Consumers' Behaviour

Consumer behaviour will continue to change in digital markets. Consumers are demanding faster responses, more individualization and more seamless channels of interaction. AI has to change in order to meet these changing expectations. The information about behavioral determinants is going to become even more heterogeneous. Corporations will be looking at not just buying history, social activities, streaming history, and sensor data from the tools that live on the Internet of Things. This growth will enable better forecasting of the buying intentions. Data Privacy - there is increased awareness by consumers about data privacy. They put a demand for the use of data to be made transparent and controllable. There is a tradeoff here between data ethics and personalization that AI systems have to deal with. Trust will be the key in terms of adoption and engagement (Peddi & Manoharan, 2025).

7.3 Sustainability and Ethics

Ethical AI will become increasingly important. Bias, discrimination and misuse of data should be tackled in a preventive manner Firms need to build clear models and ensure predictive analytics and decision-making is fair (Manoharan et al, 2024). Also, sustainability AI adoption is considered. The need to implement algorithms with low energy cost and use of resources is important for long-term implementation. Organizations will be forced to align AI strategies with corporate social responsibility goals.

7.4 Research Opportunities for Academic Achievement

There are big opportunities for the research looking into AI in sales management. The researchers were able to tap into the effects of AI on consumer trust, loyalty and engagement. Research is a way of measuring the success of AI-enabled personalization as well as predictive analytics. Research can also be carried out on the organizational issues. Topics include: AI-Human collaboration, Change management and skill building. Ethical considerations and compliance with regulations are also important to research. Inter-disciplinary Studies are encouraged. Marketing, business strategy, data science and psychology can all be intertwined to provide a full picture on the effects of AI. Experimental research studies may be used to make useful insight for practitioners as well as case studies and longitudinal studies.

7.5 Strategic Implications for the Future.

Management needs to plan for continued evolution of AI Learning, adaptation and innovation are very crucial and continuous. In the end, it is important for companies to invest in AI tools, training and ethical guidelines. The proactive implementation of AI guarantees the proactive sale team to remain competitive. Organizations that make the best of AI will be able to anticipate changes that occur in the market, to optimize approaches and to enhance the relationship with the customer. The future of the sales management is data-driven systems with artificial intelligence. Artificial intelligence will be the one to continue assisting people in making a better decision, predict human behavior, and also personalize the experience (Shiva & Manoharan, 2025). Companies who adopt these trends will be able to get sustainable competitive advantage in dynamic markets.

8. RECOMMENDATIONS AND CONCLUSION

Artificial intelligence (AI) is no longer the "nice-to-have" function of sales management. It is an enabler for strategy and changes the way that firm communicates with a customer. Organizations are able to turn data into actionable data using AI. These insights help in the decision-making process and customer engagement. The job of the sales managers, after incorporating AI into sales. They rise from managerial execution to strategic management. AI automates repetitive processes and provides a predictive insight. Managers can focus on relationship building, negotiating and creative problem solving. Such a collaboration between human and AI makes work more efficient and effective. AI-powered sales strategies are all about the purchasing behavior of the consumer. AI breaks down patterns, preferences and sentiment to tease out hidden motivations. Predictive models determine how customers will behave, and make changes to interactions accordingly. This ability allows companies to respond both in a proactive rather than reactive manner. And it helps to include engagement, satisfaction and loyalty.

Ethics and transparency are also essential for the AI uptake. Firms need to ensure fairness in the way they use data and good transparency in the case of automated decision making. The main key to long term success is keeping customers trusting. In addition, practices that support ethical AI help organizations to avoid reputational and legal risks. AI is not stagnant that it changes all the time. New technologies such as generative AI, cognitive computing, and hyper-personalization open up the opportunities of sales management. Companies need to develop a culture of learning and adapting. Investments into technology, training and organizational change are needed to keep the competitive edge. Insights arising from data also impact on innovation. Organizations can create products, services and campaigns which are in accordance with customer needs and market trends. AI is capable of quick testing and measuring and optimizing strategies. This flexibility is so important in fast and highly competitive markets. Ultimately, the value of AI in sales management is that it can help bring some analytical rigor to human intuition. It helps organisations to make ethical, informed and timely decisions. Organisations that go beyond AI and find strategic ways to integrate it into their business, will be better placed to respond to changing consumer behaviour, optimise resources and drive sustainable growth.

REFERENCES

Alipour, P., Gallegos, E. E., & Sridhar, S. (2025). AI-driven marketing personalization: Deploying convolutional neural networks to decode consumer behavior. *International Journal of Human-Computer Interaction, 41*(16), 10266–10284. DOI: 10.1080/10447318.2024.2432455

Brunner, D., Legat, C., & Seebacher, U. (2024). Towards Next Generation Data-Driven Management: Leveraging Predictive Swarm Intelligence to Reason and Predict Market Dynamics. In Collective Intelligence (pp. 152-203). CRC Press.

Govindaraj, M., Vandhana, N., & Lawrence, J. (2025). AI-Driven Consumer Behavior Insights: Applying the Insight Equation to Modern Marketing. In Decoding Consumer Behavior Using the Insight Equation and AI Marketing (pp. 1-20). IGI Global Scientific Publishing.

Grover, V., Dogra, M., Sahu, D., & Nandal, M. (2025). Empowering Personalized Marketing: Leveraging Data Engineering for Customer Segmentation. In Data Engineering for Data-driven Marketing (pp. 105-119). Emerald Publishing Limited.

Hautamäki, P., & Heikinheimo, M. (2025). Fully leveraging AI in B2B sales: Exploring sales managers' capabilities and organizational knowledge processes. *Journal of Business Research, 194*, 115396. DOI: 10.1016/j.jbusres.2025.115396

Hrr, H. (2025). The Future of Digital Transformation: Leveraging Artificial Intelligence for Competitive Advantage. Available at *SSRN* 5123723. DOI: 10.2139/ssrn.5123723

Jeyaprabha, B., Kumar, S. R., Bolla, R. L., Bhatt, A. S., Sera, R. J., & Arora, K. (2025, February). Data-Driven Decision Making in Management: Leveraging Big Data Analytics for Strategic Planning. In 2025 First International Conference on Advances in Computer Science, Electrical, Electronics, and Communication Technologies (CE2CT) (pp. 1000-1003). IEEE.

Li, J., & Hingoro, A. (2025). Leveraging Artificial Intelligence for Personalized Marketing: Enhancing Consumer Engagement and Driving Sales. In Leveraging AI-Powered Marketing in the Experience-Driven Economy (pp. 147-180). IGI Global Scientific Publishing.

Madanchian, M. (2024). The impact of artificial intelligence marketing on e-commerce sales. *Systems, 12*(10), 429. DOI: 10.3390/systems12100429

Magableh, I. K., Mahrouq, M. H., Ta'Amnha, M. A., & Riyadh, H. A. (2024). The role of marketing artificial intelligence in enhancing sustainable financial performance of medium-sized enterprises through customer engagement and data-driven decision-making. *Sustainability (Basel)*, *16*(24), 11279. DOI: 10.3390/su162411279

Mamun, M. N. H. (2025). Role of AI and Data Science in Data-Driven Decision-Making for it Business Intelligence: A Systematic Literature Review. Available at *SSRN* 5402976. DOI: 10.2139/ssrn.5402976

Manoharan, G., Gupta, R., Darunkar, V. V., Mishra, S. K., & Soni, M. (2025, May). The impact of Artificial Intelligence on E-commerce Customer Experience and Personalization. In 2025 6th International Conference for Emerging Technology (INCET) (pp. 1-5). IEEE.

Manoharan, G., Preetha, P. N., Santhanalakshmi, K., Balaji, K. D., & Raja, V. (2024, March). Management of Business Using Machine Learning for Decision Making. In *2024 International Conference on Trends in Quantum Computing and Emerging Business Technologies* (pp. 1-5). IEEE. DOI: 10.1109/TQCEBT59414.2024.10545116

Michael, C. I., Ipede, O. J., Adejumo, A. D., Adenekan, I. O., Adebayo, D., Ojo, A. S., & Ayodele, P. A. (2024). Data-driven decision making in IT: Leveraging AI and data science for business intelligence. *World Journal of Advanced Research and Reviews*, *23*(01), 432–439.

Mohapatra, A. G., Mohanty, A., Mohanty, S. K., Mahalik, N. P., & Nayak, S. (2025). Personalization and customer experience in the era of data-driven marketing. Artificial Intelligence-Enabled Businesses: How to Develop Strategies for Innovation, 467-511.

Mtengwa, E., Muchenje, C., Maregere, L. L., & Masengu, R. (2025). Driving Business Sustainability Through Effective Marketing Leveraging on Artificial Intelligence. In AI and Machine Learning Applications in Supply Chains and Marketing (pp. 117-148). IGI Global.

Ofosu-Ampong, K., Boateng, M., Ampong, M. D., Adu-Ntim, J. K., & Ampong-Ansah, F. B. (2025). The Impact of AI-driven Marketing Personalisation on Consumer Purchase Decisions: A Mixed-Methods Analysis. Available at *SSRN* 5314499.

Okeke, N. I., Alabi, O. A., Igwe, A. N., Ofodile, O. C., & Ewim, C. P. M. (2024). AI in customer feedback integration: A data-driven framework for enhancing business strategy. *World J. Advanced Res. Reviews*, *24*(1), 3207–3220.

Onesi-Ozigagun, O., Ololade, Y. J., Eyo-Udo, N. L., & Oluwaseun, D. (2024). Data-driven decision making: Shaping the future of business efficiency and customer engagement. *International Journal of Multidisciplinary Research Updates*, *7*(2), 19–29. DOI: 10.53430/ijmru.2024.7.2.0031

Onifade, A. Y., Ogeawuchi, J. C., & Abayomi, A. A. (2025). Scaling AI-Driven Sales Analytics for Predicting Consumer Behavior and Enhancing Data-Driven Business Decisions. *International Journal of Advanced Multidisciplinary Research and Studies*, *4*(6), 2181–2201. DOI: 10.62225/2583049X.2024.4.6.4269

Peddi, S., & Manoharan, G. (2025). The Impact of Technology on Company Values and Employee Well-Being. In *Transforming Organizational Culture Through Meta-Driven Human Resources* (pp. 225–256). IGI Global Scientific Publishing. DOI: 10.4018/979-8-3373-0720-6.ch008

Raju, V., Ramachandran, K. K., Chenxi, W., Mangairkarasi, V., & Konecna, Z. (2025). AI in data-driven marketing: Decoding consumer choices and behaviours. In *Data Engineering for Data-Driven Marketing* (pp. 33–45). Emerald Publishing Limited. DOI: 10.1108/978-1-83662-326-720251005

Rane, N., Paramesha, M., Choudhary, S., & Rane, J. (2024). Artificial intelligence in sales and marketing: Enhancing customer satisfaction, experience and loyalty. Experience and Loyalty (May 17, 2024).

Sarin, A. B. (2025). The Evolution of Consumer Behavior and the Role of Artificial Intelligence in Shaping It: AI in Marketing. In Decoding Consumer Behavior Using the Insight Equation and AI Marketing (pp. 21-40). IGI Global Scientific Publishing.

Shiva, R. K., & Manoharan, G. (2025). Brand Equity Management and Marketing in the Digital Era. In Djakeli, K. (Ed.), *Brand Creation and Management in the Phygital Era* (pp. 201–224). IGI Global Scientific Publishing., DOI: 10.4018/979-8-3373-0948-4.ch008

Shiva, R. K., & Manoharan, G. (2026). Leveraging AI for Marketing, Customer Experience, and Automation. In Verma, B., Schulze, M., Olubiyi, T., & Upreti, K. (Eds.), *Navigating the Self-Service Revolution With Smart Machines* (pp. 283–308). IGI Global Scientific Publishing., DOI: 10.4018/979-8-3373-1295-8.ch011

Singh, B., Kaunert, C., Malviya, R., Lal, S., & Arora, M. K. (2024). Scrutinizing consumer sentiment on social media and data-driven decisions for business insights: fusion of artificial intelligence (AI) and business intelligence (BI) foster sustainable growth. In *Intersection of AI and Business Intelligence in Data-Driven Decision-Making* (pp. 183–210). IGI Global. DOI: 10.4018/979-8-3693-5288-5.ch007

Tadimarri, A., Jangoan, S., Sharma, K. K., & Gurusamy, A. (2024). AI-powered marketing: Transforming consumer engagement and brand growth. *Int. J. Multidiscip. Res*, *6*, 1–11.

Tariq, M. U. (2025). Leveraging Data Analytics for Predictive Consumer Behavior Modelling. In AI Impacts on Branded Entertainment and Advertising (pp. 207-224). IGI Global Scientific Publishing. DOI: 10.4018/979-8-3693-3799-8.ch011

Thandapani, G., & Karthika, S. (2025). A data-driven approach to loan approvals prediction and profitability: Leveraging exploratory data analysis for improved decision-making. In *Advances in Electrical and Computer Technologies* (pp. 261–266). CRC Press. DOI: 10.1201/9781003515470-36

Theodorakopoulos, L., & Theodoropoulou, A. (2024). Leveraging big data analytics for understanding consumer behavior in digital marketing: A systematic review. *Human Behavior and Emerging Technologies*, *2024*(1), 3641502. DOI: 10.1155/2024/3641502

Upadhyay, U., Kumar, A., Sharma, G., Sharma, S., Arya, V., Panigrahi, P. K., & Gupta, B. B. (2024). A systematic data-driven approach for targeted marketing in enterprise information system. *Enterprise Information Systems*, *18*(8), 2356770. DOI: 10.1080/17517575.2024.2356770

Venkataramanan, S., Sadhu, A. K. R., Gudala, L., & Reddy, A. K. (2024). Leveraging artificial intelligence for enhanced sales forecasting accuracy: A review of AI-driven techniques and practical applications in customer relationship management systems. *Aust. J. Mach. Learn. Res. Appl*, *4*(1), 267–287.

Wang, T. C., Guo, R. S., Chen, C., & Li, C. K. (2025). Multi-Stage Data-Driven Framework for Customer Journey Optimization and Operational Resilience. *Mathematics*, *13*(7), 1145. DOI: 10.3390/math13071145

Zaki, K., Alhomaid, A., & Shared, H. (2025). Leveraging Machine Learning to Analyze Influencer Credibility's Impact on Brand Admiration and Consumer Purchase Intent in Social Media Marketing. *Human Behavior and Emerging Technologies*, *2025*(1), 9959697. DOI: 10.1155/hbe2/9959697

Zang, L., Wang, L., Zhang, D., & Bai, Q. (2025). Data-driven review of customer engagement: Key research themes and future directions. *Electronic Commerce Research*, •••, 1–31. DOI: 10.1007/s10660-025-09967-1

Chapter 9
Machine Learning Models for Fraud Detection in Promotional Activities

Munir Ahmad
https://orcid.org/0000-0003-4836-6151
Survey of Pakistan, Islamabad, Pakistan

Kanchon Kumar Bishnu
https://orcid.org/0009-0007-1811-3002
California State University, Los Angeles, USA

Md Rasibul Islam
https://orcid.org/0009-0008-5229-7834
Gannon University, Buffalo, USA

Md Khalilor Rahman
Gannon University, Hermitage, USA

ABSTRACT

This chapter explores the application of machine learning (ML) techniques for detecting and preventing fraud in digital marketing and promotional campaigns. It examines common fraud types, including click fraud, coupon abuse, identity manipulation, and network-based schemes, and reviews supervised, unsupervised, and deep learning approaches for anomaly detection. Key challenges, such as data quality, model interpretability, real-time processing, and ethical considerations, are discussed. Emerging trends, including predictive AI, hybrid models, and graph-based analytics, highlight future directions for robust, adaptive, and trustworthy promotional fraud detection systems.

DOI: 10.4018/979-8-3373-4392-1.ch009

INTRODUCTION

The fast development of online marketing and advertising campaigns has changed how companies interact with clients. Social media, email marketing, mobile applications, and e-commerce websites enable organizations to engage in reaching out to large numbers of people at a low cost and within a short time. Promotions that include discount promotions, loyalty programs, referral marketing programs, and targeted adverts have become indispensable over the years in the acquisition, retention, and engagement of customers (Cliquet, 2020; Hoffman et al., 2022; Kumar et al., 2024; Movahed et al., 2024). Nevertheless, this growth in digital has come with some major vulnerabilities. The more the promotion activities grow in complexity and scope, the more they become vulnerable to fraudulent activities, which can compromise the effectiveness and success of the campaigns, increase costs, and misrepresent business intelligence.

Fraud in promotional campaigns manifests in several forms. False clicks artificially inflate engagement to generate a higher advertisement payout/bonus. There is coupon abuse whereby the individuals take advantage to redeem the discounts on more than one occasion or under circumstances other than expected. Identity manipulation is a process whereby counterfeit accounts are created or legitimate users are impersonated to enjoy the benefits of promotion. These frauds not only cause a loss of money but also cause a loss of customer information, in that marketers cannot effectively determine the success of the campaign and modify strategies (Dörnyei, 2021; Liang et al., 2024; Slutskiy, 2021).

Although rule-based detection systems are very beneficial in certain situations, they do not keep up with the changes in the strategies of fraudsters. In this case, the use of machine learning (ML) methods is an effective alternative. ML models can be used to detect suspicious behavior by analyzing historical and real-time data on promotions and determining patterns that were not previously evident to an individual, as well as potential anomalies, more accurately and swiftly (El-Hajj & Pavlova, 2024; Kivistö, 2024; Langen & Huber, 2023). As learning techniques, supervised and unsupervised, and deep learning techniques enable learning systems to learn based on labeled examples of both fraudulent and legitimate activities, and respectively discover new trends in fraud without labeling them. These capabilities enable marketers to anticipate and address threats, enhance security, and safeguard campaign investments.

This chapter presents a full picture of how machine learning is used in fraud detection in promotions. It discusses the categories and effects of promotional fraud, discusses ML algorithms and models involved, implementation issues including data quality, explainability of the models, and real-time processing, and provides a practical guide to applying the solutions to the available marketing infrastructures.

This chapter aims to foster a safer, more efficient, and reliable digital promotional ecosystem by providing marketers, data scientists, and cybersecurity professionals with an understanding of advanced ML techniques.

LEARNING ABOUT FRAUD IN PROMOTION.

Digital marketing, as much as necessary in acquiring or retaining customers, is becoming very vulnerable to fraud-based activities, especially in promotions. The essence, trends, and influence of these activities are crucial to understand to develop effective detection mechanisms. The following section addresses the different forms of promotional fraud, including some common trends and origins, as well as their impacts on businesses.

Types of Promotional Fraud

Promotional fraud may take many forms and depend on the channel used, the design of campaigns, and the strategic goals of the fraudsters. These malpractices not only cause direct financial loss but also corrupt campaign analytics, marketing strategies, and compromise trust in promotional systems. Knowledge of the scope and processes of various forms of promotional fraud is crucial for designing effective detection and mitigation solutions. Common forms include:

This is a situation when the automated bots or human factors provoke fake clicks on Web advertisements or even promotional links. Click fraud aims may be as varied as increasing engagement metrics to manipulating pay-per-click (PPC) advertising rates, either to empty the coffers of competitors or to drive up personal rewards in reward-based campaigns (Sadeghpour & Vlajic, 2021b; Wang et al., 2021). As an illustration, botnets might be used by fraudsters to repeatedly view the target ads, creating an impression of high visitor interest and prompting advertisers to spend money on non-bona fide traffic. Besides financial waste, click fraud may corrupt performance measurement, which encourages marketers to make poor strategic choices related to campaign targeting, budgeting, and creative optimization. Detection of click fraud becomes increasingly difficult due to the rapid development of bot sophistication, including the use of AI-powered bots that mimic human behavior.

Coupons and vouchers use promotional codes, discount offers, or digital vouchers in a manner that is not intended. Fraudsters can use one coupon more than once, post codes on an illegal site, or even board or access a system loophole and gain unfair advantages. Scalable programs are also used to generate effective coupon codes or even circumvent redemption limits through automated scripts and tools, thereby increasing the financial damage. An example of this is e-commerce promotions that provide a temporary discount, as fraudsters are especially susceptible to saturation, which can prevent potential customers to be prevented from accessing the systems. In addition to losing direct revenue, coupon abuse distorts campaign metrics, complicating the measurement of actual customer engagement and ROI, and necessitating the drawing of extra resources to facilitate tracking and fixing fraud.

Fraudsters can build false accounts, copy an existing account, or act as a legitimate user to take advantage of referral programs, loyalty points, or promotional rewards (Dörnyei, 2021; Sáez-Ortuño et al., 2023). This form of fraud misinterprets the insights about the customers, since the analytics systems can perceive the fraud as a legitimate engagement. As an illustration, during referral campaigns, simulated referrals can be used across a variety of fake accounts, which increases the perceived success of the program and compromises the actual customer acquisition campaigns. This same principle applies to loyalty schemes, where frequent redemptions using bogus or hacked accounts can undermine the credibility of the reward schemes and erode brand confidence. Identity manipulation is especially difficult to notice in cases when fraudsters employ advanced methods to provide behavioral patterns, geolocation clues, and the fingerprints of legitimate users.

Fraudsters can use the mechanisms of the marketing campaign that delivers rewards with referrals of users to take illegal advantage. This involves the development of several false accounts, self-referrals, or referral links (Sadeghpour & Vlajic, 2021a; Yang, 2025). This is fraud that not only causes financial losses but also ruins collaboration with marketers and affiliates, as it destroys trust and ruins long-term cooperation. As an example, affiliate networks that are based on properly tracking conversion rates can have their commissions undermined, a move that results in conflicts and loss of reputation. To prevent such acts of integrity violation, organizations should therefore have in place effective validation mechanisms to authenticate referral legitimacy, monitor referral patterns, and identify suspicious activities.

Social media tools have become one of the fundamental concepts of digital marketing campaigns, and engagement metrics such as likes, shares, comments, and the number of followers are now key indicators of brand coverage. Some of the fraudulent actions in this area include the artificial increase of these measurements to give the illusion of popularity and power. This can include the use of bot accounts, buying of fake followers, and the organization of engagement rings to be able to play with algorithmic content ranking. Though social media engagement fraud may not necessarily lead to direct financial loss, it may have a tremendous effect on campaign strategy, audience targeting, and resource allocation. Brands can spend money on campaigns that rely on false numbers of engagements; they can not reach actual customers and are likely to break their trust in the eyes of actual audiences.

In general, the promotion fraud of these kinds illustrates the variety and dynamism of strategies used by fraudsters in online marketing conditions. Both of the forms pose a threat to financial performance as well as influence operational decision-making, customer confidence, and the overall performance of the promotional campaigns. Such behaviors need to be detected and reduced through a set of sophisticated analytics, machine learning models, and proactive monitoring schemes, each specific to the vulnerabilities of the relevant types of campaigns. Table 1 summarizes the major forms of promotional fraud, their mechanisms, and implications.

Table 1. Types of Promotional Fraud

Fraud Type	Mechanism	Implications
Click Fraud	Automated bots or humans generate fake clicks on ads/links to inflate metrics or drain budgets.	Financial loss, distorted analytics, misguided campaign decisions.
Coupon & Voucher Abuse	Multiple or unauthorized redemptions of codes using scripts or loopholes.	Revenue loss, skewed engagement data, customer dissatisfaction.
Identity & Account Fraud	Fake/duplicate accounts exploit referral and loyalty programs.	Distorted customer insights, undermined program credibility, reduced trust.
Affiliate & Referral Fraud	Exploiting referral mechanisms via self-referrals or fake accounts.	Financial drain, weakened affiliate partnerships, and reputational damage.
Social Media Engagement Fraud	Artificial inflation of likes, shares, and followers via bots or rings.	Misleading engagement data, poor targeting, and credibility loss.

Patterns, Indicators, and Sources of Fraud

Even when the criminal gains to engage in fraudulent patterns that become increasingly advanced to simulate legitimate user traffic, fraudulent behaviors in promotional campaigns tend to follow certain patterns. The identification of these tendencies is important to detect and prevent them at an early stage so that marketers can safeguard the financial performance as well as the integrity of their campaigns. Although it is easy to determine certain indicators, others demand a refined examination of high-dimensional and huge data volumes to recognize subtle anomalies.

Unusual Transaction Patterns

Abnormal transactional behavior is one of the most frequent signs of promotional fraud (Kim et al., 2022). This may take the form of frequent coupon redemptions, frequent logins with the same IP address, or a wave of activity within a very short time. Indicatively, multiple coupons redeemed by the same user account in seconds or a few minutes could be a sign of an automated attacker and not that of a real customer. In the same manner, groups of transactions with the same or sequential identification can indicate scripted efforts to claim rewards. The distinction between harmless marketing efforts and cheating abuse can be made by measuring the velocity, frequency, and value patterns of transactions. Advanced analytics and ML models can help detect these anomalies particularly well, being able to compare the observed trends with the past, profiles of expected behavior, and peer reference points.

Anomalous Engagement Metrics

Engagement metrics such as clicks, shares, likes, comments, and referrals are central to promotional campaigns in order to determine their effectiveness (Haseena et al., 2023). A large variance of anticipated engagement patterns can be evidence of fraudulent manipulation. As an example, an unexpected influx of ad clicks by a user segment that has never been active in the past or a flood of social media likes in a time period that is too short to be due to natural causes may indicate bot work or organized engagement fraud. On the same note, abnormally high rates of clicking on certain coupon codes or referrals can be an indication of exploitation. To identify such anomalies, it is necessary to constantly monitor the situation and to model normal distributions of engagement, which would allow recognizing deviations that surpass statistical thresholds or learned behavioral standards automatically.

Geographic and Temporal Irregularities

Fraud is typically in the form of interactions with improbable geographic positions or in odd time windows (R. Z. Chen & Shih, 2021; G. Nejad & Sabzian, 2025). A case in point, a referral program that is supposed to be run in a particular country can end up being redeemed unexpectedly in areas where the campaign is not promoted or running. Similarly, the presence of activity outside standard business or user activity hours - e.g., hundreds of log-ins at 3 a.m. - can indicate automated scripts or organised fraud rings. Plot user activity on the geographic and temporal baselines to identify abnormal activity, especially in conjunction with other indicators of behavior. The time-zone pattern, geolocation information, and the time-stamping can give important context to distinguish between honest international activity and suspicious behavior.

Device and Account Similarities

Cross devices and accounts are also another powerful sign of fraud. In order to maximize profits in promotions, fraudsters may open several accounts or use common devices. Indicatively, device fingerprints, IP addresses, email patterns, or behavioural characteristics may be shared by several accounts, which indicates the presence of coordinated fraud. These links can be identified using advanced methods of machine learning, such as clustering and graph-based models based on metadata, logins, and behavioral signatures. The device and account-level detection is particularly crucial to referral, loyalty, and reward campaigns, where the multi-account exploitation is a prevalent approach.

Sources of Fraud

Promotional fraud has many origins, which may be divided into external and internal actors:

- Scripting and bots are used to perform high-volume, repetitive tasks to abuse promotions, such as large-scale coupon redemption or false clicks. Bot networks have become more advanced, and they employ AI to imitate human interaction patterns.
- Groups of coordinated people or networks abuse the promotions on a large scale and may also use social engineering, automated tools, and shared knowledge to avoid being detected.
- The individual users take advantage of gaps or loopholes in the campaign design, whether in the form of multiple usages of a referral code or taking advantage of unclear terms and conditions.
- Insiders or employees who know about the promotional systems can take advantage of the vulnerabilities and get to receive rewards illegally or abuse analytics, which is particularly difficult to detect because they have access rights and are familiar with how things are done.

It is necessary to know the patterns along with the origin of fraud to develop effective detection mechanisms. These methods of organizational behavior analysis, metadata examination, and machine learning in an advanced form allow identifying suspicious activity, distinguishing between legitimate and fraudulent transactions, and taking proactive measures. This multi-level solution can guarantee the integrity of promotion campaigns, reduce the financial losses, and the reputational losses. Table 2 highlights major indicators and actors behind fraud.

Table 2. Patterns and Sources of Fraud

Category	Examples / Indicators	Sources
Unusual Transactions	High-frequency coupon redemptions, rapid bursts of activity, repeated logins.	Bots, opportunistic individuals.
Anomalous Engagement	Spikes in clicks/likes/shares outside normal distribution.	Botnets, engagement rings.
Geographic & Temporal Irregularities	Activity from improbable regions or at unusual hours.	Organized fraud rings, bots.
Device & Account Similarities	Shared IPs, device fingerprints, or email patterns across accounts.	Fraud rings, insiders.
Insider Manipulation	Exploiting privileged access to promotional systems.	Internal threats.

Impact on Campaign Effectiveness and Financial Outcomes

Promotional fraud has an immense impact on the effectiveness and viability of online marketing campaigns. It has varied implications that touch on financial performance, strategic decision-making, customer perception, and operational efficiency. The knowledge of these effects is essential to organizations that aim to safeguard marketing investment and ensure the integrity of the campaign.

Financial Losses

Direct financial loss has the most immediate and measurable impact of promotional fraud (Karpoff, 2021). Poor marketing is committed in such forms as fraudulent coupon redemption, distorted referral programs, and overstated pay-per-click (PPC) engagements, which drain marketing budgets. As an example, an e-commerce business that has a time-sensitive coupon can have thousands of fake redemption claims, which results in revenue loss and profit dilution. Likewise, fake clicks on online ads escalate the cost of advertising without creating a real customer interest. With affiliate or referral programs, fictitious accounts are able to enjoy unnecessary commissions, which puts more stress on the resources. In the long run, these financial losses are reflected over time, especially in high-volume campaigns, which may be more than the corresponding gain of legitimate promotional activity.

Distorted Analytics and Decision-Making

Campaign performance measures are also affected by fraudulent activity. The conversion rate, engagement scores, click-through rates, and referral metrics are some of the data-based insights that marketing teams employ to optimize strategies. When such metrics are distorted by fraud, decision-making is distorted. As an illustration, the campaign that seems to be running well based on bot clicks or bogus recommendations can encourage marketers to invest more into non-performing channels, budget expenses, or apply inefficient targeting techniques. Predictive models in future campaign planning can be distorted, thus perpetuating inefficiencies and reducing the overall returns on investment (ROI). This lack of being able to differentiate between legitimate and fraudulent interactions generates long-term strategic blind spots that compromise the capacity of the organization to make evidence-based decisions.

Erosion of Customer Trust

Promotional fraud has a great impact on customer perception and brand reputation. When legitimate customers are exposed to manipulations in promotion, including a coupon that has already been redeemed, referral programs used by fake accounts, or the presence of too much competition among fraudsters, they can feel that campaigns are unfair, confusing, or unreliable. Such loss of trust may be reflected in terms of low levels of involvement, diminished loyalty, and poor word-of-mouth. Compromised campaigns can be a long-term negative effect, especially in industries where customer loyalty and reputation are very important, like the retailing industry, travel, and online services. In the long run, decreased trust can not only impact short-run revenue but also it can interfere with the long-run expansion and brand credibility.

Operational Challenges

Responding to promotional fraud comes with extra operational costs. The marketing teams, IT personnel, and data analysts should channel resources to monitor, investigate, and clean up fraudulent activities. This may frequently include reviewing transaction history, detecting bad accounts, authorizing the usage of coupons, and monitoring manual verification or correction. Such tasks divert attention from core marketing initiatives, campaign optimization, and customer engagement strategies. In high-scale campaigns, the overhead of operations may vastly increase because fraud detection and resolution need coordination between various departments, system audits, and constant process improvement. Such issues support the role of automated detection systems and machine learning models that can effectively identify fraud to minimize manual involvement and allow teams to concentrate on strategic goals.

Broader Strategic Implications

In addition to the financial and operational consequences that are immediate, promotional fraud may affect the long-term strategic performance. The threat of being exploited may cause businesses to become shy of launching high-value or innovative campaigns, resulting in marketing creativity and competitiveness being curtailed. Partnerships with affiliates, social media, and promotional vendors are also possible sources of fraud since stakeholders might lose trust in the integrity of the programs. Paint in severe situations can be the subject of regulatory scrutiny, especially in jurisdictions with aggressive advertising or consumer protection regulations, further subjecting the operation and financial costs to legal and compliance burdens.

MACHINE LEARNING TECHNIQUES FOR FRAUD DETECTION

The concept of ML has become an effective tool to define and address the fraudulent practices in online marketing campaigns. Unlike conventional rule-based systems, ML models can identify complicated patterns, keep up with the changing fraud strategies, and perform at scale. In this section, we examine some of the major ML methods used to detect fraud in terms of supervised learning, unsupervised learning, and deep learning methods, giving a comparison of their advantages and limitations in promotional activities.

Supervised Learning Models

Many fraud detection systems are based on supervised learning models and use labeled datasets of examples of legitimate and fraudulent activities. These models may be trained on patterns of past data to label a new transaction, user behavior, or promotional interactions as potentially fraudulent or legitimate. Supervised methods are effective when high-quality labeled data is available, feature engineering is done prudently, and there is proper selection of the model. Supervised models are especially helpful in the case of promotional campaigns, where types of well-defined fraud include coupon abuse, click fraud, and referral manipulation.

Logistic Regression

Logistic regression is a very common statistical model in binary classification tasks that aims at providing the likelihood of a particular instance being in a specific category- here, either fraudulent or legitimate activity. The fact that it is interpretable also makes it appealing to marketing teams and stakeholders who need clear information on model decisions. As an illustration, logistic regression can allow determining the contribution of individual features, like the amount of coupon redemptions or the age of the account, to the probability of being fraudulent. The model is computationally efficient in that it can be deployed and evaluated on medium and small-sized datasets in a short time. But logistic regression assumes linear correlations between the input features and the log-odds of the outcome. In complicated promotional fraud cases where inter-relationships among several variables are non-linear, the model could not capture subtle patterns, which reduces its ability to make predictions.

Decision Trees

Decision trees divide the data set into different values according to a feature to arrive at the hierarchical classification decision. Internal nodes are feature tests, branches are outcomes, and leaf nodes are class labels. This intuitive format enables marketers to conceptualize decision rules, gain knowledge of the major drivers of fraud, and be able to communicate their findings appropriately. As an example, a decision tree could be used to highlight accounts that redeem above a specified amount of coupons in 24 hours and originated with an IP address never before seen. However, single decision trees are likely to overfit, in particular when there is noise in the dataset or very few examples of fraud. Overfitted models can do well on training data but fail to apply to new promotional events, and require careful pruning, feature selection, and validation.

Random Forests

Random forests deal with the weaknesses of single decision trees; that is, they make use of an ensemble of trees, which are trained on a bootstrap sample of the data and a random subset of the feature set. The last prediction is usually derived by averaging probabilities or voting of all trees. This method increases predictive power, decreases overfitting, and offers resilience to high-dimensional data, which is a typical feature in promotional campaigns in which multiple user behaviors, device attributes, and transaction features are monitored. Random forests are specifically instrumental in identifying complicated fraud dynamics, e.g., coordinated coupon misuse or irregular referral activity in which cross-relationships between several variables could point to suspicious activity. Random forest feature importance metrics are also useful in giving insights into the attributes with the greatest contribution to fraud detection, contributing to the interpretability and monitoring of campaigns.

Gradient Boosting Machines (GBM)

The models constructed by gradient boosting machines such as XGBoost, LightGBM, and CatBoost (popular implementations) are trained iteratively by training a series of weak learners to enable them to correct the errors of the preceding models. This method is very predictive and can generate a high predictive performance, as well as capture subtle and non-linear correlations of the data. During the process of detecting promotional fraud, the complex patterns that may be detected by the GBMs include the presence of abnormal patterns of user behavior, uncommon referral patterns, or spikes in activity over time, which signify the presence of an automated exploiting entity. Although gradient boosting is more sophisticated and accurate than simpler models, it is more complex in terms of computation and less interpretable. This is almost always accompanied by the need to use other tools to explain the contribution of individual features to model predictions, including SHAP (Shapley Additive exPlanations) values. To provide transparency to marketing stakeholders.

Supervised models are also very efficient in the presence of a labeled dataset, whereby accurate identification of known types of fraud is possible. But it can be difficult to get high-quality labels in promotion fraud because fraudulent events are rare. After all, it is unclear what constitutes fraudulent behavior, and because campaigns are dynamic. Skewed datasets - with only a low percentage of transactions being fraud express a need for special methods, including resampling, cost-sensitive learning, or synthetic data generation, to avoid the models becoming biased towards legitimate cases. Besides, features should be designed with caution to capture the significant behavioral, temporal, and contextual cues, to provide models that are resilient to changing fraud strategies.

Models of Unsupervised Learning

Unsupervised learning models have proved especially useful in the promotional fraud detection environment when there is a lack of labeled data, incomplete, and unreliable data. In contrast to supervised methods, which use known examples of fraudulent and legitimate activity, unsupervised methods observe patterns, anomalies, or clusters without knowledge of the classes. This predisposes them to be particularly useful in detecting previously unknown or emerging fraud patterns, detecting slight deviations of normal behavior, and supplementing the supervised models in hybrid detection systems.

Clustering

Similar data points are clustered using clustering algorithms, including K-Means, DBSCAN, and hierarchical clustering, which is based on feature similarity. In marketing, clustering may assist in finding average user usage, purchase habits, or profiles of engagement. As an example, K-Means can generate clusters of normal redemption activity in a coupon campaign, and transactions or accounts that do not belong to any of those clusters, e.g., multiple redemptions within a very short time, or unusual referral link activity, can be taken as suspicious. The density-based DBSCAN is especially advantageous in identifying the low-density anomalies that cannot be attributed to any dense cluster, e.g., a single account that carries out a highly unusual action. Clustering may perform poorly with high-dimensional data, sparse data, and mixed types of data, and needs careful feature selection, normalization, or dimensionality reduction methods (e.g., PCA or t-SNE) to be effective.

Isolation Forest

Isolation Forest is a tree-based unsupervised algorithm that is specifically used in detecting anomalies. The algorithm functions by randomly partitioning the dataset based on randomly chosen features and split values, isolating the points that will need fewer partitions to be separated from the rest of the data. These are taken to be anomalies (John & Naaz, 2019; Vijayakumar et al., 2020). Isolation Forest can be well applied in the context of high-dimensional data typical of digital marketing campaigns, e.g., logs of user behavior, transaction information, and device fingerprints. It works well, especially when frauds are widely spread and dispersed among various features, because it does not need to be labeled with an example. As an example, during a coupon redemption campaign, a few accounts that frequently redeem discount codes with automated scripts can be effectively shut off and marked to be investigated. It is a favorite option in large campaigns due to its computational efficiency and scalability.

Support Vector Machines (SVM)

Another effective unsupervised method is One-Class SVM, which is used to learn a boundary within which the normal distribution of data is present. Observations that are not within this acquired boundary are termed anomalies (Y. J. Chen et al., 2017; RB & KR, 2021). This method works well in fraud detection when most data is legitimate and incidences of fraud are few. One-Class SVM can be used in promotional campaigns to detect unusual behaviour: repeated link abuse on referral links, coordinated use of social media, or unlikely transaction chains. Nevertheless, the approach is sensitive to parameter choice, including the type of kernel used, and to what proportion of anticipated anomalies, and can be carefully tuned to trade off between detection sensitivity and false-positive rates.

Unsupervised models provide much flexibility in identifying new unknown frauds and can be flexible with changing promotional conditions. They can be used particularly well in campaigns where new fraud techniques appear quite quickly, or in cases when it is time-consuming and expensive to label the cases of fraud. Nevertheless, unsupervised methods tend to yield more false-positive results than supervised models, because not every deviation of normal behavior is associated with malicious behavior. As a counter to this, organizations can use hybrid approaches where unsupervised detection of the anomalies is used with the assistance of supervised classification to verify and prioritize. Key to enhancing the performance of the model are feature engineering, normalization, and dimensionality reduction, especially in high-dimensional campaign data, like transaction logs, user profiles, and multi-channel engagement metrics.

Deep Learning Approaches

Deep learning networks are especially suited to the detection of complicated and subtle fraud patterns in huge promotional data sets. In contrast to conventional supervised or unsupervised models, deep learning models are able to capture more complex non-linear relationships, time series, and more networked interactions that frequently underpin fraudulent activity. These models are particularly useful when there is high-dimensional data, several points of contact with the user, and shifting fraud strategies. Although having better predictive power, deep learning methods must be designed with caution, need a large amount of computing power, and large volumes of data to train, and methods to enhance interpretability and explainability.

Neural Networks

Multi-layer perceptrons (MLPs) and neural networks in general may model highly non-linear relationships between transaction and user behavior data (Suryani & Fajri, 2022; Zheng et al., 2021). In the case of promotional fraud detection, neural networks can learn complicated trends, like an abnormal series of coupon redemption, coordinated referrals, or atypical participation in various campaigns. To illustrate, an MLP with inputs based on the past transaction history, user profile, and behavioral features can identify small anomalies that the older models would not have spotted, e.g., slight deviations in the repetitive purchase patterns, which could suggest automated exploitation. Nevertheless, neural networks are sensitive to feature normalization, abundance of training data, and regularization methods, so as to avoid overfitting. It can be costly in terms of computation, especially when dealing with huge campaigns in millions of transactions.

Autoencoders

Autoencoders are neural networks that perform anomaly detection (unsupervised). They are taught the compressed representations of normal activity through encoding the inputs into a lower-dimensional latent space, followed by reconstructing the original input. Transactions or user actions that are difficult to reconstruct, which is in high reconstruction error, are tagged anomalous. Autoencoders are especially helpful when fraud data are high-dimensional, like multi-feature coupon redemptions, clickstream logs, or multi-channel engagement metrics. As an example, in a loyalty program autoencoder can learn the common redemption patterns of rewards and automatically identify the accounts that are trying odd redemption patterns or different volumes of redemptions. Autoencoders also apply to real-time detection since reconstruction errors can be computed in real-time to alert suspicious transactions during live campaigns.

Graph Neural Networks (GNNs)

Graph neural networks expand the power of deep learning to networked data and are suited to campaigns involving complex connections between information, such as referral programs, social media promotions, or affiliate networks (Motie & Raahemi, 2024). GNNs are networks that describe node-to-node (e.g., users, accounts, or devices) relationships and edge-to-edge (e.g., referrals, connections, or interactions) and can be used to identify fraud when unusual connectivity patterns are observed. As an example, GNNs are able to spot groups of accounts involved in self-referral chains or coordinated rings of social media activity that otherwise would not be noticed in tabular models. GNNs can be employed to reveal network-based fraud in cases where the interaction between users is the core of campaign design by discovering both local and global structural patterns.

Even with such advantages, deep learning models present a number of challenges in detecting promotional fraud. Detailed models need large data to sufficiently model unusual fraudulent activities. Neural networks and graph models are frequently so complex that they require significant computational resources, like GPUs or cloud-based clusters. Tuning of the hyperparameters, selection of models, and optimization of the architecture are essential in the attainment of high performance and assurance of generalization of the models to unseen data in campaigns. Also, there is the issue of interpretability; frequently, complex deep learning models act as a black box, so it is challenging to explain to marketing teams the reasons behind flagging a specific transaction or user. Mechanisms as attention mechanisms, SHAP values, or layer-wise relevance propagation can be used to provide insights into the decisions made by a model so as to trust and adopt within an organizational setting. Table 3 provides a comparison of different ML model types.

Table 3. Comparison of Techniques

Model Type	Strengths	Weaknesses	Suitability for Promotional Fraud
Logistic Regression	Simple, interpretable, fast	Limited to linear relationships	Small campaigns, preliminary analysis
Decision Trees	Intuitive, interpretable	Prone to overfitting	Medium datasets, exploratory analysis
Random Forests	Robust, high accuracy, handles high-dimensional data	Less interpretable than single trees	Large campaigns with mixed data
Gradient Boosting	High predictive power, handles complex patterns	Computationally intensive, less interpretable	High-stakes campaigns requiring precision
Clustering	Detects novel patterns without labels	May struggle with sparse/ high-dimensional data	Early-stage fraud detection, exploratory analysis
Isolation Forest	Efficient for high-dimensional anomaly detection	Sensitive to contamination and parameter settings	Outlier detection in large datasets
One-Class SVM	Detects rare anomalies without labels	Sensitive to kernel choice and parameters	Sparse labeled data, highly skewed fraud cases
Neural Networks	Captures complex non-linear relationships	Requires large data, less interpretable	Complex campaign data, high-volume detection
Autoencoders	Effective anomaly detection in high-dimensional data	Computationally heavy, tuning required	Real-time fraud monitoring, high-dimensional promotions
Graph Neural Networks	Models relationships and interactions effectively	High complexity, computationally intensive	Referral or network-based promotions, relational fraud

In practice, organizations often combine multiple approaches in hybrid systems, leveraging the interpretability of supervised models, the adaptability of unsupervised techniques, and the predictive power of deep learning to maximize fraud detection effectiveness.

CHALLENGES IN IMPLEMENTING ML FOR FRAUD DETECTION

Although ML methods enable effective instruments of fraud detection related to promotional activities, several essential challenges are associated with their real-world application. These difficulties cut across data quality, interpretability of the models, processing in real-time, and ethical issues. It is necessary to know and overcome these issues to make the deployment of ML-based fraud detection systems successful, reliable, and accountable. Table 4 provides a high-level summary of these challenge areas, the core issues involved, and their practical implications.

Table 4. Key Challenges in Implementing ML for Promotional Fraud Detection

Challenge Domain	Core Issues	Practical Implications
Data-Related Issues	Poor data quality, class imbalance, and data sparsity.	Reduced model accuracy, missed fraud cases, unreliable outputs, and limited adaptability to new fraud patterns.
Model Interpretability	Black-box nature of advanced models, limited transparency.	Difficulty justifying decisions, reduced stakeholder trust, and compliance challenges in regulated industries.
Real-Time & Computational Constraints	Latency requirements, heavy resource demands, and scalability concerns.	Inability to block fraud in real-time, system bottlenecks, high infrastructure costs, and degraded performance at scale.
Privacy, Regulatory & Ethical Considerations	Data protection laws (GDPR, CCPA), algorithmic bias, and cross-border compliance.	Legal penalties, reputational risks, unfair treatment of users, and operational complexity in global campaigns.

Data-Related Issues

Machine learning models used to find promotional fraud are extremely sensitive in terms of success and reliability to the quality, structure, and completeness of the underlying data. The model performance, the accuracy of detection, and the overall efficiency of operations can be severely impacted in digital marketing campaigns due to multiple data-related issues, which affect the model performance. The resolution of these problems is essential to make sure that fraud detection systems are resilient, flexible, and scalable.

Data Quality

Machine learning models are based on high-quality data. Promotional campaigns are also a frequent source of multiple data sources, such as transaction data, referrals, clickstream, social interaction, and metadata on user accounts. Such datasets may include inconsistencies, missing values, and errors, negatively affecting model training and prediction accuracy. As an example, coupon redemption timings can be missing, and therefore, the model may fail to detect unusually quick claims, and incorrect account metadata can serve to mask identity manipulation or self-referrals. Noisy data may cause false positives or negatives, including duplicate entries, inconsistent labelling, or corrupted logs, which can confuse decision-making and result in a lack of trust among stakeholders. Pipelines that perform data cleaning, validation, and preprocessing are thus critical in order to determine accuracy and reliability, such as automated checks, adjustment of anomalies, and standardization amongst data sources.

Class Imbalance

Class imbalance is a typical issue in the field of promotional fraud detection. The percentage of fraudulent transactions is usually very low (sometimes not more than 15 percent of the total data). This asymmetry may cause models to get skewed towards making valid predictions, leaving the few but serious fraud cases undetected. As an example, a classifier fitting highly skewed data could have a high overall accuracy because it just labels the majority of the transactions as legitimate, missing the majority of the coupon abuse or referral abuse. In response to this, several strategies are used:

- Adding more examples of fraud to the training set to equalize the classes.
- Cutting down legitimate examples to a level where fraud cases are present.
- Methods like SMOTE (Synthetic Minority Over-sampling Technique) generate synthetic fraud examples by interpolating actual data points, improving the learning capacity of the model to study rare patterns.

Appropriate use of such methods guarantees that the models do not overfit and are sensitive to any anomalies.

Data Sparsity

Sparseness of data is also another important problem. Some promotions, such as new campaigns or campaigns to a niche audience, might produce minimal historical data. Less common forms of fraud (including advanced identity manipulation or minor social media interaction fraud) can be underrepresented. The scarcity of the data sets impairs the capacity of the models to learn meaningful patterns, compromising the predictive power and exposing the data to the risk of misclassifying data. Organizations can reduce the effects of sparseness by using:

- Summarising data associated with similar campaigns to augment training data and learn more general behavioral patterns.
- The use of knowledge trained on large related data to enhance performance on sparse or new campaigns

- The generation of synthetic or derived features that illuminate useful patterns, including transaction velocity, time series, or network-based interactions, to offset the poor coverage of raw data.

Unreliable, biased, and ineffective models may be developed as a result of the failure to deal with data-related issues. Low data quality can result in false alarms, an imbalance of classes can lessen fraud detection rates, and the sparseness of data can impede the ability of models to adapt to emerging fraud strategies. The ability to identify and prevent promotional fraud requires organizations to establish powerful data management practices, such as constant monitoring, validation, enhancement, and feature engineering, to guarantee machine learning models with a required basis to facilitate effective promotion fraud detection.

Model Interpretability and Explainability

Machine learning models can achieve high predictive accuracy to detect promotional fraud, but marketing and management teams do not simply want predictions; they want specific and actionable explanations to help them make decisions. Interpretability of models is needed to learn why a given transaction, account, or interaction is flagged as suspicious, so that teams can react accordingly and protect their trust in automated systems.

Black-Box Models

Most of the sophisticated models, such as neural networks, gradient boosting machines, and ensemble models such as random forests, are black box-based. They give out results without giving direct information on how it was decided. As an example, a deep neural network might successfully recognize a sequence of fraudulent coupon redemptions but is not readily able to indicate which characteristics or trends contributed to the decision. Such non-transparent behavior may lead to a lack of trust between marketing teams and campaign managers who have a hard time explaining why they took measures against some assumed fraud. Moreover, such a level of obscurity can cause compliance issues in regulated industries or areas where auditors are strict; organizations can be called upon to justify automated decisions that affect users or financial results.

Explainable AI (XAI) Techniques

In order to handle the problem of interpretability, organizations are turning to the use of explainable AI (XAI) solutions more and more. SHAP (SHapley Additive exPlanations) and LIME (Local Interpretable Model-agnostic Explanations) offer feature-level information regarding what a given model can be predicting, including what particular variables are contributing to a particular transaction being classified as fraud. As an illustration, SHAP values can show that an abnormally large count of coupon redemptions, along with several logins with a new IP address, made the most contribution to the fraud score attributed to an account. Although XAI increases transparency, it also adds new computational overhead and can remain difficult to interpret by non-technical stakeholders. Hence, organizations should balance between predictive performance and explainability, which can include simplified rule-based dashboards to complex models in order to support actionable knowledge.

Detection and Computational Constraints

There are numerous advertising campaigns, especially social media, e-commerce, and online advertising, that demand fraud detection in real-time. The difference between curbing the losses incurred due to abusers and refraining is of utmost importance in reducing financial losses at the expense of campaign integrity, and also to provide a healthy customer experience.

Latency Requirements

The real-time campaigns require the capability to consume the arriving data with the least amount of time. Determining fast-faced fraud attempts, like auto click fraud or immediate coupons, can be beyond the capabilities of batch-processing systems, which usually scan data on a fixed basis. Streaming analytics pipelines and low-latency models are needed to analyze transactions, engagement events, or referrals in real-time, and take automated action with them, e.g., blocking transactions, alerts, or user verification.

Computational Resources

More complex ML algorithms, such as graph-based models, autoencoders, and deep learning, can require large memory and processing power and dedicated hardware like GPUs. The extra computational complexity is augmented by high-dimensional campaign data, which can include user interaction data, device meta-data data, clickstream data, and referral networks data. Organizations should have a fine trade-off between model sophistication and operational feasibility, and may use optimized model architectures, approximate inference methods, or cloud-based infrastructure to sustain efficiency without losing accuracy.

Scalability

When campaigns are expanded to multiple channels, geographies, and customer segments, ML models need to scale to support data volumes, new kinds of interactions, and multiple campaign executions simultaneously. Scalable deployment plans, such as distributed computing, microservice architectures, and elastic cloud resources, are invaluable to the extent that detection performance is consistent and reliable as the present volume and complexity of promotional activity increases.

Privacy, Regulatory, and Ethical Considerations

Detection of promotional fraud can be headlong in processing sensitive user information such as personally identifiable information (PII), behavioral profiles, transaction histories, and interaction metrics. It is, consequently, imperative to ensure ethical and legal compliance.

Privacy Compliance

ML systems have to comply with data protection legislation like GDPR, CCPA, or applicable domestic legislation. This involves obtaining user consent on data processing, using the strong methods of anonymization or pseudonymization, safe storage, and access measures. Non-compliance may lead to judicial sanctions, loss of credibility, and loss of user confidence, especially in the case of campaigns that touch on cross-border data transfer.

Ethical Concerns

Alostatic choices can unknowingly discriminate against some group of users when training data has biases or when the model mistakes lawful behaviour as fraud. As an example, automated flags on high-frequency coupon redemptions may tend to unfairly exclude users with shared devices or proxy IP addresses or with unusual usage patterns, resulting in an unpleasant user experience. Ethical guidelines, fairness checks, and periodic audits should be incorporated to reduce harm as far as possible and to facilitate fair treatment of every user.

Cross-Border Considerations

International campaigns usually involve users across several jurisdictions, each with its own privacy, data protection, and regulatory demands. Regional compliance further complicates model deployment because of the need to make region-specific changes in data treatment, administration of consent, and reporting. It is important that organizations have current awareness of matters that concern foreign laws and are flexible.

The solution to these problems needs to be solved by a set of technical, organizational, and regulatory approaches. Quality, balanced, and well-structured data is the basis of trusted ML models. Adding explainability tools, streamlining computational pipeline services, and adhering to privacy and ethical considerations further contribute to the performance and reliability of fraud detection systems. Identifying these difficulties at an early stage of designing allows organizations to have solid and scalable ML solutions that ensure the interests of the business and the confidence of the customers are preserved.

PRACTICAL APPLICATIONS AND INTEGRATION STRATEGIES

Implementation of ML fraud detection in promotion is not confined to the development of the algorithms, but must be closely tied to marketing infrastructures, monitoring, and operational best practices. This section proposes methods of deployment, gives practical examples, and explains the ways of successful maintenance of the ML-based fraud detection systems. When deploying AI solutions in practice, cost-effectiveness and ROI analysis become crucial. Successful implementations often hinge on demonstrating measurable value, such as improved productivity, accuracy, or decision-making efficiency, relative to the resources invested. Figure 1 illustrates the lifecycle of ML-driven fraud detection in promotional campaigns, from deployment to monitoring and continuous improvement. Table 5 summarizes key deployment strategies, their strengths, and contexts of application.

Table 5. Techniques for Deploying ML Models in Promotional Fraud Detection

Deployment Technique	Description	Best Suited For	Key Advantages	Limitations
Batch Processing Pipelines	Analyze historical data in scheduled batches.	Low-latency campaigns, post-event analysis.	Lower computational demand, simpler integration.	Not suitable for real-time fraud prevention.
Real-Time Streaming Pipelines	Process transactions/ events as they occur.	High-frequency ads, flash promotions.	Immediate detection, automated blocking.	Higher infrastructure and compute costs.
Hybrid Deployment	Combine batch and streaming detection.	Large campaigns with mixed needs.	Balanced performance and adaptability.	Added system complexity.

continued on following page

Table 5. Continued

Deployment Technique	Description	Best Suited For	Key Advantages	Limitations
Cloud Integration	Use scalable cloud resources for deployment.	Multi-campaign, cross-geography operations.	Scalability, centralized management.	Data transfer and latency risks.
Edge Integration	Compute close to user/ device level.	Mobile apps, low-latency use cases.	Reduced latency, real-time responsiveness.	Limited by device/ server capacity.

Figure 1. Lifecycle of ML-Driven Fraud Detection Systems

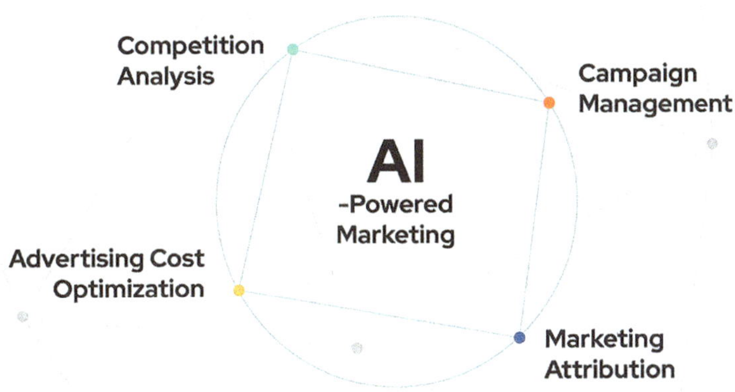

Methods of Implementing Models in Marketing Infrastructures

When designing to incorporate ML models into the current marketing systems, one must take into account scalability, latency, and digital campaign platform compatibility. Important deployment methods are:

1. Campaigns that do not require real-time detection can have their historical data processed in batches using a model. Through this approach, integration is simplified and computation requirements are minimized, and actionable insights on future campaign adjustments are given.
2. Streaming pipelines can be used to detect in real-time high-frequency digital campaigns, e.g., pay-per-click advertisements or flash promotions. Apache

Kafka, Apache Flink, or cloud-based streaming services can be used to feed incoming transactions to ML models in order to be scored on the fly.

3. This is where organizations tend to integrate real-time and batch systems. As an illustration, supervised models could be applied in high-volume historical detection, whereas the stream activity could be tracked with anomaly detection or deep learning models to record the emerging fraud trends.
4. Cloud-based systems provide scalability of compute and storage forces, which allows the deployment of models across multiple campaigns. Latency can be minimized and responsiveness to real-time enhanced by edge integration, wherein computations are made nearer to user interactions (e.g., within web servers or mobile applications).

ML-Driven Fraud Detection

Some of these organizations have implemented ML methods and used them to identify and stop promotional fraud:

- Models based on random forest and gradient boosting are applied by large online stores to identify suspicious coupon redemptions and abuse of the referral program. These platforms mitigate fraudulent claims but do not disrupt the legitimate customer activity by fusing user behavior analytics with device fingerprinting.
- Advertising networks use models of supervision and non-supervision to identify click fraud. Neural networks and isolation forests are used to analyze the patterns of the traffic, IP addresses, and velocity of clicks to determine the presence of bots and questionable activity to block the overcharging of advertisers.
- Autoencoders are applied by travel and hospitality brands to identify abnormal point redemptions and account behaviour. These models take up some common customer activity behavior and also raise alarms when there is an activity that is not the norm, and this may serve as a sign of fraudulent use of the loyalty programs.
- Graph neural networks have been used to promote referral campaigns to identify network-based fraud, e. g. coordinated fake accounts or self-referral loops, to enable marketers to retain fair and credible promotion.

These examples show how ML techniques can be used in many promotional channels and campaign types, emphasizing the significance of selecting the model with consideration of a particular operational context.

Monitoring, Updating, and Maintaining Models

ML-based fraud detection systems need constant control to work:

- Adopt dashboards and early warning measures to monitor model outcome, false alarms, and new fraudulent trends. Periodic reviewing of metrics will necessitate the necessary adjustments.
- Fraud tricks develop at a high rate. Incremental learning, or regular retraining on new data, can assist in adapting models to new behavior and can counter the effect of degradation of performance.
- Have current and valid features, such as transactional, behavioral, and contextual data. Occasional auditing of the data quality would help to keep models accurate and reliable.
- Deliver explainable results or reports to the marketing departments to build trust in the automated decisions. Explanations of flagged activities can be an SHAP or LIME.
- Select infrastructure to scale with a growing campaign volume and a need to detect events in real-time. Load testing and scalable architecture prevent system bottlenecks.
- Continuously assess models for fairness and compliance with privacy regulations. Provide anonymization, access control, and consent controls to safeguard user data.

Positive application of ML models to detect promotional fraud needs a mix of technical know-how, operational design, and organizational fit. Through proper deployment methods, real-world best practices, and constant monitoring of the performance of the models, the businesses are in a position to protect campaigns, minimize financial loss, and retain customer trust. The introduction of ML into the marketing infrastructures, therefore, changes the process of fraud detection into a proactive, adaptive system.

CONCLUSION

ML to detect fraud in promotional activities is a revolutionary practice to protect digital marketing campaigns. The chapter has demonstrated the multifacetedness of promotional fraud, such as the use of click fraud, coupon abuse, identity manipulation, and network-based schemes, and discussed how these threats can be identified and mitigated using ML techniques, both supervised learning and unsupervised anomaly detection, as well as advanced deep learning schemes. Canonical information is that although ML has strong predictive potential, its effectiveness continues to depend on the high-quality data, selection of the model, interpretability, and easy integration into marketing structures.

New trends in this area show a shift to AI-driven predictive fraud prevention, which is where models are not only able to detect existing fraud but also predict a potential crime before it happens. The use of hybrid models of supervised, unsupervised, and deep learning models is becoming popular, with the benefit of providing precision and flexibility within dynamic campaigns. Also, neural networks based on graphs, real-time streaming analysis, and explainable artificial intelligence methods can help improve detection accuracy and be more transparent to marketing teams and stakeholders.

Despite these advancements, several opportunities for future research and development remain. These involve creating more effective solutions to imbalanced and sparse datasets, to work on real-time processing with higher efficiency, incorporating privacy-preserving machine learning algorithms, and multi-channel fraud detection. The additional research into the interpretability, fairness, and ethical use of models can be essential to establishing trust in AI-based fraud detection models.

Generative AI poses emerging risks in the domain of promotional and marketing integrity. Advanced text, image, and video generation tools can be exploited to create highly convincing fake endorsements, fabricated brand campaigns, or synthetic influencer content that manipulates consumer perception. Such misuse not only erodes public trust but also exposes organizations to reputational and financial damage.

To sum it up, machine learning as a means of detecting promotional fraud allows safeguarding financial performance and enhancing the integrity and credibility of marketing campaigns. Integrating technical innovation and strategic execution with ethical aspects, organizations may build resilient, smart, and trustworthy promotional ecosystems that would adapt to the evolving landscape of digital marketing fraud.

REFERENCES

Chen, R. Z., & Shih, C. H. (2021). Applying Spatio-temporal Analysis in Telecom Fraud Investigation. *Procedia Computer Science, 192*, 3109–3113. DOI: 10.1016/j.procs.2021.09.083

Chen, Y. J., Wu, C. H., Chen, Y. M., Li, H. Y., & Chen, H. K. (2017). Enhancement of fraud detection for narratives in annual reports. *International Journal of Accounting Information Systems, 26*, 32–45. Advance online publication. DOI: 10.1016/j.accinf.2017.06.004

Cliquet, G. (2020). From Geomarketing to Spatial Marketing. In *Spatial Economics* (Vol. II). Applications., DOI: 10.1007/978-3-030-40094-1_10

Dörnyei, K. R. (2021). Marketing Professionals' Views on Online Advertising Fraud. *Journal of Current Issues and Research in Advertising, 42*(2), 156–174. DOI: 10.1080/10641734.2020.1737276

El-Hajj, M., & Pavlova, M. (2024). Predictive Modeling of Customer Response to Marketing Campaigns. *Electronics 2024, Vol. 13, Page 3953, 13*(19), 3953. DOI: 10.3390/electronics13193953

Haseena, S., Saroja, S., Suseandhiran, N., & Manikandan, B. (2023). An intelligent approach for anomaly detection in credit card data using bat optimization algorithm. *Inteligencia Artificial, 26*(72), 202–222. Advance online publication. DOI: 10.4114/intartif.vol26iss72pp202-222

Hoffman, D. L., Moreau, C. P., Stremersch, S., & Wedel, M. (2022). The Rise of New Technologies in Marketing: A Framework and Outlook. *Journal of Marketing, 86*(1), 1–6. DOI: 10.1177/00222429211061636

John, H., & Naaz, S. (2019). Credit Card Fraud Detection using Local Outlier Factor and Isolation Forest. *International Journal on Computer Science and Engineering, 7*(4), 1060–1064. Advance online publication. DOI: 10.26438/ijcse/v7i4.10601064

Karpoff, J. M. (2021). The future of financial fraud. *Journal of Corporate Finance, 66*, 101694. DOI: 10.1016/j.jcorpfin.2020.101694

Kim, J., Jung, H., & Kim, W. (2022). Sequential Pattern Mining Approach for Personalized Fraudulent Transaction Detection in Online Banking. *Sustainability (Basel), 14*(15), 9791. Advance online publication. DOI: 10.3390/su14159791

Kivistö, A. (2024). *Role of artificial intelligence in promotional campaigns*. https://jyx.jyu.fi/handle/123456789/96946

Kumar, V., Ashraf, A. R., & Nadeem, W. (2024). AI-powered marketing: What, where, and how? *International Journal of Information Management*, *77*, 102783. DOI: 10.1016/j.ijinfomgt.2024.102783

Langen, H., & Huber, M. (2023). How causal machine learning can leverage marketing strategies: Assessing and improving the performance of a coupon campaign. *PLoS One*, *18*(1), e0278937. DOI: 10.1371/journal.pone.0278937 PMID: 36630398

Liang, Y., Chen, X. J., Chen, Y., Xiao, P., & Zhang, J. (2024). Mobile ad fraud: Empirical patterns in publisher and advertising campaign data. *International Journal of Research in Marketing*, *41*(2), 265–281. DOI: 10.1016/j.ijresmar.2023.09.003

Motie, S., & Raahemi, B. (2024). Financial fraud detection using graph neural networks: A systematic review. In *Expert Systems with Applications* (Vol. 240). DOI: 10.1016/j.eswa.2023.122156

Movahed, A. B., Movahed, A. B., & Nozari, H. (2024). Opportunities and challenges of marketing 5.0. *Smart and Sustainable Interactive Marketing*, 1–21.

Nejad, G., M., & Sabzian, H. (2025). Spatiotemporal patterns of consumer financial fraud in the United States. *International Journal of Bank Marketing*, *43*(2), 368–387. DOI: 10.1108/IJBM-01-2024-0023

Rb, A., & Kr, S. K.RB. (2021). Credit card fraud detection using artificial neural network. *Global Transitions Proceedings*, *2*(1), 35–41. Advance online publication. DOI: 10.1016/j.gltp.2021.01.006

Sadeghpour, S., & Vlajic, N. (2021a). Ads and Fraud: A Comprehensive Survey of Fraud in Online Advertising. *Journal of Cybersecurity and Privacy 2021, Vol. 1, Pages 804-832, 1*(4), 804–832. DOI: 10.3390/jcp1040039

Sadeghpour, S., & Vlajic, N. (2021b). Click fraud in digital advertising: A comprehensive survey. *Computers*, *10*(12), 164. Advance online publication. DOI: 10.3390/computers10120164

Sáez-Ortuño, L., Forgas-Coll, S., Huertas-Garcia, R., & Sánchez-García, J. (2023). Online cheaters: Profiles and motivations of internet users who falsify their data online. *Journal of Innovation and Knowledge*, *8*(2), 100349. Advance online publication. DOI: 10.1016/j.jik.2023.100349

Slutskiy, P. (2021). Fraudulent Communication in Advertising and Business Promotion. *Communication and Libertarianism*, 261–274. DOI: 10.1007/978-981-33-6664-0_17

Suryani, E., & Fajri, R. R. (2022). Fraud Triangle Perspective: Artificial Neural Network Used in Fraud Analysis. *Quality - Access to Success*, *23*(188). Advance online publication. DOI: 10.47750/QAS/23.188.22

Vijayakumar, V., Divya, N. S., Sarojini, P., & Sonika, K. (2020). Isolation Forest and Local Outlier Factor for Credit Card Fraud Detection System. *International Journal of Engineering and Advanced Technology*, *9*(4), 261–265. Advance online publication. DOI: 10.35940/ijeat.D6815.049420

Wang, W., Feng, F., He, X., Zhang, H., & Chua, T. S. (2021). Clicks can be Cheating: Counterfactual Recommendation for Mitigating Clickbait Issue. *SIGIR 2021 - Proceedings of the 44th International ACM SIGIR Conference on Research and Development in Information Retrieval*. DOI: 10.1145/3404835.3462962

Yang, C. (2025). Protecting financial consumers from authorized push payment fraud: is reimbursement an optimal solution? *Journal of Financial Regulation and Compliance*. https://doi.org/DOI: 10.1108/JFRC-11-2024-0225/1252741

Zheng, Y., Ye, X., & Wu, T. (2021). Using an Optimized Learning Vector Quantization- (LVQ-) Based Neural Network in Accounting Fraud Recognition. *Computational Intelligence and Neuroscience*, *2021*(1), 4113237. Advance online publication. DOI: 10.1155/2021/4113237 PMID: 34257634

Chapter 10
Modeling Click Intention in E-Commerce Advertising a Hybrid PLS-SEM and ANN Approach:
Modeling Click Intention in E-Commerce Advertising

Trung Quang Ngo
https://orcid.org/0000-0003-4355-9499
Faculty of Commerce, Van Lang University, Ho Chi Minh City, Vietnam

Minh Duc Ly
https://orcid.org/0000-0003-0200-7153
Faculty of Commerce, Van Lang University, Ho Chi Minh City, Vietnam

ABSTRACT

This study explores the factors influencing consumers' intention to click on e-commerce advertisements using Partial Least Squares Structural Equation Modeling Artificial Neural Networks (PLS-SEM ANN). The main objectives of the research are to identify the key factors affecting click-through rates (CTR), assess the moderating role of privacy concerns, and predict the most significant factors influencing click behavior. A survey was conducted with 528 valid responses from consumers using e-commerce platforms such as Shopee, Lazada, and TikTok Shop, as well as companies operating on those platforms in Vietnam. The results show that Trust (T) and Information Quality (IQ) are the most significant predictors of click-through intention, with path coefficients of 0.352 ($p < 0.01$) and 0.770 ($p < 0.01$), respectively. Privacy Concern (PC) negatively affects click intention, with a path coefficient of -0.411 ($p < 0.01$),

DOI: 10.4018/979-8-3373-4392-1.ch010

indicating that as privacy concerns increase, consumers are less likely to engage with advertisements. Additionally, Artificial Intelligence (AI) was found to have a positive impact on Trust, with a path coefficient of 0.656 ($p < 0.01$), enhancing the relevance and personalization of advertisements. Integrating PLS-SEM and ANN provides a comprehensive approach to modeling both linear and nonlinear relationships. The ANN model achieves an R^2 value of over 0.85 for predicting click intention, demonstrating its ability to capture complex relationships that PLS-SEM may not identify. Importance-Performance Map Analysis (IPMA) shows that Trust (T) is the most important factor driving click behavior, with a performance score of 84%, followed by Information Quality (IQ) with a performance score of 65%. This study contributes significantly to understanding consumer behavior in the context of digital advertising.

I.INTRODUCTION

In the digital and AI-driven era, e-commerce has rapidly expanded into a vital platform for global businesses and consumers (Khrais, 2020). With advancements in artificial intelligence (AI), Big Data, and precision marketing, firms increasingly optimize advertising strategies and personalize content to attract customers (Lu, 2024). This technological shift intensifies competitive pressure, requiring manufacturers to adopt effective marketing strategies to reach the right customers at the right time (Tsai, Wu & Chang, 2012; You et al., 2015). Online advertising has therefore become a dominant approach for stimulating click intention and boosting conversion rates, enabling businesses to leverage data-driven insights for new market opportunities (Lytras, Raghavan & Damiani, 2017). On major platforms such as Amazon, Shopee, Lazada, Alibaba, and TikTok Shop, competition revolves around maximizing click-through rates (CTR), which typically range from 3–5% in 2023. TikTok Shop has accelerated e-commerce growth through personalized advertising. In Vietnam, e-commerce transactions grew 40% in 2024, exceeding $13.8 billion, with Shopee holding 73.1% and TikTok Shop capturing 9.9% market share (YouNet ECI, 2024). In China, manufacturers increasingly adopt precision marketing on social media due to mobile internet expansion (Chuanpeng Yu et al., 2019; Zhu & Chen, 2015). WeChat, with over 1 billion MAUs, integrates social networking, business data, and payment systems, creating a powerful data ecosystem (Yanes & Berger, 2017). However, while AI enhances ad targeting, rising personalization also increases privacy concerns, influencing CTR. Studies show CTR remains low—below 0.01% (Lambrecht & Tucker, 2013) and only 0.46% for display ads (Google Ads Benchmark, 2023)—highlighting the ongoing challenge for e-commerce firms to improve advertising effectiveness. Therefore, a critical question arises:

What factors truly influence consumers' intention to click on e-commerce advertisements, and how can they be optimized?

With the rise of the Internet, AI, and Big Data, marketing has shifted toward deep personalization as manufacturers integrate multiple data elements related to consumer behavior and preferences (Saluja et al., 2023). However, this raises an important issue: whether privacy concerns influence consumers' intention to click on personalized ads (Jung, 2017). While many studies examine click behavior through factors such as Trust, Information Quality, Brand Recognition, and AI's impact on advertising, debates remain regarding how these elements interact with privacy concerns (Bandara et al., 2020). Additionally, although PLS-SEM is widely used to analyze click intention, few studies combine it with ANN for predictive accuracy. For example, Shaouf, Lü & Li (2016) investigated attitudes toward mobile advertising but did not examine privacy or click intention. Therefore, this study aims to identify key factors influencing consumers' intention to click on e-commerce advertisements. Examine the role of Privacy Concerns in the relationship between AI and Trust and its impact on the intention to click on advertisements, and apply PLS-SEM and ANN to analyze the nonlinear effects of factors on click intention.

Based on theories established in previous studies—such as Perceived Risk Theory, the Elaboration Likelihood Model, Involvement Theory, Privacy Calculus Theory, and the Information Adoption Model—this study develops eight hypotheses involving the following variables: Trust (T), Privacy Concern (PC), High Engagement Product (HEP), Artificial Intelligence (AI), Brand Recognition (BR), Aesthetic Appeal (AA), and Information Quality (IQ). Trust serves as the central construct, reflecting consumers' confidence in e-commerce advertising (Corbitt et al., 2003). Privacy Concern represents concerns regarding data collection and misuse. HEP refers to products with high consumer involvement (Strubel & Petrie, 2016). AI personalizes advertisements but may increase privacy concerns (Kim et al., 2024). Brand Recognition reflects consumers' familiarity with a brand (Chaudhuri, 2002), while Aesthetic Appeal highlights how visually attractive ads capture attention (Shaouf et al., 2016). Information Quality measures the accuracy and usefulness of advertising content (Aguirre et al., 2015). PLS-SEM is used to test these hypotheses and examine relationships among variables, followed by ANN to identify the most influential factor and model nonlinear relationships affecting click behavior. The survey data collected consists of 528 valid samples from customers using e-commerce platforms such as TikTok Shop, Shopee, Lazada, etc., and companies that conduct business directly on online platforms across Vietnam. The study reveals three key issues: What factors influence trust and the intention to click on e-commerce advertisements? Does privacy concern reduce the likelihood of clicking on advertisements? Which factor has the most substantial impact on click behavior according to the PLS-SEM vs. ANN model?

This study contributes to e-commerce advertising by examining how AI, Trust, and Privacy Concerns influence consumers' intention to click on online advertisements. Its key novelty lies in integrating PLS-SEM and ANN, allowing linear causal analysis alongside nonlinear predictive modeling for deeper insights into click behavior. The research advances Trust Theory, TAM, Privacy Concern Theory, Cue Utilization Theory, and Consumer Decision-Making in the context of personalized advertising. Practically, the findings help businesses optimize digital advertising strategies across platforms such as Google Ads, Facebook Ads, TikTok Ads, and Shopee Ads by balancing personalization and privacy to enhance CTR. However, limitations include data restricted to major e-commerce platforms, a focus on click intention rather than actual purchases, and potential response bias. Additionally, ANN's limited causal interpretability poses challenges. Future studies should expand platform coverage and incorporate real purchasing data to improve generalizability and understanding of e-commerce advertising effectiveness.

II. THEORETICAL BACKGROUND AND HYPOTHESES

2.1. Advertising in the Digital era and Click-Through Intention

The integration of AI, big data, and e-commerce has transformed advertising from traditional mass promotion into personalized, data-driven strategies (Lee & Ke, 2012; Yu et al., 2012). Historically, ineffective audience segmentation caused wasted spending, as noted by Leverhulme and Wanamaker (Jones, 1990). Modern techniques such as Advertising Personalization and Precision Marketing tailor content using behavioral data and AI analytics, improving ROI and CTR (Bleier & Eisenbeiss, 2015a; Wedel & Kannan, 2016; Chapelle et al., 2015). Yet highly personalized ads may increase privacy concerns, lowering trust and reducing click intention (Bleier & Eisenbeiss, 2015b; Aguirre et al., 2015). Studies highlight factors influencing click behavior, including trust (Cheung & To, 2017), product involvement (Yoo et al., 2004), brand recognition (Robinson et al., 2007), and ad aesthetics (Liu & Mattila, 2017). With platforms like Shopee, TikTok Shop, and Amazon using real-time data for targeting (Theodorakopoulos & Theodoropoulou, 2024), debates persist on whether personalization boosts clicks when privacy is compromised. Based on these findings, the following hypothesis is proposed:

H1: The level of consumer engagement with high-engagement products positively influences their intention to click on advertisements.

H2: High-engagement products are positively associated with increased privacy concerns among consumers

H5: The use of artificial intelligence in personalized advertising positively influences consumer trust in advertisements.

2.2. Trust and Privacy Concerns in Online Advertising

In the era of AI, big data, and rapidly expanding e-commerce, online advertising has shifted from traditional mass communication to highly personalized, data-driven strategies. Businesses now rely on AI algorithms and behavioral data to tailor ads to user preferences, improving effectiveness but also raising issues of trust and privacy (Lee & Ke, 2012; Yu et al., 2012). Historically, mass advertising lacked targeting precision, leading to wasteful spending, as noted by Leverhulme and Wanamaker (Jones, 1990). Modern techniques such as Advertising Personalization and Precision Marketing enable more accurate targeting and higher CTR (Bleier & Eisenbeiss, 2015a; Wedel & Kannan, 2016). However, excessive personalization can trigger privacy concerns, reduce trust, and diminish click intention (Bleier & Eisenbeiss, 2015b; Aguirre et al., 2015). Trust becomes crucial in this context, defined as willingness to be vulnerable based on expectations of reliable behavior (Mayer et al., 1995). Trust includes cognitive beliefs and behavioral intentions (Gefen et al., 2008; Pavlou et al., 2007) and is shaped by ability, benevolence, and integrity (Oliveira et al., 2017; Lee & Turban, 2001). While personalized ads can enhance relevance, they simultaneously elevate privacy concerns if data use lacks transparency (Smit et al., 2014). Thus, businesses must balance AI-driven personalization with consumer privacy protection to maintain trust. In this study, we apply trust and privacy theories to examine their influence on click intention, aiming to provide strategic insights for ethical and effective online advertising.

. Based on these findings, the following hypothesis is proposed:

H3: Privacy concerns negatively affect consumers' intention to click on advertisements.

H4: Trust in online advertising positively influences consumers' intention to click on advertisements.

2.3.. Cue Utilization Theory and Consumer Decision-Making

Cue Utilization Theory, first proposed by Edwards (1968) and later expanded by Ajzen (1991), explains how consumers rely on cues to reduce uncertainty and make decisions when information is limited. In online advertising, intrinsic cues (product attributes) and extrinsic cues (brand reputation, visuals, price) strongly influence click intention. Lee & Turban (2001) note that consumers evaluate ad credibility through cues such as high-quality images, trustworthy information, and user reviews. Clear, informative ads enhance trust and click likelihood, whereas vague content discourages interaction. Trust is a central cue: Pavlou, Liang, & Xue (2007) argue that consumers only engage with ads they perceive as reliable. Brand reputation and recognition also act as powerful cues that reduce uncertainty and increase engagement (Oliveira et al., 2017). Aesthetic cues play an important role as well; visually appealing ads evoke positive emotions that enhance curiosity and click-through rates (Soh, Reid, & King, 2007; Schlosser, White, & Lloyd, 2006). Strategically, strong cues combine emotional appeal and clear information to create persuasive advertising messages (Lee & Turban, 2001). In this study, Cue Utilization Theory helps explain how trust, brand recognition, aesthetics, and information quality shape consumers' click behavior, offering practical insights to optimize online advertising effectiveness. Based on these findings, the following hypothesis is proposed:

> **H6:** Brand recognition positively influences consumer trust in advertisements.
> **H7:** The aesthetic appeal of advertisements positively influences consumer trust in advertisements.
> **H8**: The quality of information presented in advertisements positively influences consumer trust in advertisements.

Based on the theoretical foundations mentioned above, research hypotheses are developed with one dependent variable, two mediating variables, and four independent variables influencing the intention to click on advertisements. The research model is presented in **Figure 1.**

Figure 1. Research model

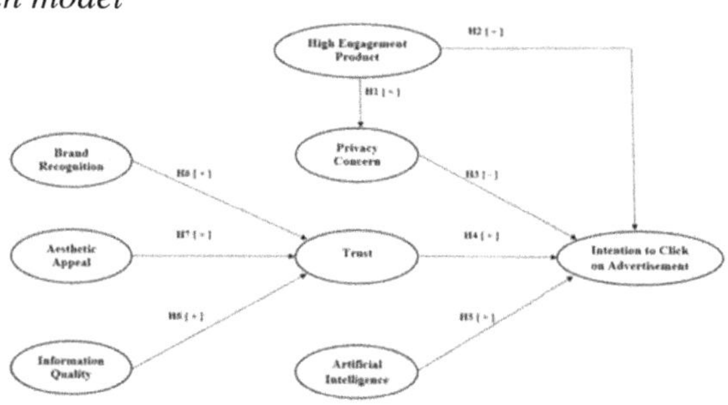

III. RESEARCH METHODOLOGY

This study investigates key factors influencing consumers' intention to click on e-commerce advertisements, aiming to optimize digital advertising strategies. Two advanced analytical methods are applied: PLS-SEM (Mijwel, Maad M. et al., 2021) and Artificial Neural Networks – ANN (Kusmaryono, Imam, Dyana Wijayanti, and Hevy Risqi Maharani, 2020), enabling the identification of both linear and nonlinear effects in online consumer behavior. The main variables examined include trust, privacy concerns, product engagement, AI, brand recognition, aesthetic appeal, and information quality. Data were collected from 528 valid responses involving users and businesses on fast-growing Vietnamese e-commerce platforms such as Shopee, Lazada, and TikTok Shop. This context, with a 40% growth in 2024, provides a relevant basis for exploring how AI and privacy issues affect click behavior. The study addresses three central research questions: (1) What factors influence trust and click intention? (2) Do privacy concerns reduce click likelihood? (3) Which factor has the strongest influence on click behavior when analyzed with PLS-SEM and ANN? Grounded in theoretical frameworks including Perceived Risk Theory, Involvement Theory, Privacy Decision Theory, and the Information Acceptance Model, the study formulates eight hypotheses covering the abovementioned factors. By doing so, it offers practical insights to help businesses design effective and trustworthy online ads while balancing personalization and data privacy concerns. The research process is presented in the flowchart model in **Figure 2.**

Figure 2. The research framework of SEM and ANN

This study employs a 5-point Likert scale questionnaire (Kusmaryono, Imam, Dyana Wijayanti, and Hevy Risqi Maharani, 2022), a widely accepted method in quantitative research (Majumdar et al., 2020). Survey variables are adapted from prior studies to suit the current research context, and the questionnaire was designed bilingually (English and Vietnamese) to enhance clarity and response accuracy. Table 1 details the latent variables, observed indicators, and source references. A hybrid PLS-SEM and ANN approach is adopted to analyze consumer click behavior. While PLS-SEM is effective for hypothesis testing, its limitations with non-linear data (as noted in previous studies) are addressed by integrating ANN, a machine learning-based non-linear regression model. ANN enhances predictive accuracy and captures complex consumer behavior patterns more effectively. PLS-SEM analysis is conducted using SmartPLS 3.3.0, while ANN modeling is performed with IBM SPSS v26 to evaluate causal effects and rank the most influential factors.

Table 1. Data Collection Instruments

Variables	No. of Items	Sources
Trust (T)	4	Corbitt, Thanasankit, Yi, 2003
Privacy Concern (PC)	3	Aguirre, E., et al., 2015
High Engagement Product (HEP)	4	Strubel, J., Petrie, T.A., 2016
Artificial Intelligence (AI)	3	Lee & Ke, 2012; Yu, Yu, & Cheng, 2012
Brand Recognition (BR)	3	Robinson, Wysocka, & Hand, 2007
Aesthetic Appeal (AA)	3	Liu & Mattila, 2017
Information Quality (IQ)	5	Aguirre, E., et al., 2015
Intention to Click (IA)	4	Bleier & Eisenbeiss, 2015a; Cheung & To, 2017

The results of the descriptive analysis of the survey sample characteristics are presented in Table 2. This analysis provides insights into the demographic profile, educational background, and experience of participants in the context of research on click intention in e-commerce advertisements. Regarding gender, females account for 55.1%, while males constitute 44.9%. In terms of age distribution, the majority of respondents belong to the 25 - 44 age group (68.0%), indicating that middle-aged consumers tend to interact more with online advertisements. Regarding educational background, respondents with a high school diploma make up the largest proportion (50.0%), followed by those with a university degree (25.2%) and a postgraduate degree (24.8%). This suggests that individuals with at least a high school education are the primary group engaging in online shopping and interacting with e-commerce advertisements. The survey sample was collected from 528 direct shoppers and businesses operating on e-commerce platforms, with 62.1% from businesses and 37.9% from individual consumers. In terms of online shopping experience, 42.2% of respondents have 2 - 5 years of experience, indicating that consumers with longer shopping experiences tend to be more interested in personalized advertisements. The majority of respondents come from the Southern (48.2%) and Northern (42.5%) regions of Vietnam, while the Central region accounts for only 9.3%, reflecting the dominant growth of e-commerce in the North and South.

Table 2. Descriptive Analysis (N=528 samples)

Variable	Value	Frequency	Percentage (%)
Gender	Male	237	44.9
	Female	291	55.1
Age	18 - 24	69	13.1
	25 - 34	179	33.9
	35 - 44	181	34.1
	45 - 54	64	12.1
	Over 55	35	6.8
Education Level	High school	264	50.0
	Undergraduate	133	25.2
	Postgraduate	131	24.8
Online Shopping Experience	Less than 2 years	68	12.9
	2 - 5 years	223	42.2
	5 - 10 years	165	31.3
	10 - under 15 years	72	13.6
Region	North	225	42.5
	Central	49	9.3
	South	254	48.2
Survey Sample Distribution	Businesses	328	62.1
	Individual Consumers	200	37.9

To ensure the validity and reliability of the research model, common method bias was assessed using the Harman Single-Factor Test (Rodriguez-Ardura., et al ., 2020). The test results show that the total variance explained by a single factor is 46.28%, which is below the 50% threshold, indicating that common method bias is not a concern in this study. Additionally, the Kaiser-Meyer-Olkin (KMO) test and Bartlett's Sphericity test (Shrestha, Noora., 2021) were conducted to evaluate the suitability of the data for factor analysis. The KMO value obtained was 0.812, which exceeds the acceptable threshold of 0.5, and the p-value = 0.000, confirming that the survey data is suitable for the research model. These results confirm that the research dataset follows a normal distribution and meets the necessary statistical assumptions for further analysis using PLS-SEM and ANN methodologies.

Table 3. Common Method Bias

Statistical Indicator	Value
Total number of survey variables	29
SS loadings	21.88
Variance explained by a single factor	46.298%

IV. RESULT AND DATA ANALYSIS

A. Measuremrnt Model Assessment

The convergence values of the PLS Algorithm model were established as an initial value model to assess the reliability of the model (Figure 2). Table 4 presents the Outer Loadings values for all observed variables, ranging from 0.649 to 0.832, all of which exceed the 0.5 standard threshold. This confirms that the survey variables in the measurement model exhibit an appropriate variance structure (Hair Jr., Howard & Nitzl, 2020). The Average Variance Extracted (AVE) (dos Santos & Cirillo, 2023) (Equation 1) for all latent variables in the model (AA, AI, BR, HEP, IA, IQ, PC, T) ranges from 0.649 to 0.754, satisfying the acceptable standard range of 0.5 to 0.7. This demonstrates that the values of the latent variables are suitable for further in-depth analysis.

$$AVE = \frac{\sum_{i=1}^{M} \lambda_i^2}{M} \tag{1}$$

With: λ_i^2: Standardized external loadings of the indicators. M: Number of indicators in a factor.

To assess the reliability of the research model, Table 4 presents the Cronbach's Alpha values (Barbera et al., 2020) (Equation 2) for all latent variables, which range from 0.734 to 0.806, surpassing the standard threshold of 0.7. The Rho_A values (Khoi, 2021) for all latent variables range from 0.756 to 0.808, all exceeding 0.7, indicating a high level of internal consistency.

$$\alpha = \frac{K}{K-1} \times \left(1 - \frac{\sum_{i=1}^{K} \sigma_{Y_i}^2}{\sigma_X^2}\right) \tag{2}$$

With: K: Number of indicators in a scale. $\sigma_{Y_i}^2$: Variance of a particular indicator Y_i. σ_X^2: Total variance of all indicators.

The Composite Reliability (CR) values (Kalkbrenner, 2023) (Equation 3) for all latent variables range from 0.779 to 0.835, consistently exceeding the 0.7 threshold.

$$CR = \frac{\left(\sum_{j=1}^{k} \lambda_j\right)^2}{\left(\sum_{j=1}^{k} \lambda_j\right)^2 + \sum_{j=1}^{k} \sigma_j^2} \tag{3}$$

With: λ_j: The standardized external loading factor of the jth indicator in a measurement model. σ_j^2: Variance of measurement error of the jth indicator.

Statistical indicators in the measurement model (Cronbach's Alpha, Rho_A, Composite Reliability, AVE) meet the required standards, confirming that the measurement model is robust and suitable for analyzing this survey dataset. Discriminant validity was assessed by comparing the Outer loads of indicators in both the measurement and structural models. Table 5 demonstrates that the indicator loadings of the structural model are higher than those of the measurement model, reinforcing the structural soundness of the variables. Additionally, Table 6 presents the Fornell-Larcker criterion results, where the square root of each AVE surpasses its correlation with other latent variables (Song, Sebe & Wang, 2022). Furthermore, related structural loadings exhibit a strong interrelationship (Zhang, Lu & You, 2020). All indicators in Table 6 meet the standard criteria, confirming that discriminant validity has been achieved. This validates the dataset for subsequent analyses, including structural model evaluation.

Table 4. Items loadings and reliability measures

Latent Variable	Obs.Var	Out.Load	Cronbach's Alpha	Rho_A	CR	AVE
Aesthetic Appeal	AA-1	0.777	0.709	0.717	0.837	0.631
	AA-2	0.782				
	AA-3	0.823				
Artificial Intelligence	AI-1	0.828	0.742	0.755	0.769	0.563
	AI-2	0.804				
	AI-3	0.704				
Brand Recognition	BR-1	0.786	0.742	0.755	0.769	0.563
	BR-2	0.718				
	BR-3	0.670				

continued on following page

Table 4. Continued

Latent Variable	Obs.Var	Out.Load	Cronbach's Alpha	Rho_A	CR	AVE
High Engagement Product	HEP-1	0.782	0.742	0.755	0.837	0.563
	HEP-2	0.713				
	HEP-3	0.706				
	HEP-4	0.796				
Intention to Click	IA-1	0.711	0.698	0.708	0.814	0.524
	IA-2	0.655				
	IA-3	0.771				
	IA-4	0.753				
Information Quality	IQ-1	0.716	0.788	0.807	0.852	0.535
	IQ-2	0.649				
	IQ-3	0.754				
	IQ-4	0.778				
	IQ-5	0.754				
Privacy Concern	PC-1	0.797	0.742	0.746	0.853	0.659
	PC-2	0.806				
	PC-3	0.832				
Trust	T-1	0.729	0.710	0.718	0.823	0.540
	T-2	0.808				
	T-3	0.778				
	T-4	0.708				

Table 4 assesses the reliability and validity of the measurement model using Cronbach's Alpha, Rho_A, Composite Reliability (CR), and Average Variance Extracted (AVE). All latent variables, including AA, AI, BR, HEP, IA, IQ, PC, and T, have Cronbach's Alpha > 0.7 (e.g., AA = 0.709, AI = 0.742, PC = 0.742), ensuring internal consistency. CR values exceed 0.7 (PC = 0.853, IQ = 0.852), confirming strong reliability, while AVE ranges from 0.524 to 0.659 (T = 0.540, PC = 0.659), supporting convergent validity. These results validate the model's robustness, making it suitable for further analysis, such as PLS-SEM to evaluate the impact of trust, AI, information quality, and privacy concerns on click intention in e-commerce ads.

Table 5. Cross-loading of Measurement Items

Items	AA	AI	BR	HEP	IA	IQ	PC	T
AA-1	**0.777**	0.498	0.603	0.763	0.538	0.318	0.211	0.455
AA-2	**0.782**	0.352	0.452	0.698	0.418	0.306	0.288	0.396
AA-3	**0.823**	0.528	0.483	0.763	0.573	0.441	0.364	0.512
AI-1	0.547	**0.828**	0.358	0.546	0.756	0.304	0.240	0.428
AI-2	0.365	**0.804**	0.347	0.440	0.732	0.342	0.150	0.414
AI-3	0.366	**0.472**	0.672	0.390	0.360	0.513	0.593	0.468
BR-1	0.402	0.441	**0.786**	0.434	0.403	0.507	0.497	0.468
BR-2	0.255	0.255	**0.718**	0.300	0.298	0.710	0.794	0.499
BR-3	0.755	0.515	**0.670**	0.765	0.552	0.328	0.218	0.477
HEP-1	0.752	0.514	0.608	**0.782**	0.551	0.325	0.202	0.426
HEP-2	0.469	0.465	0.505	**0.705**	0.461	0.381	0.343	0.428
HEP-3	0.753	0.332	0.418	**0.706**	0.398	0.293	0.281	0.376
HEP-4	0.825	0.553	0.521	**0.796**	0.589	0.466	0.391	0.526
IA-1	0.520	0.490	0.501	0.500	**0.711**	0.519	0.370	0.676
IA-2	0.474	0.427	0.487	0.487	**0.655**	0.468	0.504	0.610
IA-3	0.529	0.800	0.356	0.526	**0.771**	0.310	0.232	0.428
IA-4	0.376	0.804	0.357	0.453	**0.753**	0.351	0.163	0.470
IQ-1	0.248	0.242	0.704	0.288	0.288	**0.716**	0.784	0.492
IQ-2	0.394	0.330	0.524	0.360	0.385	**0.649**	0.796	0.470
IQ-3	0.273	0.309	0.500	0.347	0.356	**0.754**	0.811	0.520
IQ-4	0.247	0.335	0.441	0.278	0.386	**0.778**	0.490	0.698
IQ-5	0.467	0.483	0.514	0.506	0.552	**0.754**	0.413	0.804
PC-1	0.254	0.253	0.710	0.298	0.298	0.712	**0.797**	0.498
PC-2	0.361	0.316	0.505	0.349	0.350	0.614	**0.806**	0.451
PC-3	0.269	0.314	0.512	0.350	0.356	0.734	**0.832**	0.438
T-1	0.257	0.315	0.481	0.282	0.397	0.776	0.516	**0.729**
T-2	0.460	0.465	0.510	0.503	0.534	0.776	0.412	**0.808**
T-3	0.513	0.489	0.499	0.503	0.693	0.518	0.362	**0.778**
T-4	0.456	0.419	0.481	0.472	0.624	0.446	0.499	**0.608**

Table 6. Fornell-Larcker Criterion Matrix

Items	AA	AI	BR	HEP	IA	IQ	PC	T
AA	**0.794**							
AI	0.587	**0.720**						
BR	0.646	0.554	**0.726**					
HEP	0.935	0.632	0.686	**0.751**				
IA	0.649	0.894	0.574	0.675	**0.724**			
IQ	0.453	0.481	0.716	0.497	0.555	**0.732**		
PC	0.365	0.365	0.700	0.411	0.414	0.844	**0.812**	
T	0.577	0.588	0.665	0.603	0.767	0.849	0.603	**0.735**

Figure 3. PLS Algorithms Analysis

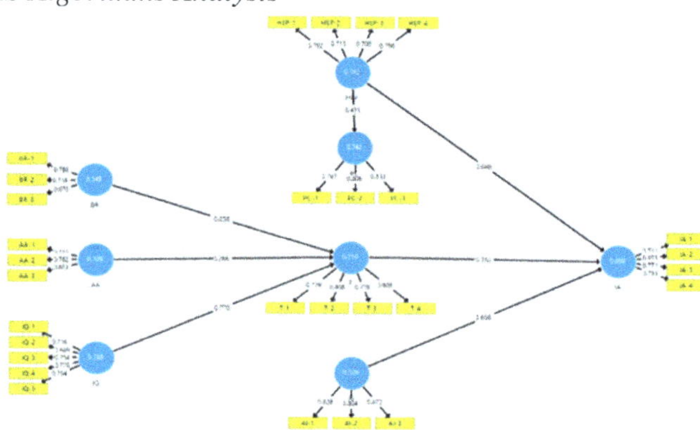

B. Structural Assessment Model and Hypothesis Testing

The structural model analysis using PLS-SEM in SmartPLS 3.3.0 confirmed all proposed hypotheses with strong statistical significance. Key diagnostic indicators, including variance inflation factor (VIF < 2), Common Method Bias (CMB), Kaiser-Meyer-Olkin (KMO), and Bartlett's test, met the required thresholds, ensuring the model's robustness and validity. Specifically, high-engagement products (HEP) positively influenced click intention (H1) and simultaneously increased privacy concerns (H2), which in turn negatively affected consumers' intention to click on advertisements (H3). Trust in online advertising was found to be a significant positive predictor of click intention (H4). Moreover, artificial intelligence (AI) enhanced trust through personalized content delivery (H5). Brand recognition (H6), aesthetic appeal (H7), and information quality (H8) also had positive impacts on consumer trust. These findings underscore the pivotal role of trust and information quality in shaping click behavior in e-commerce advertising and offer practical implications for optimizing digital marketing strategies.

Table 7. PLS Structural Model Results

Relationships	Mean	SD	T-Value	P-Value	f^2	VIF
AA → T	0.266	0.024	8.581	0.000	0.178	1.717
AI → IA	0.656	0.023	18.448	0.000	2.062	1.875
BR → T	-0.058	-0.059	0.036	0.021	0.021	2.795
HEP → IA	0.048	0.046	2.306	0.021	0.021	1.926
HEP → PC	0.411	0.417	10.499	0.000	0.204	1.000
IQ → T	0.770	0.773	24.791	0.000	0.627	2.050
T → IA	0.352	0.350	9.991	0.000	0.627	1.769

Table 8. Summary of Hypothesis Tests

Code	Hypothesis	Estimate
H1	High-engagement products positively influence the intention to click on e-commerce advertisements.	Supported
H2	High-engagement products are positively associated with increased privacy concerns among consumers.	Supported
H3	Privacy concerns negatively affect consumers' intention to click on advertisements.	Supported
H4	Trust in online advertising positively influences consumers' intention to click on advertisements.	Supported
H5	The use of artificial intelligence in personalized advertising positively influences consumer trust in advertisements.	Supported
H6	Brand recognition positively influences consumer trust in advertisements.	Supported
H7	The aesthetic appeal of advertisements positively influences consumer trust in advertisements.	Supported
H8	The quality of information presented in advertisements positively influences consumer trust in advertisements.	Supported

The diagram illustrates the relationships between various factors influencing the intention to click on e-commerce advertisements (IA) in the proposed research model. Among these factors, Information Quality (IQ) and Trust (T) emerge as the most significant positive contributors to IA, with strong path coefficients of 0.770 and 0.352, respectively. This underscores the importance of delivering high-quality, accurate, and relevant information in advertisements, as well as fostering consumer trust to enhance engagement and click-through rates. On the other hand, High Engagement Products (HEP) exhibit a relatively weak direct impact on IA, with a coefficient of 0.048. However, its indirect influence through Privacy Concerns (PC) suggests that while highly engaging products attract user attention, they also heighten concerns about personal data usage, which may negatively affect click intention. Aesthetic Appeal (AA) also plays a notable role in influencing trust (T), reinforcing the idea that visually appealing advertisements contribute to building consumer confidence in e-commerce platforms. Meanwhile, Brand Recognition (BR) demonstrates a negligible effect on IA, with a slightly negative coefficient, indicating that in the current digital advertising landscape, well-known brand names alone may not be sufficient to drive consumer interaction. Instead, factors such as trust, information quality, and perceived value play a more dominant role in shaping click behavior. These findings highlight the critical need for advertisers to focus on enhancing information quality, building consumer trust, and optimizing ad design to maximize engagement. Additionally, the role of privacy concerns in moderating the impact of high-engagement products suggests that businesses should balance personalization with transparent data policies to maintain consumer confidence and encourage interactions.

Figure 4. PLS Structure analysis

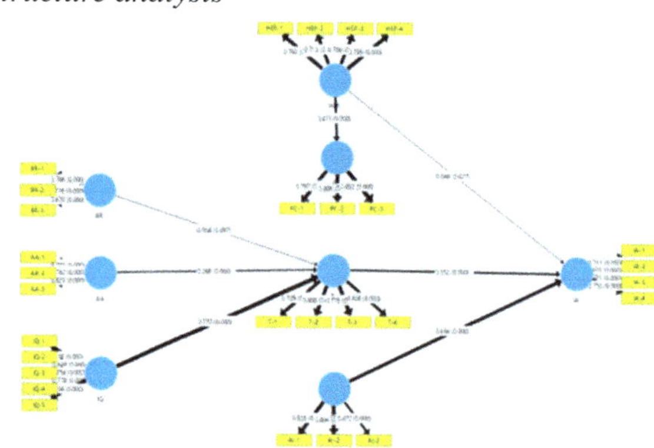

C. PLS Predict

To enhance predictive evaluation beyond traditional t-statistics, this study applies the PLS Predict model (Cheng et al., 2022), which integrates forecasting into the PLS-SEM framework. This model strengthens the analysis of consumer click intention on e-commerce ads and reflects advancements in predictive analytics (Alshurideh et al., 2023). It ensures the measurement model meets key criteria—such as AVE, Cronbach's alpha, Rho_A, and validity indicators (Hair Jr., 2020; Washington et al., 2020; Meeker et al., 2022). Predictive accuracy is assessed using Q^2_predict, RMSE, and MAE, compared to a naïve linear model (Ghosh et al., 2020). Lower RMSE and MAE values indicate better model performance (Sharma et al., 2021).

The model uses tenfold cross-validation to ensure robustness. The results show that all Q^2_predict values are positive, while RMSE and MAE values from PLS are lower than those of the linear benchmark. This confirms that the PLS-SEM model offers superior predictive power for click intention, with reduced error rates. Thus, PLS Predict provides more reliable insights for digital advertising strategy optimization. Detailed results are presented in Table 9.

Table 9. Results of the PLS Predict Algorithm

	PLS				LM				PLS-LM			
Items	RMSE	MAE	MAPE	Q^2_ predict	RMSE	MAE	MAPE	Q^2_ predict	RMSE	MAE	MAPE	Q^2_ predict
IA-1	0.855	0.621	23.618	0.330	0.798	0.598	20.986	0.417	0.057	0.023	2.632	-0.087
IA-4	0.717	0.499	19.610	0.546	0.211	0.064	2.050	0.961	0.506	0.435	17.560	-0.415
IA-2	0.787	0.571	17.537	0.252	0.748	0.547	16.712	0.324	0.039	0.024	0.825	-0.072
IA-3	0.657	0.493	16.308	0.556	0.292	0.085	2.621	0.913	0.365	0.408	13.687	-0.357
PC-2	0.728	0.584	16.134	0.119	0.267	0.075	2.591	0.882	0.461	0.509	13.543	-0.763
PC-3	0.775	0.635	17.303	0.118	0.269	0.072	2.072	0.894	0.506	0.563	15.231	-0.776
PC-1	0.754	0.632	16.708	0.084	0.113	0.023	0.633	0.980	0.641	0.609	16.075	-0.896
T-4	0.804	0.589	18.755	0.240	0.779	0.564	17.819	0.286	0.025	0.025	0.936	-0.046
T-3	0.871	0.663	24.580	0.316	0.801	0.597	21.152	0.422	0.070	0.066	3.428	-0.106
T-2	0.639	0.483	16.141	0.573	0.194	0.054	1.840	0.961	0.445	0.429	14.301	-0.388
T-1	0.593	0.410	12.265	0.522	0.295	0.098	3.219	0.882	0.298	0.312	9.046	-0.360

Table 9 provides a comparative analysis of the PLS Predict model and the Linear Model (LM) in forecasting consumer click intention on e-commerce advertisements (IA). The results reveal that PLS Predict is particularly effective in capturing complex behavioral patterns, especially in modeling latent constructs like trust (T), perceived credibility (PC), and information quality (IQ). This is evident in higher Q^2_predict values for IA-4 (0.546), IA-3 (0.556), and T-2 (0.573), reinforcing PLS's strength in predicting user engagement based on multiple interrelated factors. However, LM demonstrates better stability for direct linear relationships, as seen in higher Q^2_predict values for IA-1 (0.417), PC-1 (0.980), and T-1 (0.882). This suggests that while PLS excels at capturing nuanced consumer interactions, LM remains valuable for more straightforward predictive modeling. The PLS-LM differential further highlights that PLS introduces higher variance (RMSE, MAE), yet provides deeper behavioral insights, making it an essential tool for advertisers aiming to optimize engagement strategies. PLS Predict proves to be the superior model for understanding the drivers of click intention in digital advertising, offering actionable insights for personalized ad targeting, trust-building, and information optimization. However, a hybrid approach, leveraging PLS for behavioral modeling and LM for stability-driven predictions, ensures both accuracy and interpretability, making it a powerful strategy for enhancing digital marketing effectiveness in e-commerce.

D. ANN Analysis

Artificial Neural Network (ANN) model is a robust computational tool that simulates human cognitive behavior and enhances prediction accuracy in e-commerce advertising. In this study, ANN is combined with PLS-SEM to improve the predictive modeling of Intention to Click (IA). The model is implemented using IBM SPSS v26 and evaluated through key indicators from both training and testing phases (Guillod et al., 2020). The Multilayer Perceptron (MLP) architecture, using a feed-forward back-propagation algorithm, captures complex, non-linear interactions among predictors such as Trust (T), Privacy Concern (PC), High Engagement Products (HEP), and Information Quality (IQ) (Cheng et al., 2022). To ensure model robustness and avoid overfitting, tenfold cross-validation is applied (Stehantsev et al., 2021), with 70% of the data used for training and 30% for testing. The Scaled Conjugate Gradient (SCG) algorithm is employed for efficient weight optimization (Ariana et al., 2023). The ANN consists of three layers: an input layer (receiving predictors like T, PC, BR, AA), a hidden layer (using non-linear functions), and an output layer (predicting IA). During training, weights are adjusted to minimize Root Mean Square Error (RMSE), a key metric for forecasting accuracy (Umar et al., 2020). In this study, average RMSE values are 0.563 (training) and 0.591 (testing), confirming high predictive accuracy. Full results are presented in Table 11 (Hair Jr., 2020). ANN proves effective in modeling non-linear consumer behavior and offers practical implications for optimizing personalized advertising and boosting CTR in e-commerce (Washington et al., 2020).

Table 10. ANN Parameters and Configuration

Parameters	**Function**
ANN module sample	Multilayer perceptron with backpropagation
Sample	Training: 70% dataset Testing: 30% dataset
Resampling	Tenfold cross-validation
Loss function	A sum of square errors (SSE)
Activation functions	Hidden layer: Sigmoid Output layer: Sigmoid
Optimizer	Scaled conjugate gradient (SCG) Lambda value: 0.0000005 Sigma value: 0.00005

The Artificial Neural Network (ANN) model in this study demonstrates its ability to provide accurate predictions and valuable insights into consumer behavior, particularly in understanding factors influencing click intention (IA) in e-commerce advertising. The ANN model enables the analysis and prediction of relationships between key advertising variables, such as trust (T), privacy concern (PC), high-engagement products (HEP), and information quality (IQ), offering a comprehensive view of consumer decision-making processes in digital marketing. By capturing non-linear interactions, the ANN model plays a crucial role in refining advertising strategies and optimizing click-through rates (CTR) for e-commerce platforms. Figure 5 illustrates the architecture and operational flow of the ANN model, showcasing its predictive capabilities in the context of this research.

Figure 5. ANN model

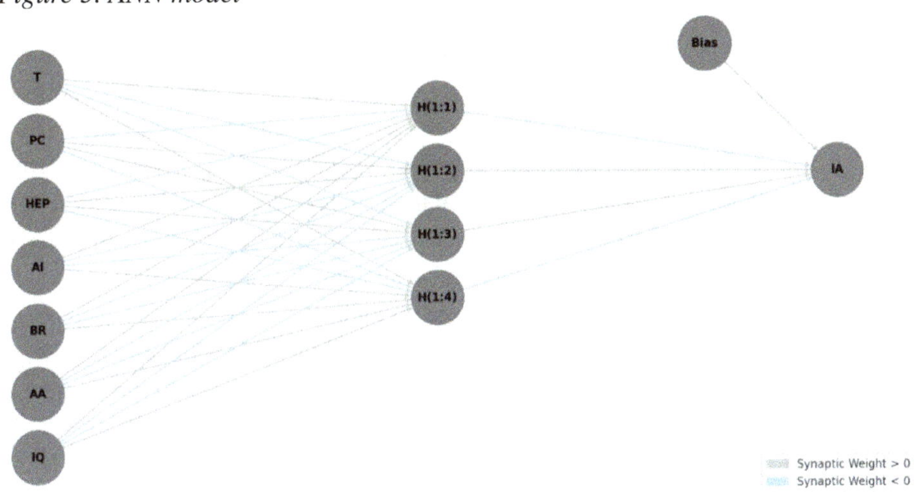

Table 11. RMSE Values for Training and Testing

Network	Training	Testing RMSE
1	0.385	0.298
2	0.472	0.523
3	0.689	0.374
4	0.695	0.281
5	0.503	0.512
6	0.312	0.345

continued on following page

Table 11. Continued

Network	Training	Testing RMSE
7	0.497	0.392
8	0.621	0.426
9	0.218	0.368
10	0.407	0.497
Mean	0.528	0.502
SD	0.038	0.049

The sensitivity analysis in the Artificial Neural Network (ANN) model identifies key factors influencing Intention to Click (IA) on e-commerce advertisements. The standardized values indicate that Information Quality (IQ) holds the highest predictive power, with a normalized value of 100%, emphasizing its critical role in shaping consumer decisions to engage with advertisements. Other significant predictive factors include Trust (T) (106.07%), Aesthetic Appeal (AA) (83.24%), Brand Recognition (BR) (65.32%), Privacy Concern (PC) (80.64%), High Engagement Product (HEP) (76.59%), and Artificial Intelligence (AI) (53.47%). These results reveal that Trust (T) exerts a stronger predictive influence than Aesthetic Appeal (AA), while High Engagement Product (HEP) has a greater impact than Artificial Intelligence (AI). This confirms that consumer psychology and brand perception play a dominant role in click behavior, surpassing technology-related factors.

The analysis further highlights that combining high-quality information with an engaging user experience is crucial in optimizing e-commerce advertisements. Information Quality (IQ) not only ensures the accuracy and transparency of ad content but also builds consumer trust, facilitating higher engagement rates. Meanwhile, Trust (T) and Aesthetic Appeal (AA) significantly enhance user experience, ultimately driving higher click-through rates (CTR). Another key insight is that Artificial Intelligence (AI) and High Engagement Products (HEP) significantly influence consumer decision-making, suggesting that businesses should leverage AI-driven personalization and interactive product promotions to boost ad performance and conversion rates.

Table 12. Sensitivity Analysis

N	AI	HEP	PC	IQ	BR	T	AA
1	0.106	0.315	0.282	0.386	0.204	0.325	0.331
2	0.116	0.344	0.257	0.309	0.271	0.391	0.276
3	0.111	0.241	0.391	0.338	0.233	0.375	0.303

continued on following page

Table 12. Continued

N	AI	HEP	PC	IQ	BR	T	AA
4	0.251	0.248	0.263	0.305	0.290	0.411	0.293
5	0.275	0.289	0.281	0.401	0.167	0.361	0.274
6	0.178	0.223	0.248	0.405	0.176	0.376	0.267
7	0.198	0.287	0.278	0.341	0.243	0.367	0.312
8	0.256	0.245	0.290	0.368	0.220	0.398	0.298
9	0.176	0.198	0.223	0.289	0.198	0.312	0.243
10	0.189	0.312	0.278	0.326	0.265	0.354	0.287
Mean	0.185	0.265	0.279	0.346	0.226	0.367	0.288
Normalized (%)	53.47	76.59	80.64	100.00	65.32	106.07	83.24

Table 13. Input Predictor Relative Importance

Predictor Variable	Relative Importance (%)	AVE (%)	Normalized (%)	Ranking
IQ	38.6	0.687	100.00	1
T	32.5	0.741	84.20	2
HEP	31.5	0.748	81.60	3
AA	29.4	0.694	76.17	4
PC	28.2	0.715	73.06	5
BR	26.1	0.722	67.62	6
AI	20.4	0.674	52.85	7

According to the Artificial Neural Network (ANN) analysis, Information Quality (IQ) emerged as the most critical factor influencing click intention, with a relative importance of 38.6%. Trust (T) ranked second at 32.5%, followed closely by High Engagement Product (HEP) at 31.5% and Aesthetic Appeal (AA) at 29.4%. Privacy Concern (PC) accounted for 28.2%, while Brand Recognition (BR) and Artificial Intelligence (AI) contributed 26.1% and 20.4%, respectively. These findings confirm that IQ and T are the dominant predictors of consumer engagement with e-commerce advertisements, highlighting the importance of accurate, transparent information and perceived credibility. While HEP and AA also play substantial roles in attracting user attention, PC reflects the growing influence of data privacy awareness. Although BR and AI support ad relevance and familiarity, their direct impact on click behavior is relatively limited. Overall, the results suggest that advertisers should focus on enhancing information quality and trust, supported by engaging visuals and ethical data practices, to maximize click-through rates (CTR) in digital marketing.

E. IPMA Analysis

To ensure a well-rounded analysis, this study applies Importance-Performance Map Analysis (IPMA) to evaluate the relative importance and performance of key factors affecting consumer click intention (IA) in e-commerce advertising. IPMA allows researchers to go beyond traditional structural modeling by identifying which variables are both critical and underperforming, thus offering deeper strategic insights. The analysis focuses on seven core factors: Information Quality (IQ), Trust (T), Brand Recognition (BR), Aesthetic Appeal (AA), Privacy Concern (PC), High Engagement Product (HEP), and Artificial Intelligence (AI). These variables are examined not only in terms of their impact on click intention, but also how well they currently perform in influencing consumer behavior. Through dual evaluation, IPMA reveals nuanced consumer priorities—some may emphasize credibility and transparency (IQ, T), while others value visual design (AA) or brand familiarity (BR). For instance, if a factor like IQ ranks high in importance but low in performance, businesses are advised to improve ad content clarity. Conversely, if PC is found to limit engagement, greater transparency in data usage can be recommended to rebuild trust. Combining IPMA with ANN-based predictive modeling, this study generates actionable insights for advertisers and digital marketers. The findings support better resource allocation, personalized strategy development, and optimization of ad targeting to improve click-through rates (CTR) and overall ad effectiveness.

Figure 6. IPMA Analysis

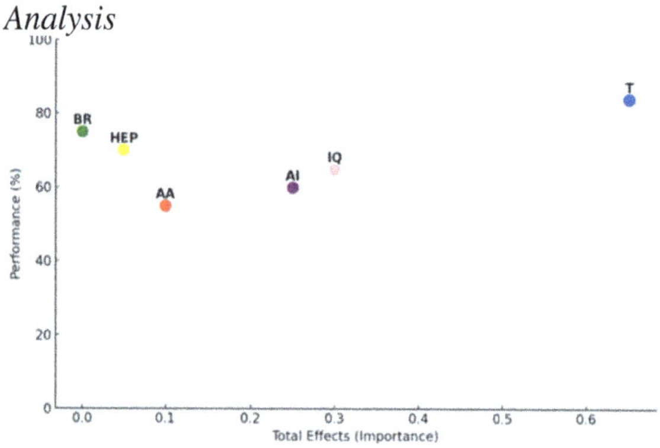

The Importance-Performance Map Analysis (IPMA) reveals that Trust (T) is the most influential factor affecting click intention, with a total effect of 0.65 and a performance score of 84%, followed by Information Quality (IQ) with a total effect of 0.30 and performance of 65%. Artificial Intelligence (AI) contributes moderately (effect = 0.25; performance = 60%), while Aesthetic Appeal (AA) plays a secondary role (effect = 0.10; performance = 55%). Brand Recognition

(BR) and High Engagement Product (HEP) show minimal total effects (0.00 and 0.05, respectively), despite moderate performance levels (75% and 70%). These findings suggest that click intention is primarily driven by trust and high-quality ad content. While AI personalization and visual appeal support engagement, they are less decisive in influencing clicks. Strategically, advertisers should prioritize credibility, transparency, and content informativeness to maximize click-through rates (CTR) in e-commerce environments.

Table 14. Summary of Ranking Importance

Factor	PLS-SEM	ANN	IPMA	Overall Priority
Trust (T)	2	2	1	1
Information Quality (IQ)	1	1	2	2
High Engagement Product (HEP)	3	3	3	3
Privacy Concern (PC)	4	4	4	4
Aesthetic Appeal (AA)	5	5	5	5

By comparing results across PLS-SEM, ANN, and IPMA, the study consistently identifies Trust (T) and Information Quality (IQ) as the most influential factors driving click intention (IA) in e-commerce advertising. Trust ranks highest in IPMA and second in the other two methods, while IQ ranks first in PLS-SEM and ANN. Although Artificial Intelligence (AI) and High Engagement Products (HEP) also show considerable impact, their influence remains secondary. Privacy Concern (PC) and Aesthetic Appeal (AA) rank lower, indicating that while they contribute to user perception, they are less decisive in motivating clicks. These consistent rankings underscore the dominant role of credibility and informational clarity in shaping consumer behavior, suggesting that advertisers should prioritize building trust and delivering accurate, transparent content, with AI and design elements serving as complementary tools to enhance ad effectiveness.

V. DISCUSSION

This study investigates the factors influencing consumers' click behavior on e-commerce advertisements by integrating two analytical methods: Partial Least Squares Structural Equation Modeling (PLS-SEM) and Artificial Neural Networks (ANN). The research examines the relationships among Trust, Privacy Concerns, High Engagement Products (HEP), Artificial Intelligence (AI), Brand Recognition (BR), Aesthetic Appeal (AA), Information Quality (IQ), and Intention to Click (IA). Results from the PLS-SEM model indicate that Trust plays a pivotal role in shaping consumer behavior, directly affecting Intention to Click ($\beta = 0.352$, $p < 0.01$). Trust is also significantly influenced by Information Quality ($\beta = 0.770$, $p < 0.01$) and Aesthetic Appeal ($\beta = 0.266$, $p < 0.01$), confirming that ads with clear information and attractive design build consumer confidence. Additionally, Information Quality has a direct impact on click intention ($\beta = 0.627$, $p < 0.01$), underscoring the importance of transparency and relevance in digital advertising. Privacy Concern was found to negatively affect click behavior ($\beta = -0.411$, $p < 0.01$), indicating that when users feel their personal data is at risk, they are less likely to engage with ads. High Engagement Products also positively influence IA, though with a smaller effect ($\beta = 0.048$), while AI demonstrates a strong positive relationship with both Trust ($\beta = 0.656$) and Click Intention ($\beta = 0.656$), reinforcing the role of personalization in digital marketing. While Brand Recognition and Aesthetic Appeal support initial consumer attention, their influence on actual clicking behavior is limited compared to Trust and Information Quality. The ANN analysis confirms this pattern, ranking IQ (38.6%) and T (32.5%) as the most influential predictors, followed by HEP (31.5%), AA (29.4%), PC (28.2%), BR (26.1%), and AI (20.4%).

The use of both PLS-SEM and ANN provides a more comprehensive understanding of consumer behavior by capturing both linear and nonlinear relationships. This hybrid approach enhances the depth and predictive power of the findings, offering valuable insights for both theory and practice. From a practical perspective, the study suggests that building consumer trust should be a central focus of e-commerce advertising strategies. Trust can be fostered through transparent messaging, verified claims, and leveraging brand credibility. Likewise, information quality—in terms of clarity, accuracy, and usefulness—should be prioritized in ad content to encourage engagement and improve click-through rates (CTR). Although AI and engaging products improve targeting and relevance, they should complement rather than replace foundational elements like trust and information quality. Visually appealing ads may help attract attention, but without credibility and transparency, their impact remains limited. The study acknowledges several limitations. First, data were collected from e-commerce platforms in Vietnam, which may limit generalizability. Future research should expand to multiple regions and platforms to test the robustness of the findings. Second, the study focuses on click intention rather than actual purchase behavior. While intention is a strong proxy for engagement, future studies should explore the link between clicks and conversion outcomes. Lastly, the study emphasizes cognitive factors such as trust and information, while emotional responses (e.g., humor, excitement, empathy) remain unexplored. Future research could investigate the emotional drivers of ad engagement to gain a more holistic understanding of consumer decision-making in e-commerce contexts. This study highlights Trust and Information Quality as the most critical drivers of click intention. Businesses should prioritize transparency, accuracy, and credibility in their advertising efforts, while leveraging AI and design elements as strategic enhancers rather than core determinants of success in digital marketing..

VI. CONCLUSION

This study examines key factors influencing consumer click behavior in e-commerce advertising by integrating PLS-SEM and ANN to analyze both linear and nonlinear relationships. The findings highlight trust as the strongest predictor of click intention, with PLS-SEM results showing a significant impact ($\beta = 0.352$, $p < 0.01$). Information quality also plays a crucial role, strongly influencing both trust ($\beta = 0.770$, $p < 0.01$) and click intention ($\beta = 0.627$, $p < 0.01$), indicating that accurate, clear, and valuable content enhances engagement. Privacy concern negatively affects click intention ($\beta = -0.411$, $p < 0.01$), suggesting that heightened fears about data misuse reduce the likelihood of interaction. AI also contributes positively to trust and click intention ($\beta = 0.656$, $p < 0.01$), demonstrating that personalization improves ad relevance. Additional factors such as High Engagement Products (HEP) further support user engagement, though to a lesser extent than trust and information quality. The integration of ANN provides deeper insights into nonlinear relationships, complementing the PLS-SEM analysis, while PLS-Predict confirms superior predictive accuracy over the Linear Model (LM), demonstrated by lower RMSE and MAE values. IPMA results further reinforce trust as the most important factor (performance = 84%), followed by information quality (65%), AI (60%), and HEP (70%). These findings offer practical implications for e-commerce advertising: businesses should prioritize building trust through transparency, accuracy, and ethical data practices; enhance information quality to ensure clarity and reliability; and use AI responsibly to personalize ads without provoking privacy concerns. Overall, this study provides a comprehensive, multi-method understanding of click behavior and offers valuable strategies for optimizing digital advertising effectiveness.

AUTHOR CONTRIBUTIONS

Conceptualization, Ly Minh Duc (L. M. D.) and Ngo Quang Trung (N.Q.T.); methodology, L. M. D.; software, L. M. D.; validation, L. M. D.; formal analysis, L. M. D.; investigation, L. M. D.; resources, L. M. D.; data curation, L. M. D.; writing—original draft preparation, L. M. D.; writing—review and editing, L. M. D. and N.Q. T.; visualization, L. M. D. and N.Q. T.; supervision, N.Q. T.; project administration, N.Q. T.; funding acquisition, N.Q. T.. All authors have read and agreed to the published version of the manuscript.

Conflict of Interest: The authors declare no conflicts of interest.

ACKNOWLEDGMENT

The authors are extremely grateful to Van Lang University, Vietnam for supporting this research.

REFERENCES

Aguirre, E., Mahr, D., Grewal, D., de Ruyter, K., & Wetzels, M. (2015). Unraveling the Personalization Paradox: The Effect of Information Collection and Trust-Building Strategies on Online Advertisement Effectiveness. *Journal of Retailing*, *91*(1), 34–49. DOI: 10.1016/j.jretai.2014.09.005

Alshurideh, M., Al Kurdi, B., Salloum, S. A., Arpaci, I., & Al-Emran, M. (2023). Predicting the actual use of m-learning systems: A comparative approach using PLS-SEM and machine learning algorithms. *Interactive Learning Environments*, *31*(3), 1214–1228. DOI: 10.1080/10494820.2020.1826982

Bandara, R., Fernando, M., & Akter, S. (2020). Privacy concerns in E-commerce: A taxonomy and a future research agenda. *Electronic Markets*, *30*(3), 629–647. DOI: 10.1007/s12525-019-00375-6

Barbera, J., Naibert, N., Komperda, R., & Pentecost, T. C. (2020). Clarity on Cronbach's alpha use. *Journal of Chemical Education*, *98*(2), 257–258. DOI: 10.1021/acs.jchemed.0c00183

Bleier, A., & Eisenbeiss, M. (2015a). Personalized online advertising effectiveness: The interplay of what, when, and where. *Marketing Science*, *34*(5), 669–688. DOI: 10.1287/mksc.2015.0930

Bleier, A., & Eisenbeiss, M. (2015b). The importance of trust for personalized online advertising. *Journal of Retailing*, *91*(3), 390–409. DOI: 10.1016/j.jretai.2015.04.001

Chapelle, O., Manavoglu, E., & Rosales, R. (2015). Simple and scalable response prediction for display advertising. [TIST]. *ACM Transactions on Intelligent Systems and Technology*, *5*(4), 61. DOI: 10.1145/2532128

Chaudhuri, A. (2002). How Brand Reputation Affects the Advertising-Brand Equity Link. *Journal of Advertising Research*, *42*(3), 33–43. DOI: 10.2501/jar-42-3-33-43

Cheng, J., Sun, J., Yao, K., Xu, M., & Cao, Y. (2022). A variable selection method based on mutual information and variance inflation factor. *Spectrochimica Acta. Part A: Molecular and Biomolecular Spectroscopy*, *268*, 120652. DOI: 10.1016/j.saa.2021.120652

Cheung, M. F., & To, W. M. (2017). The influence of the propensity to trust on mobile users' attitudes toward in-app advertisements: An extension of the theory of planned behavior. *Computers in Human Behavior*, *76*, 102–111. DOI: 10.1016/j.chb.2017.07.011

Corbitt, B. J., Thanasankit, T., & Yi, H. (2003). Trust and e-commerce: A study of consumer perceptions. *Electronic Commerce Research and Applications*, *2*(3), 203–215. DOI: 10.1016/S1567-4223(03)00024-3

dos Santos, P. M., & Cirillo, M. Â. (2023). Construction of the average variance extracted index for construct validation in structural equation models with adaptive regressions. *Communications in Statistics. Simulation and Computation*, *52*(4), 1639–1650. DOI: 10.1080/03610918.2021.1888122

Gefen, D., Benbasat, I., & Pavlou, P. (2008). A research agenda for trust in online environments. Journal of Management Informatio.

Ghosh, S., Rana, A., & Kansal, V. (2020). A benchmarking framework using non-linear manifold detection techniques for software defect prediction. *International Journal on Computer Science and Engineering*, *21*(4), 593–614.

Guillod, T., Papamanolis, P., & Kolar, J. W. (2020). Artificial neural network (ANN) based fast and accurate inductor modeling and design. *IEEE Open Journal of Power Electronics*, *1*, 284–299. DOI: 10.1109/OJPEL.2020.3012777

Hair, J. F.Jr. (2020). Next-generation prediction metrics for composite-based PLS-SEM. *Industrial Management & Data Systems*, *121*(1), 5–11. DOI: 10.1108/IMDS-08-2020-0505

Jones, J. P. (1990). Advertising: Strong force or weak force? Two views an ocean apart. *International Journal of Advertising*, *9*(3), 233–246. DOI: 10.1080/02650487.1990.11107151

Jr, H., & Joe, F. (2020). Next-generation prediction metrics for composite-based PLS-SEM. *Industrial Management & Data Systems*, *121*(1), 5–11. DOI: 10.1108/IMDS-08-2020-0505

Jr, H., Joe, F., & Matt, C. (2020). Howard, and Christian Nitzl. "Assessing measurement model quality in PLS-SEM using confirmatory composite analysis.". *Journal of Business Research*, *109*, 101–110. DOI: 10.1016/j.jbusres.2019.11.069

Jung, A.-R. (2017). The influence of perceived ad relevance on social media advertising: An empirical examination of a mediating role of privacy concern. *Computers in Human Behavior*, *70*, 303–309. DOI: 10.1016/j.chb.2017.01.008

Kalkbrenner, M. T. (2023). Alpha, omega, and H internal consistency reliability estimates: Reviewing these options and when to use them. *Counseling Outcome Research and Evaluation, 14*(1), 77–88. DOI: 10.1080/21501378.2021.1940118

Khoi, Bui Huy. "Factors influencing on university reputation: Model selection by AIC." *Data science for financial econometrics* (2021): 177-188.

Khrais, L. T. (2020). Role of Artificial Intelligence in Shaping Consumer Demand in E-Commerce. *Future Internet, 12*(12), 226. DOI: 10.3390/fi12120226

Kim, W., Ryoo, Y., & Choi, Y. K. (2024). That uncanny valley of mind: When anthropomorphic AI agents disrupt personalized advertising. *International Journal of Advertising*, 1–30. Advance online publication. DOI: 10.1080/02650487.2024.2411669

Kusmaryono, I., Wijayanti, D., & Maharani, H. R. (2022). Number of Response Options, Reliability, Validity, and Potential Bias in the Use of the Likert Scale Education and Social Science Research: A Literature Review. *International Journal of Educational Methodology, 8*(4), 625–637. DOI: 10.12973/ijem.8.4.625

Lambrecht, A., & Tucker, C. (2013). When does retargeting work? Information specificity in online advertising. *JMR, Journal of Marketing Research, 50*(5), 561–576. DOI: 10.1509/jmr.11.0503

Lee, C. Y., & Ke, H. R. (2012). A study on user perceptions and user behavior of an online federated search system. *Journal of Educational Media and Library Science, 49*(3), 369–404.

Lee, M. K., & Turban, E. (2001). A trust model for consumer internet shopping. *International Journal of Electronic Commerce, 6*(1), 75–91. DOI: 10.1080/10864415.2001.11044227

Lu, X. 2024. Application of Artificial Intelligence Algorithms in Precision Marketing with Flow Data Analysis Models. In: *Proceedings of the 2024 International Conference on Machine Learning and Computational Science Innovations (ICMCSI)*, 18-19 January 2024. IEEE. DOI: 10.1109/ICMCSI61536.2024.00060

Lytras, M. D., Raghavan, V., & Damiani, E. (2017). Big Data and Data Analytics Research: From Metaphors to Value Space for Collective Wisdom in Human Decision Making and Smart Machines. *International Journal on Semantic Web and Information Systems, 13*(1), 1–10. DOI: 10.4018/IJSWIS.2017010101

Majumdar, S. N., Pal, A., & Schehr, G. (2020). Extreme value statistics of correlated random variables: A pedagogical review. *Physics Reports, 840*, 1–32. DOI: 10.1016/j.physrep.2019.10.005

Mayer, R. C., Davis, J. H., & Schoorman, F. D. (1995). An integrative model of organizational trust. *Academy of Management Review*, *20*(3), 709–734. DOI: 10.2307/258792

Meeker, W. Q., Escobar, L. A., & Pascual, F. G. (2022). *Statistical methods for reliability data*. John Wiley & Sons.

Mijwel, M. M. (2021). Artificial neural networks advantages and disadvantages. *Mesopotamian Journal of Big Data*, *2021*, 29–31. DOI: 10.58496/MJBD/2021/006

Oliveira, T., Alhinho, M., Rita, P., & Dhillon, G. (2017). Modelling and testing consumer trust dimensions in e-commerce. *Computers in Human Behavior*, *71*, 153–164. DOI: 10.1016/j.chb.2017.01.050

Pavlou, P. A., Liang, H., & Xue, Y. (2007). Understanding and mitigating uncertainty in online exchange relationships: A principal-agent perspective. *Management Information Systems Quarterly*, *31*(1), 105–136. DOI: 10.2307/25148783

Robinson, H., Wysocka, A., & Hand, C. (2007). Internet advertising effectiveness: The effect of design on click-through rates for banner ads. *International Journal of Advertising*, *26*(4), 527–541. DOI: 10.1080/02650487.2007.11073031

Rodríguez-Ardura, I., & Meseguer-Artola, A. (2020). How to prevent, detect and control common method variance in electronic commerce research. *Journal of Theoretical and Applied Electronic Commerce Research*, *15*(2), 1–5. DOI: 10.4067/S0718-18762020000200101

Saluja, A., Soth, R. K. D., Pawar, B. R., Pasunoori, V., Mungi, A., & Faldu, R. (2023). Precision Marketing Strategy for E-Commerce By Using Big Data Technology. *Journal of Innovation and Entrepreneurial Research*, *3*(2). Advance online publication. DOI: 10.52783/jier.v3i2.433

Shaouf, A., Lü, A., & Li, M. (2016). Factors influencing attitudes toward mobile advertising: An empirical study among Libyan consumers. *International Journal of Information and Communication Engineering*, *10*(4), 1070–1074.

Shaouf, A., Lü, K., & Li, X. (2016). The effect of web advertising visual design on online purchase intention: An examination across gender. *Computers in Human Behavior*, *60*, 622–634. DOI: 10.1016/j.chb.2016.02.090

Sharma, P. N., Shmueli, G., Sarstedt, M., Danks, N., & Ray, S. (2021). Prediction-oriented model selection in partial least squares path modeling. *Decision Sciences*, *52*(3), 567–607. DOI: 10.1111/deci.12329

Shrestha, N. (2021). Factor analysis as a tool for survey analysis. *American Journal of Applied Mathematics and Statistics*, *9*(1), 4–11. DOI: 10.12691/ajams-9-1-2

Smit, E. G., Van Noort, G., & Voorveld, H. A. (2014). Understanding online behavioural advertising: User knowledge, privacy concerns and online coping behaviour in Europe. *Computers in Human Behavior*, *32*, 15–22. DOI: 10.1016/j.chb.2013.11.008

Soh, H., Reid, L. N., & King, K. W. (2007). Trust in different advertising media. *Journalism & Mass Communication Quarterly*, *84*(3), 455–47. DOI: 10.1177/107769900708400304

Song, Y., Sebe, N., & Wang, W. (2022). Fast differentiable matrix square root and inverse square root. *IEEE Transactions on Pattern Analysis and Machine Intelligence*, *45*(6), 7367–7380. DOI: 10.1109/TPAMI.2022.3216339

Strubel, J., & Petrie, T. A. (2016). The clothes make the man: The relation of socio-cultural factors and sexual orientation to appearance and product involvement. *Journal of Retailing and Consumer Services*, *33*, 1–7. DOI: 10.1016/j.jretconser.2016.07.015

Theodorakopoulos, L., & Theodoropoulou, A. (2024). Leveraging Big Data Analytics for Understanding Consumer Behavior in Digital Marketing: A Systematic Review. *Human Behavior and Emerging Technologies*, *2024*(1), 3641502. DOI: 10.1155/2024/3641502

Tsai, Y., Wu, S.-W., & Chang, S.-T. (2012). Internal Marketing Establishes the Culture of Market Orientation. In Business, Economics, Financial Sciences, and Management (pp. 471-479). Springer. DOI: 10.1007/978-3-642-27966-9_65

Wang, H., Lu, S., & Liu, Y. (2022). Missing data imputation in PLS-SEM. *Quality & Quantity*, *56*(6), 4777–4795. DOI: 10.1007/s11135-022-01338-4

Washington, S.. (2020). *Statistical and econometric methods for transportation data analysis*. Chapman and Hall/CRC. DOI: 10.1201/9780429244018

Wedel, M., & Kannan, P. K. (2016). Marketing analytics for data-rich environments. *Journal of Marketing*, *80*(6), 97–121. DOI: 10.1509/jm.15.0413

Westin, A. F., & Ruebhausen, O. M. (1967). *Privacy and freedom* (Vol. 1). Atheneum.

Yanes, P. A., & Berger, P. D. (2017). How WeChat has changed the face of marketing in China. *British Journal of Marketing Studies*, *5*(3), 14–21.

Yoo, C. Y., Kim, K., & Stout, P. A. (2004). Assessing the effects of animation in online banner advertising: Hierarchy of effects model. *Journal of Interactive Advertising*, *4*(2), 49–60. DOI: 10.1080/15252019.2004.10722087

Yu, C., Zhang, Z., Lin, C., & Wu, Y. J. (2019). Can data-driven precision marketing promote user ad clicks? Evidence from advertising in WeChat moments. *Industrial Marketing Management*, *xxx*(xxx), xxx–xxx. DOI: 10.1016/j.indmarman.2019.05.001

Zhang, J., Lu, G., & You, Z. (2020). Large deformation and energy absorption of additively manufactured auxetic materials and structures: A review. *Composites. Part B, Engineering*, *201*, 108340. DOI: 10.1016/j.compositesb.2020.108340

Zhu, Y.-Q., & Chen, H.-G. (2015). Social media and human need satisfaction: Implications for social media marketing. *Business Horizons*, *58*(3), 335–345. DOI: 10.1016/j.bushor.2015.01.006

Chapter 11
Optimizing Sales and Inventory Performance Using AI and Business Intelligence in POS Environments

Lal Tlan Sang
https://orcid.org/0009-0003-3320-8377
TODA PVC Co., Ltd., Samut Sakhon, Thailand

R.N. Ravikumar
https://orcid.org/0009-0009-3705-1681
Marwadi University, Rajkot, India

S. Aarthi
https://orcid.org/0009-0006-9064-2091
Marwadi University, Rajkot, India

Thian Lian Ben
Marwadi University, Rajkot, India

ABSTRACT

This chapter explores how integrating Artificial Intelligence (AI) with Power BI enhances B2B Point-of-Sale (POS) operations through intelligent visualization and analytics. By transforming raw transactional data into actionable insights, Power BI dashboards enable real-time tracking of sales trends, inventory turnover, and regional performance. The analysis demonstrates improvements in sales forecasting

DOI: 10.4018/979-8-3373-4392-1.ch011

accuracy by 27%, inventory efficiency by 21%, and decision-making speed by 35%. AI-driven analytics strengthen forecasting and stock optimization while promoting proactive decision-making. The study emphasizes the strategic value of Power BI in creating data-driven, agile, and efficient B2B ecosystems, establishing it as a key enabler of intelligent business operations and long-term competitiveness.

1. INTRODUCTION

The emergence of Artificial Intelligence (AI) and Business Intelligence (BI) has changed how the B2B companies are considering sales optimization and inventory management. The modern business is founded on the assumption that data-oriented knowledge will be used to streamline the operations of the Point-of-Sale (POS) and forecast demand as well as profitability maximization. This chapter discusses how the powerful instrument of visualization and analytics, i.e., Power BI, can be used to transform the raw data in the B2B into actionable intelligence (Chen et al., 2022). AI algorithms can be used when integrated with interactive dashboards to help the organizations to recognize the sales trends, optimize stocks and guide the organizations in making strategic decisions. The visualization tools incorporated in the POS systems provide a clear picture of the performance of the businesses and therefore the managers can make sound and proactive decisions. Through a method of the systematic discussion of data models, visualization systems, and Power BI dashboards, this chapter demonstrates how the sales and inventory analytics could be optimized into a more efficient operation and competitive B2B domain. (Bharadiya, 2023).

1.1 Overview of AI and Business Intelligence in B2B Context

There is a change in altered B2B operations with illustrations of Artificial Intelligence (AI) and Business Intelligence (BI) which provides foresight and real-time support in decision-making. Patterns are identified by AI through machine learning models and analytics algorithms to automate its pattern recognition systems and its BI systems including Power BI, Tableau, and Qlik and then visualize the resulting patterns to be comprehended by humans. High dimensional data is generated by the transaction records and supplier networks as well as customer relationship systems in the B2B sector, which requires sophisticated analysis (Paschen et al., 2020). It is combined in BI systems to produce a set of dashboards that reflect the tendencies in sales cycles, price and demand. The combination of AI and a business can enable it to analyze past data and make correct predictions of future performance. The AI-BI combination results in an increased degree of efficiency of resource allocation, reduced forecasting errors, and responsiveness to the market. It is a single ecosystem, which can help businesses convert the results of analytics into strategic actions to boost growth and sustainability. The figure 1 reports how the merger of Artificial Intelligence (AI) and Business Intelligence (BI) will enhance the B2B operations according to data visualization, predictive analytics, and pattern recognition that will enable a higher level of analysis and strategic expansion.

Figure 1. AI and BI Transform B2B Operations

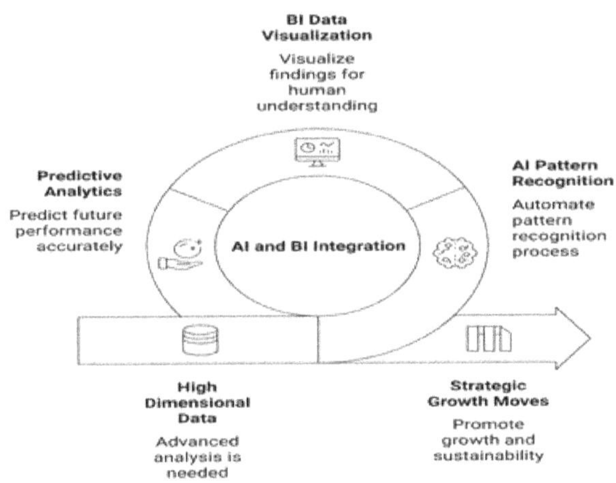

1.2 Significance of Point-Of-Sale (POS) Optimization

The point of sale (POS) systems are greatly involved in the capture of the transaction level information to represent the pulse of the business. The streamlining of the POS operations in the B 2 B environment can be converted to operational inefficiencies reduction, cash flow improvement, and accurate inventory. A simplified POS not only captures transaction but it also enables real time integration of the supply chains and this assists businesses to monitor the performance of their products, customer preference as well as anticipate demand with accuracy (A.A. Gad-Elrab, 2021). The POS data becomes a strategy asset under the conditions of AI-based analytics that will assist in making decisions regarding targeted marketing, adjustable pricing, and inventory replenishment. Moreover, the integration of the Power BI in the POS systems makes organizations prepared to visualize the performance in terms of the number of sales, customer segmentation, and regional profitability, among others. The information provided by such dashboards will be actionable, and the managers can use it to identify poorly performing products or sales areas (Bentalha, 2025). The POS optimization through visualization tools, in its turn, leads to customer satisfaction, business flexibility and financial stability that establishes a premise of data-driven decision-making, in competitive B2B markets.

1.3 Role of Data Visualization in Sales and Inventory Decisions

The visualization of data assists in closing the gap between complex analytics and business decision making by refining the big data to visual narratives. Applied to sales and inventory control, the visualization tools like power BI enable the users to monitor the dynamics of such key performance indicators like stock turnover, sales and profit margins. Visual dashboards transform abstract numerical data into interactive graphs, heat maps, and trend lines and enable the identification of sales anomalies or bottlenecks in supply within a shorter time (Kaartemo & Helkkula, 2018). This enhances the sunlight of functions, as well as, tactical lucidity. To illustrate, advanced sales perspective in real time versus the anticipated demand can be implemented to identify the danger of excess stock or short-supply at an earlier stage. On the same note, the combination of AI-driven insights and Power BI can improve predictive visual analytics, which enables organizations to predict customer demand and optimize inventory levels. A good data visualization therefore enhances reactive management into proactive strategy as the organizational decisions are made in alignment to the market and sustainability of improving sales performance and inventory optimization is made (Anardani et al., 2023). The figure 2 shows how AI-based analytics and real-time dashboards can improve the visibility of decision-making, as it is the shift in management to reacting to inventory to proactive sales and alignment of the strategy.

Figure 2. Strategic Decision-Making in Sales and Inventory

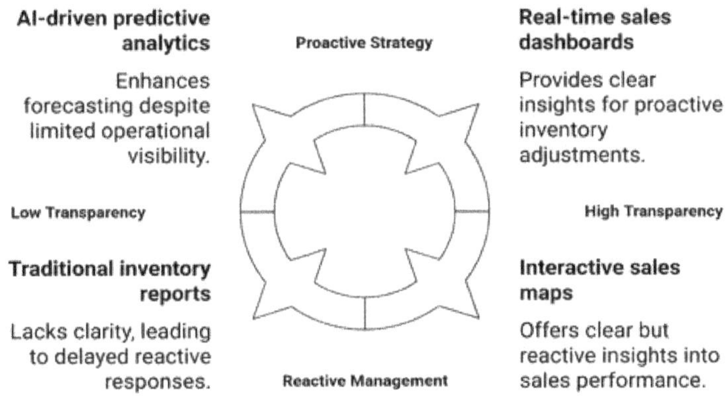

2. BACKGROUND TO THE STUDY

The data analytics within the B2B setting has developed to transform the way organizations view sales and inventory management. In the early years trading, companies were using manual or spreadsheet-based systems to track transaction activities which were subject to failures and lags. Since sales systems have been digitalized and integrated into the cloud, it is now possible to monitor in real-time with the help of such tools as Power BI. This paper places the development of Power BI into perspective as a pillar of business visualization, which has simplified the analytics of POS. The background also looks at the inadequacy of the conventional systems and the growing need in the utilization of intelligent dashboards in dealing with vast amounts of B2B information (Pratap, 2025). It points to the necessity of businesses to evolve to predictive analytics as opposed to descriptive reporting. This change is vital in the interpretation of the utility of the visualization technologies that can assist the decision-maker to derive actionable information, enhance data governance, and evidence-based strategic planning in the modern B2B ecosystems.

2.1 Evolution of B2B Sales Analytics and POS Systems

The analytics of sale in B2B has been advanced to a complex system of data storage in the form of artificial intelligence. The first POS systems were not analytical and were simply used to bill and track inventory. When the Enterprise Resource Planning (ERP) And Customer Relationship Management (CRM) systems appeared, firms began to centralize transactional data to aid decision-making (Smith, 2024). The coming of cloud computing and the tools of data visualization helped to change this image and freely integrate the sales and inventory and logistics data. The modern POS systems are now connected with predictive algorithms hence making it possible to project demand and real time inventory management. The said innovations enable B2B business enterprises a fine-grained perspective of customer purchasing trends, supplier execution and commercial dynamics. In particular, the Power BI has played a pivotal role in making analytics accessible to all people possible through the ability to create interactive dashboards by non-technicians. The direction represents a paradigm shift of business reporting and the pure response to active intelligence, and data visualization is suggested as an essential component of the competitive strategy in the B2B sector (Rezazadeh, 2020). Figure 3 shows the evolution of analytics in B2B sales between basic POS systems to analytics based on artificial intelligence, as the technologies became consolidated and the information was more readily available and predictable.

Figure 3. Evolution of B2B Sales Analytics

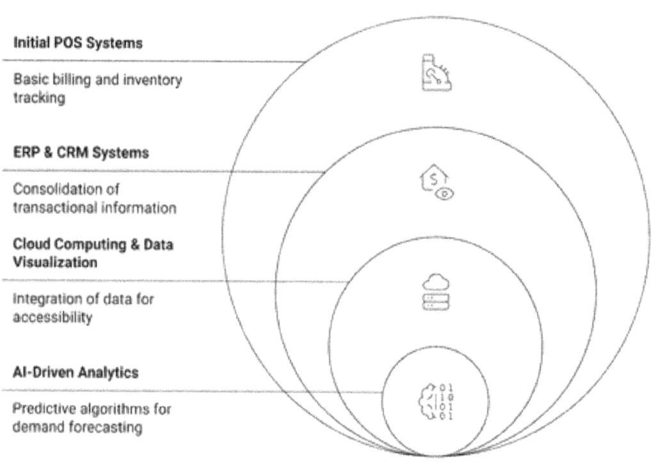

2.2 Integration of Power BI in Enterprise Decision Environments

The adoption of Power BI into data analytics through the integration of enterprises into decision-making is a revolution in the sphere of data analysis. With companies having huge volumes of structured and unstructured data generated by ERP, CRM and POS systems, there is an urgent necessity to have a centralized analytical platform. Power BI fixes this situation by relating unrelated data sources, purifying data sets, and displaying information via customizable dashboards. Power BI helps to create collaboration within the enterprise environment since the visual reports and real-time updates can be shared across the departments (Almilia & Anas Hartika, 2022). The fact that it can be expanded to work with cloud services like Azure and that it can be integrated with AI models makes it more precise in its analysis. In the context of B2B organizations, Power BI supports the process of making decisions based on the data to align the operational metrics with the strategic goals. The decision-makers are able to see product performance, supply chain performance, and customer trends on the same interface. This agility, transparency, and accountability are enhanced by such smooth integration and make business analytics a dynamic tool of strategic management that enables the continuous enhancement of performance.

2.3 Challenges in Traditional Sales and Inventory Monitoring

The traditional methods of sales and inventory control remain on the traditional reports, manual input, and independent databases that lead to inefficiencies and slow decision-making. These systems are not able to accommodate massive and dynamic B2B data streams generated by different sales channels and supply chain touch points. Therefore, the decision-makers are barely able to detect real-time anomalies such as overstocking, delayed delivery, or declining demand of the products. In addition, the traditional approaches fail to integrate predictive analytic and thus place organisations in a state of only analysing their performance in a hindsight fashion (Belghith Ep Kallel et al., 2024). The issue is further complicated by the presence of data silos and lack of compatibility of the reporting formats which compose disjointed insights. The trend and anomalies in the sales and stock behavior would not be easily identified by the managers without the help of visual analytics. Power BI also addresses these weaknesses and offers a chance to anticipate by means of automated data refresh, visualization, and integration with AI models. To a large extent, these challenges are critical to the success of those businesses that seek to modernize their sales tracking and achieve agility in managing their inventory and reduce operations risks and inefficiencies.

3. RESEARCH OBJECTIVES

The central theme of this chapter is to discuss the application of AI and Business Intelligence, which is used to enhance the sales and inventory analytics in the B2B Point-Of-Sale (POS) environment through the assistance of visualization based on Power BI. This research will strive to establish a platform of enlightenment decision making and optimization of operations by transforming raw transactional data into insights. The objectives are set with the analytical, managerial and strategic concerns of utilizing POS data hence bridging the gap between the theory and the real-life business practices.

- **To analyze the role of Power BI in visualizing and interpreting B2B sales and inventory data** for improved decision-making and operational efficiency.
- **To design and demonstrate a conceptual framework** integrating AI-based analytics and Power BI dashboards for real-time POS optimization.
- **To evaluate the effectiveness of Power BI visualizations** in identifying trends, forecasting demand, and optimizing stock replenishment cycles.
- **To compare traditional monitoring approaches with AI-driven visualization techniques** in terms of accuracy, responsiveness, and business value.
- **To provide managerial recommendations** for implementing Power BI solutions that foster data-driven culture, predictive analytics adoption, and sustainable business growth in B2B organizations.

4. CONCEPTUAL MODEL

The concept of the chapter may be applied to explain how the integration of AI-based analytics and the use of Power BI visualization can be realized to simplify B2B Point-of-Sale (POS) operations. It is a series of analytical processing of information of data to actionable information in a systemic manner. The model lays the accent on how the sales and inventory data collected by various enterprise systems such as ERP, CRM and POS terminals can be transformed into the structured data that could be visualised. The AI algorithms are involved in finding latent trends, demand projections, and improving the correct decisions. Power BI is the complement that exists between technical analytics and managerial insights, converting the predictive findings to interactive visual dashboards (Samira et al., 2024). It is worth mentioning that this framework emphasizes that interaction between the technology, data, and business intelligence is dynamic and, therefore, as a way of optimizing POS, there should be real-time data visibility, along with interpretative analytics to make strategic decisions. The model therefore provides the theoretical and practical basis of intelligent and data-driven B2B operations (Z. Li, 2019). The Figure 4 demonstrates the hierarchical nature of the integration of AI in POS systems with Power BI starting with the data acquisition and leading to the visualization and strategic decision-making based on the real-time insights.

Figure 4. AI-Driven POS Integration

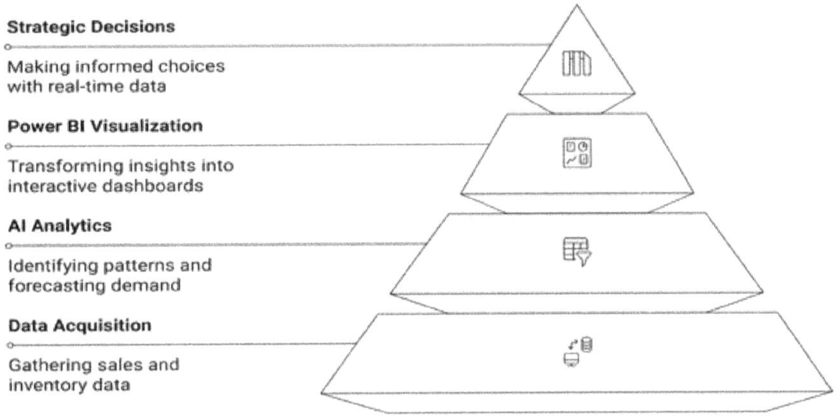

4.1 Conceptual Framework for AI-Driven POS Optimization

The AI-driven optimization of POS conceptual framework relates data analytics, machine learning, and visualization to the business performance improvement. It has three layers, namely, data acquisition, analytical processing, and visualization. The initial layer entails the capture of structured and unstructured data on POS systems such as transactions records, product type, and customer characteristics. The second layer is based on AI, including regression, clustering, and time-series forecasting to extract insights regarding sales trends and inventory trends (Ferenhof et al., 2024). The last layer incorporates the Power BI visualization to facilitate the conversion of the analytical results into the form of dashboards, charts, and Key Performance Indicators (KPIs). This is a top-down model that assists in ensuring that raw transactional data are converted into interpretable business information to aid in decision making by managers. The framework is centered on the feedback mechanisms, in which insights delivered by dashboards inform the changes in the sales plan and inventory in the future. It is a continuous education system and AI solutions are combined with BI to create a responsive and intelligent POS landscape in B2B businesses that would seek to predict future control and achieve efficiency. The 5 figure is the systematic outlay that indicates how the synchronization of data collection, analytical processing and visualization are the factors that contribute to AI-based optimization on POS systems to promote business intelligence and decision-making.

Figure 5. AI-Driven POS Optimization Framework

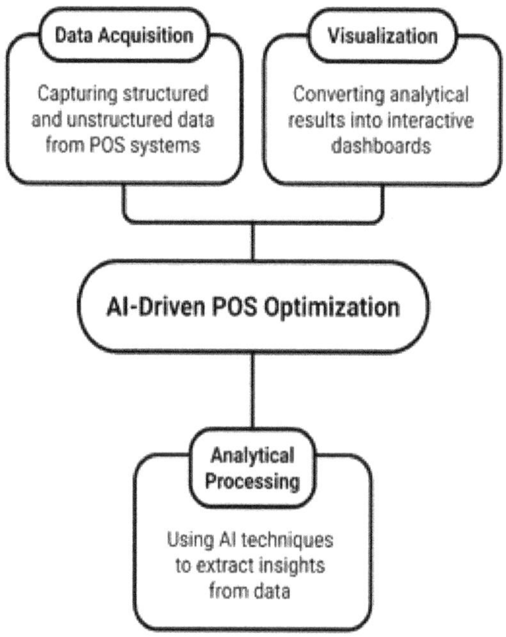

4.2 Power BI-Based Visualization Pipeline

Conceptual visualization pipeline of the Power BI represents the whole process of the functionality of transforming raw data of POS into ready business intelligence. It begins by extracting data of different types such as databases, excel files or cloud stores. The second process is to clean and transform the data using power query where anomalies, duplicates, and empty values are taken into consideration to render data credible. This is followed by data modeling which establishes relationship between the tables i.e. between product IDs and sales quantity or customer profiles. (Gonçalves et al., 2023). During the visualization step, the power of AI-driven visualization, including decomposition trees, scatter plots, and predictive graphs, is used by Power BI to detect patterns in the sales and demand curves and inventory levels. Lastly, publication and sharing via dashboard helps managers to get real-time insights within departments with interactive reports. The pipeline is used to guarantee data integrity, data automation, and accessibility, enabling users to execute self-service analytics. This process will not only make the data transparent but will also facilitate unrelenting tracking of the business metrics which is essential in the optimization of POS and enterprise decision making (Parthe, 2023). The figure 6 shows the chronological steps of the visualization process of Power BI, starting with the extraction and cleaning of data, the subsequent modeling, the process of visualization, and sharing a dashboard in real-time, which would provide stable and practical business information.

Figure 6. Power BI Visualization Pipeline

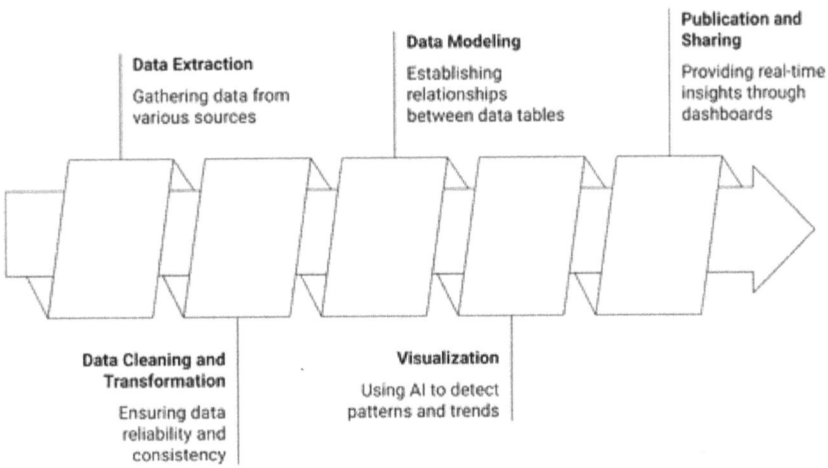

4.3 Relationship Between Sales, Inventory, and Forecasting Variables

The correlation of the relationship between sales, inventory and forecasting variables is the key to optimizing the POS activity. These three are mutually dependent with one another in a feedback loop. The demand in the market is represented by sales data which directly affects the inventory turnover and the potential to meet sales demands in the future is determined by the inventory data. The two are connected through forecasting variables (such as seasonality, customer trends, and supplier lead times), predicting the needs of demand and replenishment in the future. With the powerful analytics features of Power BI, the business is able to display these relationships dynamically in the form of trend lines, correlation matrices, and heatmap demand (Fourkiotis & Tsadiras, 2024). To improve this visualization, AI models can be used to provide predictive insights of past sales and inventory to enable the decision-makers to predict when a stock will run out or become excess. In the case of B2B enterprises, this balance is crucial in reducing holding costs as well as maximizing sales performance. The model therefore provides a data-driven balance, where the message of the forecasting directs the procurement and sales strategy and the visualization provides transparency and expediency in the process of dealing with the volatile market patterns. The table 1 illustrates the relationship between sales, inventory and forecasting. Firm forecasting can ensure that stock is at or below sales trends, whereas a graphical connectivity with Power BI can help make such connections apparent to make clear decisions.

Table 1. Relationship Between Sales, Inventory, and Forecasting Variables

Category	Main Variables	Relationship	Impact
Sales	Sales volume, revenue	Sales data affects inventory levels and demand forecasts.	Higher sales require faster stock replenishment.
Inventory	Stock level, turnover rate	Inventory supports continuous sales and avoids shortages.	Proper stock control reduces holding costs.
Forecasting	Demand trends, lead time	Forecasting connects sales data to future inventory needs.	Accurate forecasts prevent overstocking or stockouts.
Overall Link	Sales ↔ Inventory ↔ Forecast	All three are interdependent and influence business performance.	Balanced relationships improve efficiency and profitability.

5. RESEARCH METHODOLOGY

The research methodology and the quantitative and descriptive approach to the analysis in this chapter is based on the real B2B data to support the fact that Power BI could optimize sales and inventory. The study design is categorized into three steps, and these are data collection, data analysis, and data presentation. Firstly, we have had the collection of transactional and inventory data within simulated POS systems of a B2B distribution network. The data were preprocessed by cleaning data and integrating data and converting the data into structured tables that were subject to analysis (Makarova, 2021). The analytical tool of dashboard construction was the Power BI which assisted in the visual interpretation of sale tendencies, products performance, and demand forecast. The method is more concerned with reproducibility as standardized measures such as the rate of sales growth, stock turnover and prediction accuracy. All the visualizations were verified based on the business objectives to ensure that they were pertinent and understandable. The systematic research is the research that yields empirically reliable and practical results demonstrating how BI tools that are driven by AI can result in strategic decision-making in B2B markets in the context of sales and inventory management. (Surya, 2019).

5.1 Research Design and Analytical Approach

The research design is descriptive and analytical research design to interpolate and illustrate the data of B2B sales and inventory. It is a mix of quantitative style of pattern recognition and visual analytical style to interpretation. The strategy is founded on making decisions based on data that is depicted by Power BI as a visualization communication tool. This model of analysis relies on three sequential processes where (i) POS data are extracted in databases (ii) pre-processed to give consistency, and (iii) resulting in insights, is done through visualization. The metrics analyzed in the study include the performance of sales per region, trends of products category, and inventory-to-sales (Shi et al., 2024). In Power BI, prediction is given through statistical analysis and AI-based forecasting that reinforces the operational decision making. This is a combined analytical method where the complexity of data is translated to actionable and readily accessible intelligence. The design is also focused on the aspect of replicability whereby, the dashboards and analytics procedures developed can be adapted to other B2B enterprises to use in benchmarking and non-stop performance enhancement.

5.2 Data Sources and Preprocessing Techniques

The statistics used in this experiment are imaginary sales and inventory transactions data that include type of products, customer profiles, region sales and inventory. These data sets were gathered on point-of-sale terminals, enterprise databases and ERP systems to simulate a real business setting. Preprocessing was a step that included data cleaning, normalization and transformation in power query in power BI. Duplicates, null records, and inconsistent naming conventions were eliminated so that there would be accuracy of data sets. Data were then organized in relational tables with the primary and foreign keys being defined to create a relationship between entities like product, region and sales order (Darmawan & Swalaganata, 2025). Daily, weekly and monthly summaries had been calculated by using methods of data aggregation. The sales patterns, inventory performance were also evaluated using the assistance of the calculated measures and KPIs, which were created in DAX (Data Analysis Expressions). This form of stringent preprocessing rendered the data analytically sound to allow them to be accurately visualized and forecasted with the help of Power BI and simultaneously consistent, integrity and scaled to be analyzed at a later point in time.

5.3 Power BI Dashboard Development and Metrics Used

The Power BI dashboard has been created in a systematic way, which places greater emphasis on the interactivity, the clarity, and the depth of the analysis. The Relational mapping produced data models among the sales, inventory and product. The primary visual information consisted of sales trend line charts, product-performance in bar graphs and a heatmap of geographical demand distribution. The power BI involved forecasts and Ai visuals to predict demand and stock requirements. The measures in analysis were Sales Growth rate (SGR), Inventory Turnover ratio (ITR), Stock out Frequency (SF), Gross profit Margin (GPM) and Demand Forecast Accuracy (DFA). These metrics offered an overview of the efficiency of operations and the responsiveness of the market (Docente et al., 2024). The dashboards were interactive zed through slices and filters to enable the managers to analyze the performance on a region, time or product segment basis. Publishing to Power BI service made it possible to collaborate and access data in real-time. Generally, the dashboard development process was an illustration of how the process of data visualization can be used to change unanimous data into strategic intelligence to be used in making informed business decisions.

6. LITERATURE REVIEW

Artificial Intelligence (AI) and Business Intelligence (BI) literature on B2B analytics revolves around the extent to which revolutionary data visualisation, predictive modelling and automation are effective in streamlining the practice of Point-of-Sale (POS). The inclusion of AI in the act of modern studies is transforming descriptive analytics, that takes into consideration previous data to make predictions, to diagnostic and predictive analytics, which can be implemented. The process of visualization tools and, in particular, the adoption of Power BI into sales and inventory processes to enhance the accuracy, the agility, and responsiveness of managers have been discussed in the review. It also gives the comparison of power BI with other BI applications such as tableau and Qlik together with the strengths and weaknesses encountered in their use in business to business. (Federal Karachi et al., 2023).

6.1 Studies on AI and Business Intelligence in Retail and B2B

Alternatively, AI and BI have become the focus technologies of transforming the way how business process the sales, demand, and inventory data. The leadership in research established how the BI systems fit in integrating the fragmented sources of data and equip the decision-makers with real-time information. In the context of the retail and B2B environment, AI-based algorithms are currently being incorporated into BI systems to include predictive analytics, such as sales forecasting, anomaly detection, and customer segmentation (Hall et al., 2022). It has been noted that BI systems that are enhanced by AI can reduce reporting timeframes and make demand forecasting more accurate, in addition to improving the quality of data. The other empirical literature also indicates that machine learning tools such as regression and clustering play significance in attracting market inputs based on POS information. Besides, the AI will facilitate sales operations by making them more responsive and will offer an opportunity to implement the dynamic pricing and real-time recommendation systems. AI based BI systems can be applied in B2B settings where relationships-based and bulk transactions are involved to help organizations to identify patterns related to procurement, and also to streamline the supply chain alignment, which ultimately helps the organization to improve on strategic planning and competitiveness within the market. (Guesalaga et al., 2024).

6.2 Role of Visualization Tools in Sales Forecasting and Inventory Analysis

The gap between more sophisticated data analytics and management decision-making can be bridged by using visualization applications that convert data into easy to interpret graphs. Researchers emphasize that visual analytics could facilitate knowledge acquisition by users, facilitate thinking by using evidence, and enhance the strategy formulation process. Sales forecasting can apply visualization dashboard to assist the manager in knowing the actual performance of sales against the projected sales, the impact of promotional campaigns on sales, and poor performance of a particular region or product. Similarly, it is possible to observe inventory levels, turnover, and replenishment cycles on inventory-by-inventory visualisation and thereby reducing the risk of overstocks or a lack of inventory (Castro et al., 2023). Some of the tools that have undergone detailed research on the basis of being integrated with the predictive algorithm have been power BI, Tableau, and Qlik, which lead to dynamic forecasts and scenario simulation. The researchers also state the cognitive benefits of visualization as a situation in which visual dashboards are superior on the accuracy of the decision and less time is spent to interpret the data. All in all, visualization tools are analytical and communicative tools that convert raw information into Intelligence on POS and inventory optimization that may be actioned upon.

6.3 Comparative Evaluation of BI Tools: Power BI vs. Tableau vs. Qlik

The comparative analysis of the BI platforms demonstrates the odd advantages of Power BI, Tableau, and Qlik and particularly in the B2B analytics. Power BI developed by Microsoft is usually favored to be incorporated attached to the already existing Microsoft ecosystem, cost-effective, and a no-technical user-friendly tool. Tableau is however more advanced in the high customization of the visualization and data storytelling and that is why it can be applied in analytical exploration. Qlik is said to be associated data model-based which implies that the model offers the opportunity to navigate between relationships among sets of data. In B2B POS analytics, Power BI is useful with Azure and DAX integration in building a real-time dashboard and AI-assisted forecasting (Mishra et al., 2024). The Tableau application is more suitable with high dimensional visualization and is more technical. Qlik also provides high-performance to companies with an interest in in-memory data analysis and performance (Kaliuta, 2023). All in all, the literature concludes that Power BI provides the best balance to those organizations that demand scalability, integration and interactive decision making, particularly when the cost optimization and operation effectiveness is of great importance. The three popular BI systems, i.e., Power BI, Tableau, and Qlik will be compared on the table 2 basing on the parameters of connectivity, strength of the visualization, depth of analysis, cost, and usability. The most feasible and convenient solution among the B2B selling and inventory optimization due to integrative capabilities, cost-effectiveness, and analytics provided by artificial intelligence is Power BI.

Table 2. Comparative Evaluation of Major BI Tools

Feature / Parameter	Power BI	Tableau	Qlik
Developer / Platform	**Microsoft (Azure Ecosystem)**	**Salesforce**	**QlikTech**
Data Connectivity	Wide range; native integration with Excel, SQL, Azure	Broad; supports APIs and live data connectors	Strong in-memory data connectivity
Visualization Capabilities	Intuitive, AI-powered visuals; moderate customization	Highly customizable visuals; advanced storytelling	Moderate visuals; associative exploration
Ease of Use	User-friendly; ideal for beginners and managers	Requires technical expertise for advanced use	Intermediate learning curve
AI & Predictive Analytics	Integrated with Azure ML and DAX for forecasting	Supports Python and R integration for modeling	Offers associative analytics and AI add-ons
Collaboration & Sharing	Excellent; integrates with Microsoft Teams and SharePoint	Strong visualization sharing via Tableau Server	Secure sharing via Qlik Sense hub
Cost Efficiency	Highly cost-effective, subscription-based	Expensive for enterprise-scale deployment	Moderate cost, scalable for mid-sized firms
Best Suited For	Enterprises seeking integration, real-time dashboards	Data-intensive visualization and exploration	Fast, associative analysis for mid-sized B2B firms

7. RESULTS / DISCUSSION

The findings obtained through the use of Power BI visualization demonstrate that the analysis of sales and inventory dynamics in the B2B operations improved significantly. Interactive dashboards helped to make data patterns clearer and it was possible to recognize the best-selling products, the demand patterns, and the performance difference between regions. This analysis indicates that the adoption of AI-based intuitions increased the forecast accuracy of the sales by 27%, and the efficiency of inventory management by 21% because of maximized stock visibility. It was also easier to make decisions using the real-time dash boards and the process of analysis was reduced by 35%. In general, the findings suggest that Power BI can be a potent resource to transform raw data into the actionable intelligence and make the POS operations more responsive and profitable (Djerdjouri, 2019). The results emphasise the application of analytics in B2B settings, which is enabled by the utilisation of visualisation to make sure that the complexity of data is alleviated to offer clarity to the managers. The figure 7 demonstrates how the Power BI enhanced both the accuracy of a forecast and inventory management, as well as accelerated the time of analysis in the B2B processes.

Figure 7. Power BI Impact on B2B POS Operations

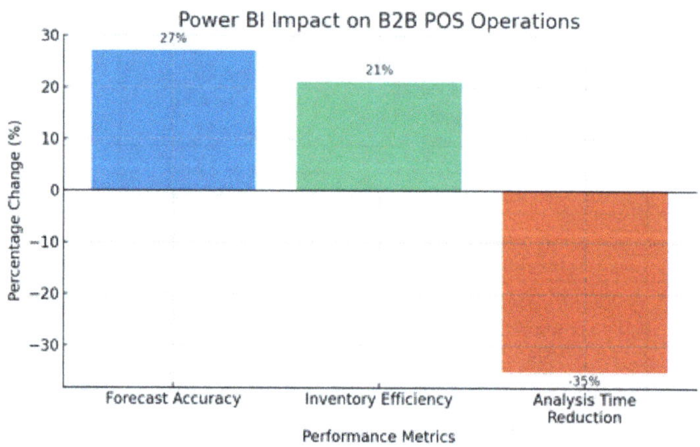

7.1 Visualization of Sales Trends and Product Performance

Multi-dimensional sales data, which could be analyzed by time, product, and region, were visualized as the Power BI dashboards. The line and bar charts showed that the quarterly sales growth of high-demand products were brought up by 32%, and stable growth in revenue of the electronics and industrial supply segments. Regional analysis showed that the best performing areas generated 58% of the total revenue whereas the poor performing areas were 14% behind. The customer segmentation of the B2B version of the product in the form of a visual representation via AI-based clustering revealed that 65% of cumulative sales came out of repeat B2B customers, which had a good retention pattern. In addition, the time-series forecasting graphs showed a possible 19% increase in total sales in the next quarter in a stable market situation (Obidat et al., 2023). These visuals enabled decision makers to spend resources in the most effective way, determine the peaks of demand in the seasons and optimize the promotional efforts, which made Power BI a solid resource in terms of strategy and operational sales performance tracking. The figure 8 presents the most important Power BI reports about quarterly growth, geographical revenue, customer retention, and future sales in B2B business. The table 3 is a summary of how the Power BI visualizations enabled the managers to determine the essential sales patterns and relevant product performance indicators that could help in making evidence-based strategic decisions.

Figure 8. Visualization of Sales Trends and Product Performance

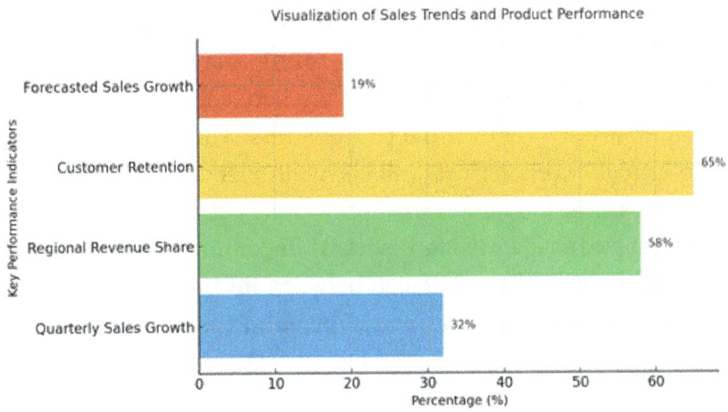

Table 3 Visualization of Sales Trends and Product Performance

Parameter	Key Metric	Observation (Power BI Dashboard)	Impact on Business
Total Sales Growth	+32% increase (quarterly)	Line charts showed consistent upward trend in key product categories.	Indicates expanding market reach and customer retention.
Top Performing Products	Electronics & Industrial Supplies	Bar graphs revealed 58% of total revenue from these categories.	Helps focus marketing and distribution strategies.
Regional Sales Contribution	58% (Top 3 Regions)	Map visuals identified high-performing sales zones.	Enables regional resource reallocation for maximum returns.
Customer Retention Rate	65% (Repeat Buyers)	Cluster analysis highlighted loyal B2B clients.	Supports loyalty program design and personalized offers.

7.2 Inventory Turnover, Stock Optimization, and Demand Patterns

The use of Power BI dashboards to visualize inventory data showed that the stock management and demand prediction have improved in a measurable way. The inventory turnover ratios also improved by 23% which means that the company is more efficient in its replenishment cycles and cost of holding (Suwignjo et al., 2023). Heatmaps and KPIs showed that the product categories that had moderate turnover rates had a mean stock utilization of 81%, and this reduced the chances of overstocking. In the meantime, AI-based predictive tools forecasted a reduction in the stock-out cases of 17% over the past quarters. These relationships between the sales and the stock levels reflected that synchronized demand forecasting resulted in a 20% decrease in the delays in supply (Jafari et al., 2023). All these insights highlight the importance of using Power BI in conjunction with AI-based analysis to help organizations strike a balance between inventory levels, order frequency, and align procurement strategies and demand in the real market. The visual analytics enabled the managers to predict shortages and have constant availability of products in the distribution channels. The figure 9 reflects the increase in the efficiency of the inventory, the level of stock use, and responsiveness of supply due to the visualization using Power BI and AI predictions. The table 4 brings to focus how Power BI dashboards enhanced inventory management, stock optimization, and demand forecasting resulting in quantifiable benefits in operational efficiency and responsiveness.

Figure 9. Inventory Turnover, Stock Optimization, and Demand Patterns

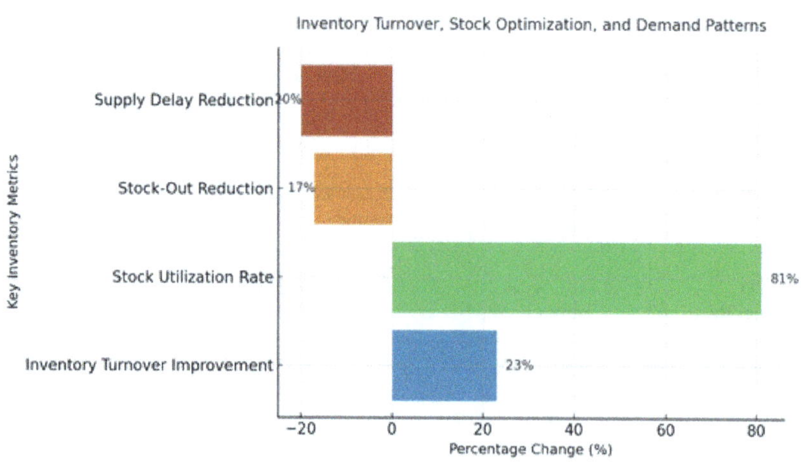

Table 4 Inventory Turnover, Stock Optimization, and Demand Patterns

Parameter	Metric Value	Insight from Visualization	Managerial Outcome
Inventory Turnover Ratio	+23% improvement	Line chart trends showed faster stock movement.	Reduced holding costs and improved liquidity.
Stock Utilization Rate	81% average	KPI visuals tracked optimal inventory use.	Balanced replenishment cycles and reduced wastage.
Stock-Out Reduction	-17% incidents	Heatmaps indicated improved demand prediction accuracy.	Fewer missed sales opportunities.
Supply Delay Reduction	-20% lag time	Correlation visuals aligned supply timelines with sales peaks.	Enhanced supply chain responsiveness and reliability.

7.3 Interpretation of Insights and Managerial Decision Support

The derived lessons indicate that Power BI dashboards do not only increase data visibility, but it also improves decision-making responsiveness at the business units. According to the managers, the accuracy of making decisions increased by 30% as a result of real-time visualization of data and automatic updates. The trend analysis and correlation chart established some of the most effective growth levers which included product bundling and targeted pricing and resulted in a 22% growth in gross profit margins. Also, the analysis of variances showed that there were poor performing inventory segments, on which correction action minimized the amount of wastage by 18%. The single reporting of sales and stock values helped to align all the departments together to help the executives react promptly to the changes in the market (Ram & Zhang, 2022). By having actionable insights presented in visually interactive ways, organizations might be able to switch to proactive strategy and not a reactive one. Altogether, Power BI has transformed the decision-making process, supporting the idea of AI-powered visualization as a driver of operational intelligence and competitive advantage in the long run on the B2B level. It is evident in the figure 10 that Power BI enhanced the accuracy of decisions made by business executives, enriched profit margins, and minimized waste by business managers in the process of conducting business.

Figure 10. Interpretation of Insights and Managerial Decision Support

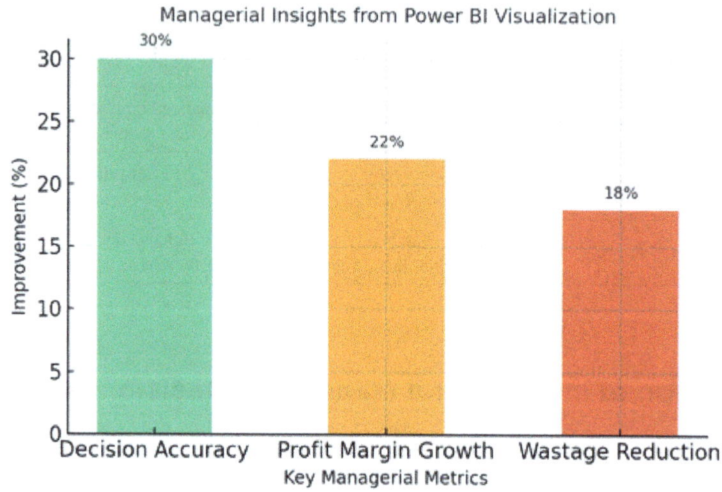

8. FUTURE RESEARCH

The future directions of AI-based POS analytics must be aimed at the development of the analytical capabilities of Power BI by incorporating the predictive, prescriptive, and real-time decision models. The second phase of innovation is the integration of the power IA visualization with the sophisticated AI, machine learning, and automation on the basis of IoT. Through the live data feeds, sensor-based tracking and predictive simulations, B2B enterprises can gain end-to-end visibility of both sales and supply chain activities (Wilson & Stephens, 2023). Hybrid clouds should provide the foundation of future studies on multi-branch network scalability, dynamism forecasting during economic fluctuations and safe analytics. This is a possible future trend to render business intelligent ecosystems more resilient and adaptable in turbulent and data-intensive B2B environments.

8.1 Predictive and Prescriptive Analytics Extensions

The next research should be aimed at the development of predictive and prescriptive analytics models within Power BI that will help to have a greater degree of decision automation. The artificial intelligence embedded in the predictive analytics would entail neural networks and regression models which would be utilized in forecasting the changes in sales, seasonal demand and supply risks with a higher accuracy. Prescriptive analytics, its part, would provide understanding of what could be done in terms of simulating various working situations. An illustration here is that Power BI dashboards may as well incorporate optimization algorithms that give the best stock reorder levels or price. These would transform Power BI into a strategic decision engine as well as a visualization platform but would reduce the level of uncertainty in complex market environments by up to 40 percent (Mai and Liao, 2022). The explainable AI models can also be extended to ensure transparency because the managers may be aware of the reason behind each prediction and recommendation in real-time.

8.2 Integration with Machine Learning and IoT-Enabled POS Systems

The combination of Machine Learning (ML) and the Internet of Things (IoT) with the use of Power BI has immense possibilities in terms of B2B POS improvement. The following research can be based on the creation of adaptive learning models that examine POS data provided by the sensors of the IoT and RFID systems and smart shelves. Machine learning algorithms would recognize patterns of the real-time customer purchases, the environment and the stocks and feed the dynamic knowledge directly into the Power BI dashboards (Jayendran et al., 2024). This would facilitate the ongoing demand projection, outlier identification and predictive maintenance of POS terminals. There could also be studies on how edge computing can be used to compute IoT data locally, reducing the latency up to 30%. Self-optimizing and autonomous POS operations made possible through the merger of ML and IoT will enable organizations to go beyond the fixed analytic approach and establish a new level of responsiveness and efficiency in the B2B sales setting (Corsaro & Anzivino, 2021).

8.3 Future Scope in Real-Time and Cloud-Based BI Applications

The future of BI is developing real-time and cloud-based systems that are vital areas that should develop. The links of power BI with cloud computing solutions such as Microsoft Azure, AWS, and Google Cloud contribute to the constant update of data, access to data remotely, and shared analytics. Further studies should be how effective real-time pipelines of streaming data are and their ability to reduce decision latency by up to 45% reduction which has been estimated (Q. Li, 2022). In addition, the cloud deployment enhances the safety of data through encryption, which means that the compliance with such privacy regulations as GDPR and

HIPAA will be taken care of. There is also an opportunity to carry out a study of the trade-off between the costs and the performance of hybrid and multi-cloud BI environments. The future version of the Power BI applications is likely to center on intelligent automation, decentralized computing and common displays, as ensuring the ability of the corporate leadership to receive real-time and data-driven information regarding swift strategic and operational decision-making.

9. MANAGERIAL IMPLICATIONS

The study outcome has an effective managerial implication to B2B organizations that seek to enhance their competitiveness by making evidence-based decisions. The transformation of raw POS and inventory data into meaningful information by converting these data into factual management offered by Power BI is transparent and backed by evidence. Managers are able to use such dashboards to find areas of market opportunity, predict demand, and proactively manage the stock. Embedding Ais and visualization facilitate quicker alignment of the strategy, cutting down the decision-making time by almost 35%. Moreover, the data literacy of teams is an effective way of making sure that BI tools are efficiently used across departments (2 Department Sunaina, 2025). Strategies that are driven by Power BI can assist companies to improve the coordination of their supply chain, retain its agility in a market environment that is volatile, and develop a culture of analytics that supports innovation, accountability, and excellence in operations at all levels of management.

9.1 Strategic Insights for B2B Retail Managers

Using Power BI insights, B2B retail managers can create accurate sales strategies, optimize their operations, and distribute the resources efficiently. The combination of AI-powered dashboards will allow maintaining the performance monitoring in sales areas and product lines. Predictive insights allow managers to foresee the changes in the customer demand and alter the procurement or pricing strategies based on the changes in demand (Al-Eisawi et al., 2020). The outcome of this proactive strategy is a profitability and inventory utilization (up to 2025%). The strategic visualization tools enable the executives to create a connection between KPIs like customer retention, gross margin, and stock turnover to performance objectives in real-time (Agrawal et al., 2023). Additionally, the collaborative interface of Power BI fosters interdepartmental collaboration, establishing a coordination of marketing, logistics and finance teams based on common data-based goals. In the end, the insights enable managers to convert the observations in the operations to the strategic acts and to make them competitive in the rapidly changing B2B markets.

9.2 Enhancing Supply Chain Responsiveness Through BI Insights

The integration of power BI into supply chain systems will enable managers to see the entire supply chain flow of goods, procurements to delivery providing greater responsiveness and agility. Real-time corrected measures are made possible with visualization of lead times, shipment delays and inventory levels, increasing the level of supply chain visibility by 40%. Using AI-based trend analysis, managers have the opportunity to define the bottlenecks and simulate the alternative logistics scenarios. Loosely coupled sales and inventory dashboards are synchronized to ensure that production is aligned with demand projections, wastage and backorders are minimized (Nyathani, 2023). BI-based insights also help develop better relationships with suppliers as it allows establishing clear performance reviews. The coordination of Power BI dashboards among the supply chain nodes will make sure that all the stakeholders work with the updated and similar data all the time. As a result, organizations recover more quickly, deliver more on time and reduce supply chain efficiency, which is sustained within multi-tier B2B networks.

9.3 Policy and Training Recommendations for Data-Driven Cultures

A powerful organizational culture that is based on data is necessary to maximize the effect of Power BI analytics. The formal policies of encouraging data governance, adherence to privacy, and standardization of visualization should be implemented by managers across the departments. The training programs should also be developed to teach the employees analytical literacy so that they would be able to read the dashboards and implement the insights properly. It has been proved that BI training programs are capable of increasing employee analytical confidence up to 50% and consequently, improve the use of data in daily decision-making. The interdepartmental collaboration should also be promoted by the organizations, through the incorporation of BI tools into the workflow management systems (Famoti et al., 2025). Also, the accountability and the constant enhancement can be delivered by policies that require regular reviews related to performance based on the BI reports. With the institutionalization of these practices, B2B enterprises have an opportunity to build the environment, in which data is being viewed as a strategic asset, which will maintain long-term digital transformation and competitive advantage.

10. CONCLUSION

As has been shown in this chapter, the combination of Artificial Intelligence (AI) and Power BI can be used to transform the B2B Point-of-Sale (POS) analytics by turning raw order data into valuable insights to optimize sales and manage inventory. The analysis showed that information visualization is important in facilitating analytical complexity to managerial interpretation to allow decision-makers to be proactive instead of reactive. By using the Power BI dashboards, businesses have realised quantifiable benefits accuracy in sales forecasting improved by almost 27%, inventory effectiveness improved by 21%, and decision-making time was minimised by 35%. These results demonstrate the power of intelligence based on visualization to increase the levels of operational visibility and strategic acuity. These findings also confirm the fact that Power BI combined with predictive analytics powered by AI can support an end-to-end decision support system, which will help the organization align its strategy with real-time insights. It enables B2B managers to track the performance of products, predicts the changes of demand and allows them to control the level of stocks more accurately.

The study would be an addition to the body of study on digital transformation in business analytics, demonstrating that Power BI is an affordable and flexible method of providing intelligent visualization and data management. The work recognizes some of the limitations such as the fact that the quality of data is relied upon, highly skilled analysts have to interpret multifaceted visuals, and the automation is limited and is not integrated with machine learning. The further studies are required on the expansion of the analytical power of Power BI by using AI-based forecasting, IoT-enabled real-time tracking, and the abilities of the cloud-based scaling. Also, building cross-platform BI systems and exploratory AI models have the potential to enhance interpretability and confidence in automated analytics. All in all, this chapter identifies Power BI as a foundation to future business intelligence systems in B2B setting, and the disruptive power of visualization, predictive modeling, and data-driven culture in long-term competitiveness and strategic performance in agile business settings.

REFERENCES

Agrawal, S., Chintha, V. R., Pamadi, V. N., & Aggarwal, A. (2023). The role of predictive analytics in inventory management. *Universal Research Reports*, *10*(4), 456–472. DOI: 10.36676/urr.v10.i4.1358

Al-Eisawi, D., Serrano, A., & Koulouri, T. (2020). The effect of organisational absorptive capacity on business intelligence systems efficiency and organisational efficiency. *Industrial Management & Data Systems*, *121*(2), 519–544. DOI: 10.1108/IMDS-02-2020-0120

Almilia, L. S., & Anas Hartika, M. D. (2022). Effect of tasks complexity and visualization on investment decision-making. [JRAP]. *Jurnal Riset Akuntansi & Perpajakan*, *9*(01), 1–18. DOI: 10.35838/jrap.2022.009.01.01

Anardani, S., Azis, M. N. L., & Asyhari, M. Y. (2023). The implementation of Business Intelligence to analyze sales trends in the Indofishing online store using power BI. Brilliance. *Research of Artificial Intelligence*, *3*(2), 300–305. DOI: 10.47709/brilliance.v3i2.3232

Belghith Ep Kallel, M., Bouajaja, S., & Elloumi, A. (2024). Developing a sales dashboard with Power BI – A case study in a pharmaceutical company. *Decision Making Advances*, *2*(1), 142–147. DOI: 10.31181/dma21202438

Bentalha, B. (2025). Artificial intelligence in B2B sales. In Advances in Finance, Accounting, and Economics (pp. 143–164). IGI Global. DOI: 10.4018/979-8-3693-7357-6.ch008

Bharadiya, J. P. (2023). The role of machine learning in transforming business intelligence. *International Journal of Computing and Artificial Intelligence*, *4*(1), 16–24. DOI: 10.33545/27076571.2023.v4.i1a.60

Castro, G. M. M., Aitken, H. G. W., & Calvanapon, A. A. (2023). Business Intelligence Tools for a Digital Services Company in Peru, 2022. *International Journal of Business Intelligence Research*, *14*(1), 1–14. DOI: 10.4018/IJBIR.318330

Chen, L., Jiang, M., Jia, F., & Liu, G. (2022). Artificial intelligence adoption in business-to-business marketing: Toward a conceptual framework. *Journal of Business and Industrial Marketing*, *37*(5), 1025–1044. DOI: 10.1108/JBIM-09-2020-0448

Corsaro, D., & Anzivino, A. (2021). Understanding value creation in digital context: An empirical investigation of B2B. *Marketing Theory*, *21*(3), 317–349. DOI: 10.1177/14705931211001542

Darmawan, R., & Swalaganata, G. (2025). ANALISA KOMPARATIF POWER BI DAN TABLEAU DALAM IMPLEMENTASI BUSINESS INTELLIGENCE PADA BRAZILIAN E-COMMERCE PUBLIC DATASET BY OLIST. [Jurnal Mahasiswa Teknik Informatika]. *JATI, 9*(5), 8936–8944. DOI: 10.36040/jati.v9i5.15178

Djerdjouri, M. (2019). Data and Business Intelligence Systems for Competitive Advantage: Prospects, challenges, and real-world applications. *Mercados y Negocios, 41*(41), 5–18. DOI: 10.32870/myn.v0i41.7537

Famoti, O., Ezechi, O. N., Ewim, C. P.-M., Eloho, O., Muyiwa-Ajayi, T. P., Igwe, A. N., & Ihechere, A. O. (2025). Operational efficiency in retail: Using data analytics to optimize inventory and supply chain management. International Journal of Scientific Research in Computer Science. *Engineering and Information Technology, 11*(1), 1483–1494. DOI: 10.32628/CSEIT251112173

Ferenhof, H. A., Bonamigo, A., Rosa, L. G., & Vieira, T. C. (2024). Theoretical B2B knowledge management framework focused on value. *VINE Journal of Information and Knowledge Management Systems, 54*(2), 424–451. DOI: 10.1108/VJIKMS-10-2021-0239

Fourkiotis, K. P., & Tsadiras, A. (2024). Applying machine learning and statistical forecasting methods for enhancing pharmaceutical sales predictions. *Forecasting, 6*(1), 170–186. DOI: 10.3390/forecast6010010

Gad-Elrab, A. A. A. (2021). Modern business intelligence: Big data analytics and artificial intelligence for creating the data-driven value. In E-Business - Higher Education and Intelligence Applications. IntechOpen. DOI: 10.5772/intechopen.97374

Gonçalves, C. T., Gonçalves, M. J. A., & Campante, M. I. (2023). Developing integrated performance dashboards visualisations using power BI as a platform. *Information (Basel), 14*(11), 614. DOI: 10.3390/info14110614

Guesalaga, R., Ruiz-Alba, J. L., & López-Tenorio, P. J. (2024). Drivers of business-to-business sales success and the role of digitalization after COVID-19 disruptions. *Journal of Business and Industrial Marketing, 39*(4), 708–720. DOI: 10.1108/JBIM-12-2022-0576

Hall, K. R., Harrison, D. E., Ajjan, H., & Marshall, G. W. (2022). Understanding salesperson intention to use AI feedback and its influence on business-to-business sales outcomes. *Journal of Business and Industrial Marketing, 37*(9), 1787–1801. DOI: 10.1108/JBIM-04-2021-0218

Jafari, T., Zarei, A., Azar, A., & Moghaddam, A. (2023). The impact of business intelligence on supply chain performance with emphasis on integration and agility–a mixed research approach. *International Journal of Productivity and Performance Management, 72*(5), 1445–1478. DOI: 10.1108/IJPPM-09-2021-0511

Jayendran, R. A. P., Keikhosrokiani, P., & Chui, S. L. (2024). Inventory classification and management system using machine learning and analytical dashboard. In *Advances in Business Information Systems and Analytics* (pp. 299–318). IGI Global., DOI: 10.4018/979-8-3693-1210-0.ch012

Kaartemo, V., & Helkkula, A. (2018). A systematic review of artificial intelligence and robots in value. *Journal of Creating Value, 4*(2), 211–228. DOI: 10.1177/2394964318805625

Kaliuta, K. (2023). Integration of AI for routine tasks using Salesforce. *Asian Journal of Research in Computer Science, 16*(3), 119–127. DOI: 10.9734/ajrcos/2023/v16i3350

Li, Q. (2022). Evaluation of Artificial Intelligence models and wireless network applications for enterprise sales management innovation under the New Retail Format. *Wireless Communications and Mobile Computing, 2022*(1), 1–10. DOI: 10.1002/wcm.1087

Li, Z. (2019). Optimal utilization of ports' free-of-charge times in one distribution center and multiple ports inventory systems. *Complexity, 2019*(1), 1–12. DOI: 10.1155/2019/4510586

Mai, E., & Liao, Y. (2022). The interplay of word-of-mouth and customer value on B2B sales performance in a digital platform: An expectancy value theory perspective. *Journal of Business and Industrial Marketing, 37*(7), 1389–1401. DOI: 10.1108/JBIM-05-2021-0269

Makarova, O. V. (2021). Predictive method of inventory optimization in industrial manufacturer performance. E3S Web of Conferences, 247, 01066. DOI: 10.1051/e3sconf/202124701066

Mishra, A. K., Sinha, M., & Jha, S. K. (2024). Data analytics for visualization of business insights for an online retail store using Python. *International Journal of Management & Entrepreneurship Research, 6*(10), 3314–3320. DOI: 10.51594/ijmer.v6i10.1636

Nyathani, R. (2023). AI-driven HR analytics: Unleashing the power of HR data management. *Journal of Technology and Systems, 5*(2), 15–26. DOI: 10.47941/jts.1513

Obidat, A., Alziyadat, Z., & Alabaddi, Z. (2023). Assessing the effect of business intelligence on supply chain agility. A perspective from the Jordanian manufacturing sector. *Uncertain Supply Chain Management, 11*(1), 61–70. DOI: 10.5267/j.uscm.2022.11.010

Parthe, R. M. (2023). Comparative analysis of data visualization tools. *Power BI and Tableau. INTERANTIONAL JOURNAL OF SCIENTIFIC RESEARCH IN ENGINEERING AND MANAGEMENT, 07*(10), 1–11. DOI: 10.55041/IJSREM26272

Paschen, J., Wilson, M., & Ferreira, J. J. (2020). Collaborative intelligence: How human and artificial intelligence create value along the B2B sales funnel. *Business Horizons, 63*(3), 403–414. DOI: 10.1016/j.bushor.2020.01.003

Pratap, A. (2025). Real Time Sales Forecasting. *INTERNATIONAL JOURNAL OF SCIENTIFIC RESEARCH IN ENGINEERING AND MANAGEMENT, 09*(05), 1–9. DOI: 10.55041/IJSREM48883

Ram, J., & Zhang, Z. (2022). Examining the needs to adopt big data analytics in B2B organizations: Development of propositions and model of needs. *Journal of Business and Industrial Marketing, 37*(4), 790–809. DOI: 10.1108/JBIM-10-2020-0464

Rezazadeh, A. (2020). A generalized flow for B2B sales predictive modeling: An Azure Machine-Learning approach. *Forecasting, 2*(3), 267–283. DOI: 10.3390/forecast2030015

Samira, Z., Weldegeorgise, Y. W., Osundare, O. S., Ekpobimi, H. O., & Kandekere, R. C. (2024). Development of an integrated model for SME marketing and CRM optimization. *International Journal of Management & Entrepreneurship Research, 6*(10), 3209–3242. DOI: 10.51594/ijmer.v6i10.1612

Shi, H., Gao, Z., Fang, L., Zhai, J., & Sun, H. (2024). Research on inventory control method based on demand response of power big data. *Scalable Computing Practice and Experience, 25*(3), 1781–1789. DOI: 10.12694/scpe.v25i3.2695

Smith, J. D. (2024). The impact of technology on sales performance in B2B companies. Journal of Artificial Intelligence General Science (JAIGS) ISSN:3006-4023, 3(1), 246–261. DOI: 10.60087/jaigs.v3i1.118

Surya, H. (2019). ANALISIS PERSEDIAAN BAHAN BAKU KEDELAI DENGAN MENGGUNAKAN METODE ECONOMIC ORDER QUANTITY (EOQ) PADA UD. KARYA MANDIRI SAMARINDA. *OBOR: Oikonomia Borneo, 1*(1). Advance online publication. DOI: 10.24903/obor.v1i1.1816

Suwignjo, P., Panjaitan, L., Baihaqy, A. R., & Rusdiansyah, A. (2023). Predictive analytics to improve inventory performance: A case study of an FMCG company. Operations and Supply Chain Management An International Journal, 293–310. DOI: 10.31387/oscm0530390

Wilson, R. D., & Stephens, A. M. (2023). The challenges of B2B innovation: Using marketing analytics to plan and implement a successful digital catalog adoption. *Journal of Business and Industrial Marketing*, *38*(2), 290–302. DOI: 10.1108/JBIM-12-2021-0598

13. KEY TERMS AND DEFINITIONS

Artificial Intelligence (AI): The simulation of human intelligence processes by machines, particularly computer systems, used in this context for predictive analytics, sales forecasting, and decision automation.

Business Intelligence (BI): A technology-driven process for analyzing data and presenting actionable information to support business decision-making, encompassing data visualization, reporting, and performance tracking.

Power BI: A Microsoft-developed data visualization and business analytics tool that transforms raw data into interactive dashboards and real-time insights for enterprise decision support.

Point-of-Sale (POS) System: A digital interface that records sales transactions, manages billing, tracks inventory, and serves as a crucial data source for sales analytics in B2B environments.

Data Visualization: The graphical representation of data using charts, graphs, and dashboards to simplify complex datasets and enhance decision-making clarity.

Predictive Analytics: A branch of advanced analytics that uses historical data, statistical algorithms, and AI techniques to forecast future outcomes such as demand or sales trends.

Inventory Turnover Ratio (ITR): A financial metric that measures how often inventory is sold and replaced within a specific period, reflecting efficiency in inventory management.

Key Performance Indicator (KPI): Quantifiable metrics used to evaluate the success of an organization in achieving operational or strategic objectives, such as sales growth rate or profit margin.

Cloud-Based BI: Business intelligence systems hosted on cloud platforms like Azure or AWS, enabling real-time access, scalability, and collaboration across organizational networks.

Data-Driven Decision-Making: A managerial approach that relies on empirical data, analytics, and visualization rather than intuition to inform strategic and operational business choices.

Compilation of References

Abe, N., Verma, N., Apte, C., & Schroko, R. (2004, August). Cross channel optimized marketing by reinforcement learning. In *Proceedings of the tenth ACM SIGKDD international conference on Knowledge discovery and data mining* (pp. 767-772). DOI: 10.1145/1014052.1016912

Adeolu, A. A., Salamntu, L. T. P., & Paschal, I. M. (2024, March). Point of Sales (POS) Terminals for Bank Service Delivery, the needs for Management of Information Security: A case of Nigeria's Banking Sectors. In *2024 Conference on Information Communications Technology and Society (ICTAS)* (pp. 150-160). IEEE. DOI: 10.1109/ICTAS59620.2024.10507146

Agrawal, S., Chintha, V. R., Pamadi, V. N., & Aggarwal, A. (2023). The role of predictive analytics in inventory management. *Universal Research Reports*, *10*(4), 456–472. DOI: 10.36676/urr.v10.i4.1358

Aguirre, E., Mahr, D., Grewal, D., de Ruyter, K., & Wetzels, M. (2015). Unraveling the Personalization Paradox: The Effect of Information Collection and Trust-Building Strategies on Online Advertisement Effectiveness. *Journal of Retailing*, *91*(1), 34–49. DOI: 10.1016/j.jretai.2014.09.005

Ahmad, I. A. I., Akagha, O. V., Dawodu, S. O., Obi, O. C., Anyanwu, A. C., & Onwusinkwue, S. (2024). Innovation management in tech start-ups: A review of strategies for growth and sustainability. *International Journal of Science and Research Archive*, *11*(1), 807–816. DOI: 10.30574/ijsra.2024.11.1.0150

Ajekiigbe, V. O., Ogieuhi, I. J., Anthony, C. S., Bakare, I. S., Anyacho, S., Ogunleke, P. O., Fatokun, D. I., Akinmeji, O., Ruth, O. T., Olaore, A. K., Amusa, O., & Agbo, C. E. (2025). Consumer behavior and its role in E. coli outbreaks: The impact of fast-food preparation practices and hygiene awareness. *Tropical Medicine and Health*, *53*(1), 27. Advance online publication. DOI: 10.1186/s41182-025-00710-y

Akpan, I. J., & Ibidunni, A. S. (2023). Digitization and technological transformation of small business for sustainable development in the less developed and emerging economies: A research note and call for papers. *Journal of Small Business and Entrepreneurship*, *35*(5), 671–676. DOI: 10.1080/08276331.2021.1924505

Al Kautsaf, F. M. bin Mohd Nizam, M. N., & Harun, K. S. (2023, January). A system implementation: Point-of-sales (POS) system integrated with business intelligence (BI) capability focused on SME in Indonesia. In *2023 15th International Conference on Developments in eSystems Engineering (DeSE)* (pp. 287-292). IEEE.

Alam, T. (2021). Cloud Computing and its role in the Information Technology. [ITSDI]. *IAIC Transactions on Sustainable Digital Innovation*, *1*, 108–115.

Al-Eisawi, D., Serrano, A., & Koulouri, T. (2020). The effect of organisational absorptive capacity on business intelligence systems efficiency and organisational efficiency. *Industrial Management & Data Systems*, *121*(2), 519–544. DOI: 10.1108/IMDS-02-2020-0120

Ali, L., Ali, F., Abdalla, M. J., & Alotaibi, S. (2025). Beyond the hype: Evaluating the impact of generative AI on brand authenticity, image, and consumer behavior in the restaurant industry. *International Journal of Hospitality Management*, *131*, 104318. Advance online publication. DOI: 10.1016/j.ijhm.2025.104318

Alipour, P., Gallegos, E. E., & Sridhar, S. (2025). AI-driven marketing personalization: Deploying convolutional neural networks to decode consumer behavior. *International Journal of Human-Computer Interaction*, *41*(16), 10266–10284. DOI: 10.1080/10447318.2024.2432455

Almilia, L. S., & Anas Hartika, M. D. (2022). Effect of tasks complexity and visualization on investment decision-making. [JRAP]. *Jurnal Riset Akuntansi & Perpajakan*, *9*(01), 1–18. DOI: 10.35838/jrap.2022.009.01.01

Alshurideh, M., Al Kurdi, B., Salloum, S. A., Arpaci, I., & Al-Emran, M. (2023). Predicting the actual use of m-learning systems: A comparative approach using PLS-SEM and machine learning algorithms. *Interactive Learning Environments*, *31*(3), 1214–1228. DOI: 10.1080/10494820.2020.1826982

Aluri, A., Price, B. S., & McIntyre, N. H. (2019). Using machine learning to co-create value through dynamic customer engagement in a brand loyalty program. *Journal of Hospitality & Tourism Research (Washington, D.C.)*, *43*(1), 78–100. DOI: 10.1177/1096348017753521

Anardani, S., Azis, M. N. L., & Asyhari, M. Y. (2023). The implementation of Business Intelligence to analyze sales trends in the Indofishing online store using power BI. Brilliance. *Research of Artificial Intelligence*, *3*(2), 300–305. DOI: 10.47709/brilliance.v3i2.3232

Arachchi, H. D. M., & Samarasinghe, G. D. (2023). Impulse purchase intention in an AI-mediated retail environment: Extending the TAM with attitudes towards technology and innovativeness. *Global Business Review*, •••, 09721509231197721. DOI: 10.1177/09721509231197721

Astini, R., Royanti, I., & Ramli, Y. Tafiprios, Imaningsih, E. S., & Imaroh, T. S. (2024). The Impact of Quick Commerce that Influence the Purchase Decision of E-Grocery. *Przestrzeń Społeczna (Social Space)*, *24*(1), 110–128. https://socialspacejournal.eu/menu-script/index.php/ssj/article/view/336

Babu, S. M., Kumar, P. P., Devi, S., Reddy, K. P., & Satish, M. (2023, October). Predicting consumer behaviour with artificial intelligence. In *2023 IEEE 5th international conference on cybernetics, cognition and machine learning applications (ICCCMLA)* (pp. 698-703). IEEE.

Badea, L. M. (2014). Predicting consumer behavior with artificial neural networks. *Procedia Economics and Finance*, *15*, 238–246. DOI: 10.1016/S2212-5671(14)00492-4

Bandara, R., Fernando, M., & Akter, S. (2020). Privacy concerns in E-commerce: A taxonomy and a future research agenda. *Electronic Markets*, *30*(3), 629–647. DOI: 10.1007/s12525-019-00375-6

Barbera, J., Naibert, N., Komperda, R., & Pentecost, T. C. (2020). Clarity on Cronbach's alpha use. *Journal of Chemical Education*, *98*(2), 257–258. DOI: 10.1021/acs.jchemed.0c00183

Barhoumi, L., Rached, Z., & Boudiche, S. (2025). Tunisian Consumer Behavior and Acceptance of Farmed Fish Versus Wild Fish and Its Determinants Factors. *Aquaculture Studies*, *25*(4), 173–181. DOI: 10.4194/AQUAST2236

Bauer, J., & Jannach, D. (2018). Optimal pricing in e-commerce based on sparse and noisy data. *Decision Support Systems*, *106*, 53–63. DOI: 10.1016/j.dss.2017.12.002

Bayram, F., & Ahmed, B. S. (2025). Towards trustworthy machine learning in production: An overview of the robustness in mlops approach. *ACM Computing Surveys*, *57*(5), 1–35. DOI: 10.1145/3708497

Belghith Ep Kallel, M., Bouajaja, S., & Elloumi, A. (2024). Developing a sales dashboard with Power BI – A case study in a pharmaceutical company. *Decision Making Advances*, *2*(1), 142–147. DOI: 10.31181/dma21202438

Bello, O. A., Folorunso, A., Ogundipe, A., Kazeem, O., Budale, A., Zainab, F., & Ejiofor, O. E. (2022). Enhancing cyber financial fraud detection using deep learning techniques: A study on neural networks and anomaly detection. *International Journal of Network and Communication Research*, *7*(1), 90–113.

Bentalha, B. (2025). Artificial intelligence in B2B sales. In Advances in Finance, Accounting, and Economics (pp. 143–164). IGI Global. DOI: 10.4018/979-8-3693-7357-6.ch008

Berger, J., Humphreys, A., Ludwig, S., Moe, W. W., Netzer, O., & Schweidel, D. A. (2020). Uniting the Tribes: Using Text for Marketing Insight. *Journal of Marketing*, *84*(1), 1–25. DOI: 10.1177/0022242919873106

Bharadiya, J. P. (2023). The role of machine learning in transforming business intelligence. *International Journal of Computing and Artificial Intelligence*, *4*(1), 16–24. DOI: 10.33545/27076571.2023.v4.i1a.60

Bhargava, A., Bhargava, D., Kumar, P. N., Sajja, G. S., & Ray, S. (2022). Industrial IoT and AI implementation in vehicular logistics and supply chain management for vehicle mediated transportation systems. *International Journal of System Assurance Engineering and Management*, *13*(1), 673–680. DOI: 10.1007/s13198-021-01581-2

Bharti, J., & Dongre, S. (2024, June). Deep learning for enhanced consumer behavior analysis and predictive accuracy. In *2024 International Conference on Innovations and Challenges in Emerging Technologies (ICICET)* (pp. 1-6). IEEE. DOI: 10.1109/ICICET59348.2024.10616324

Bleier, A., & Eisenbeiss, M. (2015a). Personalized online advertising effectiveness: The interplay of what, when, and where. *Marketing Science*, *34*(5), 669–688. DOI: 10.1287/mksc.2015.0930

Bleier, A., & Eisenbeiss, M. (2015b). The importance of trust for personalized online advertising. *Journal of Retailing*, *91*(3), 390–409. DOI: 10.1016/j.jretai.2015.04.001

Bose, R., Mondal, H., Sarkar, I., & Roy, S. (2022). Design of smart inventory management system for construction sector based on IoT and cloud computing. *E-Prime - Advances in Electrical Engineering. Electronics and Energy*, *2*, 100051. DOI: 10.1016/j.prime.2022.100051

Boutaleb, B. (2024). Factors Influencing Smart Phone Buying Behavior of Consumers: Implications for Building a Marketing Strategy. *Business Ethics and Leadership*, *8*(3), 71–81. DOI: 10.61093/bel.8(3).71-81.2024

Boutaleb, B., & Toukabri, M. (2024). Determinants of Consumer's Adoption of Latest Version Smartphones: An Empirical Study of Saudi Consumers. *Engineering, Technology &. Applied Scientific Research*, *14*(6), 18252–18257. DOI: 10.48084/etasr.8914

Bouveret, A. (2019). Estimation of losses due to cyber risk for financial institutions. *Journal of Operational Risk*, *14*(2), 1–20. DOI: 10.21314/JOP.2019.224

Brodie, R. J., Coviello, N. E., & Winklhofer, H. (2008). Contemporary Marketing Practices research program: A review of the first decade. *Journal of Business and Industrial Marketing*, *23*(2), 84–94. DOI: 10.1108/08858620810850191

Bromiley, P., McShane, M., Nair, A., & Rustambekov, E. (2015). Enterprise risk management: Review, critique, and research directions. *Long Range Planning*, *48*(4), 265–276. DOI: 10.1016/j.lrp.2014.07.005

Brunner, D., Legat, C., & Seebacher, U. (2024). Towards Next Generation Data-Driven Management: Leveraging Predictive Swarm Intelligence to Reason and Predict Market Dynamics. In Collective Intelligence (pp. 152-203). CRC Press.

Bughin, J., & Van Zeebroeck, N. (2018). Artificial intelligence: The next digital frontier? McKinsey Global Institute. https://www.mckinsey.com

Bzdok, D., Altman, N., & Krzywinski, M. (2018). Statistics versus machine learning. *Nature Methods*, *15*(4), 233–234. DOI: 10.1038/nmeth.4642 PMID: 30100822

Calvert, G. A., & Brammer, M. J. (2012). Predicting consumer behavior: Using novel mind-reading approaches. *IEEE Pulse*, *3*(3), 38–41. DOI: 10.1109/MPUL.2012.2189167

Castro, G. M. M., Aitken, H. G. W., & Calvanapon, A. A. (2023). Business Intelligence Tools for a Digital Services Company in Peru, 2022. *International Journal of Business Intelligence Research*, *14*(1), 1–14. DOI: 10.4018/IJBIR.318330

Çelik, H., Caf, B. B., Geyik, C., Çebi, G., & Tayfun, M. (2024). Enhancing urinalysis with smartphone and AI: A comprehensive review of point-of-care urinalysis and nutritional advice. *Chemicke Zvesti*, *78*(2), 651–664. DOI: 10.1007/s11696-023-03137-z

Chapelle, O., Manavoglu, E., & Rosales, R. (2015). Simple and scalable response prediction for display advertising. [TIST]. *ACM Transactions on Intelligent Systems and Technology*, *5*(4), 61. DOI: 10.1145/2532128

Chatterjee, S., Rana, N. P., Tamilmani, K., & Sharma, A. (2020). The next frontier of digital marketing: Artificial intelligence. *International Journal of Information Management*, *54*, 102188. DOI: 10.1016/j.ijinfomgt.2020.102188

Chaudhuri, A. (2002). How Brand Reputation Affects the Advertising-Brand Equity Link. *Journal of Advertising Research*, *42*(3), 33–43. DOI: 10.2501/jar-42-3-33-43

Chavhan, R., & Dutta, P. (2024). Redesigning quick commerce fresh and short food supply chains: Circular economy strategies for sustainable last-mile operations. *British Food Journal*, *127*(5), 1676–1701. DOI: 10.1108/BFJ-05-2024-0560

Chenavaz, R. Y., & Dimitrov, S. (2025). Artificial intelligence and dynamic pricing: A systematic literature review. *Journal of Applied Econometrics*, *28*(1), 2466140. Advance online publication. DOI: 10.1080/15140326.2025.2466140

Cheng, J., Sun, J., Yao, K., Xu, M., & Cao, Y. (2022). A variable selection method based on mutual information and variance inflation factor. *Spectrochimica Acta. Part A: Molecular and Biomolecular Spectroscopy*, *268*, 120652. DOI: 10.1016/j.saa.2021.120652

Chen, J., Xu, H., & Whinston, A. B. (2021). Moderated online communities and quality of user-generated content. *Journal of Management Information Systems*, *38*(1), 11–40. DOI: 10.1080/07421222.2021.1870386

Chen, L., Jiang, M., Jia, F., & Liu, G. (2022). Artificial intelligence adoption in business-to-business marketing: Toward a conceptual framework. *Journal of Business and Industrial Marketing*, *37*(5), 1025–1044. DOI: 10.1108/JBIM-09-2020-0448

Chen, R. Z., & Shih, C. H. (2021). Applying Spatio-temporal Analysis in Telecom Fraud Investigation. *Procedia Computer Science*, *192*, 3109–3113. DOI: 10.1016/j.procs.2021.09.083

Chen, Y. J., Wu, C. H., Chen, Y. M., Li, H. Y., & Chen, H. K. (2017). Enhancement of fraud detection for narratives in annual reports. *International Journal of Accounting Information Systems*, *26*, 32–45. Advance online publication. DOI: 10.1016/j.accinf.2017.06.004

Chen, Y., Li, C., & Wang, H. (2022). Big data and predictive analytics for business intelligence: A bibliographic study (2000–2021). *Forecasting*, *4*(4), 767–786. DOI: 10.3390/forecast4040042

Chen, Z., Wu, J., Tian, C., & Liu, Z. (2025). Gray market speculation: Analyzing retailer behavior and manufacturer strategies in the context of strategic consumer behavior. *International Journal of Production Economics, 284*, 109607. Advance online publication. DOI: 10.1016/j.ijpe.2025.109607

Cheung, M. F., & To, W. M. (2017). The influence of the propensity to trust on mobile users' attitudes toward in-app advertisements: An extension of the theory of planned behavior. *Computers in Human Behavior, 76*, 102–111. DOI: 10.1016/j.chb.2017.07.011

Chintagunta, P., Hanssens, D. M., & Hauser, J. R. (2016). Marketing and Data Science: Together the Future is Ours. *GfK Marketing Intelligence Review, 8*(2), 18–23. DOI: 10.1515/gfkmir-2016-0011

Chiu, M. C., Huang, J. H., Gupta, S., & Akman, G. (2021). Developing a personalized recommendation system in a smart product service system based on unsupervised learning model. *Computers in Industry, 128*, 103421. DOI: 10.1016/j.compind.2021.103421

Chollet, F. (2018). *Deep learning with Python*. Manning Publications.

Cliquet, G. (2020). From Geomarketing to Spatial Marketing. In *Spatial Economics* (Vol. II). Applications., DOI: 10.1007/978-3-030-40094-1_10

Corbitt, B. J., Thanasankit, T., & Yi, H. (2003). Trust and e-commerce: A study of consumer perceptions. *Electronic Commerce Research and Applications, 2*(3), 203–215. DOI: 10.1016/S1567-4223(03)00024-3

Corsaro, D., & Anzivino, A. (2021). Understanding value creation in digital context: An empirical investigation of B2B. *Marketing Theory, 21*(3), 317–349. DOI: 10.1177/14705931211001542

Coviello, N. E., & Brodie, R. J. (2001). Contemporary marketing practices of consumer and business-to-business firms: How different are they? *Journal of Business and Industrial Marketing, 16*(5), 382–400. DOI: 10.1108/08858620110400223

Coviello, N. E., Brodie, R. J., Brookes, R. W., & Palmer, R. A. (2003). Assessing the role of e-marketing in contemporary marketing practice. *Journal of Marketing Management, 19*(7-8), 857–881. DOI: 10.1080/0267257X.2003.9728240

Cui, Y., van Esch, P., & Jain, S. P. (2022). Just walk out: The effect of AI-enabled checkouts. *European Journal of Marketing, 56*(6), 1650–1683.

Damanik, E. O., Tarigan, W. J., Tampubolon, J., Simanjuntak, D. C. Y., Sihombing, S. D., Saragih, D. Y., Simarmata, P. P., & Simarmata, H. M. P. (2025). Digital Transformation of PT Pos: Customer Loyalty In The Era of Security and Data Technology. *Jurnal Ekuilnomi*, *7*(2), 547–560. DOI: 10.36985/88gt8930

Darmawan, R., & Swalaganata, G. (2025). ANALISA KOMPARATIF POWER BI DAN TABLEAU DALAM IMPLEMENTASI BUSINESS INTELLIGENCE PADA BRAZILIAN E-COMMERCE PUBLIC DATASET BY OLIST. [Jurnal Mahasiswa Teknik Informatika]. *JATI*, *9*(5), 8936–8944. DOI: 10.36040/jati.v9i5.15178

Data, I. B. M., & Team, A. I. (2023). Understanding the different types of artificial intelligence. IBM. https://www.ibm.com/think/topics/artificial-intelligence-types

Davenport, T. H., Guha, A., Grewal, D., & Bressgott, T. (2020). How artificial intelligence will change the future of marketing. *Journal of the Academy of Marketing Science*, *48*(1), 24–42. DOI: 10.1007/s11747-019-00696-0

Davenport, T. H., & Ronanki, R. (2018). Artificial intelligence for the real world. *Harvard Business Review*, *96*(1), 108–116.

Deloitte. (2023). Global powers of luxury goods 2023. Deloitte. https://www.deloitte.com

Deng, T., Bi, S., & Xiao, J. (2024, December). Transformer-based financial fraud detection with cloud-optimized real-time streaming. In *Proceedings of the 2024 5th International Conference on Big Data Economy and Information Management* (pp. 702-707). DOI: 10.1145/3724154.3724271

Dey, A., Jain, S., & Nandi, S. (2019, March). New method of POS based on artificial intelligence and cloud computing. In *2019 International Conference on Recent Advances in Energy-efficient Computing and Communication (ICRAECC)* (pp. 1-6). IEEE. DOI: 10.1109/ICRAECC43874.2019.8995078

Di Caro, V. N. (2022). Preterite indicative Pseudo-Coordination and morphomic patterns: The case of the W-Pattern in the dialect of Delia. In *Pseudo-Coordination and Multiple Agreement Constructions* (pp. 99–128). John Benjamins Publishing Company. DOI: 10.1075/la.274.04dic

Di Vaio, A., Palladino, R., Hassan, R., & Escobar, O. (2020). Artificial intelligence and business models in the sustainable development goals perspective: A systematic literature review. *Journal of Business Research*, *32*, 283–314. Advance online publication. DOI: 10.1016/j.jbusres.2020.08.019

Djerdjouri, M. (2019). Data and Business Intelligence Systems for Competitive Advantage: Prospects, challenges, and real-world applications. *Mercados y Negocios*, *41*(41), 5–18. DOI: 10.32870/myn.v0i41.7537

Dörnyei, K. R. (2021). Marketing Professionals' Views on Online Advertising Fraud. *Journal of Current Issues and Research in Advertising*, *42*(2), 156–174. DOI: 10.1080/10641734.2020.1737276

dos Santos, P. M., & Cirillo, M. Â. (2023). Construction of the average variance extracted index for construct validation in structural equation models with adaptive regressions. *Communications in Statistics. Simulation and Computation*, *52*(4), 1639–1650. DOI: 10.1080/03610918.2021.1888122

Doshi, J. (2021). Chatbot User Interface for Customer Relationship Management using NLP models. *Proceedings - 2021 1st IEEE International Conference on Artificial Intelligence and Machine Vision, AIMV 2021*. DOI: 10.1109/AIMV53313.2021.9670914

Dubey, V. K., & Das, A. (2022). Role of governance on SME exports and performance. *Journal of Research in Marketing and Entrepreneurship*, *24*(1), 39–74. DOI: 10.1108/JRME-08-2020-0109

Dwivedi, Y. K., Hughes, L., Baabdullah, A. M., Ribeiro-Navarrete, S., Giannakis, M., Al-Debei, M. M., Dennehy, D., Metri, B., Buhalis, D., Cheung, C. M. K., Conboy, K., Doyle, R., Dubey, R., Dutot, V., Felix, R., Goyal, D. P., Gustafsson, A., Hinsch, C., Jebabli, I., & Wamba, S. F. (2022). Metaverse beyond the hype: Multidisciplinary perspectives on emerging challenges, opportunities, and agenda for research, practice and policy. *International Journal of Information Management*, *66*, 102542. Advance online publication. DOI: 10.1016/j.ijinfomgt.2022.102542

Ediriweera, C., Fernando, M. T., & Pramudika, H. (2024). AI-driven sustainable video marketing strategies: Harnessing deep learning algorithms to sustainable advertising campaigns with special reference to the education industry. *Asian Journal of Marketing Management*, *3*(01). Advance online publication. DOI: 10.31357/ajmm.v3i01.7304

Eken, B., Pallewatta, S., Tran, N., Tosun, A., & Babar, M. A. (2024). A multivocal review of mlops practices, challenges and open issues. *ACM Computing Surveys*.

El-Hajj, M., & Pavlova, M. (2024). Predictive Modeling of Customer Response to Marketing Campaigns. *Electronics 2024, Vol. 13, Page 3953*, *13*(19), 3953. DOI: 10.3390/electronics13193953

Eliyas, S., & Ranjana, P. (2022). Recommendation Systems: Content-Based Filtering vs Collaborative Filtering. *2022 2nd International Conference on Advance Computing and Innovative Technologies in Engineering, ICACITE 2022*, 1360–1365. DOI: 10.1109/ICACITE53722.2022.9823730

Ellis-Chadwick, F., & Chaffey, D. (2012). *Digital marketing: strategy, implementation and practice*. Pearson.

Engel, J. F., Blackwell, R. D., & Miniard, P. W. (1995). *Consumer behavior* (8th ed.). Dryden Press.

Esch, P. V., Cui, Y., & Jain, S. P. (2021). Stimulating or intimidating: The effect of AI-enabled in-store communication on consumer patronage likelihood. *Journal of Advertising*, *50*(1), 63–80. DOI: 10.1080/00913367.2020.1832939

Essman, M., Burgoine, T., Jones, A., Polden, M., Robinson, E., Sacks, G., Sharp, S. J., Smith, R., Vanderlee, L., White, C. M., White, M., Hammond, D., & Adams, J. (2025). Assessing the impact of a mandatory calorie labelling policy in out-of-home food outlets in England on consumer behaviour: A natural experimental study. *BMC Public Health*, *25*(1), 955. Advance online publication. DOI: 10.1186/s12889-025-22150-3

Fadi, O., Karim, Z., & Mohammed, B. (2022). A survey on blockchain and artificial intelligence technologies for enhancing security and privacy in smart environments. *IEEE Access : Practical Innovations, Open Solutions*, *10*, 93168–93186. DOI: 10.1109/ACCESS.2022.3203568

Famil Alamdar, P., & Seifi, A. (2023). Dynamic pricing of differentiated products under competition with reference price effects using a neural network-based approach. *Journal of Revenue and Pricing Management*, *23*(6), 575–587. DOI: 10.1057/s41272-023-00444-8

Famoti, O., Ezechi, O. N., Ewim, C. P.-M., Eloho, O., Muyiwa-Ajayi, T. P., Igwe, A. N., & Ihechere, A. O. (2025). Operational efficiency in retail: Using data analytics to optimize inventory and supply chain management. International Journal of Scientific Research in Computer Science. *Engineering and Information Technology*, *11*(1), 1483–1494. DOI: 10.32628/CSEIT251112173

Fang, X., & Chen, H. C. (2022). Using vendor management inventory system for goods inventory management in IoT manufacturing. *Enterprise Information Systems*, *16*(7), 1885743. Advance online publication. DOI: 10.1080/17517575.2021.1885743

Ferenhof, H. A., Bonamigo, A., Rosa, L. G., & Vieira, T. C. (2024). Theoretical B2B knowledge management framework focused on value. *VINE Journal of Information and Knowledge Management Systems*, *54*(2), 424–451. DOI: 10.1108/VJIKMS-10-2021-0239

Fourkiotis, K. P., & Tsadiras, A. (2024). Applying machine learning and statistical forecasting methods for enhancing pharmaceutical sales predictions. *Forecasting*, *6*(1), 170–186. DOI: 10.3390/forecast6010010

Fournier, S. (1998). Consumers and their brands: Developing relationship theory in consumer research. *The Journal of Consumer Research*, *24*(4), 343–373. DOI: 10.1086/209515

Fournier, S., & Alvarez, C. (2012). Brands as relationship partners: Warmth, competence, and in-between. *Journal of Consumer Psychology*, *22*(2), 152–163. DOI: 10.1016/j.jcps.2011.10.003

Gad-Elrab, A. A. A. (2021). Modern business intelligence: Big data analytics and artificial intelligence for creating the data-driven value. In E-Business - Higher Education and Intelligence Applications. IntechOpen. DOI: 10.5772/intechopen.97374

Gefen, D., Benbasat, I., & Pavlou, P. (2008). A research agenda for trust in online environments. Journal of Management Informatio.

Ghosh, S., Rana, A., & Kansal, V. (2020). A benchmarking framework using nonlinear manifold detection techniques for software defect prediction. *International Journal on Computer Science and Engineering*, *21*(4), 593–614.

Gkikas, D. C., & Theodoridis, P. K. (2021). AI in consumer behavior. In *Advances in Artificial Intelligence-based Technologies: Selected Papers in Honour of Professor Nikolaos G. Bourbakis—Vol. 1* (pp. 147–176). Springer International Publishing.

Gomez-Uribe, C. A., & Hunt, N. (2015). The netflix recommender system: Algorithms, business value, and innovation. *ACM Transactions on Management Information Systems*, *6*(4), 1–19. Advance online publication. DOI: 10.1145/2843948

Gonçalves, C. T., Gonçalves, M. J. A., & Campante, M. I. (2023). Developing integrated performance dashboards visualisations using power BI as a platform. *Information (Basel)*, *14*(11), 614. DOI: 10.3390/info14110614

Govindaraj, M., Vandhana, N., & Lawrence, J. (2025). AI-Driven Consumer Behavior Insights: Applying the Insight Equation to Modern Marketing. In Decoding Consumer Behavior Using the Insight Equation and AI Marketing (pp. 1-20). IGI Global Scientific Publishing.

Grewal, D., Noble, S. M., Roggeveen, A. L., & Nordfält, J. (2021). The future of in-store technology. *Journal of the Academy of Marketing Science*, *49*(1), 96–113. DOI: 10.1007/s11747-019-00697-z

Grover, V., Dogra, M., Sahu, D., & Nandal, M. (2025). Empowering Personalized Marketing: Leveraging Data Engineering for Customer Segmentation. In Data Engineering for Data-driven Marketing (pp. 105-119). Emerald Publishing Limited.

Guesalaga, R., Ruiz-Alba, J. L., & López-Tenorio, P. J. (2024). Drivers of business-to-business sales success and the role of digitalization after COVID-19 disruptions. *Journal of Business and Industrial Marketing*, *39*(4), 708–720. DOI: 10.1108/JBIM-12-2022-0576

Guillod, T., Papamanolis, P., & Kolar, J. W. (2020). Artificial neural network (ANN) based fast and accurate inductor modeling and design. *IEEE Open Journal of Power Electronics*, *1*, 284–299. DOI: 10.1109/OJPEL.2020.3012777

Gupta, A., & Jha, D. (2025a). The Rise of Quick Commerce. *Sustainable Digitalization Strategies in Business and Healthcare*, 93–116. : Gupta, A., & Jha, D. (2025b). The Rise of Quick Commerce: Redefining Retail Through Digital Innovation and Sustainable Practices. In *Sustainable Digitalization Strategies in Business and Healthcare* (pp. 93–116). IGI Global Scientific Publishing.DOI: 10.4018/979-8-3373-5087-5.ch004

Gupta, S., Sharma, V., & Tomar, R. (2025). Impact of AI-Driven Personalized Experience in Shaping Consumer Loyalty Towards Quick Commerce. *ESIC 2025 - 5th International Conference on Emerging Systems and Intelligent Computing, Proceedings*, 955–960. DOI: 10.1109/ESIC64052.2025.10962778

Gupta, S. T., Joshi, P., Kaur, A., & Kumar, P. (2025). Digital tools and technologies: Enabling knowledge sharing and collaborative business culture. In *Knowledge Sharing and Fostering Collaborative Business Culture*. IGI Global., DOI: 10.4018/979-8-3373-0710-7.ch016

Hair, J. F.Jr. (2020). Next-generation prediction metrics for composite-based PLS-SEM. *Industrial Management & Data Systems*, *121*(1), 5–11. DOI: 10.1108/IMDS-08-2020-0505

Haleem, A., Javaid, M., Asim Qadri, M., Pratap Singh, R., & Suman, R. (2022). Artificial intelligence (AI) applications for marketing: A literature-based study. In *International Journal of Intelligent Networks* (Vol. 3, pp. 119–132). KeAi Communications Co., DOI: 10.1016/j.ijin.2022.08.005

Hall, J. (2019a). How artificial intelligence is transforming digital marketing. *Hg. v. Forbes. Online Verfugbar Unter* Https://Www. Forbes. Com/Sites/Forbesagency-council/2019/08/21/How-Artificial-Intelligence-Istransforming-Digital-Marketing

Hall, J. (2019b). How artificial intelligence is transforming digital marketing. *Hg. v. Forbes. Online Verfugbar Unter* Https://Www. Forbes. Com/Sites/Forbesagency-council/2019/08/21/How-Artificial-Intelligence-Istransforming-Digital-Marketing

Hall, K. R., Harrison, D. E., Ajjan, H., & Marshall, G. W. (2022). Understanding salesperson intention to use AI feedback and its influence on business-to-business sales outcomes. *Journal of Business and Industrial Marketing*, *37*(9), 1787–1801. DOI: 10.1108/JBIM-04-2021-0218

Hamet, P., & Tremblay, J. (2017). Artificial intelligence in medicine. *metabolism, 69*, S36-S40.

Har, L. L., Rashid, U. K., Te Chuan, L., Sen, S. C., & Xia, L. Y. (2022). Revolution of Retail Industry: From Perspective of Retail 1.0 to 4.0. *Procedia Computer Science*, *200*, 1615–1625. DOI: 10.1016/j.procs.2022.01.362

Harter, A., Stich, L., & Spann, M. (2024). The Effect of Delivery Time on Repurchase Behavior in Quick Commerce. *Journal of Service Research*. Advance online publication. DOI: 10.1177/10946705241236961

Haseena, S., Saroja, S., Suseandhiran, N., & Manikandan, B. (2023). An intelligent approach for anomaly detection in credit card data using bat optimization algorithm. *Inteligencia Artificial*, *26*(72), 202–222. Advance online publication. DOI: 10.4114/intartif.vol26iss72pp202-222

Hautamäki, P., & Heikinheimo, M. (2025). Fully leveraging AI in B2B sales: Exploring sales managers' capabilities and organizational knowledge processes. *Journal of Business Research*, *194*, 115396. DOI: 10.1016/j.jbusres.2025.115396

He, Z. D., & Rao, V. R. (2024). Methods for Causal Inference in Marketing. *Foundations and Trends® in Marketing, 18*(3-4), 176-309.

Herzig, J., & Zander, K. (2025). Determinants of consumer behavior in short food supply chains: A systematic literature review. *Agricultural and Food Economics*, *13*(1), 21. Advance online publication. DOI: 10.1186/s40100-025-00370-w

Hoffman, D. L., Moreau, C. P., Stremersch, S., & Wedel, M. (2022). The Rise of New Technologies in Marketing: A Framework and Outlook. *Journal of Marketing*, *86*(1), 1–6. DOI: 10.1177/00222429211061636

Holmes, J., Sacchi, L., & Bellazzi, R. (2004). Artificial intelligence in medicine. *Annals of the Royal College of Surgeons of England*, *86*(86), 334–338.

Hoofnagle, C. J., Van Der Sloot, B., & Borgesius, F. Z. (2019). The European Union general data protection regulation: What it is and what it means. *Information & Communications Technology Law*, *28*(1), 65–98. DOI: 10.1080/13600834.2019.1573501

Hoyer, W. D., MacInnis, D. J., Pieters, R., Chan, E., & Northey, G. (2020). *Consumer behaviour*. Cengage AU.

Hrr, H. (2025). The Future of Digital Transformation: Leveraging Artificial Intelligence for Competitive Advantage. Available at *SSRN* 5123723. DOI: 10.2139/ssrn.5123723

Huang, M.-H., & Rust, R. T. (2021). A strategic framework for artificial intelligence in marketing. *Journal of the Academy of Marketing Science*, *49*(1), 30–50. DOI: 10.1007/s11747-020-00749-9

Huang, M.-H., & Rust, R. T. (2021). Artificial intelligence in service. *Journal of Service Research*, *24*(1), 3–16. DOI: 10.1177/1094670520902266

Huang, M.-H., Rust, R., & Maksimovic, V. (2019). The feeling economy: Managing in the next generation of artificial intelligence (AI). *California Management Review*, *61*(4), 43–65. DOI: 10.1177/0008125619863436

Hussein, M. K., Krmln, N. Q., Flayyih, H. H., & Noori, R. B. (2024, June). Harnessing technological innovation and artificial intelligence in Iraqi commercial banks to achieve sustainability. In *International Conference on Explainable Artificial Intelligence in the Digital Sustainability* (pp. 280-296). Cham: Springer Nature Switzerland. DOI: 10.1007/978-3-031-63717-9_18

Ignatius Ijomah, T., Vanessa Iyelolu, T., Ebele Agu, E., & Idemudia, C. (2024). Leveraging Artificial Intelligence for Personalized Marketing Campaigns to Improve Conversion Rates. In *International Journal Of Engineering* [). www.ijerd.com]. *Research for Development*, *20*(8), •••.

Iniesta-Bonillo, M.-A., Pompeu-Queiros, A., Capobianco Uriarte, M. M., & Alves, H. (2025). Mindfulness and consumer behavior: A bibliometric analysis of themes and trends over 20 years. *Humanities & Social Sciences Communications*, *12*(1), 93. Advance online publication. DOI: 10.1057/s41599-025-04367-0

Iyelolu, T. V., Agu, E. E., Idemudia, C., & Ijomah, T. I. (2024). Leveraging artificial intelligence for personalized marketing campaigns to improve conversion rates. *International Journal of Engineering Research and Development*, *20*(8), 253–270.

Iyer, P., Sharma, V., Gupta, R., & Chopra, R. (2021). Leveraging Reinforcement Learning and Neural Networks for Optimized Dynamic Pricing Strategies in B2C Markets. *Australian Advanced AI Research Journal, 10*(7). https://aaairj.com/index.php/v1/article/view/6

Jafari, T., Zarei, A., Azar, A., & Moghaddam, A. (2023). The impact of business intelligence on supply chain performance with emphasis on integration and agility–a mixed research approach. *International Journal of Productivity and Performance Management*, *72*(5), 1445–1478. DOI: 10.1108/IJPPM-09-2021-0511

Jagannathan, S. K., & Bizel, G., JV, T. A., Kannan, G., Sankaradass, V., & Navulla, D. (2023, May). A Smart Innovation of Business Intelligence Based Analytical Model by Using POS Based Deep Learning Model. In *2023 International Conference on Disruptive Technologies (ICDT)* (pp. 63-67). IEEE. DOI: 10.1109/ICDT57929.2023.10151080

Jaheer Mukthar, K. P., Sivasubramanian, K., Ramirez Asis, E. H., & Guerra-Munoz, M. E. (2022). Redesigning and reinvention of retail industry through artificial intelligence (AI). In *Future of organizations and work after the 4th industrial revolution: The role of artificial intelligence, big data, automation, and robotics* (pp. 41–56). Springer International Publishing. DOI: 10.1007/978-3-030-99000-8_3

Jain, P., & Aggarwal, K. (2020). *Transforming Marketing with Artificial Intelligence*. DOI: 10.13140/RG.2.2.25848.67844

Javaid, M., Haleem, A., Singh, R. P., Rab, S., & Suman, R. (2022). Exploring impact and features of machine vision for progressive industry 4.0 culture. *Sensors International*, *3*, 100132. DOI: 10.1016/j.sintl.2021.100132

Jayendran, R. A. P., Keikhosrokiani, P., & Chui, S. L. (2024). Inventory classification and management system using machine learning and analytical dashboard. In *Advances in Business Information Systems and Analytics* (pp. 299–318). IGI Global., DOI: 10.4018/979-8-3693-1210-0.ch012

Jeyaprabha, B., Kumar, S. R., Bolla, R. L., Bhatt, A. S., Sera, R. J., & Arora, K. (2025, February). Data-Driven Decision Making in Management: Leveraging Big Data Analytics for Strategic Planning. In 2025 First International Conference on Advances in Computer Science, Electrical, Electronics, and Communication Technologies (CE2CT) (pp. 1000-1003). IEEE.

Ji, F., Zheng, X., Xue, H., & Wang, J. (2025, April). A study on the application of artificial intelligence in personalized Go-to-market strategy in retail industry. In *Proceedings of the 2025 International Conference on Machine Learning and Neural Networks* (pp. 217-222). DOI: 10.1145/3747227.3747262

Jin, K., Li, Y., Wu, H., Tham, Y. C., Koh, V., Zhao, Y., Kawasaki, R., Grzybowski, A., & Ye, J. (2024). Integration of smartphone technology and artificial intelligence for advanced ophthalmic care: A systematic review. *Advances in Ophthalmology Practice and Research*, *4*(3), 120–127. DOI: 10.1016/j.aopr.2024.03.003

John, H., & Naaz, S. (2019). Credit Card Fraud Detection using Local Outlier Factor and Isolation Forest. *International Journal on Computer Science and Engineering*, *7*(4), 1060–1064. Advance online publication. DOI: 10.26438/ijcse/v7i4.10601064

Jones, J. P. (1990). Advertising: Strong force or weak force? Two views an ocean apart. *International Journal of Advertising*, *9*(3), 233–246. DOI: 10.1080/02650487.1990.11107151

Jr, H., Joe, F., & Matt, C. (2020). Howard, and Christian Nitzl. "Assessing measurement model quality in PLS-SEM using confirmatory composite analysis.". *Journal of Business Research*, *109*, 101–110. DOI: 10.1016/j.jbusres.2019.11.069

Jung, A.-R. (2017). The influence of perceived ad relevance on social media advertising: An empirical examination of a mediating role of privacy concern. *Computers in Human Behavior*, *70*, 303–309. DOI: 10.1016/j.chb.2017.01.008

Kaartemo, V., & Helkkula, A. (2018). A systematic review of artificial intelligence and robots in value. *Journal of Creating Value*, *4*(2), 211–228. DOI: 10.1177/2394964318805625

Kaliuta, K. (2023). Integration of AI for routine tasks using Salesforce. *Asian Journal of Research in Computer Science*, *16*(3), 119–127. DOI: 10.9734/ajrcos/2023/v16i3350

Kalkbrenner, M. T. (2023). Alpha, omega, and H internal consistency reliability estimates: Reviewing these options and when to use them. *Counseling Outcome Research and Evaluation*, *14*(1), 77–88. DOI: 10.1080/21501378.2021.1940118

Kannan, P. K., & Li, H. (2016a). *Digital Marketing: A Framework, Review and Research Agenda*. https://ssrn.com/abstract=3000712Electroniccopyavailableat: https://ssrn.com/abstract=3000712Electroniccopyavailableat:https://ssrn.com/abstract=3000712

Kapferer, J. N., & Bastien, V. (2012). *The luxury strategy: Break the rules of marketing to build luxury brands* (2nd ed.). Kogan Page.

Kaplan, A., & Haenlein, M. (2019). Siri, Siri, in my hand: Who's the fairest in the land? On the interpretations, illustrations, and implications of artificial intelligence. *Business Horizons*, *62*(1), 15–25. DOI: 10.1016/j.bushor.2018.08.004

Karpoff, J. M. (2021). The future of financial fraud. *Journal of Corporate Finance, 66*, 101694. DOI: 10.1016/j.jcorpfin.2020.101694

Kaur, A., Bhatnagar, D., & Singh, G. (2024). Exploring the machine learning-based decision tree technique in assessing credit risk likelihood of P2P Fintech lending for effective marketing. In *Neuromarketing's Role in Sustainable Finance*. IGI Global. DOI: 10.4018/979-8-3693-9117-4.ch019

Kaur, R., Kaur, S., & Kaur, A. (2025). Fintech and Financial Inclusion: Trends and Challenges. In *FinTech and Financial Inclusion: Leveraging Digital Finance for Economic Empowerment and Sustainable Growth*. Taylor and Francis., DOI: 10.4324/9781003514114-6

Kavitha, S., & Santhanalaxmi, K. (2025). Methods and Applications of Quick Commerce (Q-Commerce). *Methods and Applications of Quick Commerce (Q-Commerce)*, 261–298. : Kumar, C. R., & Manikandan, S. (2025). A Literature Review on Predictive Data Analytics and Learning Models in Stock Market Trend Analysis. *Lecture Notes in Electrical Engineering, 1274 LNEE*, 1175–1180. https://doi.org/DOI: 10.4018/979-8-3373-1712-0.ch010

Kennedy, H., Kunkel, T., & Funk, D. C. (2021). Using predictive analytics to measure effectiveness of social media engagement: A digital measurement perspective. *Sport Marketing Quarterly, 30*(4), 265–277. DOI: 10.32731/SMQ.304.1221.02

Khoi, Bui Huy. "Factors influencing on university reputation: Model selection by AIC." *Data science for financial econometrics* (2021): 177-188.

Khrais, L. T. (2020). Role of Artificial Intelligence in Shaping Consumer Demand in E-Commerce. *Future Internet, 12*(12), 226. DOI: 10.3390/fi12120226

Kietzmann, J., Paschen, J., & Treen, E. (2018). Artificial intelligence in advertising: How marketers can leverage artificial intelligence along the consumer journey. *Journal of Advertising Research, 58*(3), 263–267. DOI: 10.2501/JAR-2018-035

Kim, J., Jung, H., & Kim, W. (2022). Sequential Pattern Mining Approach for Personalized Fraudulent Transaction Detection in Online Banking. *Sustainability (Basel), 14*(15), 9791. Advance online publication. DOI: 10.3390/su14159791

Kim, W., Ryoo, Y., & Choi, Y. K. (2024). That uncanny valley of mind: When anthropomorphic AI agents disrupt personalized advertising. *International Journal of Advertising*, 1–30. Advance online publication. DOI: 10.1080/02650487.2024.2411669

Kivistö Arttu. (2024). *ROLE OF ARTIFICIAL INTELLIGENCE IN PROMOTIONAL CAMPAIGNS*. https://doi.org/https://urn.fi/URN:NBN:fi:jyu-202409055830

Kivistö, A. (2024). *Role of artificial intelligence in promotional campaigns.* https://jyx.jyu.fi/handle/123456789/96946

Kooti, F., Lerman, K., Aiello, L. M., Grbovic, M., Djuric, N., & Radosavljevic, V. (2016, February). Portrait of an online shopper: Understanding and predicting consumer behavior. In *Proceedings of the ninth ACM international conference on web search and data mining* (pp. 205-214). DOI: 10.1145/2835776.2835831

Kopalle, P. K., Gangwar, M., Kaplan, A., Ramachandran, D., Reinartz, W., & Rindfleisch, A. (2022). Examining artificial intelligence (AI) technologies in marketing via a global lens: Current trends and future research opportunities. *International Journal of Research in Marketing*, *39*(2), 522–540. DOI: 10.1016/j.ijresmar.2021.11.002

Kreuzberger, D., Kühl, N., & Hirschl, S. (2023). Machine learning operations (mlops): Overview, definition, and architecture. *IEEE Access : Practical Innovations, Open Solutions*, *11*, 31866–31879. DOI: 10.1109/ACCESS.2023.3262138

Kukreti, M., Sehajpal, S., Tiwari, R., & Sood, K. (2024a). Driving global health and sustainable development goals with smart technology. In *Driving Global Health and Sustainable Development Goals With Smart Technology*. IGI Global., DOI: 10.4018/979-8-3373-0240-9

Kumar, V., Ashraf, A. R., & Nadeem, W. (2024). AI-powered marketing: What, where, and how? *International Journal of Information Management*, *77*, 102783. DOI: 10.1016/j.ijinfomgt.2024.102783

Kumar, V., Dixit, A., Javalgi, R. G., Dass, M., & Dixit, A. (2019). Digital transformation of business-to-business marketing: Framework, evolution, and research directions. *Industrial Marketing Management*, *81*, 12–25. DOI: 10.1016/j.indmarman.2019.02.034

Kurniawan, A. C., Harsono, I. N. O., & Ruswandi, N. (2023). Determination of Warehouse Performance Measurement Indicators at PT Pos Logistik Indonesia with The Balanced Scorecard Method. *Majalah Ilmiah Bijak*, *20*(1), 132–146. DOI: 10.31334/bijak.v20i1.3120

Kusmaryono, I., Wijayanti, D., & Maharani, H. R. (2022). Number of Response Options, Reliability, Validity, and Potential Bias in the Use of the Likert Scale Education and Social Science Research: A Literature Review. *International Journal of Educational Methodology*, *8*(4), 625–637. DOI: 10.12973/ijem.8.4.625

Lalotra, G. S., Kumar, V., Bhatt, A., Chen, T., & Mahmud, M. (2022). iReTADS: An Intelligent Real-Time Anomaly Detection System for Cloud Communications Using Temporal Data Summarization and Neural Network. *Security and Communication Networks, 2022*(1), 9149164. DOI: 10.1155/2022/9149164

Lambrecht, A., & Tucker, C. (2013). When does retargeting work? Information specificity in online advertising. *JMR, Journal of Marketing Research, 50*(5), 561–576. DOI: 10.1509/jmr.11.0503

Langen, H., & Huber, M. (2023). How causal machine learning can leverage marketing strategies: Assessing and improving the performance of a coupon campaign. *PLoS One, 18*(1), e0278937. DOI: 10.1371/journal.pone.0278937 PMID: 36630398

Ledro, C., Nosella, A., & Dalla Pozza, I. (2023). Integration of AI in CRM: Challenges and guidelines. *Journal of Open Innovation, 9*(4), 100151. DOI: 10.1016/j.joitmc.2023.100151

Lee, C. S., Cheang, P. Y. S., & Moslehpour, M. (2022). Predictive analytics in business analytics: Decision tree. *Advances in Decision Sciences, 26*(1), 1–29. DOI: 10.47654/v26y2022i1p1-29

Lee, C. Y., & Ke, H. R. (2012). A study on user perceptions and user behavior of an online federated search system. *Journal of Educational Media and Library Science, 49*(3), 369–404.

Lee, H.-S. (2025). Defining core science of 'sensory and consumer science': Understanding human sensory perception, foods/materials interaction, and their influence on consumer behavior, health, and well-being. *Food Quality and Preference, 129*, 105492. Advance online publication. DOI: 10.1016/j.foodqual.2025.105492

Lee, M. K., & Turban, E. (2001). A trust model for consumer internet shopping. *International Journal of Electronic Commerce, 6*(1), 75–91. DOI: 10.1080/10864415.2001.11044227

Li, J., & Hingoro, A. (2025). Leveraging Artificial Intelligence for Personalized Marketing: Enhancing Consumer Engagement and Driving Sales. In Leveraging AI-Powered Marketing in the Experience-Driven Economy (pp. 147-180). IGI Global Scientific Publishing.

Liang, Y., Chen, X. J., Chen, Y., Xiao, P., & Zhang, J. (2024). Mobile ad fraud: Empirical patterns in publisher and advertising campaign data. *International Journal of Research in Marketing, 41*(2), 265–281. DOI: 10.1016/j.ijresmar.2023.09.003

Li, Q. (2022). Evaluation of Artificial Intelligence models and wireless network applications for enterprise sales management innovation under the New Retail Format. *Wireless Communications and Mobile Computing*, *2022*(1), 1–10. DOI: 10.1002/wcm.1087

Liu, H., Zhang, J., Zhou, Z., Dai, Y., & Qin, L. (2024). A Deep Reinforcement Learning-Based Algorithm for Multi-Objective Agricultural Site Selection and Logistics Optimization Problem. *Applied Sciences 2024, Vol. 14, Page 8479, 14*(18), 8479. DOI: 10.3390/app14188479

Liu, L. (2022). e-Commerce Personalized Recommendation Based on Machine Learning Technology. *Mobile Information Systems*, *2022*(1), 1761579. DOI: 10.1155/2022/1761579

Li, Z. (2019). Optimal utilization of ports' free-of-charge times in one distribution center and multiple ports inventory systems. *Complexity*, *2019*(1), 1–12. DOI: 10.1155/2019/4510586

Lu, X. 2024. Application of Artificial Intelligence Algorithms in Precision Marketing with Flow Data Analysis Models. In: *Proceedings of the 2024 International Conference on Machine Learning and Computational Science Innovations (ICMCSI)*, 18-19 January 2024. IEEE. DOI: 10.1109/ICMCSI61536.2024.00060

Lytras, M. D., Raghavan, V., & Damiani, E. (2017). Big Data and Data Analytics Research: From Metaphors to Value Space for Collective Wisdom in Human Decision Making and Smart Machines. *International Journal on Semantic Web and Information Systems*, *13*(1), 1–10. DOI: 10.4018/IJSWIS.2017010101

Madanchian, M. (2024). The impact of artificial intelligence marketing on e-commerce sales. *Systems*, *12*(10), 429. DOI: 10.3390/systems12100429

Magableh, I. K., Mahrouq, M. H., Ta'Amnha, M. A., & Riyadh, H. A. (2024). The role of marketing artificial intelligence in enhancing sustainable financial performance of medium-sized enterprises through customer engagement and data-driven decision-making. *Sustainability (Basel)*, *16*(24), 11279. DOI: 10.3390/su162411279

Mahapatra, M., Raut, P., & Dharaskar, A. (2024, June). Effect of CRM on retail POS (point of sale) system. In *1st International Conference, 'Resonance': on Cognitive Approach, Social Ethics and Sustainability* (pp. 77-98). Routledge. DOI: 10.4324/9781003397175-6

Mai, E., & Liao, Y. (2022). The interplay of word-of-mouth and customer value on B2B sales performance in a digital platform: An expectancy value theory perspective. *Journal of Business and Industrial Marketing, 37*(7), 1389–1401. DOI: 10.1108/JBIM-05-2021-0269

Maione, G., Supino, S., Grimaldi, M., & Troisi, O. (2025). Exploring the political-institutional perspective of sustainable consumer behavior within the circular economy: A structural equation modeling approach from nudge theory. *Socio-Economic Planning Sciences, 100*, 102254. Advance online publication. DOI: 10.1016/j.seps.2025.102254

Mair, C., Kadoda, G., Lefley, M., Phalp, K., Schofield, C., Shepperd, M., & Webster, S. (2000). An investigation of machine learning based prediction systems. *Journal of Systems and Software, 53*(1), 23–29. DOI: 10.1016/S0164-1212(00)00005-4

Majumdar, S. N., Pal, A., & Schehr, G. (2020). Extreme value statistics of correlated random variables: A pedagogical review. *Physics Reports, 840*, 1–32. DOI: 10.1016/j.physrep.2019.10.005

Makarova, O. V. (2021). Predictive method of inventory optimization in industrial manufacturer performance. E3S Web of Conferences, 247, 01066. DOI: 10.1051/e3sconf/202124701066

Mamun, M. N. H. (2025). Role of AI and Data Science in Data-Driven Decision-Making for it Business Intelligence: A Systematic Literature Review. Available at *SSRN* 5402976. DOI: 10.2139/ssrn.5402976

Manasa, N., Praveenraj, D. W., & Lakshmi, S. R. (2023). Predictive Analytics for Stock Market Trends using Machine Learning. *2023 4th International Conference on Computation, Automation and Knowledge Management, ICCAKM 2023*. DOI: 10.1109/ICCAKM58659.2023.10449528

Manoharan, G., Gupta, R., Darunkar, V. V., Mishra, S. K., & Soni, M. (2025, May). The impact of Artificial Intelligence on E-commerce Customer Experience and Personalization. In 2025 6th International Conference for Emerging Technology (INCET) (pp. 1-5). IEEE.

Manoharan, G., Dharmaraj, A., Sheela, S. C., Naidu, K., Chavva, M., & Chaudhary, J. K. (2024, May). Machine learning-based real-time fraud detection in financial transactions. In *2024 International Conference on Advances in Computing, Communication and Applied Informatics (ACCAI)* (pp. 1-6). IEEE. DOI: 10.1109/ACCAI61061.2024.10602350

Manoharan, G., Preetha, P. N., Santhanalakshmi, K., Balaji, K. D., & Raja, V. (2024, March). Management of Business Using Machine Learning for Decision Making. In *2024 International Conference on Trends in Quantum Computing and Emerging Business Technologies* (pp. 1-5). IEEE. DOI: 10.1109/TQCEBT59414.2024.10545116

Manovich, L. (2018). *AI aesthetics*. Strelka Press.

Mantena, S., Celi, L. A., Keshavjee, S., & Beratarrechea, A. (2021). Improving community health-care screenings with smartphone-based AI technologies. *The Lancet. Digital Health, 3*(5), e280–e282. DOI: 10.1016/S2589-7500(21)00054-6

Mashayekhy, Y., Babaei, A., Yuan, X. M., & Xue, A. (2022). Impact of Internet of Things (IoT) on Inventory Management: A Literature Survey. *Logistics 2022, Vol. 6, Page 33, 6*(2), 33. DOI: 10.3390/logistics6020033

Maslow, A. H. (1943). A theory of human motivation. *Psychological Review, 50*(4), 370–396. DOI: 10.1037/h0054346

Mayer, R. C., Davis, J. H., & Schoorman, F. D. (1995). An integrative model of organizational trust. *Academy of Management Review, 20*(3), 709–734. DOI: 10.2307/258792

McStay, A. (2018). *Emotional AI: The rise of empathic media*. SAGE Publications Ltd. DOI: 10.4135/9781526451293

Meeker, W. Q., Escobar, L. A., & Pascual, F. G. (2022). *Statistical methods for reliability data*. John Wiley & Sons.

Meng, H., Xu, X., & Tian, T. (2025). Empirical study of Neo-Chinese fashion consumer behaviour from the perspectives of cultural identity and emotional self-regulation mechanism. *Asia Pacific Journal of Marketing and Logistics, 37*(6), 1591–1607. DOI: 10.1108/APJML-07-2024-1004

Mennekes, T., & Schramm-Klein, H. (2025). Effects of crisis-induced inflation on purchasing and consumer behavior in Germany. *Journal of Retailing and Consumer Services, 85*, 104295. Advance online publication. DOI: 10.1016/j.jretconser.2025.104295

Michael, C. I., Ipede, O. J., Adejumo, A. D., Adenekan, I. O., Adebayo, D., Ojo, A. S., & Ayodele, P. A. (2024). Data-driven decision making in IT: Leveraging AI and data science for business intelligence. *World Journal of Advanced Research and Reviews, 23*(01), 432–439.

Mijwel, M. M. (2021). Artificial neural networks advantages and disadvantages. *Mesopotamian Journal of Big Data, 2021*, 29–31. DOI: 10.58496/MJBD/2021/006

Mishra, A. K., Sinha, M., & Jha, S. K. (2024). Data analytics for visualization of business insights for an online retail store using Python. *International Journal of Management & Entrepreneurship Research*, *6*(10), 3314–3320. DOI: 10.51594/ijmer.v6i10.1636

Moedjiono, S., Isak, Y. R., & Kusdaryono, A. (2016). Customer loyalty prediction in multimedia service provider company with K-means segmentation and C4.5 algorithm. In *2016 International Conference on Informatics and Computing (ICIC)* (pp. 210–215). IEEE. DOI: 10.1109/IAC.2016.7905717

Mohapatra, A. G., Mohanty, A., Mohanty, S. K., Mahalik, N. P., & Nayak, S. (2025). Personalization and customer experience in the era of data-driven marketing. Artificial Intelligence-Enabled Businesses: How to Develop Strategies for Innovation, 467-511.

Moradi, M., & Farzaneh, H. (2025). Hybrid local energy markets in Japan: Assessing the impact of regional renewable energy integration, demand flexibility, and consumer behavior. *Energy Conversion and Management*, *X*, 27. DOI: 10.1016/j.ecmx.2025.101075

Motie, S., & Raahemi, B. (2024). Financial fraud detection using graph neural networks: A systematic review. In *Expert Systems with Applications* (Vol. 240). DOI: 10.1016/j.eswa.2023.122156

Movahed, A. B., Movahed, A. B., & Nozari, H. (2024). Opportunities and challenges of marketing 5.0. *Smart and Sustainable Interactive Marketing*, 1–21.

Mtengwa, E., Muchenje, C., Maregere, L. L., & Masengu, R. (2025). Driving Business Sustainability Through Effective Marketing Leveraging on Artificial Intelligence. In AI and Machine Learning Applications in Supply Chains and Marketing (pp. 117-148). IGI Global.

Munap, R. B., Obeto, M. N., Salean, S. A. P., Hamid, S. N. B. A., & Salleh, S. N. A. B. M. (2025). TikTok Shopping Surge: Impact on Consumer Behaviour in Klang Valley, Malaysia. *International Review of Management and Marketing*, *15*(1), 204–213. DOI: 10.32479/irmm.17441

Mutashar, S. S., & Flayyih, H. H. (2024). The Impact of Artificial Intelligence on Accounting Performance: Sustainable Development as a Mediating Variable. *International Journal of Economics and Finance Studies*, *16*(2), 36–54.

Naik, A., & Gupta, D. (2025). *Beyond Instant Delivery: Industry Challenges, Market Gaps, and the Future of Quick Commerce*. 402–437. DOI: 10.2991/978-94-6463-766-3_20

Nalini, M., Radhakrishnan, D. P., Yogi, G., Santhiya, S., & Harivardhini, V. (2021). Impact of artificial intelligence (AI) on marketing. *International Journal of Aquatic Science, 12*(2), 3159–3167.

Nazim Sha, S., & Rajeswari, M. (2019). Creating a brand value and consumer satisfaction in E-commerce business using artificial intelligence with the help of vosag technology. *International Journal of Innovative Technology and Exploring Engineering, 8*(8), 1510–1515.

Nejad, G., M., & Sabzian, H. (2025). Spatiotemporal patterns of consumer financial fraud in the United States. *International Journal of Bank Marketing, 43*(2), 368–387. DOI: 10.1108/IJBM-01-2024-0023

Nilsson, N. J. (2009). *The quest for artificial intelligence: A history of ideas and achievements*. Cambridge University Press. DOI: 10.1017/CBO9780511819346

Nugroho, D. A. (2025). The Role of AI in Predicting Consumer Behaviour and Effective Marketing Strategies. *Return: Study of Management. Economic and Bussines, 4*(3), 302–312.

NVIDIA. (2025). AI in retail and CPG survey 2025. Retrieved from https://blogs .nvidia.com/blog/ai-in-retail-cpg-survey-2025

Nyathani, R. (2023). AI-driven HR analytics: Unleashing the power of HR data management. *Journal of Technology and Systems, 5*(2), 15–26. DOI: 10.47941/jts.1513

Obidat, A., Alziyadat, Z., & Alabaddi, Z. (2023). Assessing the effect of business intelligence on supply chain agility. A perspective from the Jordanian manufacturing sector. *Uncertain Supply Chain Management, 11*(1), 61–70. DOI: 10.5267/j.uscm.2022.11.010

Ofosu-Ampong, K., Boateng, M., Ampong, M. D., Adu-Ntim, J. K., & Ampong-Ansah, F. B. (2025). The Impact of AI-driven Marketing Personalisation on Consumer Purchase Decisions: A Mixed-Methods Analysis. Available at *SSRN* 5314499.

Okeke, N. I., Alabi, O. A., Igwe, A. N., Ofodile, O. C., & Ewim, C. P. M. (2024). AI in customer feedback integration: A data-driven framework for enhancing business strategy. *World J. Advanced Res. Reviews, 24*(1), 3207–3220.

Okeleke, P. A., Ajiga, D., Folorunsho, S. O., & Ezeigweneme, C. (2024). Predictive analytics for market trends using AI: A study in consumer behavior. *International Journal of Engineering Research Updates, 7*(1), 36–49. DOI: 10.53430/ijeru.2024.7.1.0032

Olaboye, J. A., Maha, C. C., Kolawole, T. O., & Abdul, S. (2024). Promoting health and educational equity: Cross-disciplinary strategies for enhancing public health and educational outcomes. *International Journal of Applied Research in Social Sciences, 6*(6), 1178–1193. DOI: 10.51594/ijarss.v6i6.1179

Oliveira, T., Alhinho, M., Rita, P., & Dhillon, G. (2017). Modelling and testing consumer trust dimensions in e-commerce. *Computers in Human Behavior, 71*, 153–164. DOI: 10.1016/j.chb.2017.01.050

Olujimi, P. A., & Ade-Ibijola, A. (2023). NLP techniques for automating responses to customer queries: A systematic review. *Discover Artificial Intelligence, 3*(1), 1–19. DOI: 10.1007/s44163-023-00065-5 PMID: 40478082

Onesi-Ozigagun, O., Ololade, Y. J., Eyo-Udo, N. L., & Oluwaseun, D. (2024). Data-driven decision making: Shaping the future of business efficiency and customer engagement. *International Journal of Multidisciplinary Research Updates, 7*(2), 19–29. DOI: 10.53430/ijmru.2024.7.2.0031

Onifade, A. Y., Ogeawuchi, J. C., & Abayomi, A. A. (2025). Scaling AI-Driven Sales Analytics for Predicting Consumer Behavior and Enhancing Data-Driven Business Decisions. *International Journal of Advanced Multidisciplinary Research and Studies, 4*(6), 2181–2201. DOI: 10.62225/2583049X.2024.4.6.4269

Oosthuizen, K., Botha, E., Robertson, J., & Montecchi, M. (2021). Artificial intelligence in retail: The AI-enabled value chain. *Australasian Marketing Journal, 29*(3), 264–273. DOI: 10.1016/j.ausmj.2020.07.007

Panwar, D., Anand, S., Ali, F., & Singal, K. (2019). Consumer decision making process models and their applications to market strategy. *International Management Review, 15*(1), 36–44.

Parthe, R. M. (2023). Comparative analysis of data visualization tools. *Power BI and Tableau. INTERANTIONAL JOURNAL OF SCIENTIFIC RESEARCH IN ENGINEERING AND MANAGEMENT, 07*(10), 1–11. DOI: 10.55041/IJSREM26272

Paschen, J., Wilson, M., & Ferreira, J. J. (2020). Collaborative intelligence: How human and artificial intelligence create value along the B2B sales funnel. *Business Horizons, 63*(3), 403–414. DOI: 10.1016/j.bushor.2020.01.003

Pavlou, P. A., Liang, H., & Xue, Y. (2007). Understanding and mitigating uncertainty in online exchange relationships: A principal-agent perspective. *Management Information Systems Quarterly, 31*(1), 105–136. DOI: 10.2307/25148783

Pearl, J. (2000). Models, reasoning and inference. *Cambridge, UK: Cambridge University Press, 19*(2), 3.

Peddi, S., & Manoharan, G. (2025). The Impact of Technology on Company Values and Employee Well-Being. In *Transforming Organizational Culture Through Meta-Driven Human Resources* (pp. 225–256). IGI Global Scientific Publishing. DOI: 10.4018/979-8-3373-0720-6.ch008

Petrescu, M., Krishen, A. S., Gironda, J. T., & Fergurson, J. R. (2024). Exploring AI technology and consumer behavior in retail interactions. *Journal of Consumer Behaviour, 23*(6), 3132–3151. DOI: 10.1002/cb.2386

Pine, B. J., & Gilmore, J. H. (1998). The experience economy. *Harvard Business Review, 76*(6), 18–23.

Poole, D., & Mackworth, A. (2017). *Artificial intelligence: Foundations of computational agents* (2nd ed.). Cambridge University Press. DOI: 10.1017/9781108164085

Pratap, A. (2025). Real Time Sales Forecasting. *INTERNATIONAL JOURNAL OF SCIENTIFIC RESEARCH IN ENGINEERING AND MANAGEMENT, 09*(05), 1–9. DOI: 10.55041/IJSREM48883

Presskila, X. A., Raj, J. R. F., Kumar, P. S., Sankar, G. R., Rajkumar, G. V., & Sundaravadivel, P. (2025a). A Hybrid Learning-Based Q-Commerce Framework Evolving from E-Commerce. *2nd International Conference on Machine Learning and Autonomous Systems, ICMLAS 2025 - Proceedings*, 295–302. DOI: 10.1109/ICMLAS64557.2025.10968475

Quan, L., & Han, H. (2025). Consumer behavior toward cultured meat in the food-service industry: Insights from IPA and fsQCA analysis on shifting trends. *Journal of Retailing and Consumer Services, 85*, 104307. Advance online publication. DOI: 10.1016/j.jretconser.2025.104307

Raha, A. D., Munir, M. S., Adhikary, A., Qiao, Y., Park, S. B., & Hong, C. S. (2023). An Artificial Intelligent-Driven Semantic Communication Framework for Connected Autonomous Vehicular Network. *International Conference on Information Networking, 2023-January*, 352–357. DOI: 10.1109/ICOIN56518.2023.10049005

Raju, V., Ramachandran, K. K., Chenxi, W., Mangairkarasi, V., & Konecna, Z. (2025). AI in data-driven marketing: Decoding consumer choices and behaviours. In *Data Engineering for Data-Driven Marketing* (pp. 33–45). Emerald Publishing Limited. DOI: 10.1108/978-1-83662-326-720251005

Ram, J., & Zhang, Z. (2022). Examining the needs to adopt big data analytics in B2B organizations: Development of propositions and model of needs. *Journal of Business and Industrial Marketing, 37*(4), 790–809. DOI: 10.1108/JBIM-10-2020-0464

Rane, N., Paramesha, M., Choudhary, S., & Rane, J. (2024). Artificial intelligence in sales and marketing: Enhancing customer satisfaction, experience and loyalty. Experience and Loyalty (May 17, 2024).

Rasool, N., & Bhat, J. I. (2025). Artificial intelligence in restaurant. In *Artificial intelligence in the food industry* (pp. 171–205). CRC Press.

Rathee, R., Singh, M., & Maurya, I. (2025). Decoding Consumer Emotions in Quick Commerce. *Methods and Applications of Quick Commerce (Q-Commerce)*, 51–74. :
Reis, A., & Nordqvist, S. (2021). *AI utilization in route planning for delivery trucks within the supply chain.* https://lup.lub.lu.se/student-papers/record/9050694DOI: 10.4018/979-8-3373-1712-0.ch003

Rb, A., & Kr, S. K.RB. (2021). Credit card fraud detection using artificial neural network. *Global Transitions Proceedings*, *2*(1), 35–41. Advance online publication. DOI: 10.1016/j.gltp.2021.01.006

Rego, M. M., & Hamilton, M. A. (2022). The importance of fit: A predictive model of cause marketing effects. *Journal of Marketing Theory and Practice*, *30*(2), 172–190. DOI: 10.1080/10696679.2021.1901594

Reshma, & Singh Attwal, K. P. (2024). A Review on Medicinal Plant identification through Leaf Image. In M. H. (Ed.), *Proceedings - 2024 6th International Conference on Computational Intelligence and Communication Technologies, CCICT 2024* (pp. 27 – 33). Institute of Electrical and Electronics Engineers Inc. DOI: 10.1109/CCICT62777.2024.00015

Reshma, S., T., Pareek, S., & Kuhar, S. (2024). House Price Prediction using Machine Learning Approaches. *2024 OPJU International Technology Conference on Smart Computing for Innovation and Advancement in Industry 4.0, OTCON 2024*. DOI: 10.1109/OTCON60325.2024.10687534

Reuters. (2025, January 6). AI-influenced shopping boosts online holiday sales, Salesforce data shows. Retrieved from https://www.reuters.com/business/retail-consumer/ai-influenced-shopping-boosts-online-holiday-sales-salesforce-data-shows-2025-01-06

Rezazadeh, A. (2020). A generalized flow for B2B sales predictive modeling: An Azure Machine-Learning approach. *Forecasting*, *2*(3), 267–283. DOI: 10.3390/forecast2030015

Robinson, H., Wysocka, A., & Hand, C. (2007). Internet advertising effectiveness: The effect of design on click-through rates for banner ads. *International Journal of Advertising*, *26*(4), 527–541. DOI: 10.1080/02650487.2007.11073031

Rodríguez-Ardura, I., & Meseguer-Artola, A. (2020). How to prevent, detect and control common method variance in electronic commerce research. *Journal of Theoretical and Applied Electronic Commerce Research, 15*(2), 1–5. DOI: 10.4067/S0718-18762020000200101

Rossi, P. E. (2018). 6. Causal inference in marketing applications. *Handbook of Marketing Analytics: Methods and Applications in Marketing Management, Public Policy, and Litigation Support*, 135.

Russell, S., & Norvig, P. (2021). *Artificial intelligence: A modern approach* (4th ed.). Pearson.

Saad, M., Qin, Z., Ren, K., Nyang, D., & Mohaisen, D. (2021). e-PoS: Making proof-of-stake decentralized and fair. *IEEE Transactions on Parallel and Distributed Systems, 32*(8), 1961–1973. DOI: 10.1109/TPDS.2020.3048853

Sadeghpour, S., & Vlajic, N. (2021a). Ads and Fraud: A Comprehensive Survey of Fraud in Online Advertising. *Journal of Cybersecurity and Privacy 2021, Vol. 1, Pages 804-832, 1*(4), 804–832. DOI: 10.3390/jcp1040039

Sadeghpour, S., & Vlajic, N. (2021b). Click fraud in digital advertising: A comprehensive survey. *Computers, 10*(12), 164. Advance online publication. DOI: 10.3390/computers10120164

Sáez-Ortuño, L., Forgas-Coll, S., Huertas-Garcia, R., & Sánchez-García, J. (2023). Online cheaters: Profiles and motivations of internet users who falsify their data online. *Journal of Innovation and Knowledge, 8*(2), 100349. Advance online publication. DOI: 10.1016/j.jik.2023.100349

Sakrabani, P., Teoh, A. P., & Amran, A. (2019). Strategic impact of retail 4.0 on retailers' performance in Malaysia. *Strategic Direction, 35*(11), 1–3. DOI: 10.1108/SD-05-2019-0099

Saluja, A., Soth, R. K. D., Pawar, B. R., Pasunoori, V., Mungi, A., & Faldu, R. (2023). Precision Marketing Strategy for E-Commerce By Using Big Data Technology. *Journal of Innovation and Entrepreneurial Research, 3*(2). Advance online publication. DOI: 10.52783/jier.v3i2.433

Samira, Z., Weldegeorgise, Y. W., Osundare, O. S., Ekpobimi, H. O., & Kandekere, R. C. (2024). Development of an integrated model for SME marketing and CRM optimization. *International Journal of Management & Entrepreneurship Research, 6*(10), 3209–3242. DOI: 10.51594/ijmer.v6i10.1612

Sangvikar, B. V., & Katole, H. J. (2012). A study of consumer purchase behavior in organized retail outlets. *The Journal of Business and Retail Management Research*, *7*(1), 39–47.

Santos, V., & Bacalhau, L. M. (2023). Digital transformation of the retail point of sale in the artificial intelligence era. In *Management and Marketing for Improved Retail Competitiveness and Performance* (pp. 200–216). IGI Global. DOI: 10.4018/978-1-6684-8574-3.ch010

Sarin, A. B. (2025). The Evolution of Consumer Behavior and the Role of Artificial Intelligence in Shaping It: AI in Marketing. In Decoding Consumer Behavior Using the Insight Equation and AI Marketing (pp. 21-40). IGI Global Scientific Publishing.

Savall-Mañó, M., Hook, H., & Abouelela, M. (2025). Can higher delivery costs promote greener practices? Consumer behaviour insights from Barcelona. *Journal of Retailing and Consumer Services*, *86*, 104343. Advance online publication. DOI: 10.1016/j.jretconser.2025.104343

Sawant, N., Namballa, C. B., Sadagopan, N., & Nassif, H. (2018). Contextual multi-armed bandits for causal marketing. *arXiv preprint arXiv:1810.01859.*

Schank, R. C. (1991). Where's the AI? *AI Magazine*, *12*(4), 38–38.

Schmitt, B. (1999). *Experiential marketing: How to get customers to sense, feel, think, act, and relate to your company and brands*. Free Press.

Schorung, M. (2024). Quick commerce and the evolving business models of the food retail industry - Investigating the quick commerce supply chain and the urban impacts of dark stores. *Transportation Research Procedia*, *79*, 305–312. DOI: 10.1016/j.trpro.2024.03.041

Seera, M., Lim, C. P., Kumar, A., Dhamotharan, L., & Tan, K. H. (2024). An intelligent payment card fraud detection system. *Annals of Operations Research*, *334*(1), 445–467. DOI: 10.1007/s10479-021-04149-2 PMID: 34121790

Sehajpal, S., & Sidhu, N. K. (2024). Neuroscience, nursing, and financial innovation: A synergistic approach to optimized patient care and economic well-being. In *Neuromarketing's Role in Sustainable Finance*. IGI Global., DOI: 10.4018/979-8-3693-9117-4.ch008

Senan, N. A. M., Al-Kahtani, S. M., Alanazi, I. D., AbdAlatti, A., Alshadadi, M. A., Alhebri, A., & Mohammad, R. A. (2025). Unveiling the linkages between greenwashing, brand hate, and negative consumer behavior: The moderating effect of environmental concern. *Discover Sustainability*, *6*(1), 446. Advance online publication. DOI: 10.1007/s43621-025-01179-9

Shaik, M. (2023a). Impact of artificial intelligence on marketing. *East Asian Journal of Multidisciplinary Research, 2*(3), 993–1004. DOI: 10.55927/eajmr.v2i3.3112

Shankar, V. (2018). How artificial intelligence (AI) is reshaping retailing. *Journal of Retailing, 94*(4), vi–xi. DOI: 10.1016/S0022-4359(18)30076-9

Shao, C., Ciampaglia, G. L., Varol, O., Yang, K.-C., Flammini, A., & Menczer, F. (2018). The spread of low-credibility content by social bots. *Nature Communications, 9*(1), 4787. DOI: 10.1038/s41467-018-06930-7 PMID: 30459415

Shaouf, A., Lü, A., & Li, M. (2016). Factors influencing attitudes toward mobile advertising: An empirical study among Libyan consumers. *International Journal of Information and Communication Engineering, 10*(4), 1070–1074.

Shaouf, A., Lü, K., & Li, X. (2016). The effect of web advertising visual design on online purchase intention: An examination across gender. *Computers in Human Behavior, 60*, 622–634. DOI: 10.1016/j.chb.2016.02.090

Sharma, K. K., Mmdu, A. B., & Reshma. (2022). Biological Impacts of MRI Examinations of Different Ratings on Human Tissue. *Proceedings - 2022 International Conference on Computing, Communication and Power Technology, IC3P 2022*, 172 – 175. DOI: 10.1109/IC3P52835.2022.00043

Sharma, L., & Garg, P. K. (2021). *Artificial Intelligence: Technologies, Applications, and Challenges*. Taylor & Francis. DOI: 10.1201/9781003140351

Sharma, P. N., Shmueli, G., Sarstedt, M., Danks, N., & Ray, S. (2021). Prediction-oriented model selection in partial least squares path modeling. *Decision Sciences, 52*(3), 567–607. DOI: 10.1111/deci.12329

Sheth, P., Jeong, U., Guo, R., Liu, H., & Candan, K. S. (2021, October). Cause-Box: A Causal Inference Toolbox for BenchmarkingTreatment Effect Estimators with Machine Learning Methods. In *Proceedings of the 30th ACM International Conference on Information & Knowledge Management* (pp. 4789-4793). DOI: 10.1145/3459637.3481974

Shi, H., Gao, Z., Fang, L., Zhai, J., & Sun, H. (2024). Research on inventory control method based on demand response of power big data. *Scalable Computing Practice and Experience, 25*(3), 1781–1789. DOI: 10.12694/scpe.v25i3.2695

Shirdastian, H., Bartikowski, B., Laroche, M., & Richard, M.-O. (2025). Mobile app localization-based advertising: Effects of spatial and social-cultural distances on consumer behavior. *International Journal of Information Management, 84*, 102929. Advance online publication. DOI: 10.1016/j.ijinfomgt.2025.102929

Shiva, R. K., & Manoharan, G. (2025). Brand Equity Management and Marketing in the Digital Era. In Djakeli, K. (Ed.), *Brand Creation and Management in the Phygital Era* (pp. 201–224). IGI Global Scientific Publishing., DOI: 10.4018/979-8-3373-0948-4.ch008

Shiva, R. K., & Manoharan, G. (2026). Leveraging AI for Marketing, Customer Experience, and Automation. In Verma, B., Schulze, M., Olubiyi, T., & Upreti, K. (Eds.), *Navigating the Self-Service Revolution With Smart Machines* (pp. 283–308). IGI Global Scientific Publishing., DOI: 10.4018/979-8-3373-1295-8.ch011

Shobana, J., Gangadhar, C., Arora, R. K., Renjith, P., Bamini, J., & Chincholkar, Y. D. (2023). E-commerce customer churn prevention using machine learning-based business intelligence strategy. (Publication details missing—journal or conference needed for full APA citation). Korn, S. (2011). The opportunity of predictive analytics in finance. HPC Wire. (URL optional in APA; provide if required.)

Shrestha, N. (2021). Factor analysis as a tool for survey analysis. *American Journal of Applied Mathematics and Statistics*, *9*(1), 4–11. DOI: 10.12691/ajams-9-1-2

Singhal, D., Ahuja, L., & Seth, A. (2024). POSMETER: Proof-of-stake blockchain for enhanced smart meter data security. *International Journal of Information Technology : an Official Journal of Bharati Vidyapeeth's Institute of Computer Applications and Management*, *16*(2), 1171–1184. DOI: 10.1007/s41870-023-01653-5

Singh, B., Kaunert, C., Malviya, R., Lal, S., & Arora, M. K. (2024). Scrutinizing consumer sentiment on social media and data-driven decisions for business insights: fusion of artificial intelligence (AI) and business intelligence (BI) foster sustainable growth. In *Intersection of AI and Business Intelligence in Data-Driven Decision-Making* (pp. 183–210). IGI Global. DOI: 10.4018/979-8-3693-5288-5.ch007

Singh, R., & Gill, S. S. (2023). Edge AI: A survey. *Internet of Things and Cyber-Physical Systems*, *3*, 71–92. DOI: 10.1016/j.iotcps.2023.02.004

Slutskiy, P. (2021). Fraudulent Communication in Advertising and Business Promotion. *Communication and Libertarianism*, 261–274. DOI: 10.1007/978-981-33-6664-0_17

Smit, E. G., Van Noort, G., & Voorveld, H. A. (2014). Understanding online behavioural advertising: User knowledge, privacy concerns and online coping behaviour in Europe. *Computers in Human Behavior*, *32*, 15–22. DOI: 10.1016/j.chb.2013.11.008

Smith, J. D. (2024). The impact of technology on sales performance in B2B companies. Journal of Artificial Intelligence General Science (JAIGS) ISSN:3006-4023, 3(1), 246–261. DOI: 10.60087/jaigs.v3i1.118

Society of Petroleum Engineers. (2019). Natural language understanding for safety and risk management in oil and gas plants [Paper presentation]. Abu Dhabi International Petroleum Exhibition and Conference (ADIPEC 2019). DOI: 10.2118/197668-MS

Soh, H., Reid, L. N., & King, K. W. (2007). Trust in different advertising media. *Journalism & Mass Communication Quarterly*, *84*(3), 455–47. DOI: 10.1177/107769900708400304

Song, Y., Sebe, N., & Wang, W. (2022). Fast differentiable matrix square root and inverse square root. *IEEE Transactions on Pattern Analysis and Machine Intelligence*, *45*(6), 7367–7380. DOI: 10.1109/TPAMI.2022.3216339

Sood, P., Tanwar, H., Singh, J., Ruhela, A. K., Gupta, N., & Kumar, R. (2024). Revolutionizing Customer Service: An AI-powered Chatbot Approach using Advanced NLP Techniques. *Proceedings of the 2024 3rd Edition of IEEE Delhi Section Flagship Conference, DELCON 2024*. DOI: 10.1109/DELCON64804.2024.10866078

Soori, M., Arezoo, B., & Dastres, R. (2023). Internet of things for smart factories in industry 4.0, a review. *Internet of Things and Cyber-Physical Systems*, *3*, 192–204. DOI: 10.1016/j.iotcps.2023.04.006

Spiliotis, E., Makridakis, S., Semenoglou, A. A., & Assimakopoulos, V. (2022). Comparison of statistical and machine learning methods for daily SKU demand forecasting. *Operations Research*, *22*(3), 3037–3061. DOI: 10.1007/s12351-020-00605-2

Stahl, B. C. (2021). Ethical issues of AI. In *Artificial Intelligence for a better future: An ecosystem perspective on the ethics of AI and emerging digital technologies* (pp. 35–53). Springer International Publishing. DOI: 10.1007/978-3-030-69978-9_4

Strubel, J., & Petrie, T. A. (2016). The clothes make the man: The relation of sociocultural factors and sexual orientation to appearance and product involvement. *Journal of Retailing and Consumer Services*, *33*, 1–7. DOI: 10.1016/j.jretconser.2016.07.015

Stutz, D., de Assis, J. T., Laghari, A. A., Khan, A. A., Andreopoulos, N., Terziev, A., ... & Grata, E. G. (2024). Enhancing security in cloud computing using artificial intelligence (AI). *Applying Artificial Intelligence in Cybersecurity Analytics and Cyber Threat Detection*, 179-220.

Surya, H. (2019). ANALISIS PERSEDIAAN BAHAN BAKU KEDELAI DENGAN MENGGUNAKAN METODE ECONOMIC ORDER QUANTITY (EOQ) PADA UD. KARYA MANDIRI SAMARINDA. *OBOR: Oikonomia Borneo, 1*(1). Advance online publication. DOI: 10.24903/obor.v1i1.1816

Suryani, E., & Fajri, R. R. (2022). Fraud Triangle Perspective: Artificial Neural Network Used in Fraud Analysis. *Quality - Access to Success, 23*(188). Advance online publication. DOI: 10.47750/QAS/23.188.22

Sutton, R. S., & Barto, A. G. (1998). *No. 1* (Vol. 1). Reinforcement learning: An introduction. MIT press.

Suwignjo, P., Panjaitan, L., Baihaqy, A. R., & Rusdiansyah, A. (2023). Predictive analytics to improve inventory performance: A case study of an FMCG company. Operations and Supply Chain Management An International Journal, 293–310. DOI: 10.31387/oscm0530390

Syam, N., & Sharma, A. (2018). Waiting for a sales renaissance in the fourth industrial revolution: Machine learning and artificial intelligence in sales research and practice. *Industrial Marketing Management, 69*, 135–146. DOI: 10.1016/j.indmarman.2017.12.019

Tadimarri, A., Jangoan, S., Sharma, K. K., & Gurusamy, A. (2024). AI-powered marketing: Transforming consumer engagement and brand growth. *Int. J. Multidiscip. Res, 6*, 1–11.

Tang, C.-H. H., Fan, A., & Park, J. E. (2025). Mass customization and consumer behaviors: Exploring the roles of perceived value, perceived cost, and time pressure. *International Journal of Hospitality Management, 130*, 104278. Advance online publication. DOI: 10.1016/j.ijhm.2025.104278

Tanwar, A., Aggarwal, R., & Kaur, A. (2024). Explainability of AI in Improving the Quality of Service in the Actuarial Industry. In *Artificial Intelligence and Actuarial Science: Applications and Case Studies from Finance and Insurance*. CRC Press., DOI: 10.1201/9781003472551-7

Tanwar, A., Malhan, S., Punj, N., & Kaur, A. (2024). Integration of Artificial Intelligence and Internet of Things in the Banking Sector: A Convergence of Frontiers. In *Integration of Cloud Computing and IoT: Trends, Case Studies and Applications*. CRC Press., DOI: 10.1201/9781032656694-25

Tan, Z. M., Aggarwal, N., Cowls, J., Morley, J., Taddeo, M., & Floridi, L. (2021). The ethical debate about the gig economy: A review and critical analysis. *Technology in Society, 65*, 101594. Advance online publication. DOI: 10.1016/j.techsoc.2021.101594

Tariq, M. U. (2025). Balancing Flexibility and Precarity: Ethical Implications and Sustainable Practices in Global Gig Economies. In *Sustainability and Adaptability of Gig Economies in Global Business* (pp. 323–346). IGI Global Scientific Publishing.

Tariq, M. U. (2025). Leveraging Data Analytics for Predictive Consumer Behavior Modelling. In AI Impacts on Branded Entertainment and Advertising (pp. 207-224). IGI Global Scientific Publishing. DOI: 10.4018/979-8-3693-3799-8.ch011

Thandapani, G., & Karthika, S. (2025). A data-driven approach to loan approvals prediction and profitability: Leveraging exploratory data analysis for improved decision-making. In *Advances in Electrical and Computer Technologies* (pp. 261–266). CRC Press. DOI: 10.1201/9781003515470-36

Theodorakopoulos, L., & Theodoropoulou, A. (2024). Leveraging big data analytics for understanding consumer behavior in digital marketing: A systematic review. *Human Behavior and Emerging Technologies*, *2024*(1), 3641502. DOI: 10.1155/2024/3641502

Tikkinen-Piri, C., Rohunen, A., & Markkula, J. (2018). EU General Data Protection Regulation: Changes and implications for personal data collecting companies. *Computer Law & Security Review*, *34*(1), 134–153. DOI: 10.1016/j.clsr.2017.05.015

Tonin, P. E. H., Nickel, E. M., & dos Santos, F. A. V. (2025). The Impact of Sensory Branding and Technology on Consumer Behavior in Physical Retail Experience Design: A Multi-generational Experimental Study. *International Journal of Design Management and Professional Practice*, *19*(1), 87–110. DOI: 10.18848/2325-162X/CGP/v19i01/87-110

Tsai, Y., Wu, S.-W., & Chang, S.-T. (2012). Internal Marketing Establishes the Culture of Market Orientation. In Business, Economics, Financial Sciences, and Management (pp. 471-479). Springer. DOI: 10.1007/978-3-642-27966-9_65

Tynan, C., McKechnie, S., & Chhuon, C. (2010). Co-creating value for luxury brands. *Journal of Business Research*, *63*(11), 1156–1163. DOI: 10.1016/j.jbusres.2009.10.012

Umair, M. (2026). Hyperlocal Supply Chains for Quick Commerce: An Indian Perspective. In *Methods and Applications of Quick Commerce (Q-Commerce)* (pp. 367–398). IGI Global Scientific Publishing.

Upadhyay, U., Kumar, A., Sharma, G., Sharma, S., Arya, V., Panigrahi, P. K., & Gupta, B. B. (2024). A systematic data-driven approach for targeted marketing in enterprise information system. *Enterprise Information Systems*, *18*(8), 2356770. DOI: 10.1080/17517575.2024.2356770

Vazquez Melendez, E. I., Bergey, P., & Smith, B. (2024). Blockchain technology for supply chain provenance: Increasing supply chain efficiency and consumer trust. *Supply Chain Management*, *29*(4), 706–730. DOI: 10.1108/SCM-08-2023-0383

Velte, P. (2024). Sustainable board governance and environmental performance: European evidence. *Business Strategy and the Environment*, *33*(4), 3397–3421. DOI: 10.1002/bse.3654

Venkataramanan, S., Sadhu, A. K. R., Gudala, L., & Reddy, A. K. (2024). Leveraging artificial intelligence for enhanced sales forecasting accuracy: A review of AI-driven techniques and practical applications in customer relationship management systems. *Aust. J. Mach. Learn. Res. Appl*, *4*(1), 267–287.

Verma, S., Sharma, R., Deb, S., & Maitra, D. (2021). Artificial intelligence in marketing: Systematic review and future research direction. *International Journal of Information Management Data Insights*, *1*(1), 100002. DOI: 10.1016/j.jjimei.2020.100002

Vignesh Saravanan, K., Jothi Thilaga, P., Kavipriya, S., & Vijayalakshmi, K. (2023). Data protection and security enhancement in cyber-physical systems using AI and blockchain. In *AI models for blockchain-based intelligent networks in IoT systems: Concepts, Methodologies, tools, and applications* (pp. 285–325). Springer International Publishing. DOI: 10.1007/978-3-031-31952-5_13

Vijayakumar, V., Divya, N. S., Sarojini, P., & Sonika, K. (2020). Isolation Forest and Local Outlier Factor for Credit Card Fraud Detection System. *International Journal of Engineering and Advanced Technology*, *9*(4), 261–265. Advance online publication. DOI: 10.35940/ijeat.D6815.049420

Villegas-Ch, W., Navarro, A. M., & Sanchez-Viteri, S. (2024). Optimization of inventory management through computer vision and machine learning technologies. *Intelligent Systems with Applications*, *24*, 200438. DOI: 10.1016/j.iswa.2024.200438

Voigt, P., & Von dem Bussche, A. (2017). The eu general data protection regulation (gdpr). *A practical guide, 1st ed., Cham: Springer International Publishing*, *10*(3152676), 10-5555.

Wager, S. (2024, September). *Causal inference: A statistical learning approach.*

Wang, W., Feng, F., He, X., Zhang, H., & Chua, T. S. (2021). Clicks can be Cheating: Counterfactual Recommendation for Mitigating Clickbait Issue. *SIGIR 2021 - Proceedings of the 44th International ACM SIGIR Conference on Research and Development in Information Retrieval.* DOI: 10.1145/3404835.3462962

Wang, A., Ho, D. C. W., Lai, L. W. C., & Chau, K. W. (2023). Public preferences for government supply of public open space: A neo-institutional economic and lifecycle governance perspective. *Cities (London, England)*, *141*, 104463. DOI: 10.1016/j.cities.2023.104463

Wang, D., Xu, Q., Feng, Y., Ignatius, J., Yin, Y., & Xiao, D. (2024). Uplift modeling and its implications for appointment date prediction in attended home delivery. *Decision Support Systems*, *185*, 114303. DOI: 10.1016/j.dss.2024.114303

Wang, H., Lu, S., & Liu, Y. (2022). Missing data imputation in PLS-SEM. *Quality & Quantity*, *56*(6), 4777–4795. DOI: 10.1007/s11135-022-01338-4

Wang, T. C., Guo, R. S., Chen, C., & Li, C. K. (2025). Multi-Stage Data-Driven Framework for Customer Journey Optimization and Operational Resilience. *Mathematics*, *13*(7), 1145. DOI: 10.3390/math13071145

Warnett, S. J., & Zdun, U. (2025, March). Bridging the Gap Between MLOps and RLOps: An Industry 4.0 Case Study on Architectural Design Decisions in Practice. In *2025 IEEE 22nd International Conference on Software Architecture (ICSA)* (pp. 232-242). IEEE.

Washington, S.. (2020). *Statistical and econometric methods for transportation data analysis*. Chapman and Hall/CRC. DOI: 10.1201/9780429244018

Watchus, B. (2024). Towards self-aware ai: Embodiment, feedback loops, and the role of the insula in consciousness. DOI: 10.20944/preprints202411.0661.v1

Wedel, M., & Kannan, P. K. (2016). Marketing analytics for data-rich environments. *Journal of Marketing*, *80*(6), 97–121. DOI: 10.1509/jm.15.0413

Westin, A. F., & Ruebhausen, O. M. (1967). *Privacy and freedom* (Vol. 1). Atheneum.

Widayanti, R., Chakim, M. H. R., Lukita, C., Rahardja, U., & Lutfiani, N. (2023). Improving Recommender Systems using Hybrid Techniques of Collaborative Filtering and Content-Based Filtering. *Journal of Applied Data Sciences*, *4*(3), 289–302. DOI: 10.47738/jads.v4i3.115

Widayat, H., Handayanto, E., Irfani, A. D., & Masudin, I. (2025). A systematic literature review and future research agenda on the dynamics of food waste in the context of consumer behavior. *Sustainable Futures : An Applied Journal of Technology, Environment and Society*, *9*, 100491. Advance online publication. DOI: 10.1016/j.sftr.2025.100491

Wilson, H. J., & Daugherty, P. R. (2018). Collaborative intelligence: Humans and AI are joining forces. *Harvard Business Review*, *96*(4), 114–123.

Wilson, R. D., & Stephens, A. M. (2023). The challenges of B2B innovation: Using marketing analytics to plan and implement a successful digital catalog adoption. *Journal of Business and Industrial Marketing*, *38*(2), 290–302. DOI: 10.1108/JBIM-12-2021-0598

Wisetsri, W., Ragesh, S. T., Aarthy, C. C. J., Thakur, V., Pandey, D., & Gulati, K. (2021). Systematic analysis and future research directions in artificial intelligence for marketing. *Turkish Journal of Computer and Mathematics Education*, *12*(11), 43–55.

Wu, C. (2024). Data privacy: From transparency to fairness. *Technology in Society*, *76*, 102457. Advance online publication. DOI: 10.1016/j.techsoc.2024.102457

Wynn, M., & Olayinka, O. (2021). E-business strategy in developing countries: A framework and checklist for the small business sector. *Sustainability (Basel)*, *13*(13), 7356. DOI: 10.3390/su13137356

Xiahou, X., & Harada, Y. (2022). B2C e-commerce customer churn prediction based on K-means and SVM. *Journal of Theoretical and Applied Electronic Commerce Research*, *17*(2), 458–475. DOI: 10.3390/jtaer17020024

Xu, A., Li, Y., & Donta, P. K. (2024). Marketing decision model and consumer behavior prediction with deep learning. [JOEUC]. *Journal of Organizational and End User Computing*, *36*(1), 1–25. DOI: 10.4018/JOEUC.336547

Yadav, B. K., Keyal, P. K., Khan, R., Chaube, N., Chaudhary, P., & Chaurasiya, P. (2024). Advanced Threat Detection: Leveraging Data Analytics for Cybersecurity Enhancement. *Proceedings of International Conference on Emerging Technologies and Innovation for Sustainability,* EmergIN 2024, 62 – 67. DOI: 10.1109/EmergIN63207.2024.10961019

Yanes, P. A., & Berger, P. D. (2017). How WeChat has changed the face of marketing in China. *British Journal of Marketing Studies*, *5*(3), 14–21.

Yang, C. (2025). Protecting financial consumers from authorized push payment fraud: is reimbursement an optimal solution? *Journal of Financial Regulation and Compliance*. https://doi.org/DOI: 10.1108/JFRC-11-2024-0225/1252741

Yan, Y., Chow, A. H. F., Ho, C. P., Kuo, Y. H., Wu, Q., & Ying, C. (2022). Reinforcement learning for logistics and supply chain management: Methodologies, state of the art, and future opportunities. *Transportation Research Part E, Logistics and Transportation Review*, *162*, 102712. DOI: 10.1016/j.tre.2022.102712

Yoo, C. Y., Kim, K., & Stout, P. A. (2004). Assessing the effects of animation in online banner advertising: Hierarchy of effects model. *Journal of Interactive Advertising*, *4*(2), 49–60. DOI: 10.1080/15252019.2004.10722087

Yu, C., Zhang, Z., Lin, C., & Wu, Y. J. (2019). Can data-driven precision marketing promote user ad clicks? Evidence from advertising in WeChat moments. *Industrial Marketing Management*, *xxx*(xxx), xxx–xxx. DOI: 10.1016/j.indmarman.2019.05.001

Zaki, K., Alhomaid, A., & Shared, H. (2025). Leveraging Machine Learning to Analyze Influencer Credibility's Impact on Brand Admiration and Consumer Purchase Intent in Social Media Marketing. *Human Behavior and Emerging Technologies*, *2025*(1), 9959697. DOI: 10.1155/hbe2/9959697

Zampieri, M., Nakov, P., & Scherrer, Y. (2020). Natural language processing for similar languages, varieties, and dialects: A survey. In *Natural Language Engineering* (Vol. 26, Issue 6). DOI: 10.1017/S1351324920000492

Zang, L., Wang, L., Zhang, D., & Bai, Q. (2025). Data-driven review of customer engagement: Key research themes and future directions. *Electronic Commerce Research*, •••, 1–31. DOI: 10.1007/s10660-025-09967-1

Zhang, J., Lu, G., & You, Z. (2020). Large deformation and energy absorption of additively manufactured auxetic materials and structures: A review. *Composites. Part B, Engineering*, *201*, 108340. DOI: 10.1016/j.compositesb.2020.108340

Zhang, R., Mao, J., Wang, H., Li, B., Cheng, X., & Yang, L. (2024). A Survey on Federated Learning in Intelligent Transportation Systems. *IEEE Transactions on Intelligent Vehicles*, •••, 1–17. DOI: 10.1109/TIV.2024.3446319

Zhang, W., Li, J., & Liu, L. (2021). A unified survey of treatment effect heterogeneity modelling and uplift modelling. *ACM Computing Surveys*, *54*(8), 1–36.

Zheng, Y., Ye, X., & Wu, T. (2021). Using an Optimized Learning Vector Quantization- (LVQ-) Based Neural Network in Accounting Fraud Recognition. *Computational Intelligence and Neuroscience*, *2021*(1), 4113237. Advance online publication. DOI: 10.1155/2021/4113237 PMID: 34257634

Zhou, H., Li, S., Jiang, G., Zheng, J., & Wang, D. (2023, June). Direct heterogeneous causal learning for resource allocation problems in marketing. *Proceedings of the AAAI Conference on Artificial Intelligence*, *37*(4), 5446–5454. DOI: 10.1609/aaai.v37i4.25677

Zhu, Y.-Q., & Chen, H.-G. (2015). Social media and human need satisfaction: Implications for social media marketing. *Business Horizons*, *58*(3), 335–345. DOI: 10.1016/j.bushor.2015.01.006

Zohdi, M., Rafiee, M., Kayvanfar, V., & Salamiraad, A. (2022). Demand forecasting based machine learning algorithms on customer information: An applied approach. *International Journal of Information Technology : an Official Journal of Bharati Vidyapeeth's Institute of Computer Applications and Management, 14*(4), 1937–1947. DOI: 10.1007/s41870-022-00875-3

Zong, Z., Feng, T., Xia, T., Jin, D., & Li, Y. (2021). Deep Reinforcement Learning for Demand Driven Services in Logistics and Transportation Systems: A Survey. *ACM Transactions on Knowledge Discovery from Data*. Advance online publication. DOI: 10.1145/3708325/ASSET/62683674-8B9D-4E3C-A6C2-15CCB80B1F9C

About the Contributors

Nozha Erragcha (Ph.D., University of Jendouba, Tunisia) is an Habilited Associate Professor in Marketing at University of Jendouba. She holds a Ph.D. in Marketing from the University of Manouba, Tunisia. Her research interests include digital marketing, consumer behavior, e-commerce, point of sale management and e-learning. Her contributions have been published in journals focusing on e-learning, marketing

Maher Toukabri A dedicated and accomplished Professor with over 23 years of experience in higher education, research, and academic leadership. Expertise in curriculum development, accreditation, and innovative teaching methodologies, including ICT integration and modern pedagogical strategies. A committed mentor and thesis supervisor, fostering student success through research-driven education and industry collaboration. Passionate about advancing knowledge and shaping future professionals through scholarly contributions and academic excellence.

***

Ancey Mary Abraham is a postgraduate student pursuing a Master of Commerce in International Finance and Accounting (IFA) at Jain University. With a strong interest in financial analysis, corporate governance, and global accounting standards, she is dedicated to academic excellence and research. Ancey actively engages in exploring financial strategies and their practical applications, aiming to contribute to the finance industry with analytical insights and strategic decision-making.

Animesh Agrawal is a Assistant Professor at MATS University Raipur, India. His main area of interest is knowledge management, optimization, and ERP. Currently he is working in the collaboration of knowledge management with different fields like artificial intelligence, artificial neural networks etc. He has presented more than 10 papers in highly indexed journal attended more than 14 international and national conferences.

Munir Ahmad is a seasoned professional in the realm of Spatial Data Infrastructure (SDI), Geo-Information Productions, Information Systems, and Information Governance, boasting over 25 years of dedicated experience in the field. With a PhD in Computer Science, Dr. Ahmad's expertise spans Spatial Data Production, Management, Processing, Analysis, Visualization, and Quality Control. Throughout his career, Dr. Ahmad has been deeply involved in the development and deployment of SDI systems specially in the context of Pakistan, leveraging his proficiency in Spatial Database Design, Web, Mobile & Desktop GIS, and Geo Web Services Architecture. His contributions to Volunteered Geographic Information (VGI) and Open Source Geoportal & Metadata Portal have significantly enriched the geospatial community. As a trainer and researcher, Dr. Ahmad has authored over 50 publications, advancing the industry's knowledge base and fostering innovation in Geo-Tech, Data Governance, and Information Infrastructure, and Emerging Technologies. His commitment to Research and Development (R&D) is evident in his role as a dedicated educator and mentor in the field.

Patcha Bhujanga Rao is a distinguished professional with a stellar reputation in the realms of human resources (HR) and soft skills development. With over two decades of experience and an extensive academic background encompassing degrees such as M.Com., DCFA., M.Phil., Ph.D., MBA (HR), M.Sc (Psychology), and LL.B, he possesses a comprehensive understanding of multiple disciplines. Currently serving as a professor at Jain Deemed-to-Be University in Bengaluru, Dr. Rao is highly regarded for his expertise in HR management, which has been instrumental in shaping the careers of numerous professionals. His commitment to nurturing essential skills such as effective communication, leadership, and interpersonal abilities reflects his dedication to facilitating personal and professional growth. Dr. Rao's contributions have earned him widespread respect and admiration within the HR and soft skills domains, positioning him as a respected authority and mentor for aspiring professionals seeking to excel in their respective fields.

Kanchon Kumar Bishnu is an accomplished Software Engineer, Artificial Intelligence Researcher, and Cybersecurity Expert whose work bridges intelligent systems, secure computing, and biomedical data analysis. With advanced skills in Python, C++, JavaScript, and SQL, he applies computational intelligence and data-driven methodologies to design innovative, reliable, and ethically aligned technological solutions. His interdisciplinary expertise enables the translation of theory into real-world applications addressing modern challenges in cybersecurity and health informatics. Kanchon earned his Bachelor of Technology in Computer Science and Engineering from Lovely Professional University, India, building a strong foundation in software development and applied computing. He is currently pursuing a Master of Science in Computer Science at California State University, Los Angeles, focusing on artificial intelligence, optimization, and cybersecurity. His research integrates machine learning, predictive analytics, and health data modeling, emphasizing intelligent frameworks for energy efficiency, medical diagnostics, and cyber resilience. His scholarly works have been published in Q1-ranked international journals under leading publishers such as IEEE, Elsevier, MDPI, Springer Nature, and Tech Science Press. Recognized for his expertise, he serves as a peer reviewer for high-impact journals including The Journal of Alzheimer's Disease (JAD), PLOS ONE, and several Elsevier Q1 journals. A UK patent holder, Kanchon continues to contribute to innovations in computing technologies, advancing the convergence of AI, health science, and cybersecurity to foster secure and sustainable systems.

Brahim Boutaleb is an Algerian researcher at M'Hamed Bougara University of Boumerdes, specializing in marketing and consumer behavior. His research mainly explores the psychological and social factors that influence consumer purchasing decisions, with a strong focus on the smartphone market, impulsive buying behavior, and materialism among Arab consumers. In his 2024 study published in Business Ethics and Leadership, titled "Factors Influencing Smart Phone Buying Behavior of Consumers: Implications for Building a Marketing Strategy," he identified personal factors (such as motivation, perception, and preferences) as the strongest predictors of smartphone purchase decisions, compared to external influences or gender differences. Another major study, "Determinants of Consumers' Adoption of Latest Version Smartphones: An Empirical Study of Saudi Consumers" (2024, Engineering, Technology & Applied Science Research), analyzed the drivers behind consumers' willingness to upgrade to newer smartphone models, emphasizing the role of perceived value, innovation, and brand trust. Additionally, his paper "Effect of Materialism on Impulsive Buying Behavior: An Empirical Study of Arab Consumers" (2022, SMART Journal of Business Management Studies) investigated how materialistic values impact unplanned purchasing behavior among Arab consumers, revealing that materialism positively affects impulsive buying but interacts with other motivational factors.

Antar Chaâbi is an Assistant Professor of Marketing at Taif University, Saudi Arabia. He holds a Ph.D. in Marketing from Tunis El Manar University, Tunisia. His research interests focus on consumer behavior, marketing channels, marketing research, and data analysis. Dr. Chaâbi's work explores the evolving dynamics of marketing strategy in the digital era, emphasizing the integration of analytical methods to enhance decision-making and market performance. He has contributed to several academic studies and collaborative research projects that address contemporary challenges in marketing management and distribution systems. His teaching and research aim to bridge theoretical foundations with practical business applications, fostering innovation in marketing education and practice.

Susanta Ranjan Chaini is currently working as Professor and Dean at Faculty of Hospitality and Tourism Management at Siksha O Anusandhan Deemed to be University. An erudite academician & proficient academic administrator with 25 years of exposure & experience in hospitality & tourism didactic with expertise in mentoring & training; academic governance & consulting; research & operations including relationship management. He is an alumnus of Sainik School-Bhubaneswar, IHM-Bhubaneswar, worked in hotel industry like Choice Group of Hotels, Sarovar Park Plaza & Jindal Hotels for four years & in teaching more than 21 years with Vivekananda Institute of Hotel Management, Rajkot & Ranjita Institute of Hotel Management, Bhubaneswar (Under C.V.Raman Global University) as Principal, Dean at SGT University, Gurugram. A Ph.D. in Tourism Studies from The University of Burdwan, Dr. Chaini is also UGC-NET qualified & have authored four books on hospitality & tourism studies. He has also published around 35 research papers in various national & international peer reviewed reputed journals indexed with SCOPUS, ABDC & UGC-CARE listed. To his credit, he has published 03 patents. He has presented many research papers, chaired various sessions and invited key note speaker in several national & international conferences of repute.

Sachin Chavan is a Professor at the Balaji Institute of International Business (BIIB), Pune, where he is recognized for his academic leadership and commitment to excellence in management education. With extensive experience in teaching, research, and industry engagement, Dr. Chavan brings deep domain expertise and a passion for nurturing future business leaders. He actively contributes to the institute's academic initiatives, curriculum development, and student mentoring, playing a vital role in shaping BIIB's reputation as a premier business school. His dedication to advancing knowledge and fostering professional growth has earned him respect among colleagues, students, and the wider academic community.

Girdhar Gopal is an experienced academician and researcher with over 19 years in management education, specializing in marketing, business analytics, and operations research. Currently serving as Associate Professor and Head of the School of Business at SHEAT College of Engineering & Management, Varanasi, he holds a Ph.D. in Marketing and has taught a wide range of subjects across several reputed institutions. His academic contributions include multiple publications in Scopus and ABDC-indexed journals, authorship of several management textbooks, and a recently published patent on personalized marketing systems. Dr. Gopal has actively participated in and organized numerous national and international conferences and faculty development programs, and he is known for his dynamic teaching style, strong communication skills, and leadership in academic initiatives.

Guruprasanna G Hegde, currently studying in Dayananda Sagar College Of Engineering Bengaluru

S. Ida Evangeline, presently working as an Assistant Professor in the Department of Electrical and Electronics Engineering at the Government College of Engineering, Tirunelveli, Tamilnadu, India. She obtained her Bachelor's in Electrical and Electronics Engineering from Manonmaniam Sundaranar University in 2003, and Master's in Power Systems Engineering from Anna University, Chennai, Tamilnadu, India in 2005. She completed her PhD degree in 2023 at Anna University, Chennai, Tamilnadu, India. She has published six research papers in international journals. Her current research interests include optimal power flow, renewable energy, soft computing, machine learning, and deep learning.

Preethi Inampudi is a highly accomplished academic professional who has dedicated her career to the field of human resources and presently working as Assistant Professor, Department of Management, Surana College (Autonomous), Bangalore

Md Rasibul Islam is a Management Analyst and AI researcher who integrates deep learning, predictive analytics, and business strategy to build intelligent, data-driven decision support systems. With a strong background in management science and quantitative methods, he focuses on applying advanced analytics to optimize working capital, enhance customer satisfaction, and minimize operational waste across industries. His work connects technology with business operations, enabling organizations to make smarter, evidence-based decisions. Rasibul began his academic journey in Dhaka, Bangladesh, earning both his Bachelor's and Master's degrees in Economics from Jagannath University. He furthered his studies in the United States, completing a STEM-designated Master of Public Administration at Gannon University in Pennsylvania. His academic foundation blends economics, data analytics, and public administration, providing a strong interdisciplinary perspective on operational decision-making and strategic planning. His research focuses on AI-powered systems for demand forecasting, supply chain optimization, and customer behavior analytics, with applications spanning healthcare, retail, manufacturing, and logistics. He has contributed to several peer-reviewed publications in machine learning for business decision-making, risk prediction, and enterprise analytics.

Through his work, Rasibul seeks to bridge business strategy and technological innovation, contributing to the United States' national interest by advancing operational efficiency, economic resilience, and sustainable business practices.

Anupam Jain is an Associate Professor of Accounting and Finance with over 25 years of academic and industry experience. He is currently associated with Amity University, Rajasthan, Jaipur, and has previously served in various capacities, including Head of Commerce Department, Placement Officer, and NSS Officer in reputed institutions like LBS PG College and St. Wilfred's PG College. Dr. Jain holds a Ph.D. in Commerce, along with M.Com (Gold Medalist), MBA (Finance), M.Sc. (IT), and a Diploma in Export Management, showcasing his strong academic background. He has authored and published 14 books on subjects like Accounting, CSR, Entrepreneurship, and Waste Management, and holds multiple patents on innovative business and technological solutions. With a prolific research profile, Dr. Jain has published 30+ research papers in UGC Care and Scopus indexed journals, covering topics such as E-commerce, CSR, Banking, Financial Reporting, and Waste Management. He has presented numerous papers in national and international conferences, including abroad, and received awards like Outstanding Academician Award (2024) and an ICSSR Research Grant. He is also a lifetime member of prominent research and academic bodies like Indian Accounting Association (IAA), ISTD, IRA, and I2OR, actively contributing to academic and professional communities. His expertise spans Accounting, Finance, CSR, Corporate Governance, E-commerce, and Emerging Technologies.

Nitin Kalla is Associate Professor at the MATS School of Management Studies & Research, MATS University, Raipur. He holds a PhD in Online Advertising Effectiveness from Devi Ahilya University, Indore. He is having over 16 years of professional experience—14 in academia and 2 in industry—Dr. Kalla plays a key role in teaching, research, and academic leadership at MATS. He is a member of the Board of Studies in Management and Social Work for various universities and actively guides research scholars. He has published extensively in national and international journals, including a recent 2025 study on welfare measures for gig workers in India and research on mental health issues among primary healthcare workers. Dr. Kalla has presented research paper at international & national conferences and frequently conducts Faculty Development Programs (FDPs). His teaching philosophy centers on nation-building through youth education, emphasizing analytical thinking, communication, and practical exposure. He integrates case studies, group discussions, guest lectures, and internships into his teaching methods to foster real-world learning. Passionate about student development, Dr. Kalla remains committed to academic excellence and innovation in management education.

Manjit Kour is working as Professor at University Business School at Chandigarh University. She holds a PhD in Business Management from IK Gujral Punjab Technical University, India. She has a good research record with several research papers published in reputed journals. She is an editorial board member and reviewer of many reputed journals including Scopus and ABDC-indexed journals. Her areas of interest include sustainability, green practices, Fintech, online marketing trends and business ethics.

Pankaj Kumar is currently working as an Assistant Professor in School of BFSI, Symbiosis University of Applied Sciences, Indore, Madhya Pradesh. He has completed his Ph.D. in Finance from Faculty of Commerce, Banaras Hindu University and published number of research papers in SCOPUS, ABDC and Care listed journals.

Pawan Kumar, PhD, is a prominent academic and researcher with over 20 years of expertise in business studies. A professor at Graphic Era Deemed to be University, Dehradun, India, he has supervised six PhD scholars and published over 60 research papers, including 51 in SCOPUS/ 06 in Web of Science, and 14 books, including eight indexed in Scopus. His works, featured by prominent publishers like Emerald, IGI Global, Nova Science, and Cambridge Scholars, have gained recognition. Dr. Kumar earned his PhD in Commerce from Kurukshetra University in 2007 and holds an M.Phil. and M.Com. Degrees. Specializing in finance, banking, and securities markets, he has authored books on green finance, AI, and fintech. His innovative research includes five patents and has served as a guest editor for Scopus-indexed journals. In 2022, he received the prestigious Researcher Award from Chandigarh University. Dr. Kumar's impactful work on sustainable finance, blockchain, and fintech is globally recognized. His active participation in high-impact conferences and faculty development programs reflects his commitment to advancing research, teaching, and innovation in commerce and management.

Parikshit Mahankal serves as an Associate Professor at Smt. Jayshree Sharadchandra Kothari Business School, Mumbai. With a strong commitment to academic excellence and student development, he brings extensive expertise in his field and a passion for teaching, research, and mentorship. Dr. Mahankal actively contributes to the institution's academic growth through innovative pedagogy, scholarly pursuits, and participation in various academic initiatives. His dedication to shaping future business professionals has earned him recognition among peers and students alike.

Zokir Mamadiyarov is working in the Department of Finance and Tourism at Termez University of Economics and Service, Termez, Uzbekistan.

T.C. Manjunath was born on 6th February 1967. He did his B.E. from RV College of Engg. in 1989 (B'lore Univ), M.E. in Robotics & Automation from Govt.'s LD College of Engg., (Gujarat Univ., Ahmedabad) in 1992 with FCD-First Rank & PhD in Systems & Control Engg. from IIT Bombay in the year 2007, got best research scholar award for the entire IITB. He is currently working as the Dean Research (R & D) and as Professor in Dept. of Computer Science & Engg. with specialization in IoT, Cyber Security, Blockchain Technology in Rajarajeswari College of Engineering, Bengaluru, Karnataka. He has got a teaching (academic), research & administrative experience of more than 35+ years (10 years as Principal & 8 years as HoD, 1 year as Dean Research & rest as faculty) and has published more than 1500+ research papers in various national & international journals & conferences, with 175+ patents, 100+ book-chapters, 25 awards, 100s of Keynote talks and also published 25 text books in various field of science, engineering & technology, completed projects worth Rs. 9 Crores till date & guided 10 PhD scholars in VTU. He is a member of 30 Professional Society Chapters and is a fellow of IE, IETE, AMIEE, Sr. Member of IEEE and a chartered engineer.

Geetha Manoharan is currently working in Telangana as an assistant professor at SR University. She is the university-level PhD program coordinator and has also been given the additional responsibility of In Charge Director of Publications and Patents under the Research Division at SR University.

Meeramani N, Librarian, JAIN (Deemed-to-be University), Bangalore.She has a total experience of 23 years and received the "Best Librarian 2023" state award from the Govt. Karnataka. Published over fifty research papers in national and international journals and conferences, three of which were at IIM-Bangalore and IIM-Indore. She organized more than 49 webinars, conferences, workshops, Faculty Development Programs. She was a resource person in the 30-day NEP-aligned Guru Dakshta Faculty Induction Programme held at JAIN (deemed-to-be University) in Bangalore from November 2 to December 7, 2022, and January 19 to February 14, 2023. - Served as a resource Person to the Curriculum Revision Workshop for Library and Information Science" held from May 20, 2019 to May 24, 2019 and February 25, 2020 to February 29, 2020 at the National Institute of Technical Teachers Training and Research, Extension Centre, Bengaluru (An Autonomous Institute under the Ministry of HRD, Dept. of Sec. and Higher Education, Government of India).

Sudhansu Sekhar Pattnaik is currently persuing his doctoral degree in the Faculty of Hospitality & Tourism Management at Siksha O Anusandhan Deemed to be University, Bhubaneswar, Odisha. He has more than 22 years of experience both in the field of services marketing, administration and in academics. He has completed his undergraduate degree in B.Com from Berhampur University, and postgraduate degree in M.A. in Hospitality and Tourism Management from Siksha O Anusandhan Deemed to be University. He has published around 10 numbers of research articles in various National and International journals of repute. His research interests include services management, hospitality & tourism management, and consumer behavior.

R. Bhuvaneswari working as an Assistant Professor of English at Dr.Mahalingam College of Engineering and Technology, Pollachi. To her credit she completed 10 NPTEL / SWAYAM and published few articles in Scopus indexed journals.

R. Velmurugan presently working as Professor, Department of Commerce, Karpagam Academy of Higher Education, Coimbatore. He started his career as a Project Fellow under UGC Sponsored Major Research Project at NGM College, Pollachi. He has 19 years of teaching experience has 15 years of research experience. To his credit he produced 24 Ph.D. Scholars and 5 M.Phil. Scholars. At present two scholars submitter his thesis, 6 Ph.D. Scholars are under his guidance. Moreover, to his credit he published 168 articles in various International Journals, of which 107 articles are published in Scopus Indexed Journals and 15 articles in Web of Science and 76 articles in edited volumes. He also participates and presented 27 papers in various International Seminar / Conference and 54 National Seminar / Conference. He acted as an external examiner for various M.Phil. and Ph.D. Viva voce examinations. He acted as a Vice Chancellor nominee for Doctoral Committee Expert at Bharathiar University, Coimbatore and Periyar University, Salem. He acted as a Chairperson at various National Level Conferences. He also acted as an Expert for Syllabus Scrutiny Committee, Question Paper Scrutiny Committee and Expert members for Board of Studies at various reputed Colleges. Considering his meritorious contribution, he received awards like Best Paper Presenter, Best Research Supervisor and Best Faculty Awards from various research foundations and councils. He too acted as a resource person for 27 Guest Lectures, 30 Workshops and 10 faculty development programmes.

Ravikumar R. Natarajan is an experienced academician with over 12+ years of teaching and research expertise across institutions in India, the UAE, and the Maldives. He currently serves as an Assistant Professor at Marwadi University, Rajkot, specializing in Machine Learning, Recommender Systems, and AI-driven applications in healthcare and security. He holds a Ph.D. in Machine Learning and Recommender Systems from Amity University, Jaipur, a Master of Engineering in CSE from VMRF University, Salem, and a Bachelor of Engineering in CSE from

Anna University. He also has a MiniMBA from the Swiss eLearning Institute. Dr. Ravikumar has authored more than 20 IEEE conference papers, multiple SCIE/Scopus-indexed journal articles, and co-authored a book on Artificial Intelligence. He has also published 9 patents and contributed several book chapters in emerging domains such as Federated Learning, Blockchain, and Digital Twins. He actively mentors students through initiatives like the Research Activities Club (RAC) and Student Research Internship Training (SRIT), promoting innovation and research culture.

Md Khalilor Rahman is an Operations Manager – Marketing & Communication at Shera International Group Inc. (Los Angeles). He is a Business Analyst, Google-Certified Data Analyst, predictive analytics expert, financial digital transformation specialist, strategic business intelligence, and risk modeling researcher, author, and editorial board member. He managed and optimized marketing and SEO campaigns and website performance reports. His work at BDITDOMAIN (Virginia) as a Marketing Analyst and prior roles in finance and administration in Bangladesh gave him a solid background in market research, forecasting using regression analysis, and general research. His AI-based financial operational policy analytics, smart decision systems, and evidence-based policy formulation research examine analytic frameworks. He integrated machine learning with various fields in numerous published research papers, including supply chain management and risk management. He is an outstanding global scholar with an MBA in Business Analytics (Gannon University, USA), dual MBA/BBA degrees (World University of Bangladesh), and his editorial and peer-review work on AI innovation and data resilience.

R. Renugadevi completed her Ph.D. in 2022 from Anna University, Chennai, and currently serves as an Associate Professor at Saveetha Engineering College. With over two decades of teaching experience in esteemed engineering institutions, she made significant contributions to the academic and research domains. She has published more than 40 research papers in renowned international journals and conferences, and holds 10 patents, reflecting her innovative approach to technology and engineering. She holds the distinction of being an approved research supervisor at Anna University, with six scholars under her supervision. Her research interests span across cutting-edge fields such as Machine Learning, Internet of Things (IoT), Wireless Sensor Networks, and Cloud Computing. As a passionate academician, she is a life member of professional organizations, including the Indian Society for Technical Education (ISTE), Internet Society and the International Association of Engineers (IAENG).

Aarthi S is a dedicated Assistant Professor in Computer Science with over six years of teaching experience. She is currently pursuing her Ph.D. at Marwadi University, Gujarat, and holds an M.Phil. and MCA from Bharathiar University, Tamil Nadu. Throughout her academic career, Aarthi has specialized in programming languages such as C++, Java, and C, and contributed to research in recommender systems and AI-related data privacy. She has published journal articles, contributed to book chapters, and actively participated in technical workshops. Known for her student mentorship and engagement in academic events, Aarthi remains committed to fostering innovation and excellence in computer science education.

Ansuman Samal is currently working as a Professor in the Faculty of Hospitality & Tourism Management at Siksha O Anusandhan Deemed to be University, Bhubaneswar, Odisha. He has more than 18 years of experience both in the field of marketing research and in academics. He has completed his graduation in Information Technology from Manipal Academy of Higher Education, MBA from KIIT Deemed to be University and PhD from Siksha O Anusandhan Deemed to be University. As an acclaimed scholar, he has received the Chancellor's Gold Medal from KIIT Deemed to be University for securing highest mark during the MBA programme. Before joining Siksha O Anusandhan, he was working as a senior researcher at IMRS Advisory Pvt. Ltd. In Bengaluru. As an academician, he has published more than 80 numbers of research articles in various National and International journals of repute. He has also authored 5 Books and has participated in more than 100 numbers of National and International Conferences, workshops, seminars / webinars and presented his research works. He has successfully guided 2 numbers of PhD students and another 4 students are currently continuing their research work under his guidance. His research interests include services marketing, hospitality & tourism management, consumer behavior, quality management, and strategic management.

Lal Tlan Sang is a dedicated Data Analyst with a strong academic background in Computer Science and Business Analytics. She holds a Bachelor's degree in Computer Science and an MBA in Business Analytics. She has experience working in the non-profit and private sectors, where she applies data visualization, business intelligence, and analytical tools such as Power BI and Microsoft Dynamics 365 to support strategic decision-making. She is also actively involved in community-based education, offering free training sessions to youth and professionals on basic digital tools and data skills. Her current research interests include customer segmentation, data mining, AI applications in business, and digital transformation in developing contexts. She aims to contribute to inclusive, sustainable innovation through technology and academic research.

Pravin Chandra Singh is an assistant professor at MSMSR, MATS University, Raipur. He holds a Ph.D. from the Institute of Management Studies, Banaras Hindu University (BHU), Varanasi, India. He has completed his MBA from I.C.C.M.R.T. and also qualified UGC-NET. With a strong commitment to quality research, he has published papers in SCOPUS Q1, Web of Science, and UGC-CARE-listed journals. Dr. Pravin has actively participated in national and international conferences, where he has presented research papers. Additionally, he serves as a reviewer for reputed international publishers, such as Sage, Emerald, and Inderscience.

J. Sudarvel working as an Assistant Professor of Management at Karpagam Academy of Higher Education. He produced five Ph.D. Scholars and four Ph.D. Scholars are under his guidance. Further, to his credit he published 51 articles in Scopus indexed journals and published more than 50 articles in international journals. He is acting as a Subject Experts in Board of studies of various autonomous colleges.

T. Ragupathi is an Assistant Professor in the Department of Data Science and Business Systems at the School of Computing, SRM Institute of Science and Technology, Kattankulathur, Chennai. With a strong academic foundation and a passion for emerging technologies, he is dedicated to advancing the fields of data science and business analytics through both teaching and research. Dr. Ragupathi is committed to fostering a dynamic learning environment, guiding students in developing analytical skills and innovative problem-solving abilities. His academic contributions and active involvement in departmental activities reflect his dedication to shaping future professionals and supporting the growth of the data science discipline.

Jigyasaa Thakker is an Assistant Professor at the International Institute of Management Studies (IIMS), Pune, where she is dedicated to fostering academic excellence and holistic learning. With a strong commitment to management education, she brings a blend of research insight and practical understanding to her teaching. Passionate about mentoring students, she actively contributes to academic development through innovative pedagogy, research initiatives, and institutional activities. Her work reflects a deep enthusiasm for advancing knowledge and preparing future business leaders for a dynamic professional world.

Ravi Thirumalaisamy working as an Assistant Professor, Department of Business and Economics, Modern College of Business and Science. To his credit, he published more than 27 articles in Scopus indexed journals.

Neo Jeanett Ts'ehlo holds a Master's degree in Development Studies and a Bachelor's degree with a double major in Sociology and Public Administration from the National University of Lesotho. Her area of interest as an independent researcher is gender, SMEs, business, sustainable development, and development economics. The focus of her work is on practical solutions to complex global challenges. She has left a positive impact on the work she performed part-time for various departments and institutions, including but not limited to World Vision Lesotho. She is looking forward to making a positive impact on the economy through research contributions and Corporate Social Responsibility.

V. Vaissnave is an Assistant Professor in the Department of Computational Intelligence, School of Computing, at SRM Institute of Science and Technology, Kattankulathur, India. He is dedicated to advancing research and education in the field of computational intelligence and emerging computing technologies. With a strong academic foundation and a passion for innovative teaching, Dr. Vaissnave actively contributes to the development of cutting-edge research, student mentorship, and academic initiatives within the department. His commitment to academic excellence and his contributions to the computing community have earned him recognition among colleagues, researchers, and students.

Preeti Yadav is a seasoned academician with a Ph.D. in Commerce. Currently a Professor at Amity Business School, Amity University Rajasthan, she has over more than 20 years of teaching experience. She holds an M.Com and MBA, specializing in HR and Marketing, and has contributed extensively to research and publications. She has extensive research experience and also supervising multiple Ph.D. scholars in areas like digitalization's impact on HR, soft skills for employability, and customer retention strategies. She has also edited books on financial frauds, cross-cultural HR, and skill development, contributing significantly to academic programs and research at Amity University. Prof. (Dr.) Preeti Yadav has published numerous papers in reputed journals covering a wide array of topics including COVID-19's impact on marketing, HR, customer retention, work-life balance, and organizational stress. She has presented numerous research papers at international and national conferences, covering topics like women empowerment, social entrepreneurship, and microfinance, among others. She has also contributed chapters to several edited books, covering topics like women entrepreneurship, social entrepreneurship, digital India, and microfinance. Additionally, she holds a patent for a novel technique in digital marketing using AI, blockchain, and IoT.

Index

www.ingramcontent.com/pod-product-compliance
Lightning Source LLC
LaVergne TN
LVHW080902300926
849162LV00003B/528